Intimate Enemies

PENNSYLVANIA STUDIES IN HUMAN RIGHTS

Bert B. Lockwood, Jr., Series Editor

A complete list of books in the series is available from the publisher.

Intimate Enemies

Violence and Reconciliation in Peru

Kimberly Theidon

PENN

UNIVERSITY OF PENNSYLVANIA PRESS

PHILADELPHIA

Published by
University of Pennsylvania Press
Philadelphia, Pennsylvania 19104-4112
www.upenn.edu/pennpress

Printed in the United States of America on acid-free paper

10 9 8 7 6 5 4 3 2 1

Library of Congress Cataloging-in-Publication Data
Theidon, Kimberly.
    Intimate enemies : violence and reconciliation in Peru / Kimberly Theidon. — 1st ed.
        p.   cm. — (Pennsylvania studies in human rights)
    Includes bibliographical references and index.
    ISBN 978-0-8122-4450-2 (hardcover : alk. paper)
    1. Postwar reconstruction—Social aspects—Peru—Ayacucho (Dept.)   2. Conflict
management—Peru—Ayacucho (Dept.)   3. Political violence—Social aspects—
Peru—Ayacucho (Dept.)   4. Political violence—Psychological aspects—Peru—
Ayacucho (Dept.)   5. War victims—Mental health—Peru—Ayacucho (Dept.)
6. Ayacucho (Peru: Dept.)—Politics and government.   I. Title.   II. Series:
Pennsylvania studies in human rights.
HN350.A96T482 2013
363.34'988098529—dc23
                                                                                                2012022597

Contents

Contents

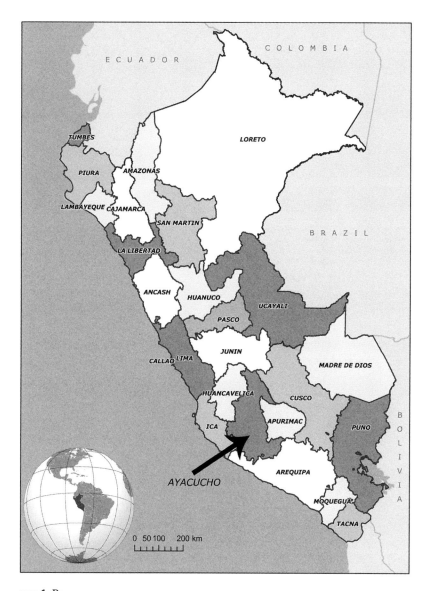

MAP 1. Peru.

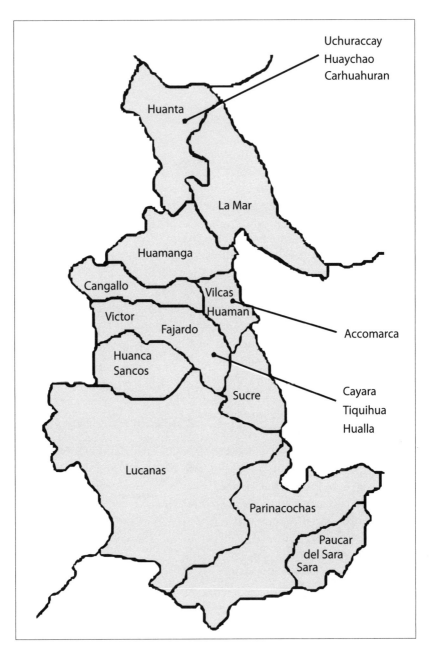

Uchuraccay
Huaychao
Carhuahuran

Huanta

La Mar

Huamanga

Cangallo

Victor

Fajardo

Vilcas
Huaman

Accomarca

Huanca
Sancos

Sucre

Cayara
Tiquihua
Hualla

Lucanas

Parinacochas

Paucar
del Sara
Sara

MAP 2. The Department of Ayacucho.

THE BRIGHTLY COLORED speck in the distance kept coming closer without increasing much in size. I stood still with a large sack of kindling slung over my shoulder, not certain who it was. It was barely dusk, so I was less frightened than curious. People had assured me that the guerrillas only walked at night, as did the other frightening creatures I had been warned about. There were the *jarjachas*—human beings who had assumed the form of llamas as divine punishment for incest. There were the *pishtacos*—beings that suck the body fat out of the poor people who cross their paths. There were also the *condenados*—the condemned dead who are sentenced to an afterlife of wandering the earth and never finding peace. All of these beings derive pleasure from inflicting their vengeance on the living. But it was still dusk. I just wanted to know who the speck in the distance was.

I finally heard a voice call out, but the wind carried the words upward to the peaks of the mountains. I dropped down to the dirt highway and began calling out my own greeting. Finally an elderly man came into focus. He wore threadbare pants and a green wool sweater, and was stooping beneath the weight of a brightly colored blanket brimming with wood. Standing as upright as his heavy load would allow him, this tiny man pushed back his hat and looked straight up at me: "*Gringacha*"—little gringa—"where is your husband?" And so I met don Jesús Romero, an altogether different sort of creature to be wary of on isolated paths.

Don Jesús was also headed to the village of Carhuahurán, so we walked back home together. It was the time of day when cooking fires sent smoke curls up from the roofs of the houses and animals crowded into their corrals for the night. The smoke curls were a prelude to intimate evening hours, when stories from that day or years past were told as families gathered around blackened cooking pots.

Efraín, my research assistant, already had our fire going by the time we arrived. I invited don Jesús to come in for a cup of coffee and a *chapla*—round wheat bread I had brought with me from the city a few days earlier. I slathered a *chapla* with butter and strawberry jam, instantly making me someone worth visiting on a regular basis.

Don Jesús began by telling us he was the oldest person we would ever meet—he was a hundred years old. His cousin Domingo Santiago would later assure me that Jesus had lied—he was only eighty-three and it was Domingo who was the oldest person we would meet because he was eighty-seven. When I asked Jesús one day about the discrepancy, he thought for a bit before distracting me with the obvious: "*Gringacha*, I'm very charming."

That first afternoon don Jesús began talking about *el tiempo de los abuelos*—the time of the grandparents. "But that was before. Traditions change because times change. Before, we never raised the flag like we do now. This is recent, just since the terrorists appeared. In *el tiempo de los abuelos*, we didn't even have a flag."

"Why do they raise the flag now?" I asked.

"We have laws now, laws to civilize us. To make us understand each other."

"And before, how was it then—weren't there laws?"

"Yeah. But everything changed."

"Changed how, don Jesús? When?"

"When the violence appeared. Before, there were laws. Before, it was forbidden to kill," he replied, wiping some jam from his face with his scratchy green sleeve.

"They didn't kill before?"

"No, it was forbidden—only with thieves who came to steal animals. But the violence appeared and people began to kill. People were dying like dogs, there was no controlling it. Like dogs people were dying and there wasn't any law."

"And now?" prompted Efraín.

"Now is another time. In our assemblies, in the Mother's Clubs—everything is changing again. It's against the law to kill now, even to attack someone. It's forbidden. Everything is changing. Time changes."

"Was there a time before *el tiempo de los abuelos*?" I asked.

Don Jesús nodded. "It was *el tiempo eterno*—time eternal. The people were different then."

"They weren't like us?" I asked.

"No, they were different. We're from *el tiempo de Dios Hijo*—the time of the Son of God."

"And the people who lived before, did they disappear?"

"Of course. We come after them."

"Did the people from *el tiempo eterno* live here?"

"Yeah. Their houses are up there," pointing toward the hills above Carhuahurán. "We've seen their houses."

"Did they have a name?"

He nodded. "The gentiles. They were *envidiosos*—envious. They disappeared in the rain of fire. Then it was *el tiempo de Dios Hijo*. That ended in the flood."

"So there have been two times?"

"Yes. There have been two judgments."

"Will there be another?"

"Oh, yes. Some people say it will happen soon. We'll end in flames."

Don Jesús finally stood up, letting us know it was time for him to head home. I looked outside and saw how dark it was. "So you aren't afraid of the dark?" I wondered out loud. "*Jarjachas, condenados. . . .*"

He shook his head. "That was before. That changed when the violence appeared. The condemned disappeared—they stopped walking. When the violence appeared, it was the time of the living damned." He lifted his blanket full of wood onto his shoulders and tied the ends tight around his chest. "We weren't afraid of the *condenados* anymore. We were terrified of our *prójimos*—terrified of our neighbors, of our brothers."

I shut the door behind don Jesús that night, but our conversation opened many others as I attempted to answer the deceptively simple questions that had stayed with me since my first visit to Peru in 1987. At that time I was an undergraduate at the University of California at Santa Cruz. With a small grant from the chancellor's fund, I headed to Peru in part to research Shining Path, the guerrilla organization that had launched its war on the Peruvian state seven years earlier. I squeaked in just months before the university shut down its study abroad program there, concerned about the safety of students amid the political violence that convulsed the country. I did not attempt to visit Ayacucho, the region that Abimael Guzmán—founder of Sendero Luminoso (Shining Path)—called the "cradle" of the revolution.[1] The guerrillas espoused a fervent anti-imperialist ideology, and the United States was on their list of enemies. Besides, by 1987 the violence extended well beyond the highlands of Ayacucho, and soon nearly half the population lived under a state of emergency, subject to the control and caprice of the Peruvian armed forces.

It was a time of rampant inflation, which led to long lines for basic necessities and to the hoarding of groceries on the shelves of the small corner stores that dotted any given neighborhood. With my host family in Pueblo Libre, a barrio in Lima, we grew accustomed to the water rationing the government implemented in an effort to make water available to the rapidly growing squatter settlements that ringed the capital city, becoming home to the tens of thousands of people who were internally displaced by the armed conflict. The rationing set us scrambling to fill all available pots and pans during the two or three hours a day that the pipes creaked and the water ran. We grew tensely accustomed to a restricted range of movement as curfews and blackouts became a common feature of daily life. Mama Clara warned us not to roam too far from the house in case the guerrillas bombed an electrical tower and we found ourselves stranded on a distant street in the pitch black of a Lima night.

Somehow the omnipresent soldiers stationed in the streets and scattered across the rooftops did not alleviate our fears. With their black woolen ski masks and machine guns, we thought they were just as frightening as the tanks that rolled through the streets or the guerrillas who sprayed their revolutionary graffiti in vivid red across random walls.

This was Peruvians killing Peruvians, some in army uniforms, others in guerrilla attire, and many more in the clothes they wore every day when they planted fields, waved to neighbors, walked their children to school, or brought their animals into the safe harbor of a family's corral. Some deceptively simple questions stayed with me across the years. How do people commit acts of lethal violence against individuals with whom they have lived for years? How can family members and neighbors become enemies one is willing to track down and kill? But it was not just the violence that gave rise to questions. More was at stake here. There was no invading army that would gather up weapons and return to some distant land. Not this war. When the killing stopped, former enemies would be left living side by side. What would happen then?

It is common these days to hear the term "new wars" used to contrast contemporary armed conflicts with conventional warfare and the battlefield strategies with which two or more nation-states trained their armies and engaged in combat.[2] These "new wars" are more likely to be civil wars fought with guerrilla tactics and counterinsurgency responses, and the front lines blur into the home front as civilians frequently bear the brunt of the violence.

One particularity of civil wars is that foreign armies do not wage the attacks. Frequently the enemy is a son-in-law, a godfather, an old schoolmate, or the community that lies just across the valley. The forms of violence suffered as well as the forms practiced matter greatly and influence the reconstruction process when the fighting subsides. The fratricidal nature of Peru's internal armed conflict means that ex-Senderistas, current sympathizers, widows, orphans, rape survivors, and army veterans live side by side. This is a volatile social world. It is a mixture of victims, perpetrators, witnesses, beneficiaries—and that sizable segment of the population that blurs the categories, inhabiting what Primo Levi called the gray zone of half tints and moral complexity.[3] The charged social landscape of the present reflects the damage done by a recent past in which people saw just what they and their neighbors could do.

I returned to Peru in 1995 in the hope of answering those deceptively simple questions. I headed to Ayacucho, the region of the country that bore the greatest loss of life and infrastructure during the internal armed conflict. I began working with Quechua-speaking communities to explore how people reconstruct individual lives and collective existence in the aftermath of war. I studied the process of social reconstruction—what some have deemed social repair.[4] Social repair involves much more than laying down weapons, reviving economies, or rebuilding infrastructure: it also consists of reconstructing the social ruins that are among the most enduring legacies of war. My years of research have convinced me that the theories and practices Peruvians have elaborated about political violence and its effects—about social life and their struggles to rebuild it—are relevant in many other contexts in which people strive to reinvent community amid landscapes steeped in blood and memory, fully aware of the danger human beings pose to one another.

Intimate Enemies

PART I

The Difficult Time

Chapter 1

"Ayacucho Is the Cradle"

The blood of the people has a rich perfume,
It smells of jasmine, violets, geraniums and daisies,
Of gunpowder and dynamite!
Carajo! Of gunpowder and dynamite!
—Refrain from "Flor de Retama," the unofficial anthem of Shining Path

IN QUECHUA PEOPLE refer to the internal armed conflict as the *sasachakuy tiempo* (difficult time). The political violence is bracketed as a finite period in which normal moral codes were suspended, people engaged in the previously unimaginable, and many individuals grew strange unto themselves. It was a time most people fervently hope will never happen again.

The *sasachakuy tiempo* began when the Communist Party of Peru-Shining Path (Sendero Luminoso) launched the armed phase of its revolution in 1980 with an attack on the Andean village of Chuschi. Militants burned the ballot boxes on the very day Peruvians were voting for the first civilian president in twelve years—and on the day that many *campesinos* (peasants) were voting for the first time since the 1979 Constitution eliminated the literacy requirement that had effectively excluded them from suffrage.

Founded in the Universidad Nacional San Cristóbal de Huamanga in Ayacucho by professor Abimael Guzmán, this band of revolutionaries positioned themselves as the vanguard in a revolution to guide the nation toward an imminent communist utopia.[1] Drawing upon Maoist theories of guerrilla warfare, they planned a top-down revolution in which the cadres of Sendero Luminoso would mobilize the peasantry, surround the cities, and strangle the urbanized coast into submission.

Initially Shining Path was considered a marginal group of fanatics. Espousing antifeudal rhetoric, hanging dead dogs from electrical posts with signs assuring passersby that a similar fate awaited enemies of the revolution—they may have raised a few eyebrows but little alarm. Even intelligence reports submitted to then president Francisco Morales Bermudez (1975–80) gave no indication there were any problems brewing with Sendero. They were wrong.[2]

After a twelve-year military regime, the civilian government of President Fernando Belaúnde was voted into power in 1980. Given the recent transition, there was reluctance to summon the armed forces to deal with the insurgents. The new government was hesitant to "knock on the barracks door" just when the armed forces had been sent back to those barracks. Sendero grew, particularly in rural areas, without confronting any coordinated response from the state and did so within the context of a democratic government.

During the initial period of Sendero's growth (1980–82), Senderista militants concentrated their efforts on political work rather than armed actions. The cadres were not yet imposing the summary execution of *campesinos* or inhabitants of popular urban barrios for being spies or "traitors to the revolution." It was during those years that Sendero launched an assault on the jail in Ayacucho, freed their political prisoners, and drew a crowd of ten thousand mourners to the burial of fallen Senderista militant Edith Lagos. Confronted with the guerrillas' dramatic display of force, the ill-equipped police withdrew from rural posts located throughout the department of Ayacucho.[3]

In the countryside, Shining Path grew in part because it filled the absence of the state. Following the Agrarian Reform (1969–75), no other authority filled the void left by the *hacendados* (large landholders). The authority that did exist was communal and limited to the jurisdiction of each individual *campesino* community.[4] The Senderista cadres began to administer their own brand of justice. In their so-called *juicios populares*, they utilized physical punishment for common crimes and a bullet to the head or knife across the throat for more serious infractions. The party's decisions were not open to appeal, thereby imposing an authoritarian order that resolved conflicts lethally—frequently with the rousing support of the *campesinos*, for whom the elusive search for justice was a feature of daily life.

The ill-conceived response of the police and the armed forces was another factor that contributed to the growth of Sendero. In their rush to "drain the water and isolate the fish," the "forces of order" practiced indiscriminate repression and committed serious human rights violations. These abuses generated resentment and a desire for revenge among various sectors of the population, and it was precisely these sentiments that the Senderista cadres channeled to their own ends.

However, only a simplistic reading would reduce this conflict to a war between the guerrillas and the armed forces. Although the Senderista leadership was composed of university-based provincial elites, the rank and file were peasants. This internal armed conflict was fought among Shining Path, the Peruvian armed forces, and the peasants themselves.[5] Without denying the pressures exerted by the Shining Path cadres as well as the armed forces, the idea of being "caught between two fires" does not help us understand the brutal violence that involved entire pueblos or the fact that there was a "third fire," comprised of peasants themselves. In the words of many villagers, "we learned to kill our brothers."

As late as 1991 there were concerns that Sendero would topple the Peruvian government. However, in September 1992, the Fujimori administration located the leader of Shining Path hiding in a safe house in Lima. The arrest of Abimael Guzmán virtually defeated the guerrilla movement. Although various would-be successors have vied for power, Sendero Luminoso remains an isolated group that has been pushed into the jungles of the coca-growing interior.

The man credited with "pacifying" the country was former president Alberto Fujimori. Elected in 1990, he campaigned on a platform of ending hyperinflation and defeating the guerrilla movements that had been waging war for a decade.[6] In fulfilling his promises, Fujimori used draconian measures, including staging a self-coup that shut down a recalcitrant Congress, rewriting the constitution, and dismantling political parties and other institutional intermediaries in the development of his self-described "direct democracy." Fujimori's popularity and vast patronage apparatus enabled him to handily win reelection in 1995; however, his authoritarian tendencies increased during his second term. To remain in power, he removed members of the Constitutional Tribunal who blocked his illegal run for a third term and reinterpreted the constitution to allow for the perpetuation of his presidency.

Following a highly tainted presidential campaign in 2000, Fujimori fled the country, faxing his resignation from Japan. The massive corruption of his two administrations had become increasingly visible. Indeed, visibility was a key component in his downfall and the subsequent political transition. Hundreds of videotapes were discovered showing both Fujimori and his crony, former head of internal intelligence Vladimiro Montesinos, bribing a cast of characters that ranged from congressmen to talk-show hosts to body builders. The corruption charges forced Fujimori from office and provided the political opening for the establishment of the truth commission by interim president Valentín Paniagua in 2001. It was his successor, Alejandro Toledo, who added the word "reconciliation" to the commission's name and mandate. That mandate was to clarify the facts of and responsibilities for the violence and human rights violations attributable to "terrorist organizations" as well as to agents of the state from 1980 to 2000.

Commissioning Truth

Wars are fought. They are also told, and the telling is always steeped in relations of power. As countries emerge from periods of violent conflict and authoritarian rule, reckoning with the past is a volatile endeavor. Memories and countermemories become both a means and an end of political struggle, and our historical époque is characterized by much faith in memory—not its infallibility but rather the work it is alleged to do in deterring future atrocities.[7] Part of contemporary memory politics involves transitional justice, a field of postwar inquiry and intervention focused on addressing the legacies of past human rights violations in the hope that doing so will build a more peaceful future.[8] Transitional justice may include tribunals, war crimes prosecutions, memorials, reparations, and truth commissions.[9]

The primary function of a truth or truth and reconciliation commission (TRC) is to collect testimonies from as many individuals as possible—including but not limited to victims, perpetrators, witnesses, political and religious leaders, institutional representatives—to clarify "the truth" of what happened during a specific episode of a country's history. These temporary bodies focus on the past, investigating patterns of abuses that resulted in the derogation of basic human rights, including acts of violence such as torture, rape, unjust imprisonment, extrajudicial killings, and disappearances.[10]

Based on these testimonies, a truth commission publishes an official public record of the past while also offering recommendations to the transitional or successor government. The recommendations may include a wide range of reforms, including moral, symbolic, and economic reparations for victims, institutional reforms, and the transfer of selected cases to the appropriate authorities for further criminal investigation.[11]

The Peruvian Truth and Reconciliation Commission (PTRC) was a two-year process that involved focus groups, in-depth interviews, fourteen Public Audiences, ethnographic research, the review of archives including those compiled by the U.S. State Department, and the collection of almost seventeen thousand testimonies from people throughout the country, many given to the commission's mobile teams that worked in rural areas.

The PTRC aimed to provide a structural analysis of the conditions that gave rise to the internal armed conflict *and* to the governmental response, as well as identify responsibility both institutionally and individually for what had occurred. Unlike other truth commissions, Peru's investigations included the identification of criminal responsibility because the Inter-American Court of Human Rights had annulled Fujimori's 1995 amnesty laws.[12] As a result, the PTRC was able to present state prosecutors with forty-two criminal cases, many of which related to human rights violations that had occurred during the Fujimori administration.

When the commission concluded its work in August 2003, it presented then president Alejandro Toledo with a nine-volume final report. Among the most striking conclusions in the report is the number of fatalities—69,280 deaths, double the number routinely cited by human rights organizations and the government prior to the PTRC.[13] During the presentation, Dr. Salomón Lerner, head of the commission, posed a rhetorical question to the crowd gathered in the Government Palace: "We Peruvians used to say, in our worst estimates, that the violence had left thirty-five thousand dead. What does it say about our political community now that we know another thirty-five thousand of our brothers and sisters were missing and we never even noticed they were gone?" I say "rhetorical" because the answer lies in the demographics of those who died. Of the total number of victims reported to the PTRC, 79 percent lived in rural areas and three of every four people killed during the internal armed conflict spoke Quechua or another native language as their mother tongue. The dead were people who—in the national imaginary—had counted for little during their lives and went largely unaccounted for in their deaths.

Equally striking are the statistics regarding accountability for these deaths. In the section of the Final Report regarding responsibility for the conflict, the commissioners state that the Shining Path guerrillas were responsible for 54 percent of the fatalities reported to the PTRC.[14] These statistics in no way diminish the atrocities committed by the armed forces; they do, however, point to a high level of civilian participation in the violence.

I collaborated with the commission in the Ayacucho office, directing research on community mental health, reconciliation, and reparations. This book is in part an exploration of the PTRC and how people interacted with this national initiative in the region of the country where the violence left its most damaging and enduring legacies. I worked with an amazing group of young researchers: Edith Del Pino Huamán, Leonor Rivera Sullqa, José Carlos Palomino Peña, Juan José Yupanqui, Dulia Lozano Noa, and Norma Salinas Mendoza. They appear throughout this book, along with two research assistants who accompanied me during my first year in Ayacucho: Efraín Loayza and Madeleine Pariona. Working with them figures among my fondest memories of Peru.

Memory Projects

It is not only a truth commission or the anthropologist who has a memory project. So do people who have lived through violent times and fiercely guard stories, secrets, and silences. Although there was technically one war, we could write many histories of the *sasachakuy tiempo*. Where to begin? Where to tease out the multiple registers of truth that may coexist yet rarely collide? The "Eight Martyrs of Uchuraccay" came to mind.

It was early in the course of Peru's internal war when eight journalists from Lima's leading newspapers headed out for the highland village of Huaychao, located in the department of Ayacucho. The men had arrived from Lima to investigate rumors that the peasants had been killing the Senderistas, who were ostensibly waging a revolution on behalf of the rural poor. Immediately following the killings of the Senderistas in Huaychao, President Belaúnde congratulated the peasants for taking action against the "terrorists" in defense of the Peruvian state. However, uncertainty about the reports—and concerns from groups on the left that the military was involved in a misinformation campaign—prompted the journalists to travel to the site to investigate. In 1983 the war in the interior still had an enigmatic quality for many residents of Lima due to the profound cleavages that characterize Peru. Indeed, in part because the war was still a mystery to many urban

Peruvians, the journalists fashioned their trip as an expedition in search of the truth.

They spent the night in the city of Huamanga before heading out at dawn the next day for the lengthy trip to Huaychao. Their route took them through Uchuraccay, where the journalists arrived in the village unannounced, accompanied by a Quechua-speaking guide. Although the sequence of events remains debatable, the photos taken by one of the journalists as he and his friends were dying established one thing: The villagers surrounded the journalists and began killing them with rocks and machetes. Their bodies were then buried facedown in shallow graves in the ravine that runs the length of the village.

At the national level, the events at Uchuraccay marked the initiation of the war in the highlands and thus the journalists' deaths became an intensely debated national theme. Although Sendero Luminoso had initiated their armed struggle three years earlier and the armed forces had been sent to Ayacucho a month prior to the killings to begin the counterinsurgency campaign, until Uchuraccay the violence had not captured significant national attention. However, the photos that were subsequently developed from the camera that had been buried with journalist Willy Retto would be placed on the cover of every major Peruvian publication, constructing a "mediatic spectacle of political violence" that would become one of the emblematic national memories of the war.[15] The "Eight Martyrs of Uchuraccay" would be commemorated annually in the press for the sacrifices they had made in their search for truth.

In the aftermath of the killings, President Belaúnde established an investigatory commission to determine what had happened and why. Headed by the novelist Mario Vargas Llosa, the commission was composed of three anthropologists, a psychoanalyst, a jurist, and two linguists who were sent to study Peru's "ethnic other" and the circumstances of the journalists' deaths.[16] The three anthropologists were well-known and respected members of the academic community and were included on the basis that anthropologists specialized in the study of "indigenous communities." And so the members of the Vargas Llosa commission accepted their charge and headed via helicopter to Uchuraccay, where they spent one morning investigating the killings as background for their final report.

In their report, the *Informe de la Comisión Investigadora de los Sucesos de Uchuraccay*, the authors begin by reviewing material on the history and ethnography of the Iquichanos, an ethnic group allegedly comprising the villages of Carhuahurán, Huaychao, Iquicha, and Uchuraccay, among others.[17] As they summarize, "This history [of the ethnic group Iquichanos] is characterized by long periods of almost total isolation and by unseasonable warlike eruptions by these communities in the events of the region or the nation."[18] The belligerence of the Iquichanos forms a central component of the history presented, as does the notion of a violent "ethnic latency." The Vargas Llosa commission's report offered a "hierarchy of causes" (truths?) that revolved around two key explanatory factors: the primitiveness of the highlanders, who allegedly lived as they had since the time of the conquest, and the intrinsically violent nature of the "Indians."[19] In the widely circulated *Informe*, the commission suggests that one could not really blame the villagers—they were just doing what came *naturally*. The commission grounded its findings in the assertion that two irreconcilable worlds coexist in Peru: modern/civilized/coastal Peru, with Lima as its center, and the traditional/savage/archaic Peru, mapped onto the highland communities, particularly Ayacucho. Somehow, in a perverse twist on John Murra's concept of *pisos ecológicos* (ecological niches), civilization had never found a way to scale up the steep mountain slopes of Peru's interior.[20]

In a subsequent interview with the journal *Caretas*, Vargas Llosa elaborated on the notion of "the two Perus" consisting of "men who participate in the 20th century and men such as these villagers of Uchuraccay who live in the 19th century, or perhaps even the 18th. The enormous distance that exists between the two Perus is what lies behind this tragedy." As such, these highland villages were akin to museum exhibits, frozen in time and placed outside history, resulting in an "Andean world that is so backwards and so violent."[21]

As one might imagine, the ensuing debates were vociferous. In response to the endemic violence arguments, a more *indigenista* perspective was elaborated, particularly by academics on the political left. This view insisted upon the harmonious nature of the villagers and the peaceful quality of *lo andino*—a cultural essence that imbued the lives of the villagers and subsumed individuality to the greater good.[22] From this perspective, if indeed the villagers had killed the journalists, certainly it was due to being *engañados*—tricked or duped—by the military.

In an insightful article regarding the *Informe* and the subsequent debates, Enrique Mayer notes, "the result was an anthropological text rather than a fact-finding report. Anthropological input into the Commission thus lent an aura of legitimate expertise concerning indigenous affairs."[23] However, although it produced an anthropological text in tone, the commission did so without utilizing the key components of anthropological methodologies—prolonged fieldwork and the embodied experiences of the people with whom we conduct our research.

Several years later, in the novel *Adiós, Ayacucho*, Julio Ortega provided a thinly veiled political commentary on these same events, suggesting that anthropology as a discipline was one of the fatalities in the aftermath of Uchuraccay.[24] As he suggests, if all anthropologists can do is offer up a mirror in which the "primitive's savagery" is reflected back to them, then it would be best to count anthropology among the dead at Uchuraccay.

These debates formed the backdrop for my early research. I decided to focus on the highlands of Huanta, the province of Ayacucho that encompasses Uchuraccay, Huaychao, and Carhuahurán.[25] I was convinced the answers to my questions about violence and its legacies did not lie in the distant colonial past—violence "then" does not explain violence "now"—or in primordial ethnic latencies. I wanted to explore how villagers understand the political violence of the 1980s and 1990s, the decision to kill that arose within the context of the war, and the communal processes employed to reclaim those who had "fallen out of humanity" and came around pleading for a way back in.

*   *   *

In a wonderful toss-away line, Luise White reminds us that history is different in different places.[26] So true! Over the years I have followed ideas, people, hunches, rumors, and the occasional consulting gig throughout Ayacucho. This movement in both time and space generated an abiding appreciation for the irreducible complexities of postwar social worlds, as well as the importance of local specificity. If I wanted to understand what motivated the revolution, this meant including communities that had been militant Shining Path bases. My work with the PTRC made that possible.

In 2002 my research team and I began working with the communities of Accomarca, Cayara, Hualla, and Tiquihua, all located in central-southern Ayacucho, the region Shining Path considered its "Principal Committee."[27] Here the Shining Path cadres had begun their political work a decade before launching the armed phase of the revolution with their 1980 attack on Chuschi. Sendero had much deeper roots in this region than in the highlands of Huanta, and this made for different memories, different truths.[28]

Importantly, the cadres were frequently *lugareños*—local people. While the revolutionary spark in the northern provinces was externally lit, the revolution burned from within these southern communities. In interviews with former militants, I sought to understand what motivated people to join or sympathize with Shining Path, how they view their participation now, and how they interact within these communities as well as with the state.

However, while insisting on the need to listen to the life histories of these former militants to understand their complex motivations for waging war, I do not lose sight of those who feel deeply aggrieved by "those people" (*huk kuna*, referring to the former militants). Daily conversations resonated with local moral idioms—detailed discussions of responsibility, degrees of guilt, and processes of redress. This is "justice talk" in another register, likely to involve references to aching hearts, lacerating ulcers, masks, faces and foreheads held shamelessly high. Local moral discourse is embodied, leading me to think in terms of a phenomenology of justice and injustice, as well as the complicated alchemy of remembering and forgetting that characterizes postwar social worlds. This local moral idiom is one of condemnation and transformation and provides great insight into how people conceptualize their elusive search for justice.

Terror's Talk: Some Notes on Fieldwork, Witches, and War

What is involved in conducting research on political violence? We ask people to speak about life and death, about pain and how it etches the heart. If and when they decide to speak with us, there is no turning back without also turning away. To paraphrase Stanley Cavell, "The utterance 'I am in pain' is my acknowledgment of pain," and it is our research participant's claim upon us. We are "forced to respond, either to acknowledge it in return or to avoid it," and any sort of shared future between the narrator and her listener is at stake.[29] In that encounter, the possibility of distance and impartiality must be surrendered.

Frankly, there is no "observation" when people are at war and you arrive asking them about it. You are, whether you wish to be or not, a participant. When terror weaves its way through a community, words are no longer mere information. Words become weapons and posing a question must mean you plan to do something with the response. How does one conduct fieldwork amid terror's talk?

* * *

It was 1997 and I had been in the village of Carhuahurán for a few weeks when I finally met Michael, the commando of Los Tigres—a special self-defense unit that was paid to stand watch each night. I was interested in why the villagers had added this additional unit and expense to the preexisting *ronda campesina* (armed peasant patrol). I approached Michael with my hand extended, commenting on how happy I was to meet him and eager to talk with him. His feet shifted into a broad stance, his rifle was hoisted more firmly over his shoulder, and he looked me straight in the eyes: "Why do you want to talk to me?"

I began to explain, feeling more nervous with each awkward word that came out of my mouth. I had been introduced by the village president at a general assembly sometime before—certainly he remembered? I tried to explain my research and why I was there. I told him I was interested in the history of the villages, how they had lived during the years of the war, and how they were now rebuilding their communities. He gave me a quizzical look. Finally I felt rescued by a group of small children who approached—I noted how adorable the girls' hats were, rimmed with flowers and ribbons. I made "small talk," not understanding just how oxymoronic the term would be.

That evening in my room, I began mulling over what was happening. My experience with Michael was not unique. When I first arrived, many people invented names for themselves when we met. My earliest field notes are peopled by a phantom cast of pseudonyms. As I would learn, for years the guerrillas had arrived in the village with lists of names. The list was read, those villagers would be separated out, and there would be a *juicio popular* (people's trial) followed by the execution of everyone whose name appeared on the list. The soldiers also arrived with their lists of supposed Senderista sympathizers; many of those named were arrested, killed, or disappeared. Giving one's name was to place oneself at risk.

But it was not just war that made naming so powerful. Added to the political violence are long-standing practices of *hechicería*—witchcraft. These traditional practices are mobilized at times to new uses, as concerns about suspicious alliances during the war give rise to concerns about wrong-doing and revenge in the present.

A key figure in diagnosing witchcraft and settling accounts in Carhua-hurán is don Teofilo, the *curandero* (healer). Teofilo is a tiny man—indeed, his nickname is El Piki (Quechua for "flea"). Teofilo is called upon to read the coca leaves and bodily symptoms; to name a perpetrator when witch-craft is determined; and to head out to the mountains and speak with the *apus*—the mountain gods who were angry that the villagers forgot them during the years of war, causing the gods to ally with the Senderistas.

Teofilo was wary of me when I first arrived, wondering what this gringa was going to do with all she learned. During one of our initial conversations, Teofilo issued a thinly veiled challenge: "So you want to know what I do? The words I use are so powerful that I could destroy you just by speaking them. Do you want me to speak them right now? Do you really think you have the power to handle my words?" He began to laugh, clearly pleased by my discomfiture. I felt very small indeed. He was, after all, the man who knew the language that allowed him to climb the sharp peaks surrounding Carhuahurán and converse with the mountain gods, soliciting advice and appeasing their anger.

The methodological challenges of conducting research during war go far beyond the routine concerns of establishing trust. Over the years, I was told of killing suffered and killing done. I knew who the ex-guerrillas were and why they had been allowed back in, their secret kept from the soldiers at the base. I knew what had happened to don Mario Quispe, the village presi-dent who demanded that the soldiers stop abusing the women—his body was never found; his widow went mad with grief. And there, in the freezing *puna*, I thought about Jeanne Favret-Saada and the French peasants with whom she had worked.

In her book *Deadly Words: Witchcraft in the Bocage*, Favret-Saada sets off to study witchcraft in the provinces of France. As she writes, "In the project for my research I wrote that I wanted to study witchcraft practices. For more than a century, folklorists had been gorging themselves on them, and the time had come to understand them. In the field, however, all I came across was language. For many months, the only empirical facts I was able to record were words."[30] As she comes to realize, "witchcraft is spoken words; but these spoken words are power, and not knowledge or information. . . . In short, there is no neutral position with spoken words: in witchcraft, words wage war."[31] And in war, words trigger terror. Rumor about who was seen where and doing what becomes a matter of life and death.

I reflected on her assertion that language is an act—the word is an act. Ethnographers frequently rely upon the spoken word as conveying information; however, witchcraft is spoken words as action. Informing the ethnographer for the sake of knowing is a contrary idea because a word can fix a fate and whoever puts herself in a position to utter the words is formidable. Knowledge is not neutral, and insisting that one is simply there to "study" keeps people guessing what purpose lies behind wanting to know.

The parallels were striking. Both witchcraft and war involve social relationships that are tense, dangerous, occult, violent, and potentially lethal. Again, there is no neutral place from which to ask, "What happened here? Tell me a bit about the war." By merely speaking, I had entered into terror's talk.

Mass violence provokes a recalibration of perceptual and moral frameworks. This world of altered perceptions and ruptured symbolic systems has been described as the "space of death."[32] In this space of death the signified and signifier come unhinged—the structuralist dream of a chainlink fence of order is disrupted, and the surplus meaning unleashed gives rise to tremendous portent. Everything becomes what it is and yet something more. The wind rustling through the laminated steel roofs of rural houses presages an imminent Senderista attack. A hollow in the mountain signals the opening in which the guerrillas slip out of view and disappear into the earth itself. Villagers assured me that it took the security forces so long to capture Abimael Guzmán because he could transform himself into a rock, a tree, a spring—and the soldiers had only thought to search for a man. Events, sounds, images—these become signs that are read for the warnings they offer or the evil they index.

The surplus of meaning also gives rise to duplicity and doubling. Villagers learned that survival might well depend on showing one face to the soldiers and another to the guerrillas. People lived their public and secret lives, masking their torn allegiances. Many people insisted that everyone became "two-faced" (*iskay uyukuna*), and one could never know which way anyone might turn. Duplicity gives rise to rumor, and rumor is divisive. As Luise White notes, "if we can historicize gossip, we can look at the boundaries and bonds of a community. Who says what about whom, to whom, articulates the alliances and affiliations of the conflicts of daily life."[33] As villagers attempt to forge community as a strategic identity that allows them to make demands upon the state—to suppress internal conflicts in order to present a unified front to state and nongovernmental organizations (NGOs)—gossip becomes explosive. In one community village authorities passed the Ley Contra Chismes (Law Against Gossip) in an attempt to control the power of words to rip the village apart. Authorities tried to control the verbal economy, recognizing that words wound.

This novice anthropologist sought to help, to heal, to demonstrate she meant no harm. I did not realize I was engaging in fields of power I did not perceive or comprehend. I had entered a world of stories, silences, secrets—a world in which trying to catch my bearings left me reeling more often than not.

Teodoro Huanaco's Eye

One day a high-pitched voice sang greetings from outside our door in Carhuahurán. A slender man with smooth skin and a tightly clenched left eye stood outside, his hands grasped in front of him. I had never seen him before, but he brought potatoes to barter for sugar, and I invited him in.

Efraín and I learned his name was Teodoro Huanaco and that he was from Pera. He had come to Carhuahurán during the violence, as had so many people from his village. As he told us, Sendero arrived killing, not talking, in Pera.

We sat sipping *miski yaku* (coffee sweetened with sugar until it reached a syrupy consistency) and chatting for quite awhile. I did not want to be rude but was more than a bit curious about his left eye. It remained closed during his entire visit. I finally asked if he felt well, hoping that might lead us to the topic. It did, and he began explaining why his eye was clenched shut, only opening from three to five o'clock each afternoon.

Several weeks earlier, don Teodoro had gotten very drunk coming home from the *feria* (open-air market) when it was still held an hour-and-a-half walk away in Huaynacancha. He fell down a steep slope and passed out, spending the night in the bitter cold. The next day, he could no longer open his eye: he had been grabbed by *daño* (an illness caused by the mountain gods).[34]

He had thought about joining the Evangelical Church to see if that would cure his eye, but he was reluctant to give up his *trago* (alcohol) and his coca.

"Without coca we can't do anything here. To work we need coca. Besides, there's nothing wrong with chewing coca—it's what the Virgin Mary gave us. During her flight when she was so tired and worried, she sat in the shadow of the coca plant and she began chewing the coca and she realized how good it was for fatigue. She said, 'This plant is good for my children, and I will make the leaves increase for them.' That's why the coca leaves grew— this is a well-known fact," don Teodoro assured us. "But I have been looking at the *libro de los hermanos* [the Bible] just in case."

Efraín and I nodded, understanding he would have to give up his coca if he joined the Evangélicos. As our Evangelical friends explained, just as coca turns the teeth green, so does it stain the soul. Chewing coca was forbidden because you cannot walk through heaven's gates with a green soul.

"Has no one been able to help?" I asked. "It must be so difficult to work."

Don Teodoro nodded. "*Arí mamacita linda*. I've tried so many things for my eye. But nothing has helped."

He left a bit later, and Efraín and I continued to wonder about his eye and why it only opened for two hours each afternoon. *Daño* worked in many ways, and evidently he had an unusual case.

A few days later, the same high voice called out, and it was Teodoro Huanaco again. He explained that he wanted to talk with us but could not do so in front of anyone else. "May I come back tonight?" he asked.

"Absolutely, we'll be here," replied Efraín. "Just come by, *papi*."

It was around eight o'clock when Teodoro appeared again in our doorway, his poncho wrapped tightly around him and the candles casting his shadow against the wall. This time, it became clearer why he wanted to speak to us alone. Teodoro wanted to know if I could cure his eye. I was a bit surprised at first—*daño* was not an illness I knew how to treat.

"I'm not certain, don Teodoro. What would help your eye?"

"We could try flowers, candles, fruit, *trago*, a *pagapu*—it would need to be after midnight. Could you try?" he asked, looking straight at me.

Efraín glanced my way and we spoke softly to each other. He had heard about how people cure *daño*, although he had never tried before. I asked him if he thought we could figure it out and he nodded, reluctantly.

I then asked Teodoro exactly what we would need and that I would try to make the purchases the following Friday at the *feria*. He thanked me repeatedly and left.

Efraín and I were curious—why me? As a gringa, I hardly seemed like a sure thing. However, I had been giving people Ibuprofen for pain, antibiotics for infections, and massages to the women when talking about the violence made them ache. In one instance, amoxicillin probably had saved a man's life.

A few weeks prior to don Teodoro's first visit, a knock at the door had sent me scrambling for my flashlight. I slept with a rock propped against my door, figuring that if the soldiers planned a nocturnal visit, at least I would have a few minutes' warning. But the voice that replied to my "Who is it?" clearly belonged to a child.

I slid the rock back, creaked open the rusty aluminum sheet, and found a little boy and his mother standing in a slender stream of moonlight, both in tears. The boy told me his father, Jesús, was very ill and asked me to come look at him. I gathered up my first aid kit and flashlight, and we made our way down past the preschool, silvery light reflecting off the roofs and barely illuminating the rocky path beneath my stumbling feet.

We entered their house and they directed me toward the heap of blankets piled on the bed. A man was lying there, breathing laboriously. I could feel the heat that emanated from his body before even touching him, and the gurgling congestion in his chest was audible with each strained breath. I thought he had bronchitis, perhaps even pneumonia. We began a seven-day treatment with antibiotics and aspirin, massages with mentholatum—and sugar, requested by his wife to give him strength.

He did recover, and the seriousness of his illness was impressed upon me during the rainy seasons I spent in Carhuahurán. The interminable rains of December–March left everything and everyone damp: we could go for days without a moment of dryness, torrents alternating with drizzles. Each rainy season the cemetery was filled with more children and adults who first had bronchitis and then, in combination with malnutrition and a reluctance to go to the health post, pneumonia. Jesús and his family insisted I had saved his life: the strips of dried beef hanging from the rafters in my room were the proof, along with the hugs and exclamations each time we crossed paths.

Thus it was not as strange as it might seem that Teodoro came to my door. Unfortunately, the Friday *feria* was poorly attended and we could not obtain all of the necessary supplies. We spoke with Teodoro and told him I would be heading for Huamanga and could make the purchases there. We agreed on this alternative plan.

When I arrived in Huamanga, I spoke with some of my Peruvian colleagues, mentioning Teodoro's eye and his request for help. They immediately asked me what in the world I was thinking. Now, this "what in the world" was not referring to what one might assume—a "what in the world" bafflement that I *could actually believe all that*. On the contrary, my colleagues were concerned that I was involving myself in forms of power and politics I clearly did not understand. They shook their heads and asked why I would want to get involved with forces I did not know how to command. As they insisted, healing such afflictions is highly specialized, and the *curanderos* zealously guard their secrets and their clientele. If I did succeed in healing don Teodoro, this would confirm my status as competition for their services and as someone to be reckoned with. They convinced me I was walking into an explosive situation, and I was both frightened by my ignorance and ashamed of what must have struck them as arrogance.

When I returned to Carhuahurán, I relayed these conversations to Efraín. He looked profoundly relieved; he also had some new information. Several villagers had come by to let him know that Teodoro Huanaco was a powerful *brujo*—one of the most powerful witches in the region. Teodoro said he used *el libro de los hermanos*, but others implied the book he used was not the Bible.[35] We were warned to be very careful—he was a dangerous man. I felt responsible for having gotten us into this mess; Efraín had a wife and a small daughter, and I apologized for placing all of them at risk. I assured him I would take care of this. I think I was also trying to reassure myself.

Sure enough, Teodoro came by later in the day. After we exchanged greetings and invited him in, I brought out the bottle of rum I had carefully carried with me from the city. I poured the first shot for Teodoro, thus sending the tin cup on its way around our small circle. Two rounds into the rum, I knew I needed to give the clumsy speech I had been practicing over and over in my head. I explained that I had felt so much sympathy for him when he first asked for help—that I could only imagine how difficult it must be to maintain his family given how much he was suffering.

"Don Teodoro, I give people some pills when they have headaches—sometimes I clean wounds with rubbing alcohol. That's really all I know how to do. I have no idea how to cure *daño* but hoped I could somehow figure it out because I wanted to help you. But I'm far too ignorant and the *apus* would never pay attention to me. I don't know the *palabras íntimas* [intimate words] to use—the *apus* would never listen to me. I'm so sorry. I'm just a gringa with some pills. I don't have any power to cure something like *daño*."

Teodoro sat back in his chair looking at me with his one unblinking eye. Slowly an expansive smile worked its way across his face. He nodded. "That's what I thought."

Why had he sought me out? Why didn't he go to El Piki, to Manuco—why me? As an outsider, why did he think I would know how to cure *daño*?

Whereas El Piki did not want to talk to me—and when he did, he used the opportunity to assure me he could do away with me simply by uttering the right words—Teodoro had another way of sizing me up.

I was being challenged to a witchcraft duel: he wanted to test me. I thought I had cured Jesús of pneumonia; as I subsequently found out, his symptoms resembled those of *daño*, and there were a number of people who were convinced I was more than just a gringa with a first aid kit. I had been climbing the hills, scrounging for kindling, in complete disregard for where I stepped or sat. And yet the angry gods had not grabbed me for my lack of respect—I was not ill, and that made me suspect. I had also been treating people's ailments, within my own limited understanding of their etiology. Teodoro wanted to see what others sorts of magic I might work. Was I truly powerful or simply a gringa with *miski yaku*, some pills, and a very large dog? The Senderistas had made pacts with the *apus*—did I have some sort of relationship with them as well?

But I did not have *palabras íntimas* that would cause the *apus* to recognize me. I can still see that big smile on Teodoro Huanaco's face when I told him I was both ignorant and powerless: he was delighted.

So in the midst of such painful and dangerous times, why should people speak at all? What is the researcher's responsibility in light of how much is at stake? If I wanted to stay, I had to take a stand and make it explicit. I had to demonstrate that I would put the knowledge shared with me to good use or get out.

Obviously I am not the first anthropologist to note the implausibility of neutrality in the face of struggle.[36] However, I am not simply noting the need to take a position as an ethical imperative; rather, I am arguing that one's presence, one's speech, elide neutrality. We are, to paraphrase Favret-Saada, already caught. Conducting fieldwork during times of armed conflict requires tremendous time—people will not speak with you if you arrive asking. Additionally, one simply cannot observe. You will not be permitted to if you ever intend to open your mouth. There will come a point when you must take a stand. People will remind you that you are far too implicated not to, just as they reminded me.

One morning I was called out of my room by gunshots and shouting. A crowd had gathered outside the *calabozo*—the room the *ronderos* (peasant patrollers) used to lock up prisoners overnight. I made my way through the crowd and found soldiers using their rifles to push away the women who were attempting to shove past them into the *calabozo*. I saw mama Juliana and mama Sosima, shouting at the soldiers. As I made my way to Juliana, I learned that her partner, Esteban, was one of the young men locked inside. *La leva* had made its way to Carhuahurán—the illegal forced "recruitment" by the army of young and primarily undocumented men. However, "men" seemed a euphemism for the adolescent boys locked inside. Juliana was distraught: Although several years her junior, Esteban was a good partner for her, bringing bright pink plastic shoes to her little daughter Shintaca. He was a kind stepfather and a hard worker. Juliana was not going to allow these soldiers to take him away. The mothers of the other two young men were also protesting, and before too long the women were grabbing the soldiers' rifles and attempting to pull them out of their hands.

People knew I had a camera and told me to run and get it. Villagers began exhorting me to take pictures of the soldiers as they struggled with the women. I began shoving my camera up close and photographing their faces. I joined in the shouting and the grabbing. The soldiers began to back down: being photographed shoving unarmed women around with their rifles may have disturbed them. The mayor came down and in front of the soldiers agreed that I should take the photos to the Defensoría del Pueblo and show them what had happened. Mayor Rimachi and the women succeeded in freeing the young men—the women simply refused to back down.

I had previously been hesitant in my dealings with the soldiers, always conscious that my actions might have unintended consequences for the villages in which I lived and worked. Although an airplane could deliver me to safety, for villagers flight would not be airborne. However, in this situation, there was only one thing to do. Had I not stood side by side with the women as they grabbed those rifles out of the soldiers' hands, who would I have been in that context when the soldiers moved on? I had spent many evenings around small cooking fires and blackened pots, listening to how the soldiers had treated the women and young girls when the military base was fully operational and positioned on the slope overlooking the village. The panopticon had brought daily life under the power of its gaze. I had heard the stories; I could choose a side or have one chosen for me.

I did indeed meet with the Defensor del Pueblo en Huamanga, as well as with the director of the Coordinadora Nacional de Derechos Humanos (CONADEH) in Lima. These groups knew that *la leva* continued despite official denial of the practice. Photos provided some proof, and the events of that day could become something more than just the routine abuse of rural villagers in the countryside. The women had made the difference; the photos were testimony to that.

Nancy Scheper-Hughes has asked, "What makes anthropology and anthropologists exempt from human responsibility to take an ethical (and even a political) stand on the working out of historical events as we are privileged to witness them?"[37] She discerns between the anthropologist as witness and the anthropologist as spectator, and I agree with her insistence on our role as committed witnesses. To merely watch is to reduce the sensuous world and high stakes of events such as this to spectacle—the optic of the distant observer for whom the world is an intellectual project rather than a world in which one is engaged.

However uneasily, I have tried to work as an advocate. I have used my research to argue for where new schools should be built and where bilingual education programs could make a critical difference. I have listened to villagers' criticisms of the NGOs and their endless surveys and workshops; I've suggested to the NGOs what "participation" might look like—distinct from the "top-down participation" that can amount to no more than a restructuring of control.[38] Whenever possible, I provided communal authorities with copies of the reports and recommendations that NGOs produced so people could have some sense of what had been promised versus what was delivered. Finally, I have used my ongoing research on sexual violence and reparations to argue for a greater measure of justice for women in the aftermath of war. "On the ground" these issues pull the anthropologist in many directions. The ethnographic particulars of the situation challenge one's intellectual paradigms, theoretical constructs, the ground on which one stands. I trust we will always be challenged.

* * *

A note about the chapters that follow. There is no conventional chronology, no "telling the sequence of events like the beads of a rosary."[39] My beads are unstrung, and that is most faithful to the way I experienced my research. This was not a simple story to follow. It was full of switchbacks, dead ends, detours, bodies found and lost, whispers, outright lies, and silences. Think of concentric circles that ripple out from those deceptively simple questions that compelled me back to Peru.

We begin with some cross-cutting themes to establish a shared vocabulary, if you will. We look at the social ills people associate with the war and how they attempted to soothe these wounds of the body and soul. We then consider two iconic figures, The Rape Victim and The War Widow, to unsettle some commonsense notions about gender and armed conflict. Then we move from the northern communities to the central-south, exploring the complex local dynamics of making enemies, learning to kill, and the efforts people have made to reconstruct social life amid intimate enemies.

Chapter 2

Sensuous Psychologies

VÍCTOR RIVERA WAS one of the people who came into the TRC office in Ayacucho each weekday, took his place in a row of cubicles, stretched the large black earphones over his head, and listened hour after hour to some of those 16,917 testimonies. The *relatores* performed several tasks in the broader scheme of data management. They translated the testimonies from Quechua into Spanish, summarizing what they heard into two- to three-page *relatos*, and introduced chronology and coding. This was emotionally difficult work. Testimonies given to a truth commission do not make for easy listening.

I interviewed eleven *relatores* about the training they had received. They explained the challenges they had initially faced when listening to emotional, rambling testimonies. As Víctor recalled, "I had a lot of trouble at first because I was accustomed to transcribing what I heard, just literally transcribing what people said in a disorderly way. They told stories—they wound around. But in the training we learned how to construct a chronological sequence: Antecedents, Facts, Actions Taken, Sequelae, and Expectations for the Future. I got so behind at first because it was hard to learn the sequence. Besides, I listened to drastic things, I'd be crying. The sadness of the testimonies was contagious."

In addition to introducing linearity into the *relatos*, the *relatores* were responsible for an initial coding process, and one task involved translating Quechua speakers' ailments into biomedical categories. Sandra, who worked on the *relatos* in addition to collecting testimonies, recounted the training she had received from the team that arrived from Lima: "The trainers told us that *campesinos* are very imaginative, and they would tell us all sorts of fabulous things. We were warned not to fall for all of that. *Susto* [soul loss due to fright], *llakis* [painful memories that fill the body and torment the soul], irritation of the heart—they told us those things were inconceivable. They don't exist."

I was baffled. "So what were you told to do when you were working on the *relatos*?"

"Well, they asked us to describe some of the symptoms—fearful, loss of appetite, painful memories. They said some things could be malnutrition, but most of it was trauma. They told us that people were suffering from trauma."

"So in the *relatos*, you categorized these ailments as trauma?"

Sandra nodded. "Yeah, these problems were coded as trauma [*estar traumado*]."

Coding for Trauma

> Among neighbors, among family members—we killed each other here. *Jesúcristo*, even now I still don't understand.
> —Moises, Tiquihua, 2003

The violence in Peru frequently involved people who lived in the same social worlds and knew each other well—or at least thought they did. In many communities, these same people find themselves forced to share spaces that were recently scenes of intimate, lethal violence. When a woman continues to live across the street from her rapist, or a son crosses paths each week at the market with the men who murdered his father, what does it mean to work on mental health? How can we best understand and respond to the psychological aftermath of war?

The discourse of trauma—and the psychiatric diagnosis of post-traumatic stress disorder (PTSD)—plays a prominent role in postconflict and humanitarian conceptions of suffering. This diagnosis was first included in the American catalogue of psychiatric disorders in 1980 with specific reference to Vietnam-era American war veterans. Over the past three decades the range of application of this diagnosis has expanded dramatically, and concepts of traumatic memory have become the dominant framework for medical engagement with social suffering both domestically and internationally.[1] There is an enormous market for trauma and an industry of trauma experts deployed to postwar countries to detect symptoms of PTSD via the use of "culturally sensitive" questionnaires. In the process of globalizing the discourse of trauma through humanitarian and postconflict interventions, the trauma narrative itself has become increasingly normative, making it difficult to think otherwise about violent events and their legacies. From Holocaust survivors to U.S. soldiers in Vietnam, from battered women in Latin America to child soldiers in the Congo and survivors of rape in the Balkans, mainstream trauma theories beguile with their alleged capacity to encompass vastly divergent experiences fraught with etiological and moral complexity.[2]

Parallel with the growth of the trauma industry, however, has been a debate regarding the diagnostic category PTSD and its underlying assumptions. The literature questioning the utility of PTSD in "non-Western" or nonclinical settings—for example, in postwar contexts—is abundant, and I will not rehearse a well-worn series of debates.[3] There is, however, a gap between academic critique and the "on the ground" world in which battles are waged over funding priorities, service design, and delivery. When I worked with the PTRC in Ayacucho, it became clear that nongovernmental organizations would be jockeying for position to work on mental health, with mental health concerns frequently reduced to "trauma." A scant three years later, many people would accuse those same NGOs of "trafficking with the blood and the pain of the people" in their efforts to secure funding during the "mental health boom."[4]

A caveat. One hackneyed anthropological move is to speak "our" cultural relativism to "their" (read: psychiatry's) universalism via a litany of examples that at times resemble a compendium of exotica.[5] I am not interested in assembling a list of sundry illness categories, pinned to the page like so many colorful butterfly wings. Rather, my aims are twofold. First, I want to question an enduring juxtaposition and its consequences: some people and groups have "theory" and others have "beliefs"; some people and groups export categories of knowledge, while others remain resolutely "culture bound." One problem with the increasingly normative trauma discourse and models such as PTSD is their pretentious scope, reducing other theories (generally called "beliefs and customs") to little more than local deviations of a universal truth. From this perspective, there would be little or nothing to learn from the sophisticated theories Quechua speakers have elaborated about violence and its effects, about social life and their struggle to rebuild it.

Second, I want to investigate the social and moral implications of framing violence and its legacies in terms of trauma.[6] I am troubled less by the relativist concern with the imposition of "Western categories" and more by what the discourse of trauma allows people to say and do. Approaching these topics in terms of the "West and the rest" is not useful, descriptively or analytically.[7] "Western categories" elide the complex ways in which people engage with global institutions and obscure how place-based engagements with these institutions involve complex, unpredictable negotiations and outcomes. Rather than assuming a "traumatized" population that homogenizes victims and perpetrators into a morally elastic category, there are more interesting and complicated stories to tell. These stories might, in turn, teach us a great deal about the individual and collective consequences of lethal, intimate violence and what is involved in reconstructing both people and place in the aftermath of war.

In this chapter and the next, I explore the discourse of trauma and how it moves in local social and political fields.[8] Trauma is, in part, a technology of commensuration designed to yield scientifically authorized categories of harm across vastly divergent lifeworlds. I discuss the implications of the PTRC's coding process and what was lost in translation. I then move on to the theories Quechua speakers have about health, illness, and healing, exploring the crucial links between the body and memory, between emotions and illness, between ethnopsychological concepts of the human and what these reveal about processes of punishment, atonement, and, at times, redemption.

*   *   *

I was proud to work with the Peruvian TRC, and their Final Report is rigorous and politically important. However, certain methodological aspects troubled me. "Coding for trauma" was one of them. How can interventions help people rebuild their lives without understanding locally salient theories of illness, health, agency, and social repair? How do we respond to the needs of survivors of war without understanding the local forms and logics of social ties and their transformation? Without understanding what makes a being human, and to whom that status is conferred or denied?

In his analysis of the data coding process employed by the South African TRC, Richard Wilson found that the desire to create legally defensible findings led to the development of an elaborate classification scheme that broke each testimony down into a series of forty-eight categories of violation. Wilson argues that "The integrity of the narrative at the data processing stage was destroyed as processors deconstructed the single narrative and 'captured' discrete acts and the details of victims, witnesses and perpetrators."[9] The creation of legally defensible findings thus came at the expense of victims' experience of telling their stories, which in turn led to the "Final Report [being] little more than a chronicle of wrong acts."[10]

Although the PTRC's Final Report moves far beyond a mere chronicle of human rights violations, I share Wilson's concerns about the systematic distortions involved in converting testimonies into evidence. Truth commissions are aware they are producing final reports for various audiences. One audience is the "international community," and this is an incentive to employ key diacritics of veracity: linear chronologies, tables and charts, quantifiable violations, dates, times—and trauma. As a technology of commensuration, the discourse of trauma is globally recognized and can "authorize the real."[11] Thus locally salient categories of affliction, which may reference radically different understandings of etiology, are coded as trauma. This entails important semantic shifts. It also simplifies complex moral and political situations.[12]

In the section of the PTRC's Final Report titled "Psychosocial Sequelae," the authors state that allusions to being traumatized are abundant in the testimonies, with trauma understood as a state of confusion or disorientation as a result of the violence.[13] They acknowledge that Quechua speakers learned the term as a result of NGO interventions. My point is that people were also "traumatized" as a result of the data coding process.

I had several meetings with the PTRC's mental health team in Lima, and our first conversation was a jolt. I presented some preliminary findings, outlining various memory afflictions, *llakis*, *susto*, irritation of the heart, *la teta asustada* (the frightened breast). At the end of my talk, there was awkward silence. I wondered what had gone awry. Someone finally explained the initial silence: with the exception of *susto*, this team of seasoned and committed mental health professionals had never heard of these ailments. As one person remarked, "It's as though you were talking about another world." What had happened?

As we talked, the reason became clear. The mental health team was analyzing the *relatos*, understandable given the number of testimonies and the time constraints. In the *relatos* people were "traumatized," and thus the various afflictions I discussed were absent. To their credit the mental health team attempted to rectify this problem. Midway through the TRC process, they obtained funds to have a sample of 401 testimonies transcribed in Quechua and subsequently translated into Spanish in an effort to capture what people had actually said they suffered from. This sample, however, was still limited because the interviews had not been designed to explicitly explore the theme of mental health; rather, the interview guide was aimed at collecting facts about the human rights violations people reported.[14]

Truth commissions have pedagogical objectives. One didactic goal is to educate both domestic and international audiences about a violent past as a means of ensuring nonrepetition: in this case, memory is understood to exercise a deterrent effect. Individual testimonies provide the raw "memory material" that is processed and from which a collective narrative is forged. In an effort to produce "intelligible results," there is a move to technologies of commensuration. This may include the standardized software program used to analyze data, the teams of international experts who move from country to country to provide technical assistance, as well as the discourse of trauma itself. These strategies are part of the globalized transitional justice industry and are marshaled in the interest of producing findings that are defensible and that allow a final report "to speak" beyond the context in which it was produced. For the PTRC, it allowed the Final Report to translate "inconceivable things" into science and thereby authorize the suffering and the text.

These are worthy goals. However, I cannot shake off some doubts. When first thinking through this material, it was tempting to assert that the discourse of trauma involves the systematic erasure of local meaning. While this is true for the *relatos* and the coding process, trauma circulated in other spheres in other ways. Although being "*traumado*" was introduced into these communities by external agents, over the years I did hear some Quechua speakers use the term. "*Estar traumado*" became part of local dynamics as people mobilized the category to different ends.[15]

Talking Trauma . . . and Other Modern Things

When I started my work in Peru, I visited various NGOs to introduce myself and learn more about their programs. From the director of an NGO in Lima, I received my first lecture on "how they do not suffer." I explained to the director that I was going to work in Ayacucho on the impact of political violence in *campesino* communities, and he responded in a tone reserved for children and gringos: "*Señorita*, what you need to understand is that they've already forgotten everything that happened." He leaned forward. "Look. We are capable of abstract thought. That's why we have suffered so much. But they only think in a concrete way—they only think about their daily food and their animals. They don't think beyond that. That's why they haven't suffered like we have. They aren't capable of it." Evidently, being such concrete thinkers, "they" only have access to a range of primary emotions, while the loftier sentiments—love for a child, grief for the murder of a loved one, hope for a different sort of future—are reserved for "us."

There is no way to approach the themes of mental health, political violence, and its legacies without addressing ethnic discrimination, a form of psychological violence that cuts across every aspect of daily life for Quechua-speaking *campesinos*. Nelson Manrique has noted there is no sense of national tragedy in Peru, and this has to do with the characteristics of those who were killed or disappeared during the violence.[16] In the politics of death in Peru, loss of life is measured according to a hierarchy of cultural and ethnic differences. So, evidently, is suffering. Pain and its expression *are* deeply cultural, and how one suffers and makes that suffering manifest will be contoured by the structures of discrimination that shape bodily experience, social hierarchies, and access to services. It is necessary to discuss ethnic discrimination, how this maps onto a geography of difference, and then situate "talking trauma" within this discussion.

I recall the *campesinos* who described their experiences as internally displaced people during the violence. They found it agonizing to "wander in foreign lands," and their poverty was extreme. As one woman recalled, "In the cities everything is money—even to urinate, they charge you fifty *céntimos*. We didn't even have money for food." However, although lamenting the poverty and hunger that characterized those years, what was poignant was her tearful insistence that "The poverty was terrible, but the mistreatment was worse. *Chuto nikurawanchik* they called us—*chutos*, filthy *chutos*." In many conversations with "returnees," the discriminatory treatment they endured in the cities enters into their motives for returning to their communities or for reconstructing them.

According to the *Diccionario de la Lengua de la Real Academia Española*, the word *chuto* comes from the Aymara *ch'utu*, which means "of thick lips." The definition continues: "Said of a crude, uncultured, dirty person; insulting; Indian of the *puna*." There is a fusion of physical and geographical characteristics, constructing both the *puna* and its inhabitants as wild, as savage. However, the dictionary definition is relatively mild when compared to how the word *chuto* is used in daily life. Among ethnic insults, *chuto* is a word that is especially lacerating, and Quechua speakers learn at an early age how deeply the insult can cut.

    *   *   *

The children came piling into our room in Huaychao and began enthusiastically spreading the colored pieces of a jigsaw puzzle across our rickety table. Active hands grabbed the pieces, locating them one way and another until a design began to emerge inside the wooden frame.

The children completed the puzzle and then dumped the pieces upside down to start all over again. While they scrambled the pieces, Edith and Juanjo explained there would be a drawing competition in Huanta, part of a commemorative event that would take place in the municipal stadium. The children were invited to paint murals on the walls of the stadium as part of an effort to reinscribe the space following the years La Marina (navy) had used it as a detention and torture center.

Their faces lit up with the idea: a trip to the city, painting, mandarin oranges, ice cream. They began to talk all at once about what they were going to paint, the volume increasing with their excitement. Suddenly, in the midst of the happiness provoked by the idea of a trip to the city, Edgar posed a question that silenced this group of boys—just little guys ranging from six to ten years old. "But if we go to Huanta, what if they call us *chutos*?"[17]

    *   *   *

Ethnic hierarchies are mapped onto geography in Peru, and despite the massive movement of people, there is a tenacious cartography underpinning discrimination.[18] While *campesinos* also mark territory and difference in a variety of ways, the capacity to define and assign inferior status to certain regions and their inhabitants follows broader power dynamics. Quechua speakers are acutely aware of where they are located (literally and metaphorically) in Peru's ethnic hierarchy. Enter "talking trauma."

One institutionalized site of racism is the Peruvian health care system.[19] In each community, people complain about the ill treatment and expired medications they receive in the health posts. During one visit to Cayara, I headed to the health post in search of a remedy for stomach cramps. In the waiting room a large sign declared the results of a needs assessment the medical staff had conducted:

> It is necessary to mention that the idiosyncrasy of the villagers makes it difficult to carry out the activities of health professionals. This is due to the still persistent taboos, myths and other customs of the community, as well as other sociological factors.[20]

There is a tendency to assume that cosmopolitan medicine—that is, biomedical models—are outside of culture, transparently reflecting a universal biology without cultural mediation. From this perspective, culture is something belonging to the "other" and serves as an obstacle to the advance of science and its double, modernity. In my interviews with personnel in rural health posts, the "beliefs" and *baja cultura* of the *campesinos* were frequently cited as barriers to service provision and compliance. As the sign hanging in that waiting room proclaims, "abandon your myths and taboos at the doorstep, all ye who enter here."

This thinking infuses program design and delivery. For instance, the government agency established to coordinate postwar reconstruction efforts—the Programa de Apoyo al Repoblamiento (PAR)—compiled the results of focus groups held throughout Ayacucho on the theme of sequelae and reparations.[21] On page 68 of the report, the authors assert it was a great "advance" that participants in their focus groups spoke of "being traumatized" and located mental health within their priorities.

The assertion that this is an "advance" is perplexing. Evidently, if before *campesinos* had their taboos and myths, now they were suffering in scientific style. If *campesinos* say they need elixirs for *daño*, offerings for the *apus*, *qayapa* ("calling the soul") for *susto*, perhaps they have not suffered, or perhaps their suffering is simply *inconceivable*.

One day during the TRC process I discussed my research project with a group of young men in Uchuraccay. They were dressed in tennis shoes, jeans, and cheap ski jackets; baseball caps sat snugly atop the brightly colored *chullos* they wore to keep their ears warm. Older people, particularly the women, referred to these young men as *moderña warmakuna* (modern young people). Often as not, the term was a lament! Several of these *moderña warmakuna* had spent part of their lives in the city, just children when their parents packed up what they could and fled during the internal armed conflict.

I discussed some of the themes that had surfaced in the research, such as *daño* and *llakis*, and was interested in hearing what they thought about these ailments. They laughed a bit, kicking the ground with their tennis shoes. Julian, one of the *moderña warmakuna*, shook his head and scoffed: "You know, I've studied in the city. I lived there and I went to school. *Daño*, *llakis*—all that's just belief. Only the ignorant and illiterate believe all that. I studied in the city and I know what we have is trauma."[22]

How one is ill both reflects and establishes social status.[23] With the influx of state and NGO interventions throughout Ayacucho, *campesinos* learned to express suffering in a language that could make their suffering legible to the experts, to "outsiders." Talking trauma legitimates their pain in the face of those who discard their afflictions as mere superstition or survivals from some distant past. One motivation for talking trauma is recognition—recognition for being someone just as capable of suffering as the person sitting on the other side of the desk in the health post, or holding a clipboard and pen, poised to complete the PTRC's questionnaire.[24]

Veena Das and Ranendra Das's comments on medical pluralism echo here: "Although biomedical categories and therapies have reached different parts of the world in very different ways, the condition of medical diversity or medical pluralism is now universal. The fact raises significant questions about how concepts of health and illness travel. How are these concepts translated, and how do people deal with different expert cultures in making intimate bodily experiences available for therapeutic intervention?"[25] In addition to asking how people translate illness categories and what sorts of claims are expressed via the identities and social dynamics these categories construct, it is worth exploring how people understand what interventions, in this case psychological services, can do.

"Too Much Memory"

One morning Edgar, the guard in the TRC's Ayacucho office, peered around my door. "Doctora Kimberly, there's someone here to see you. He says he's from Hualla."

Both Edith and I headed out to see who it was. The man standing just inside the enormous wooden portal was unknown to us, at least until he introduced himself: Hernán Pariona. Edith and I exchanged a furtive glance and anticipation tickled the back of my neck. We had never met Hernán, but we had heard so much about him from people in Hualla. He had been one of the key Shining Path militants in town and, depending upon the speaker's allegiance during the war, he was alternately described with admiration, hatred, or fear.

We invited him into our office and began some small talk as Nescafé crystals slowly dissolved in our cups of hot water. Hernán had been living in Ica for a few years, returning occasionally to Hualla to tend to the land he owned. On this trip he had come straight from Hualla to our office because he had been told about our research team.

"People said you were working on mental health, and that's what we need," he explained. "We need psychological treatment in Hualla."

I was struck by his request. It was the first time someone had placed psychological treatment on the list of needs they discussed with me. I quickly replayed some conversations in my mind. Several people in Hualla had assured us theirs was a "traumatized pueblo," describing the bitter conflicts that surfaced when people were drinking. I recalled one of José Carlos's field note entries: Several people had complained to him about how tense Hualla was. "People start insulting each other, calling each other *terrucos* [slang for "terrorists," referring to members of Shining Path]. They say, 'I know what you did.' Others threaten, reminding us just who we're living with."

I hesitated for a moment. "Hernán, tell me a bit more about the psychological treatment you want in Hualla."

He shifted in his chair and exhaled his frustration. "Life in Hualla is impossible! People argue all the time. Before we can even think about reconciliation, we need psychological treatment."

"And what is it about psychological treatment in particular that would help?" I wondered.

"Well, everybody keeps remembering everything. They keep insulting each other, especially when they're drunk. It's one big fight. If we could have professional attention—therapy with a professional—we could forget everything that happened."

"So, therapy would be necessary so you could live together again?"

Hernán nodded. "That's right. You know what the big problem in Hualla is? There's too much memory—way too much memory," repeating the line for emphasis. "With psychological treatment, we could forget everything. That way we could live together again—peacefully," he added.

Hernán's understanding of therapy and what it might achieve is fascinating. Somehow professional attention could erase the memories and assist people in achieving a state of forgetfulness. This is certainly at odds with the redemptive vision of memory that characterizes contemporary memory politics. Even more interesting was the person soliciting the therapy: a former Shining Path cadre who later assured me that ex-Senderistas were marginalized and *mal visto* (negatively viewed) in Hualla by those who blame them for the devastation of the internal armed conflict. Too much memory indeed.[26]

Returning to the section of the PTRC's Final Report in which the mental health team analyzed the 401 testimonies, there is a finding that bears upon this discussion: "Despite the lack of mental health services in the country, which carries with it a lack of information on the part of the population about the type of attention and help they could receive from this sort of service, eleven percent of the [401] testimonies analyzed registered explicit requests for psychological support to respond to the effects of the political violence."[27] What is intriguing, even more than the small percentage of people who requested psychological support, is that we do not know what that 11 percent think psychological support might do for them and for those around them.

Despite their omnipresent criticisms of their health posts, people are not rejecting medical care per se. Indeed, claiming trauma is in part a demand for services. Talking trauma is one way of constructing the intervenable subject—individually and collectively. There will be no projects providing elixirs for *daño*, no NGOs heading to the mountains with sacrifices for the *apus*. Interventions and their subjects must fit within a modernist paradigm: angry ancestors no, trauma yes. The modern subject of suffering is traumatized.

However, if the researcher listens to the concerns of survivors in these communities, then she must focus on social disorders, injustice, angry gods, witchcraft, poverty, and spiritual and moral confusion. The researcher must account for a social world that is dangerous and capable of producing affliction. Arthur Kleinman and Joan Kleinman have suggested that the ethnographer focus on what is at stake for particular people in particular situations in order to understand the social-psychological characteristics of life in local moral worlds.[28] What is at stake in postwar contexts is the reconstruction of social relationships, moral communities, cultural forms, and economic networks, and the reinvention of ritual life that allows people to make sense of suffering endured and suffering inflicted.[29]

I oriented my research around a few basic questions: What do people suffer from? What aches and why? Whom do they hold responsible and what should be done with them? How do people talk about what is wrong with their world, and how might it be set right? These questions led to the theories Quechua speakers have developed about the body and memory, about emotions and illness, and about the qualities that constitute being human.

*   *   *

Marcos was the *promotor de salud* (a layperson trained in first aid)[30] in Carhuahurán. He came by early one morning, seeking assistance in writing a request for funds to establish a "soup kitchen" for children under the age of five. Marcos brought a clean sheet of white paper and the community's rusty typewriter with him.

In the request, Marcos discussed how the political violence had severely affected Carhuahurán, prompting him to solicit funding to open the Children of Jesus Soup Kitchen. I suggested we strengthen the request by incorporating statistics from the health post indicating that 80 percent of the children in Carhuahurán and its eleven outlying annexes (*pagos*) suffered from chronic malnutrition. Marcos nodded emphatically: "Yes. You know, here we need to think of the violences," emphasizing that chronic hunger and poverty would require us to speak of violence in its plural form.[31] War and poverty had both assaulted his community, with various consequences. Violence is frequently described as senseless, which I accept with modification. Horrific violence destroys accepted meanings (while creating others) and assaults the sensory organs. Allen Feldman has referred to a "sensorium of violence" to capture how one's perceptions are altered by armed conflict and fear.[32] It is the overwhelming sentience of violence that stands out in my conversations with survivors of war. Survivors' testimonies are punctuated with syllables imitating the bombs that fell and the whipping wind of the army helicopters. Many people insisted they had cried until they had lost their vision—insisted bodies that carry so much sadness are bodies that ache and age before their time.

*   *   *

Byron Good has argued that one contribution anthropology offers to the study of psychopathology is a focus on phenomenological reality—the categories of experience associated with a particular phenomenon rather than symptom criteria presumed to reflect universal biological categories.[33] Entering into the realm of meaning and experience allows us to grasp different understandings of etiology, as well as how health and illness are socially and historically produced. Thus we can move beyond stale debates regarding universality versus cultural specificity, combining an interest in human nature with a commitment to investigating human conditions.

Drawing upon phenomenology, Thomas Csordas has suggested "embodiment" as a methodological approach in which bodily experience is understood as the existential basis of culture and of the self.[34] Embodiment begins with the assumption that all human experience is intrinsically embodied social experience, which involves a mode of presence and engagement in the world. From this perspective, the body in its various cultural configurations is used as a means of expressing emotions and states of being; what varies is how one learns both to be and to have a body as a member of any given culture.

I combine these approaches with one other: local biologies. Biology is in part a system of signs and meanings, subject to cultural transformation. For instance, Margaret Lock researched menopause in Japan and found that the end of menstruation was significantly different from what is frequently considered universal or "natural." For Japanese women, menopause was not accompanied by the array of symptoms and medicalized responses that characterize the experiences of menopausal women in Canada and the United States. Lock combines her ethnographic research with epidemiological studies of differences in the distribution of heart disease, osteoporosis, and breast cancer in Japan and in the West, leading her to insist that "local biologies" are at work.[35] These theoretical tools allow us to explore how a recent history of violence is embodied and expressed. There are local biologies of poverty, rage, fear, grief—and an array of responses that underscore the close ties between mental health, the administration of justice, and the micropolitics of reconciliation.

Local biologies mean that bodies are historical processes and historical sites. Memories sediment not only in the burned-out houses and churches that dotted the landscape when I began my work in Ayacucho but also in the bodies of the people with whom I have lived.[36] As Paul Stoller insists, "the sentient body is culturally consumed by a world of forces, smells, textures, visions, sounds and flavors that unchain, all of them, cultural memories."[37] Violent experiences leave embodied traces. These traces persist in the stiffness of a neck, the burning of nerves, or the aching of a womb.

*   *   *

It was midday when Dionisia came to my room, the folds of her skirts wrapped tightly in her hands. She called my name from the doorway and I looked up to see her unfolding the embroidered top layer to reveal two eggs her hens had laid earlier that morning. Dionisia's chickens had somehow survived the long presence of the military base that had occupied the hill overlooking Carhuahurán. When at first I had asked people why there were so few chickens in the village, they looked puzzled by a question with so obvious a response: "We don't have chickens. We have soldiers." What initially sounded like a non sequitur in fact conveyed much about civil-military relations during Peru's internal armed conflict.

I thanked her for the eggs, aware that any protein-rich food was scarce. I offered her a cup of *miski yaku*. I loved Dionisia. She was a storyteller, a self-proclaimed *bocona y reclamona*—a "big mouth" who was quite ready to voice her opinion but always with great humor. She had a crinkle-eyed laugh that made both her dangling earrings and me rock back and forth. When I was still a newcomer to the village and a source of tremendous concern and distrust, Dionisia was one of the first women to visit me. It was Dionisia who had convinced the other women that the large sack I carried with me when I went in search of kindling was not used to smuggle out their children in the depth of a moonless night.

She had come to get me so that we could walk down the mountain to her house, lay out in the sun, and talk. "Today I want to tell you about my son," she said. My research assistant Madeleine and I gathered up a few of our things and we headed down to the patch of sun that fell behind her kitchen. She went into her house to grab some blankets and began shaking them out and placing them on the ground. Dionisia began to unwind her *chumbi*, the long woven belt that women use to wrap layers of skirts around their waists.

I opened my bag and took out the massage lotion I used when talking with Dionisia. As with several other women, when the conversation turned to sadness and loss I would massage them, directing my hands to the part of their body that ached with the telling. I prepared to rub her lower back as I usually did, but she stopped me. "No, today I want to talk about my son who was killed." She rolled onto her side and placed my hands on her abdomen: "This is where I hurt."

I began to rub her gently, struck by the contrast between her wiry legs and back and the soft flesh of her stomach. Dionisia had given birth eight times and miscarried on three other occasions. Her soft stomach seemed so vulnerable beneath my hands. We had spoken many times, muscular back stretched out in the warmth of the sun. But today was different.

Teodoro had been her favorite son, the one named after her father, the one who brought her sweet mandarins from the jungle each time he returned from working on the coca plantations. Her eyes began to glisten, and she shook her head: "Better to have been a rock all of those years, better never to have felt anything." Teodoro had left one last time for the jungle and had never returned. The Shining Path guerrillas had killed him with a crushing blow to his head. "They killed people like that, just smashed their heads as though they were frogs." The glistening turned to tears, and her stomach began to heave beneath my hands. Dionisia had not been able to bring his body back for burial, but friends told her how he had died and how they had buried him as best they could so far from home.

I was also crying as we lay in the sun. Dionisia kept speaking, her face wet with tears. She told me that she had cried for so long that some of the other women in the village had told her, "Mama Dionisia, if you don't stop crying you will lose your sight. If you cry too much you'll go blind." So they prepared herbs for her and had her drink them everyday. But her tears did not subside.

The women continued to worry about her, and they insisted she must try to stop crying and cleanse her body of *llakis*. *Llakis* had been known to drive people mad. The women led her to the river where they caught the water as it ran downstream. Pouring the water into a mortar and pestle, they ground it several times and had her drink. But the *llakis* continued to make her body ache, and her *pensamientos* (thoughts) refused to stop. Her head throbbed as the *pensamientos* opened the nerves in the nape of her neck.

Finally one of the older women came to visit her and told Dionisia what she must do. She was to search her entire house and gather up every shred of her son's clothing, place it in a large burlap sack, tie it tight with rope, and walk it out behind her house. Then she would be able to forget, and her tears would finally subside.

"So I went through every bit of my house, and I gathered up everything," she said, "even the shreds of his clothes that I found hanging from the rafter above my bed. I found a large sack, put all of his clothing in it, tied it up tight, and carried the sack out to behind my corral—that's even farther than behind my house." She fell silent. My hands stopped—my entire body paused to listen. By now her stomach was heaving even harder, and Madeleine and I were crying as well. Finally I asked, "So, mama Dionisia, did it help?" Her tears turned to sobbing and she shook her head: "No. I just walked out everyday behind my corral and untied that sack."[38]

This conversation with Dionisia still unsettles me, and I have returned to it many times as I struggle to understand memory, the body, and affliction. Memory is achingly bittersweet. Of course she wants to remember her son but has tried so hard to forget the horrible way Teodoro was killed and the impossibility of mourning his death and burying him as would befit a beloved son. So she ties the sack tightly, only to open it and touch his clothes an innumerable one-last-time.

During my research in Ayacucho, various women asked, "Oh, why should we remember everything that happened? *To martirize our bodies*, and nothing else?" Others insisted their *martirio* (martyrdom) had already begun, starting with an audible rasping in the marrow of their bones. The term "martyr" shares a root with the Latin word *memor*. The martyr is one who voluntarily suffers as punishment for having been a witness. The corporality of memory is central, and the link between the body and memory is evident in the Latin root "testes," from which the words "testicle" and *testigo* (witness) are drawn. The root privileged men as the bearers and reproducers of memory, eclipsing women and their "martyred bodies." In contrast, Veena Das has suggested, "the representation of suffering is such that it is experienced metonymically as bodily pain and it is the female body that shelters this pain in its insides forever."[39] These women were lamenting the bodily toll of remembering and bearing witness.

Dionisia was plagued by *llakis*, one of the most prevalent afflictions throughout the region.[40] *Llaki*, in the singular, can be translated as "sadness" or "pain," but that scarcely does justice to this complex term. *Llakis* are painful thoughts or memories that fill the heart where they are charged with affect. These "emotional thoughts" blur the distinction between intellectual and affective faculties, just as the heart is the seat of emotion as well as memory. *Llakis* can be the product of either political violence or the poverty that serves as a trigger for remembering all that one has lost. This suffering is not merely a state of mind: it is an embodied state of being.

> The thoughts begin in your head, but they drop down to your heart. When they reach your heart, they become *llakis* because of the pain.
> —Hilario Pulido, *promotor de salud*, Accomarca

> When you have pain/sadness, thoughts arrive in your heart. Your heart opens up like a pot with no lid. Your heart cannot contain all of this, all of the *llakis*, and you become pure pain/sadness.
> —Benedicta Mendoza, Accomarca

Llakiwan kachkani can be translated as "I am in pain," consumed by sadness. *Llakis* surge from the heart, overflowing its capacity to contain so many hurtful memories. As they fill the body, "you become pure pain or sadness." This is a "hydraulic model" of the emotions; emotions rise, fall, bear down upon, and travel through the body. There was another powerful expression several women used: *Yuyaynipas tapawan* ("My memories suffocate me"). Beneath the weight of reminiscence, the person cannot breathe and their heart aches. *Llakis* can rob the person of their use of reason, leaving them *sonso* (senseless or mad). And as *llakis* mature in the body, they can be fatal.

Many people described their search for a way to cleanse their bodies of *llakis*. Among methods of cleansing are the use of guinea pigs to "scan" the body, drinking *agua de olvido* (water of forgetfulness, caught as river water runs downstream and forms whirlpools), and the faith healing that occurs in the Evangelical churches. When the women took mama Dionisia to the river and had her drink water caught in the whirlpool, they hoped to cleanse her body and relieve her suffering.[41] Another important point: to claim one is in pain is to place a demand upon others to respond.[42]

The word *llakis* frequently appears together with *pensamientos* (thoughts or worries). Señora Victoria Pariona in Cayara described the effect of *pensamientos*:

I always have *pensamientos*. I'm worried. Sometimes I'm so enraged that I cry, and I have to calm myself down. That's how I am. This *pensamiento* is very heavy, and because of this I ask myself, "What sort of life is it that God allows our destiny to be like this?" The *pensamientos* grab you, really suddenly. A *pensamiento* arrives when you're doing just anything. In that exact moment it grabs you. When you're headed to the path, walking, or sometimes at night, too, when you're tired and sleeping—you're calm and then suddenly a *pensamiento* arrives and you ask yourself again, "What sort of life is this?"

There is a temporal aspect associated with *llakis* that allows us to distinguish between *llakis* and another term that was prevalent in testimonies during the war years: *ñakariy* (to agonize).[43] One agonizes in the moment of horror, but it is with the memories and their unchecked accumulation over time that *llakis* grab the person. The person suffering from *llakis* is suffering from a memory affliction. Just as a person can possess memory, so can memory possess the person, grabbing them, filling their body, maturing to the point that their body itself becomes unbearable. So villagers emphasize their desire to forget.

I had a long conversation in 1997 with a group of women in Umaru, a community that had been virtually destroyed during the war. I was seated with the women amid the burned-out remains of someone's home, conducting a health care needs assessment for an NGO. At one point during our conversation, I asked the women which health care services were a priority in their community. Past experience indicated that a question about services needed could solicit responses that ranged from livestock to food to materials to build an Evangelical church. The women murmured briefly among themselves, and finally one woman responded on behalf of the group: "What we need most are pills to make us forget."

Forgetting is more than a strategy of the powerful over the weak. There are desired forgettings and, as Elizabeth Jelin has argued, "There are forms of forgetting that are 'necessary' for the survival and functioning of the individual subject as well as for groups and communities."[44] There is a need to open space for "positive forgetfulness" that liberates a person from an unbearable past. Forgetting and *remembering to forget* were leitmotifs throughout these communities.

These memory afflictions are different from *les maladies de la mémoire* that concerned the founders of psychotherapy and psychoanalysis.[45] The work of these analysts was situated within concerns about the reality of intrapsychic phenomenon, unclaimed traumatic experience and its recovery, and broader debates regarding the normal and the abnormal. In contrast, *llakis* and "martirizing" one's body are not experienced within a framework of individual normality or abnormality; there is no stigma conferred upon those suffering from *llakis*; nor do *llakis* isolate the sufferer. These memory afflictions do not index an internal world of private suffering but a social world that causes distress, and they invoke a chain of mutual aid and response.[46] The memory of unaddressed wrongs, of economic dispossession, of loved ones brutally killed—these memory afflictions indict a social world that is capable of making people very ill indeed.

The Frightened Breast

> My daughter was born the day after the massacre at Lloqllepampa. We were hidden in a hut. I told my husband to leave because if the soldiers came they would have killed him. I gave birth all alone. During that time we were escaping, I didn't even have milk to breastfeed my baby. How was I going to have milk when there was nothing to eat? One day the other women told me, "If you leave your baby in the mountain, *alcanzo* [also known as *daño*] will grab her and she'll die." Remembering this, I left her in the mountain so she would die. How was she going to live like that? I'd passed all of my suffering in my blood, in my milk. I watched her from a distance, but she began to cry so much I had to go back and get her so that the soldiers wouldn't hear her. If they had, they would've killed me. That's why I say my daughter is damaged because of everything that happened, and because of my milk, my blood, my *pensamientos*. Now she can't study. She's seventeen and she's still in fifth grade. She says her head hurts, it burns. What could it be? *Susto*? Ever since she was a baby she's been like this. I took her to a *curandero* and he tried to change her luck. But it's no better—it just stays the same. I took her to the health post and they gave her pills [Dioxycillin] to take everyday. What could it be? Nothing helps her.
>   —Salomé Baldeón, Accomarca

There is another reason people, particularly women, attempt to forget and spare their bodies further martyrdom.[47] Not only do toxic memories torment them; they also pose a danger to their children. Quechua speakers have elaborated a sophisticated theory regarding the transmission of suffering and *susto* from mother to child, either in utero or via the mother's breastmilk. The term used in Quechua is *mancharisqa ñuñu. Ñuñu* can mean both breast and milk depending on the context and the suffix, and *mancharisqa* refers to *susto* or fear. In my Spanish publications, I have translated the term as *la teta asustada* (the frightened breast) to capture this double meaning. *La teta asustada* conveys how strong negative emotions and memories can alter the body and how a mother can transmit these harmful emotions to her baby.[48] Quechua speakers insist the frightened breast can damage a baby, leaving the child slow-witted or predisposed to epilepsy.

In addition to Salomé's daughter, there are six other young people in Accomarca with various congenital problems: they are deaf, mute, or suffering from epileptiform attacks. These young people are collectively referred to as "children of the massacre." All of their mothers were pregnant when the soldiers entered Accomarca, rounded people up in Lloqllepampa, and killed them. The mothers of these seven young people escaped and watched the killing from their hiding places in the surrounding mountains. All seven women gave birth in the days and weeks following the atrocities.

Rather than disregard this as anecdotal evidence, it echoes the findings of a study conducted in Chile, where a team of researchers studied the impact of political violence on pregnant women. For the study, the researchers determined which barrios of Santiago had suffered the most political violence and disappearances. They selected a sample of barrios, ranging from low to high levels of political violence. They followed the pregnancies and deliveries of a group of women from each barrio and, when they controlled for confounding variables, the researchers determined that the women who had lived in the most violent barrios suffered a fivefold increase in pregnancy and delivery complications.[49] Both the epidemiological study and the pervasive theory that villagers have with respect to the damaging effects of violence, terror, and *llakis* on both a mother and her baby are suggestive and warrant further study. These women and their children provide a painful example of the violence of memory.

Rural Afflictions

When I began working with rural communities in Ayacucho, I asked people which illnesses were most common. There was an answer that has stayed with me: "Well ... coughs, colds, colic. But more than illnesses, it's the *males de campo*[50] that grab us." On several occasions I was told *los males de campo* (rural afflictions) would not grab me because I was from the city and "did not believe in them," which illustrates the ethnicized geography discussed earlier. In addition to marking territory and status, this phrasing distinguishes between the ailments that send one to the health post versus those that prompt a visit to the *curandero*.

Throughout Ayacucho, biomedically oriented health posts coexist with *curanderos*, healers whose innovative bricolage defies the term "traditional." Villagers go to the health post for the bags of fortified powdered milk the government distributes, as well as for the treatment of bronchitis and malaria and for birth control. These are considered strictly "health problems"—medical issues for which the health post may be useful. It is with the *curanderos*, however, that villagers address what is wrong with the world: ancestors who are angry, the envious neighbor who has placed a curse, the *llakis* that riddle the body with pain, ex-enemies whose presence in the village irritates the heart, and the earth itself that reaches up and grabs those who carelessly tread where they should not.

Curanderos can serve as lay psychologists by treating the relational aspects of life; they diagnose "social ills." While one may visit the health post for an acute but short-term problem, with *curanderos* there is follow-up and frequently a series of visits. Importantly, with *curanderos* there is respectful interaction. Within a population that resists the idea of spending two *soles* (roughly sixty-five cents) for a trip to the health post, patients may well pay the *curandero* with a sheep in exchange for his services.[51]

Males de campo refer to disordered social relations and to the spiritual and moral confusion that characterizes a postwar society. Indeed, these *males de campo* frequently arise from strong negative emotions. Michel Tousignant has noted that emotions are generally conceived throughout Latin America as important etiological factors of illnesses.[52] In addition to causing individual illness, certain emotions are considered socially disruptive and dangerous. Managing strong negative or retributive emotions is one part of managing conflict.

Carlos Alberto Seguín has suggested many illnesses in these communities have an "ethnoreligious" aspect.[53] In contrast with PTSD, which marginalizes the spiritual plane, these *males de campo* have a strong religious component. The separation of spheres of experience into nonporous categories (for example, natural/supernatural, secular/religious) is an obstacle to understanding the semantic world in which these villagers become ill, recover—in which they live.

"The *males de campo* grab us." The verb in Quechua is *qapiy* and deserves a few additional words. A woman in Accomarca described her pain and how difficult it is to be alone because "When I'm alone, the sadness follows and wants to grab me." Similarly, *alcanzo* can grab a person when they step or sit where they should not, angering the *apus*, who grab the person with vomiting, fever, and overall bodily pain. The harmful agent is not located within the individual: rather, the "badness" or "evil" enters and grabs the person. This exteriority is important when we consider the rehabilitation of perpetrators and the processes used to cleanse them of their evil or wrongdoing. This is one component of a complex understanding of agency, accountability, and the force of things: objects, words, and violence itself are imbued with their own agency.[54]

The healing processes used by *campesinos* emphasize cleansing and purgation. The idea of cleansing one's interior and purging the "badness" is common and is invoked at the communal level as well. Villagers often exteriorize the violence ("the violence arrived here") and the Senderistas ("they arrived here—where could they have come from?"). People attempt to locate the cause of sociopolitical problems outside the community, depicting the violence and its perpetrators as invading the collective. One long-standing sanction in communal justice is the banishment of the perpetrator, a form of "purging" the community.[55] These ideas influence the processes of rehabilitation and reconciliation. The emphasis on exteriorizing harmful agents serves psychological and social needs: it opens space for one to regain his or her humanity via cleansing and confession, and permits people to assimilate more slowly just whom they are living with. These illnesses and their alleviation figure strongly in the violence, both its making and its unmaking.

Weakness

> I'm already so old. I don't even know how old I am! Maybe eighty. Before I was happy—now, there's so much suffering. With so many *pensamientos*, with *iquyasqa* I'm so old. Those years were penitence, sacrifice. We had to hide in the hills, without eating, without sleeping. The soldiers killed my two little children when we were hiding in Lloqllepampa. We were escaping, hiding in the hills. So my little boy said, "*Mami*, I need to pee." "*Ya*, go ahead," I told him. When he was peeing, that damned soldier shot him in his penis. The bullet passed through him from behind. The same thing with my little girl—the bullet passed right through her stomach. That night I cried, holding them at my side—my little boy under one arm, my little girl under the other. I cried all night, I mourned all night. The following day I kept escaping, hiding myself in fear. Oh, some people say all of that is coming back again. If that happens, I'd rather take some poison and die. I could never live through that again! I'd rather throw myself in the river—I'd rather jump off a cliff! I can't forget. Oh, I'm so old now.
>
> —Señora Edelina Chuchón, fifty-six years old, Accomarca, 2003

In English we could translate *iquyasqa* as "weakness." It is the sensation of profound physical exhaustion, as if one did not have the energy to carry out even minimal daily activities. Women lamented, "We've cried so much we've lost our vision because of weakness." They associate this weakness with the political violence and the suffering of the *sasachakuy tiempo*. As Señora Edelina graphically described, *iquyasqa* ages the body.[56] Adult women of all ages complained of *iquyasqa*, underscoring the toll the *sasachakuy tiempo* had taken upon them. Women of reproductive age routinely stated they were so weak they "died" while giving birth and had to be resuscitated afterward. Villagers and medical personnel in the health posts both use the term "weakness" but assign a different etiology to this affliction. While the majority of "lay interviewees" locate the cause of *iquyasqa* in the upheaval of the political violence and its legacies, the medical personnel I interviewed reduced the problem to poor nutrition, erasing the psychological suffering indexed in the common usage of the term.

Here is an opportunity to analyze how the same word may have different connotations for the villagers and for the medical personnel stationed in the health posts. Malnutrition is chronic in the countryside and was exacerbated by the violence because people could not engage in normal agricultural production. However, I insist that we follow the complex meaning of the term as the women use it. *Campesinas* juxtapose their weakness now with the energy they had "during the time of meat" when "we wanted for nothing." This is not just nostalgia, and they are not referring exclusively to the material sphere: more is being remembered than simply "the time of meat." Ayacucho has always been among the poorest departments in Peru. However, that is not how people remember their lives. Villagers had homes with thick straw roofs that kept out the rain and the wind; now they have corrugated aluminum roofs that inevitably channel frigid raindrops down the back of the neck and onto a shivering back. They had livestock and fields that were continuously planted; during the war, 65 percent of land remained fallow and most villagers saw their livestock almost completely lost or killed.[57] Virtually everyone lost a family member or someone dear to them, often in brutally violent ways. Local biologies have been altered by the *sasachakuy tiempo*.

Iquyasqa—profound, bone-penetrating exhaustion. Words do not just express our experiences of loss, pain, or suffering; they orient us in the world and in our bodies. To be war-weary—*iquyasqa*—is a phenomenological reality. It also serves as powerful motivation to avoid repeating a bloody past and to engage in individual and collective practices designed to keep further conflict at bay.

Hardening the Heart

> To remember: from the Latin word *re-cordis*, to pass again through the heart.
> —Eduardo Galeano, *The Book of Embraces*

The heart is the most important organ in terms of memory, health, and affliction and plays a central role in repentance and reconciliation. We recall that *llakis* refer to painful memories that keep passing through the heart, lacerating its soft tissue. Various *curanderos* described how they treated their patients in order to "harden their hearts." With the use of herbs and by sharing examples of suffering they themselves have overcome, *curanderos* help their patients who must endure great suffering. During the internal armed conflict, hardening the heart was a means of tolerating pain and loss. As Dionisia lamented, better to have been a rock all those years, better never to have felt anything. Beyond tolerating pain, however, hardening the heart also implied the restriction of love and compassion (*caridad*) for one's fellow creatures. In a time of extremely reduced resources—and the intimate violence that distorted social relations—compassion was also diminished, reminding us there is a political economy of the emotions.[58] When people spoke about the origins of the *sasachakuy tiempo*, they emphasized that hatred (*odio*) and envy (*envidia*) played a key role in fomenting lethal violence. Additionally, as with the envious gentiles that God punished with the rain of fire, the violence was widely described as a punishment from Dios Tayta for the unbridled expression of *odio* and *envidia*.[59] *Qocha*—a polysemic Quechua word meaning "sin," "crime," or "error"—captures the porous realms of human and divine affairs and transgressions.

However, as don Jesús Romero explained, times change and so do norms. One part of recuperation is recovering the capacity to access a range of emotions and not only those associated with political violence such as fear, hatred, or rancor. This was the key theme of a communal event in Sacsamarca, located in the central-southern region of Ayacucho.

In May 2003, villagers organized a day of reconciliation in their community. The chapel in the cemetery was filled with people as one activity included a visit to the cemetery to honor "all of our war heroes." This illustrates a central theme of the day's agenda: all who died during the violence, regardless of their allegiances, were human beings. In an attempt to overcome the victim-perpetrator dichotomy, villagers imparted the message that everyone gathered in the chapel was a survivor.

In the church a member of the community addressed the crowd, flickering candles grasped between their hands. Orlando is a young man, and there was a striking contrast between his smooth complexion and the deeply wrinkled faces of the elderly women gathered in the chapel. Orlando reminded the crowd that during the violence they had all hardened their hearts. Now, in the process of reconciling, he spoke to them of the need to once again have "softened hearts"—hearts capable of feeling, loving, remembering.

> We offer this homage to our heroes, thinking of how our pueblo will be different. We are born with white [pure] hearts, and it is with a white heart that we should die, for the good of our pueblo. No one should be allowed to stain our hearts. If we stain our hearts, we will only have a lifetime of tears [*waqay vida*]. We should die with white hearts. We must forgive, ask for forgiveness, so that never again will these same things come to pass. If our heart is a rock, we must change. We are

passing one another with our hearts of rock, with our *pensamientos* that cause us such pain. Let's change. We must open our hearts because our pueblo is waiting for us so that we can all live well with our families. We must speak with one another with our white hearts. From this day forth, let's change our hearts so that we don't have *llaki vida, waqay vida* [a life of pain, a life of tears]. We must soften our hearts so that we can change.

The emphasis on softening the heart, and on change, is striking. One must learn to live with the memories, many of which are personified in the faces of family members or neighbors, without each memory overwhelming the heart's capacity to contain it.

"Changing one's life" is a central psychocultural theme. *Campesinos* visit *curanderos* to change their *suerte* (luck or destiny); congregations in the Evangelical churches pray to God so that He will change their hearts and their lives. Importantly, when the context changes, so does the person. Many people described the process of *arrepentimiento* (repentance): "After repenting, we go forth with a clean heart. We are no longer the people we were before. We are *musaq runakuna*—new people."

This was powerfully conveyed by El Piki in Carhuahurán. In the midst of a long conversation about the violence, I asked him what he thought about reconciliation. He replied by telling me about a friend whom he had known since primary school and how he had participated in Sendero. "It was difficult, but we can accept the *arrepentidos* [the ex-Senderistas, literally, 'the repentant ones']. As long as they act like *runakuna* [people] they can come back. We have to pardon them or we would hate them. Dios Tayta says we must pardon them so we can live with a tranquil heart."[60]

The idea of a tranquil heart appeared in many of our conversations and serves as one motivation for reconstructing social relationships that were distorted during the violence. Perhaps it is useful to consider the opposite— *corazoniypas irritasqa*, or irritation of the heart—which is an illness in its own right, as mama Zenaida explained to us in Hualla:

I'm sick with irritation of the heart. It grabs you when you cry, when you have *pensamientos*, sadness, rage. Before I used to be grabbed by fainting—oh, I died [*wañurqani*] for an hour at a time! That was when my irritation was just starting—it wasn't mature yet like it is now.

Because of my poverty, I died without even realizing it. I would even wake up like I was in a dream. I didn't remember absolutely anything that had happened. Now I feel like my irritation has accumulated like blood, accumulated in my stomach. It doesn't let me eat. That's why I'm drying up [*charkiqa kachkani*]. Look at my hand—I'm like a skinny cow!

Several things can produce irritation of the heart. Mama Zenaida mentioned *pensamientos*, sadness, and rage.[61] Many women lamented the toll that rage had taken on their bodies; *mal de rabia* (the illness of rage) was most often described as the sensation that one's nerves were throbbing uncontrollably, crawling just under the surface of the skin, refusing to leave the person in peace. Sadness and rage, when they grab the person and mature, result in serious, life-threatening afflictions.[62]

Finally, there is the verb *wañurqani* ("I died"). The first time a woman used this term, I was at a loss to understand her. She insisted she had died several times but now died only once in a while. As I would learn, fainting and losing consciousness are understood to be states similar to death. Both sadness and poverty can provoke fainting, as can the presence of defiant perpetrators who walk the streets of these pueblos.

Epidemic: Witches, Gods, and Bones

Several months after don Teofilo had put me in my place, he did begin to share a bit of his knowledge, although I was never fully trusted by this powerful, tiny man. He assured me there was an epidemic in the *alturas* of Huanta: there was *daño* (witchcraft); *alcanzo*, an illness caused by the *apus* (mountain gods) who punish the person who sits or steps where they should not; and *aya*, caused by coming into contact with the bones of the *gentiles* (ancestors). The *gentiles* were the people who lived before the time of Christ, and God sent down a rain of fire to punish them for being envious (*envidiosos*). They attempted to save themselves by entering the mountains, where their remains continue to cause illness to the unfortunate people whose bones they invade.[63]

These illnesses began to increase uncontrollably in 1984 when the fighting became so intense that both life and the landscape were in upheaval. People began fleeing, sleeping in caves for fear of attacks. As El Piki explained,

"In those times we escaped to the mountains, we slept in the caves. That's why we're sick. We're always getting sick. *Alcanzo* grabbed us—*aya* grabbed us. We were sleeping in caves with the bones of the *gentiles*. That's why so many people died with weakness. It's a slow wasting, until you die because the illness matures inside you."

Once military bases were established throughout the countryside, *campesinos* were obligated to live in nucleated settlements for security purposes. This new spatial practice gave rise to more *envidia* as neighbors now lived next door as opposed to a steep slope away. The fighting also made it too dangerous for El Piki to head out regularly to the mountains and place *pagapus* (offerings or sacrifices) on behalf of villagers who were requesting godly intervention in resolving problems. "I could no longer speak regularly with Madre Rasuhuillca [Mother Rasuhuillca, the highest mountain in the region]. She is *la señora de la medicina, la señora abogada* [the lady of medicine, the lady lawyer]."

In a time of profoundly conflictive social relationships—envious neighbors as well as different alliances during the war, which generated tremendous distrust—Madre Rasuhuillca grew angry that villagers had forgotten their commitments to her and to the past. She sided with the Senderistas, allowing them to hide in the clouds surrounding her peak, the shrubs clustered on her slopes, and the holes in the earth that she opened for the guerrillas when they were pursued by the *rondas campesinas*. As numerous *ronderos* recalled, "When we went out to Rasuhuillca on patrol, we found flowers, cigarettes, limes—the Senderistas took *pagapus*. They had a pact with the mountains and that was why they could hide in the hills. The mountains opened up to let them in, and then hid them."

Daño was rampant, and virtually every villager was currently suffering from *alcanzo* or had recently recovered.[64] Don Teofilo was called upon on a daily basis to climb up to the *puna* and try to repair villagers' relationships with the gods, as well as cure them of the witchcraft performed by all-too-human perpetrators. El Piki treats social strife and conflictive relations. Madre Rasuhuillca is both doctor and lawyer; healing the individual body means administering justice in the social sphere.

Curanderos are memory specialists. In diagnosing patients, they listen carefully to determine which past event might be causing illness, as well as to determine which person in the patient's life might wish to harm them via witchcraft.[65] They weave between the past and present, reminding fellow villagers of their debts to the dead and to the gods. As El Piki insisted, "The gods were angry that we forgot them during the *sasachakuy tiempo*. So I go out every day and talk with them. You must always remember them or they get angry." *Curanderos* treat tenuous relationships—between the present and the past, between human beings, and between human beings and their capricious gods.

This chapter began by asking how best to respond to the psychological aftermath of war. I have presented local idioms of suffering *and* resilience, demonstrating that ethnographic studies of postwar social worlds may not lead to psychological diagnoses but rather to the cultural logics involved in social strife and repair. People in these Andean communities are reconstructing a human way of life—the collective dimension—as well as individual lives. What is it that makes a life distinctly human?

Chapter 3

Being Human

Being is . . . not only a belonging but a becoming.
—Michael Jackson, *The Politics of Storytelling*

MY EXPERIENCES IN Peru have convinced me that the work of postconflict social repair involves reconstructing the human. Although it may sound cliché to speak about "dehumanizing violence," listening to how *campesinos* describe the *sasachakuy tiempo* confirms that dehumanizing is precisely the word that best captures how people experienced the war. People tearfully recall that "we lived and died like dogs" and "we had to leave our dead loved ones wherever they were. They ended up as animals"—referring to having seen dogs and pigs gorging themselves on the cadavers. In the aftermath of fratricidal violence—in contexts in which people are fully aware of what they and their neighbors are capable of—people ask what it means to be a human being now.[1]

In Andean communities, the status of "human being" is acquired.[2] One accumulates the characteristics that transform *criaturas* (babies and small children) into *runakuna*. Most people concurred that babies are not born with souls. With the exception of the "very Evangelicals"—as opposed to the *chawa* (halfway) Evangelicals—villagers explained that babies acquire their souls when they are about two years old. It is because their souls are not "well stuck" to their bodies that babies are very susceptible to *susto* (soul loss due to fright). In this stage, babies and toddlers are considered *sonsos* (senseless).[3]

Another characteristic *criaturas* acquire is the *uso de razón*—the use of reason, a supremely important faculty. In addition to making us more fully human, this concept is fundamental to the assessment of accountability. The term cuts across social fields: in the religious sense, it is the age at which a child can commit sin; in the political sense, it is related to accountability as a member of the community; in a legal sense, it refers to the capacity to discern right from wrong. Children are said to acquire the *uso de razón* around the age of six or seven; this is also the age at which children are said to remember things.

Just as the *uso de razón* makes *criaturas* more fully human, so does the accumulation of memory. When parents spoke about their children, they differentiated between the younger and older children by using *yuyaniyuq* for the older ones. *Yuyay* is Quechua for "remember," and the older children are described as the remembering ones, in contrast to little children who are *sonsos*. People with *mucha memoria* are considered better people, more intelligent, and they have more *conciencia*.

The question of conscience and culpability figures into legal standards as well. In the *Diccionario para Juristas*, *uso de razón* is defined as "possession of natural discernment that is acquired passing through early childhood; the time during which discernment is discovered or begins to be recognized in the acts of the child or individual."[4] *Discernimiento* refers to the capacity to judge, to choose, to distinguish. Thus *uso de razón* implies volition, memory, and the capacity to judge right from wrong. This is a central phase in becoming a moral person and entering communal life as an accountable member of the collective.

Just as one acquires humanizing qualities, so may they be lost. The mutability of identity is a central psychocultural theme. In Quechua, *uriway* refers to the transference of the essence of one life form to another. For instance, El Piki runs a *cuy* (guinea pig) over his patients as a diagnostic tool. After several passes, he cuts open the *cuy* and can read the illness there; the signs have transferred from the internal organs of his patient to the animal. Many Andean stories concern human beings who can transform themselves into animals, springs, trees—and convert themselves back into human form.[5] Recall the people who explained why it had taken the security forces so long to capture Abimael Guzmán: "He could change himself into a rock, a bird, a river—and the police only thought to look for a man." Thus the capacity to transform oneself is imbued with ambivalence: it can be dehumanizing or a form of power. This transference can also occur through no volition of one's own, with devastating results. It is how villagers explained what had happened to *wawa* Gloria.

*   *   *

Wawa Gloria (baby Gloria) was a round toddler who had caught my eye many times, her ponytail bobbing on top of her head as she half-walked, half-crawled around Carhuahurán. Yolanda, Edith, and Gloria's sister Marina would sometimes carry her over with them, bouncing her on their backs in a shawl. At other times she came on her own, pulling herself fully to her feet and peeking around the door.

One day I told the girls "I'm next in line" to give *wawa* Gloria some hugs. They passed her over, and I took her in my arms, resting my head lightly on hers. We sat in the sun, visitors coming and going as I felt the warmth of her baby breath against my chest. The women who came by began joking that I looked like I wanted to keep her. They weren't too far off.

I finally felt her stirring, her top-knot rubbing against my chin. Marina told me she would take her home since it was time to begin late afternoon water-fetching and fire-starting chores. As I passed her to Marina, I realized there were a few spots of toddler poop on my sleeve. Although babies were usually wrapped in cloth, toddlers didn't wear diapers. The moms would just lift their clothes, let them relieve themselves on the spot, and then wipe them down with a cloth.

Before going to bed that night, I threw the clothes I'd been wearing that day into a bag: sun permitting, I would wash clothes the next day. Sun did not permit, so the bag sat in the humid corner for a few days until the clouds cleared and the thought of frigid water was bearable.

I gathered up my Bolivar soap, scrub brush, and bag of clothes and walked down the hill to the river. I found my favorite small pool and rock, and went to pull my clothes out of the bag. When I opened the bag, something seemed to be moving. I recoiled: mice in my room were a constant, but I never grew accustomed to them. I kicked the bag upside down with my foot, but no furry creature emerged. Keeping my distance was part of the plan, so a stick replaced my foot. I turned the clothes over, trying to figure out what was moving. I finally narrowed the movement down to my long-sleeved green shirt, the one I had worn when cuddling *wawa* Gloria. It was moving. A few more pokes revealed why: the left sleeve—the one that I'd cradled under Gloria's little bottom—was alive with worms. They rolled over one another, squirming in the sun. That round baby belly was full of parasites.

After I washed my clothes, I headed to the health post to let them know *wawa* Gloria had a bad case of parasites. Manlio, the nurse, nodded: "Almost all of the children have them. They drink unboiled water, they eat dirt—there isn't much we can do."

"But *wawa* Gloria is so chubby. She's so big for her age," I commented, a bit perplexed.

"Kimberly, how old do you think she is?"

"A little over a year, no?"

Manlio went behind his desk and pulled out his files. Searching a bit, he found Gloria's. "Gloria is three-and-a-half years old. She's had malnutrition her whole life. She seems to have some kidney problem, which is why she is chubby. But she's terribly delayed." I was stunned. She could barely walk, didn't speak a word. Manlio winced as he saw the look on my face. "Don't waste your time on that one. It's too late to do anything."

The next day I watched her and felt awful. I was writing about it in my journal when Víctor came by. He was about eleven, shy and skinny. He frequently visited, and just as frequently sat quietly in my room, watching the endless activity of the other children.

"Víctor, what's the matter with *wawa* Gloria? What do you think she has?"

He knew. "It's *uriwasqa* [*uriway*]. Gloria must have been playing with a frog when she was littler. The frog grabbed hold of her and took her body."

"But Víctor, how do we know it was a frog?"

"It had to be a frog. Look how small she is, and she doesn't speak. It was a frog. If it had been a parrot, she would talk a lot. If it had been a cow, she'd have a huge tongue that reached up to her nose. No, it was definitely a frog that grabbed her," Víctor patiently explained. Evidently that frog never let her go.

Uriway was common and influenced how people think of life forms and human status. There were many transformations during the violence, and identities were in flux. There were the massive conversions to Evangelical Christianity that characterized the highlands of Huanta. The guerrillas could assume a variety of shapes. There were villagers who transformed into *anticristos* (the antichrists) and *malafekuna* (the people of bad faith/bad conscience), ceasing to be people. Mutability is a resource: enemies who at one time had "fallen out of humanity" can convert into people again, seeking reentry into the community of humankind.

An Emotional Education

In the *alturas* of Huanta, many people experienced the *sasachakuy tiempo* as a cultural revolution—an assault on a way of life, shared meaning, symbols, and moral codes. Tumultuous upheavals may provoke explicit discussions regarding the content of culture as individuals engage in the everyday work of social reconstruction. There was tremendous talk about who people had been—individually and collectively—before and during the violence, as well as what sort of people they would be now. This talk was part of remoralizing the world: redefining cultural norms and managing affect was one component of these discussions.

Richard Shweder and E. J. Bourne suggested the term "sociocentric" to refer to cultures that value interconnectedness among people.[6] From this perspective, we are who we are because of the social relations that define us, that give us our identity—an identity that changes according to the social context. Psychological theories predicated upon the bounded, sovereign individual have limited applicability when working with groups whose life is more oriented toward the collective. The atomized individual is neither the developmental goal nor the norm within Quechua-speaking communities, and individual members of the community will be reminded in many ways that the collective good takes precedence over individual interests.

An important part of one's emotional education includes *kuyachicuyta yachana* (learning how to make others love you). Love is something one must inspire or generate in another person rather than being a "natural" or latent emotion just looking for an object upon which to focus. For example, women were candid: some children knew how to make their mothers love them, and others did not.[7] A mother's love was not unconditional but rested in great measure upon a child learning how to be lovable and to act in such a way as to elicit that emotion.[8]

With *kuyachicuyta yachana*, boys and girls (and adults in rituals such as weddings) learn and are reminded of the centrality of exchange in social relations, as well as the importance of conflict-avoidance mechanisms. The capacity to produce positive emotions in another person is a sign of maturity in a face-to-face context in which retributive emotions are disruptive and potentially dangerous.[9] Rather than a concept of the self that places value on the degree of separation achieved from others, solidarity and interconnectedness are valued. And this solidarity and coexistence require a continual effort to maintain them. As Catherine Allen has noted, there are few channels in daily life for the direct expression of negative emotions; even brief interactions among *runakuna* are marked by elaborate expressions of mutual esteem.[10] "Harmony ideology" functions on the interpersonal and communal levels, cloaking perpetual conflict in a florid idiom of courtesy.[11]

One component of this relational model is a high level of permeability between the interior and the exterior. Rather than a model of the human being with a clearly defined internal world, there is tremendous fluidity between the social environment and the person. For instance, several *curanderos* explained how they cure *susto*. One effective treatment is *qayapa*, which consists of repeatedly calling the patient's soul, requesting that it return. Calling the soul is complemented by identifying the place in which the person suffered *susto* and taking an article of the patient's clothing to that spot. The soul, upon recognizing the clothing, "sticks" to it and can thus be reunited with the person. The clothing beckons to the soul. The theory that clothing carries something of the person's essence also plays a role in mourning and rituals of death. For Dionisia, the bits and pieces of her son's clothing strewn throughout the house made it impossible to forget the horror of his death and his distant burial. Gathering the clothing into a sealed sack was to alleviate her lacerating memories. More generally, after someone dies the soul of the deceased remains present, revisiting the sites frequented during the person's life. On the fifth day following the death, family members of the deceased wash his or her clothing so the soul can begin its journey to heaven. If the clothing is not washed, the soul cannot free itself and will continue wandering this earth without finding peace; during this transitional phase, the wandering soul is potentially dangerous to the human beings it encounters. For a year following someone's death, his or her clothing is stored in a folded shawl (*manta*). Once the year of mourning is finished, family members open the shawl and distribute the clothing the soul has left behind.

Clothing is also important for practicing the witch's craft. Because an article of clothing carries the person's essence, having it helps the witches more effectively cast their spells. The power of this was made clear when people in the highlands of Huanta described how they burned the clothing of the Senderistas they had killed: those flames finished off the *terrucos*. The essence of the person extends beyond their skin; the surface of the skin does not mark the person's bodily boundaries. That which is inside and outside are connected, and a human being is primordially defined by his or her mutable social environment. This is a thoroughly "social body." Madness is social as well.

Madness

> We were like crazy people [*loca qina karaniku*]. We went around like crazy people then.
> There was so much death! It was like another life [*huk vida*].
>   —Juliana Morales, Hualla, April 2003

If indeed *llakis* constitute the most common category of suffering, they find their complement in two expressions that dominated conversations about the *sasachakuy tiempo*: "We were like crazy people" (*loca qina kara-niku*) and "as though we were in a dream" (*muspaypi qina karaniku*).[12] We begin with two conversations about madness, attuned to how figures of madness emerged within the context of the internal armed conflict and its aftermath. The discourse of madness is a domain of knowledge that can tell us a great deal about intimate violence, cosmic upheaval, and moral transgression.

Dulia and I were talking with mama Zenaida one morning when some-one registered in my peripheral vision.[13] It was a tall woman whose hat was adorned with flowers of various colors, and she was heading toward us. Her determined stride sent the layers of her blue skirts swaying back and forth. She stopped in front of me: "Are you the people who are gathering testimo-nies about the violence?"

Dulia nodded. "Yes, we are."

She expressed her interest in talking with us, and mama Zenaida quickly excused herself and left. Her reaction was perplexing. Normally she was very friendly. I asked the woman standing before me, "What happened? Why did she act that way with you?"

Victoria looked up and down the street to see if anyone was watching us. Then she replied, "There are people here who're afraid of me because of my husband. But we can't talk here—I'm afraid. Come to my house and there we can talk woman to woman." She insisted we visit her that same afternoon.

We went to her house later that day, and one of her children let us in. At the back of the room Victoria was seated with her children and grandchil-dren, who continued playing boisterously while we talked. She offered us sheepskins so we could sit beside her and began to talk while we threshed corn. She seemed quite anxious, her words tumbling out as quickly as pos-sible. Over and over again she insisted, "I suffer so much. The violence left us poor. We were going to have work, the schools were going to improve—but when this problem began everyone left, even SINAMOS [a government agency]. Where did they go? That's how it was."

"And now—are these things still lacking, mama Victoria?" I asked.

"Yes, but hopefully they'll come back." She shrugged before adding, "If Dios Tayta wants them to return, then they will. In Matthew [chapter] 24, Dios Tayta says, 'The mother will kill her children, and the children will kill their mother.' That's how it will be when it's the end of time [*tuku-pay tiempupi*]. That's how it will be when time runs out. That's what God wanted."

"So it was a time of killing among families, neighbors?" prompted Dulia.

"Yes," she replied, emphatically nodding her head. "That's what it said in the words of God. In Matthew, those words made me understand because I was so frightened by these things. Then a woman warned me, 'Don't be afraid even when they kill in front of you because we are in the last days. We should kneel down to save our souls. We need to ask God to save us. He will save us. If He wants, not even a bullet can kill us.' She made me understand these words. It made my heart stronger. Since she warned me, I was no longer afraid. That's how I began to know the *evangelio* [Evangelical church]."

"So the *evangelio* arrived during that time?"

"Yes, since that time the *evangelio* appeared. With this violence we all went mad. There was so much death! With the violence, we were like crazy people. My head aches when I remember these things. During those years, I was like a crazy person." Her face changed and she stopped threshing the corn. She raised her hands and touched her chest forcefully, thanking God for the healing she had found in the *evangelio*. "The word of God reached my heart like water, refreshing me. And the word calmed my thirst."

She waited a moment before she began speaking again. "Señora Margarita, she also went crazy." Victoria's face grew sad as she remembered. "Ya, with her head gone mad [*uman locayarusqa*] from having seen people dying in front of her. She went crazy. She wandered from one place to another. She reached Huancapi and threw herself in front of cars. 'Let these cars kill me,' she said, and threw herself in front of them. She grabbed a knife, giving it to people so they could stab her in her chest. 'Stab me with this, I can't do it alone,' she pleaded. To the *hermanos* [members of the church] she gave them sticks and asked them to strike her in the head. 'I can't stand anymore of this!' Oh, she pleaded so desperately."

"What happens when a person goes crazy?"

"When a person goes crazy, day is no longer day, night is no longer night. It's night all of the time. That's why they like to be in the darkness, a darkness that would scare any one of us. 'I've seen hell,' she said. 'Hell reeks horribly,' she said. 'Everyone has horns there—goats with horns, cows with horns, everyone has horns in hell.' But a healthy person, healthy with God, can't see those things. That's how it is. 'Papá Dios made me see these things,' she said. That's why she also sought the word of God. 'I'm going to leave here, leave the darkness,' she said. That poor woman—morning and night she sang songs of the souls [for the dead]. She said her head burned and she kept putting mud on her head. She would wrap her head in mud because it burned, and walking in circles she'd sing the songs of the souls."

"Mama Victoria, what happened to her?" asked Dulia.

"She went crazy. She was weak in her thoughts. I also wrapped my head in a *chumbi* all of the time. At what hour will we die? That thought was in my head, and my head was wrapped day and night."

"And how was that—to feel mad? How did you feel then?"

"You don't recognize day and night. You cry, singing songs of the dead."

* * *

Juanjo and I were walking through the streets of Tiquihua, hoping to find someone home.[14] It was early afternoon and most people were either working in their *chacras* (agricultural land) or pasturing their animals. Only the tiniest children and older women were at home. Peering over a wall, I saw a woman lethargically sweeping her small patio. I greeted her and she answered, but she turned her back again and kept sweeping. We approached her house and asked if we could join her. She nodded and waved us into her house. She looked Juanjo up and down: "Those *guerrilleros* [Senderistas] came here just like you—young people. Like you," she repeated, inclining her head toward Juanjo. We explained that we were there to work, and she poured us each a cup of hot barley water (*café de cebada*).

Señora Julia Rojas was forty-five and had lived in Tiquihua during the violence. At first she had her children with her, but then her husband was brutally killed. After losing him, the political violence and poverty forced her to send her four children away to live with family members on the coast.

"My husband died, my uncles, my cousins—so many members of my family died that there weren't enough coffins to bury them." She cried as she remembered. "So my soul—I don't know where it might have gone. I was alone and the wives of the dead were crying. Their bodies were scattered around. They [the killers] had taken their ponchos and they were nude. They'd also taken their pants. They were innocent! I cried like a crazy person and I had no one. I had no one to tell." She was silent for a moment, staring at the space in front of her.

"May I ask how they killed them?"

"They shot my husband here," placing her hand on her shoulder. "When they shot him he began to cry out 'call my wife' so that I could carry him. My husband called my name. 'Julia! Come quickly.' And they told him, 'Shut up you motherfucker. Kill him, shit. Kill him,' and they killed him again in the mouth so he shut up.[15] So he didn't have a face—it was just a hole. I cried like crazy. We walked like crazy people seeing so many dead people, scattered everywhere. It was another life. We were like crazy people! I saw the dead scattered, without pants. They'd taken their good shirts."

Her crying was contagious, her tears falling across a face prematurely aged by pain. "I had to bury everyone alone, being careful they didn't come back to kill me and my children. That's why I had to send my children to Lima. They sent for me later, but it wasn't the same. I felt useless with everyone taking care of me. I decided to come back to my *chacra* because at least here I can take care of myself. When I returned, my house was empty—only the walls were standing. I fixed the roof, and I cleaned the patio. I was like a crazy person. I'm still like that. I feel different. We can't forget the dead. Seeing so many dead scattered around, full of blood! As if you wouldn't feel pain for people like you! Having so much sadness, you cry, thinking, 'That's how they'll kill me, tomorrow or the day after.' What curse could they be, those *plagakuna* [people of the plague, i.e., Senderistas] who came here? What mother or father could have given birth to them [implying the Senderistas had sprung from the devil himself]?"

*   *   *

People overwhelmingly invoked collective madness when they referred to the *sasachakuy tiempo*. Certainly villagers recognize individual pathology, which makes the emphasis on the collective nature of the madness even more striking. This emphasis on a disorder larger than one's own, larger than a personal or family issue, conveys a great deal about living through catastrophic upheaval.[16] The emergence of collective madness offers social and political commentary about a world in disarray, in which no one seemed capable of responding to villagers' demands for an end to the killing and for the reestablishment of a humane social order. At the community level many authorities were targeted for killing or co-optation. In certain regions Shining Path established "liberated zones" and appointed their own authorities, who frequently administered arbitrary and brutal forms of control. There were also armed agents of the state who at times failed in their duty to protect civilians and at others committed abuses against them. Magnifying the ambient terror was the fear that even family members and neighbors were capable of treachery. Many villagers lamented that there was no earthly authority one could turn to or trust. This was a world in which the bewildering loss of context resulted in subjects radically unmoored from the moral limits that tethered life to some sense of predictability, to "social sanity."

The searing proximity of the violence resonates with Begoña Aretxaga's work on narratives of madness in post-Franco Spain. Her research on radical nationalist youth in the ETA (Euskadi Ta Askatasuna, or Basque Homeland and Freedom) movement shares the themes of intimate violence and collective madness that haunted my conversations in Ayacucho. She found the question of madness was linked to forms of intimate violence that defied comprehension and produced profound shock. The familiarity of local youth turned perpetrators transgressed the moral boundaries of local communities, resulting in violence perpetrated by a "familiar turned stranger." Narratives of collective madness acknowledged that reality was "de-realized" all the more for occurring within the boundaries of the socially familiar. Importantly, in contrast with individual madness, which does not threaten the premises of the social order, collective madness "blurs the very distinction between madness and sanity and thus turns reality upside down."[17]

A world turned upside down can be taken literally when working with Andean communities, in which the concept *pachakuti* extends back to the time of the Incan empire. *Pacha* is a Quechua word meaning earth, time, and space, and *kuti* refers to overturning something or turning it back. *Pachakuti* is part of a millennial understanding of time and space, in which one world dramatically ends and another begins. For instance, recall the gentiles who were punished with a rain of fire for being corrupt, envious, and sinful. They were punished collectively, as a people, and their time on this earth came to an end. This historical consciousness endures, albeit under a different guise. Villagers lamented that they had become envious and hateful; that family members and neighbors were sinful; and that corruption reigned. Taken together, these signs meant the Apocalypse was at hand, and the fact the *plagakuna* and devil's children walked this earth confirmed its imminence.

For Quechua speakers, there are three *pachas*, interacting yet distinct. *Kay pacha* is "this world," the physical world we apprehend and traverse. It also constitutes a middle world lying between the *hanan pacha* (upper world, traditionally home to various deities) and the *uku pacha* (the lower or inner world, home to the wicked).[18] For the Spanish colonizers and their missionary legions, these three worlds were glossed as earth, heaven, and hell.

Although these three dimensions of time and space have always intermingled, the *sasachakuy tiempo* threw these *pachas* into disorder. The *uku pacha* is normally invisible to the living and cloaked in darkness, with spirits that may emerge at night and frequent people's dreams. However, as we see in the two conversations above, people were terrified as day and night blurred to the point of being indistinguishable and the underworld appeared in all its stench. During the *sasachakuy tiempo* it was this world (*kay pacha*) that was hellish. Magnifying the hellish aspects were the changes in norms and in moral codes, summed up by the passage from Matthew 24: "The mother will kill her children and the children will kill their mother." Family members and neighbors *were* killing each other, and many times people insisted the killing began because the Devil himself had grabbed them—or spawned them. This was a cosmic disorder.

The rituals that gave meaning to life were also interrupted and, confronted with so much death, people were unable to hold wakes or bury their loved ones properly, which had implications for the fate of their souls. They died a "bad death," which has repercussions in the lives of their loved ones.[19] Their clothes were also taken, so there was no way to tend to their souls and send them on their way to another dimension of time and space. Thus the unburied dead can become a danger to the living, either by beckoning them to follow or by placing demands from beyond. Additionally, *qala* (the Quechua word for "naked") has been used to describe *mestizos* and gringos—beings who are not *runakuna*, not "people like us." The emphasis on nakedness invokes bodies made strange, bodies rendered less than fully human.

In Ayacucho, what is termed "popular religion" played a key role both in implementing the violence and in coping with its aftermath. Bible stories have been a key semiotic resource for people confronted with "limit experiences" and have offered a language to express altered life and the rupture with reality. Religious imagery offered damnation *and* salvation amid a period of violence people commonly explained as a sign of grave spiritual disorder, a result of humankind's sins and Dios Tayta's retribution. When the outbreak of war is understood as grave spiritual disorder—as in part a question of sin and punishment—then religious signifiers may become the reiterative images of both collective madness and its superation. The concept of collective madness condenses this spiritual, moral, and political collapse and reminds us that long before madness was defined as a medical or psychological problem, it was understood to be a spiritual phenomenon.

*   *   *

When I arrived in Ayacucho in 1994, I arrived in a space full of stories, many oddly familiar to me. I was enveloped in The Greatest Story Ever Told, at times thumbing through a copy of the Bible to see what might happen next or to remind myself how a particular story might end. There is much more to be said about the Evangelical Christianities people elaborated in the context of the internal armed conflict and its aftermath. This discussion involves theologies of war and of reconciliation, involves the religious imagination and its creative exercise.[20] I agree with Daniel Philpott that "more attention to local and community level faith-based actors who help populations deal with the past would fill an important gap in our knowledge of religion and transitional justice."[21] We begin with one of the first Quechua-speaking pastors to travel throughout rural Ayacucho. He recounted the history of Evangelismo during the many hours we spent in his Clinic of the Soul.

Chapter 4

Fluid Fundamentalisms

In many rural communities, the [Evangelical] churches were the only social organizations that did not dissolve, but rather resisted and stood their ground. Faced with the totalitarian, violent message of the subversive groups and the horror, the faith that animated these churches led them to elaborate diverse responses: from not complying with the call to arms, to the articulation of a theological reflection with which they lived daily life, to those who decided to fight against the terror of Shining Path by forming the *rondas campesinas*. In all cases, they were the response of native leadership given that the majority of the foreign missionaries had to withdraw from these areas, leaving the direction of these churches in the hands of local pastors and lay people.
—PTRC, Final Report, 2003

IT WAS ABOUT nine in the morning when I headed to the *óvalo* in search of a taxi to Huanta. The *óvalo* is a transportation hub, with taxis, vans, buses, and the occasional bicyclist departing for destinations throughout Peru. The first *combis* (vans) to the *selva* (jungle) had already left, and the crew of the next *combi* out was still loading passengers and cargo when I passed by. The roof rack was piled high with boxes, burlap sacks, suitcases, and backpacks, but a young man was still optimistically squeezing in a few more boxes before securing the load with rope. The passengers had opened the windows despite the brisk morning air, perhaps thinking ahead to their twelve-hour ride into the fly-buzzing heat of the *selva*.

Shiny streaks of gasoline floated on puddles left from the previous night's rain. I dodged them as I crossed the street to a row of cars parked at odd angles. Children began coming by, carrying small cardboard boxes with carefully arranged rows of gum, candy, and bottled beverages for sale. Several women had cranked up kerosene stoves to the side of the parking lot, and sizzling *chicharrones* were sputtering in oil.

The sun warmed the streets and the puddles turned to vapor. The driver of the car stationed first in line was calling out, "Huanta, Huanta!" to the people milling about. One by one we accumulated the requisite five passengers, and the radio was blasting *huaynos* as we headed out to the "Emerald of the Andes." In every direction there are valleys, some lush green and others streaked with layers of red and brown rock. Those valleys line up one after another until the sky ends.

An hour later the taxi pulled into the town plaza, and we each paid our five *soles* for the ride. I walked down to the Sunday market, bending over to dodge colorful sheets of plastic tied to sticks with webs of twine. This patchwork sheltered produce, cheese, herbs, flowers, and a wide assortment of potatoes. The merchants, mostly women, were sitting in their stalls on upside-down plastic buckets or old wooden crates, carrying on lively conversations in Quechua with customers as well as each other.

I had come to Huanta in search of Vidal Trujillano, one of the first-generation Evangelical pastors who figured into many conversations with *comuneros* in the highlands. I was interested in the history of Evangelismo (Evangelical Christianity), one of the most important social movements in the department of Ayacucho. From the U.S. missionaries who arrived in the 1940s, established the Bible Institute in Huanta, and founded Radio Amauta, to the local theologies developed by Quechua-speaking pastors, tracing this history adds to the familiar stories of evangelical growth and conversion by capturing the multiple theologies people have developed both during war and in its aftermath, exploring a phenomenon Joel Robbins describes as "one of the greatest success stories of the current era of cultural globalization."[1]

In 1980, on the eve of the internal armed conflict, only 4 percent of the rural population identified as Evangélico.[2] A mere decade later, the majority of people in the *alturas* of Huanta were *hermanos* and *hermanas*.[3] While the Catholic churches lay in ruins, one of the priorities when people rebuilt their communities was the construction of one, two, perhaps three Evangelical churches. Some were Presbyterian, others Assembly of God, Prince of Peace, or the Pentecostal Church of Peru. However, when asked which church they belonged to, although people might point to a different rustic building, they uniformly replied they were "*evangélicos.*"

Friends had told me Pastor Vidal still lived in Callqui, referring to a small barrio on the outskirts of Huanta. Callqui was unfortunately well-known, its notoriety dating back to the early 1980s. In October 1981, former president Belaúnde declared a state of emergency, and in December of the following year the entire department of Ayacucho was placed under the control of the armed forces as the government escalated counterinsurgency measures. Army general Roberto Clemente Noel, the first political-military commander, was sent to Ayacucho in January 1983, and he began the deadliest phase of state violence in the region. That same year the Marina established their general headquarters in the municipal stadium in Huanta, converting the structure into a detention and torture center. This was the context in which a group of uniformed men knocked on the door of the Evangelical Presbyterian Church at Callqui one evening in August 1984, selected six members of the congregation, and took them out back to kill them.

I doubted I would find Pastor Vidal at home. In my previous experiences trying to locate evangelical pastors, I found they were almost always out preaching. I began with the church, but the padlock was closed and a peek through the cracks in the door confirmed no one was there. There were a few houses, but their *calamina* (corrugated aluminum) doors were also shut. Walking around, I realized there was a small store off the side of one of the houses and the door was open. As I approached, an elderly man in a red baseball cap and tennis shoes came outside, rubbing his unshaven stubble with the palm of his hand.

"Hola," I greeted him. "My name's Kimberly. I'm looking for Pastor Vidal Trujillano. Do you know if he's around?"

A smile spread across his face as his eyes squinted to tone down the sun. "That's me."

Pastor Vidal invited me into his store, introducing me to his wife, who was standing behind the counter. A glance around the store prompted me to compliment Pastor Vidal for having founded Snacker's Heaven. He burst out laughing, adding that maybe there was a paradise here on earth. Small metal display racks were sitting upon the glass counter, bags of potato chips in various sizes and flavors hanging in orderly rows. Beneath the glass were stacks of cookies, candies, and soda crackers. The shelves were lined with cans of *leche Gloria*, bottles of Kola Real, plastic bags of sugar and rice, and packages of pasta. Pastor Vidal gestured toward an elaborate armchair of deep burgundy velveteen located in the corner. The chair was covered with thick plastic to avoid wear, and I immediately demurred. "Pastor Vidal, this is a throne fit for a queen!"

He bowed deeply and his arm was my escort. "Of course . . . and here she is." His face crinkled again as he laughed, displaying a sense of humor that punch-lined our hours of conversation.

Pastor Vidal asked his wife to pass him two bottles of Kola Real to accompany the *chaplas* I had brought with me. I explained that I was an anthropologist and was living in several communities in the *alturas* of Huanta. "That's why I was looking for you. People remember you and the Bible movies you showed them."

He nodded, clearly pleased. He suggested we go next door to the church so he could show me where so many things had happened. His wife handed him an old white shoelace tied through half a dozen keys, one of which opened the padlock on the church's wooden doors. There was a small painted sign hanging above the doorway: Evangelical Presbyterian Church. We walked into a room filled with the light of a dizzying blue sky. The dirt floor was swept smooth, and six rows of wood slab pews lined each side of the aisle. Following him up that center aisle, I noticed a drum set, guitar, accordion, and amplifiers set up in the corner. It made me think of the children who said they went to church to dance.

At the front of the church was a simple table with some flowers. What caught my eye was a series of laminated posters on the wall. Pink roses and an English countryside were hung alongside a chart titled "Clínica del Alma: Médico Especialista" (Clinic of the Soul: Specialized Doctor). Big letters detailed the services rendered and by whom.

Honorary Degree	Son of God
Doctor's Assistant	The Holy Spirit
Field of Study	The Heart
Experience	Unfailing and Eternal
Doctor's Office	Everywhere
His Power	Unlimited
Specialty	The Impossible
Prescription	The Bible
Illnesses Treated	All
Guarantee	Absolute
Hospital	Anywhere
Treatment Goals	Peace and Happiness
Cost of the Visit	True Faith
Attention	24 Hours a Day
Doctor	Jesus Christ

Clinic of the Soul: Specialized Doctor

We settled in around a small table, and Vidal asked if I planned to tape our conversation: "Most people want to record what I say. I've seen a lot of things." Indeed, he was such a "practiced talker" that at times I felt I was listening to his testimony, much like the testimonies evangelicals give in church as proof of God's work.

"I'm interested in the history of these communities," I said, "how people lived through the violence, and rebuild their lives now."

Pastor Vidal nodded, removing his glasses to rub his eyes. "I'm losing my eyesight," he explained. He wore thick eyeglasses that made his eyes swim as though I was looking at him through a thick window on a drizzly day. But the glasses helped alleviate the horrible headaches he had suffered from. As he explained, prior to being fitted for his coke-bottle lenses, "I walked around weaving back and forth like a drunk." We concurred that such swerving was incompatible with his evangelical position.

"And when did you start preaching, *hermano* Vidal?"

"*Bueno*, I've been preaching for over fifty years," pausing to let those five decades sink in. "I have *el don de predicar* [a gift for preaching]."

"And where did you learn about the gospel?" I asked, a question that led us to Vidal's youth and his disenchantment with the Catholic Church.

"I lived with the Franciscans in Lima when I was young. We studied every morning until noon, and then we went out to work. But they never showed us the Bible. Never! They had us read a few little books—dogmas, that's all we read. Only they [the priests] had Hail Mary, the salvation of mass, and confession."

"Why didn't they use the Bible?"

"It was only for them."

I was perplexed. "But why only for them and not to show to everyone?"

"Well, we [the Evangelicals] talk straight out about the gospel, but they have no way in. They earn money baptizing, marrying people—money for everything."

"So they didn't want to share the Bible because of the power it gave them?"

"Exactly! Not to win souls but to earn money. The liturgy for the dead? Well, the dead were already buried so people didn't come to them for this. They were already dead! So the priests taught people that the spirits were in purgatory, their children in limbo. So people had to come and confess their sins so they wouldn't end up like that. Then they administered the Eucharist with little round cookies—the fruit of the crucifixion of Christ." He rolled his eyes. "The cookies are called '*hostias*' [communion wafers]. When people confessed, the priests gave them the Eucharist [*comulgación*]. But they were just cookies. They had coloring, but people didn't know that. They had no idea everything the Franciscans did. The *hostia* is just a colored cookie," he insisted, making a tiny "o" with his fingers to emphasize just how insignificant they were.

"What did people think the *hostia* was?"

"They thought the Father was pardoning their sins. That's why they confessed everything. The priests asked them, 'What have you done? What have you done? What have you done?'" Vidal drilled in an imperious tone, drawing his tiny self up and throwing out his chest in inquisitorial fashion. "So people confessed all of their sins. People believed salvation was coming because in the altar there were these *imágenes* [images of the saints]."

"What do you think of this practice of praying to the saints?"

Vidal shrugged. "Well, I didn't know any better. I thought the same way back then. In your heart you're accustomed to that. They don't show you the Bible."

I could see a memory flicker across his face. "You know, in the convent there was this young man. He grew grapes from Italy, and they made them into wine for the Eucharist. The priests had those grapes, but no one else could. Only them. They had so many grapes in the convent—they could have filled the streets with grapes," he marveled. "And there were always priests arriving, leaving, arriving, leaving," his head moving back and forth as though following their trail.

"Where were they from?"

"Spain—all of them were from Spain.[4] I started to study with them. They told us we would be sacristans, that we'd play the organ. Several of us went to study, and we worked. We helped the masons build classrooms. Oh, we worked hard! Well, one time we were really tired and thirsty. I kept looking at those grapes. I finally grabbed some to eat."

"Oh, I'd have done the same thing," I assured him.

He nodded. "Of course. But inside his room, through a window with bars, someone was watching me. I didn't even see him. He came out and asked me what I'd done. 'So you just came to the convent to steal, or did you come to work and learn?' He made me go with him to the boss. 'This young man stole grapes!' Oh, that priest scolded me so much." Vidal held his face in his hands as he remembered how sternly the priest had spoken to him. 'You came here to rob. You're a thief.' That's what he said to me! It was so ugly the way he attacked me. My heart couldn't stand it. They talk about love, but where was their love? I started to think about that."

"How old were you?"

"I was sixteen. It was a parochial school and I entered to be a priest. But I couldn't stand much of it. They played all sorts of tricks on me," said Vidal, with an incredulous look on his face. "Once, without permission, I started to read the Bible. Well, one of the priests saw me and practically killed me." Sitting upright in his chair, Vidal assumed a pompous, booming voice: "'Uncivilized men shouldn't touch this book. Only educated men can read the *Santa Biblia*.' That's how he scolded me. It was forbidden to touch the Bible." Vidal slumped back in disgust. "So one day when we finished work, all of us students went in and Father Zaguán closed the doors behind us. Well, I had an empty sack—it was from the sand we were using. I threw all of my things in the bag and had it waiting at the door before we came in." Vidal leaned forward, his voice lowering into a conspiratorial tone. "I had everything ready and that night I escaped. I never went back. But in the convent I'd learned to make the *imágenes* and firecrackers. So when I came back here, I went to the *selva*. I went from church to church making money from the *imágenes* and firecrackers for their fiestas. I was working for this one church and I got to know the priest. So one day—I didn't ask permission—I started to read about the birth of El Señor Jesucristo. That priest saw me and almost killed me! He was angry! 'This book is not to be touched. Only *los doctorados* [the highly educated] can read this book. It is the Bible.' That's what he said." Vidal shook his head, as though still perplexed by the priest's outrage.

"So it was forbidden to even touch the Bible?"

"Yes. After that," Vidal clasped his right hand to his chest, "my heart was wandering, and I knew it was better to leave."

Vidal's critique of the priests and their elitism was a constant in our conversations. It is also a recurrent theme in the literature on Evangelismo. Among the attractions of Pentecostal Christianity are the promise of an unmediated, personal relationship with God and the alleged egalitarianism of a religion in which virtually anyone can learn to preach or evangelize.[5] In his research on postwar Guatemala, Kevin O'Neill refers to the "spiritual intimacy" that characterizes religious practice for neo-Pentecostals who eschew the distancing formality of the Catholic Church and its ornate structures in favor of gathering around the kitchen table in a neighbor's modest home.[6]

It was to his own home that Vidal returned, his heart still wandering. But then, unexpectedly, a friend's wife died and the family found themselves preparing for the fifth day.

"*Pichqa punchaw*? The day to wash the clothes?"

"Exactly. I went to say good-bye to her, and because I had been with the priests, people thought I was a priest too. So on the fifth day they asked me to pray. We spent the night praying, smoking, and in the morning a friend—well, I told him the priests had their book that I wanted to read but they wouldn't let me. He asked me if I *really* wanted to read it and I told him of course I did. He told me he had a Bible, so I asked him to sell it to me. 'How much does it cost?' I asked him. He told me to just take it, but I traded a bottle of *trago* for it."[7]

I laughed at the irony. "So you traded *trago* for the Bible?"

"Yes," he said, his face breaking into a big smile. "I read it, but I didn't understand much. So I wrote a letter to my brother-in-law in Lima with the verses I didn't understand and asked him to come and visit. He came right away. Here, I had my *chacra* and worked alongside everyone, chewing coca and drinking. But my brother-in-law was an Evangelical and he didn't like that. So one afternoon we were talking about the Bible and he showed me his. I opened it to the New Testament and he started to teach me. Well, I had my *chacra* and had plenty of hens, duck, *yucca*. So we made a *pachamanca* and I invited all the neighbors.[8] While we were preparing everything, he shared the word of El Señor. The time came to open the *pachamanca* and we started to eat chicken and meat—there was enough for all the neighbors. We just kept inviting people, but there was still more food. The food never ended."

Vidal closed his eyes as though relishing the moment. "I delivered myself to El Señor."

I nodded as he spoke, thinking about the transformation of the fish and loaves into an abundant Andean feast. There were numerous miracles in the life history Vidal related, and the endless *pachamanca* was one of them. Those miracles paved the path to his conversion.

"We decided to build a temple right there. Then people started thinking, 'We have lots of young men and women and they need someone to marry them. We need to baptize people, and who's going to baptize them?' So we decided to vote and send a group to the Bible Institute. I was elected."

"Did you go back to Lima?"

"No, here in Huanta. I came and interviewed with don Nicholas Cochran. 'We're starting an institute here,' he told me."

I had heard so much about Nicholas Cochran and Harry Marshall, two North American Presbyterian missionaries who introduced what is categorically referred to as Evangelismo in the early 1950s. They established Radio Amauta and the Bible Institute, where they trained the first Quechua-speaking pastors, one of whom was Vidal.

"What year was that?"

"'57. They started in Huamanga but they couldn't find a place. There was no water, and they wanted a garden, fruit trees. So they came here to Huanta. Besides, they almost killed them in Huamanga."

"What? They were almost killed?"

He rolled his eyes. "Oh, they were giving out pamphlets in the street, and people tried to kill them. The police grabbed them and put them in jail—not to punish them but to save their lives. People wanted to kill them! It was against the law to preach in the open air. The government thought it was a threat to Catholicism and they wanted to stop it. The police saved their lives. They were very lucky. Back then, the missionaries were all North Americans. There were no Peruvians. The missionaries educated us."

The history Pastor Vidal told reminded me of the Catholic priests I interviewed in the late 1990s. They remained concerned about the "invasion of the sects," referring to the massive growth of Evangelical Christianity in Ayacucho. Numerous priests cautioned that the Evangelicals were a "threat to Andean culture" because Evangelical doctrine rejected the use of religious images and banned chewing coca leaves and alcohol consumption (both key elements in celebrating many religious fiestas). They were joined in their concerns by social scientists trained in the Weberian tradition; they feared the Protestant ethic would fuel the spirit of capitalism and erode communal forms of labor and reciprocity in the name of individual gain and salvation.

"How many people were studying with you at the institute?"

"There were six of us." Vidal paused. "I learned about the Bible so I could see it, so I could touch it," his voice lingering over the words. "Well, some people asked, 'How is this drunk going to be an evangelical?' I played the guitar, I sang, I danced."[9]

"Wow—you did it all!"

He threw back his head and laughed out loud. "*Hermana*, nothing escaped me. But after that, I never was out tracking down young women."

Vidal's tone turned serious. "I didn't drink. I worked hard. I wasn't fornicating—not at all. No fornication! I thought I'd just work and never touch a woman again. But I worked making firecrackers, and this young woman started talking to me. I wasn't talking, but she fell in love with me. We got married, but not because I'd been talking to her," he insisted.

"So you had *el don de predicar*, but didn't use it with her?" I teased.

"That's right, *hermana*."

"Or maybe it was the fireworks?"

He laughed, rocking back and forth in his chair.

"Ok—I'm switching topics! How did you begin evangelizing in the *selva*?" I asked.

"I studied one full year and then went out preaching." As he explained, he went out with the North American missionaries, translating into Quechua for them.

"And when you headed out to the communities to start churches, did you bring movies, pamphlets—how did you do it?"

"At first we didn't have movies. We only took pamphlets—that's how we worked. Then don Nicholas Cochran started the radio—Radio Amauta [in 1960]. It took him two or three years because the government didn't want to give him permission," he explained. "Later don Nicholas brought a thousand radios and we gave them out everywhere. They were just two band radios, Radio Amauta and Voz Cristiana, from Ecuador."

"Evangelical programs?"

"Aha. We gave them away everywhere," gesturing expansively with his outstretched arms. "I traveled all over, forming churches. Enrique [Harry] Marshall was here and I worked with him in the *selva*. There was no road then, no cars. People walked on foot and so did we."

"You walked all the way to the *selva* on foot?"

Pastor Vidal nodded. "I had a mule and I'd travel to the jungle, taking the path that runs by Rasuhuillca," referring to the highest peak in northern Ayacucho.

"And the North Americans went with you?"

He nodded. Pastor Vidal began tracing the route they followed, naming off a long list of communities in which they had founded churches from the 1950s through the 1970s. "We were always visiting. I'd work teaching them choruses, hymns, prayers. I just used a house. We would start visiting their neighbors and calling them, no? I always stayed for two or three weeks in each place. Then little by little, as they formed a group, I'd move on to the next stop. I always traveled with Enrique [Henry] Marshall."

"And the films were later?"

"Yes. First we had Radio Amauta, and then the projector. With the films, the church grew everywhere. The first time, children came during the day and we tried it. We showed one film and they all watched. So we told them that night we'd show a free film, so they should tell their friends, their parents, everyone. Tell them there'll be a free movie tonight—we won't charge a cent."

"So everyone came?"

"Uf," he threw up his hands. "The kids ran around everywhere—'Movie! Movie tonight!' *Hermana*, the temple couldn't hold everyone. So the next day we invited the missionaries to talk after the movies and there was no more room anywhere. Everyone came to watch the movie."

"And what did people say after they saw the film? How did they react?"

"They just wanted more. For the grace of God, the churches grew. And people listened to Radio Amauta everywhere too."

"I bet they'd never seen movies before?"

"Never. Such admiration. Ad-mi-ra-tion!"

"What films were they, *hermano* Vidal?"

"The birth of Señor Jesucristo, the flight from Egypt. Then the crucifixion, the universal flood." He thought for a moment. "That's why people came, to see Señor Jesucristo with their own eyes. Then they knew Jesucristo was God."

"When you arrived how did people react? Were there ever problems with the Catholics?"

Vidal sat straight up in his chair. "They wanted to kill us but they couldn't. Once in Rosario they wanted to kill me. They beat me up and left me bloody. Well, there were police stations then, so the *hermanos* got an order and they made the Catholics go to the police station. How those police looked at me! They threw them in jail—it was the *comuneros* themselves who'd beaten me. I spent three days in the hospital. I was all swollen up, blood, fever, everything."

"So it was the Catholic *comuneros* who did this?" I asked incredulously. He nodded.

"And why did they say they'd done this?"

"Because I was Evangelical, because I was preaching. They told me I had no right to preach because they were Catholic."

"Did this happen more than once?"

"Oh, they almost killed me several times."

"And the priests? The catechists?"

"They were against me too. They said, 'Those Evangelicals are enemies. Don't allow them in.' They said we were condemned. Because we denied the images, they said we were diabolic men." Vidal shook his head as he recalled those early years. "It wasn't easy at first. That's how it was, *hermana*. Later we won in spite of it all. We won against the Catholics because they became fewer and fewer in number."

"*Hermano* Vidal, did they have catechists in these communities?"

"No, nobody. They just had chapels and the priests visited once a year."

"Were there Catholic churches in the communities then?"

"Yes, in some of them."

"But now there aren't."

"No, not now. The priests traveled. They would bring the priests—people would come with horses to take the priests with them. The priests rode on horses, with saddles. The horses ran and so did the men, just looking up at them. But we didn't do that. We helped with everything."

Vidal paused, taking a swig of his Kola Real. "It was stronger then, not like now. We still go out, but we don't have any support. And that Senderismo . . . " his voice drifted off.

"What about Senderismo?"

"Because of that Senderismo, it dropped. There was nothing to eat. And there were massacres from all three sides—from the Senderistas, the military, and the *ronderos*."

"*Ronderos* too?"

He nodded. "Powerful massacres."

Things began to change in the *selva* and the *sierra*. There was another group with a message to share in their own search for converts: Sendero Luminoso. As the violence spread throughout Ayacucho, traveling in the countryside became increasingly dangerous. Being an Evangelical pastor conferred no protection, in part because Senderista militants considered the Evangélicos to be one of their key ideological enemies. As the threats mounted in the early 1980s, the North American missionaries withdrew from Peru, leaving the church in the hands of local pastors like Vidal. However, it was not only the North Americans who retreated from rural areas; many Catholic priests ceased to visit as well. One Peruvian colleague wryly noted that in many rural areas, the Catholic Church was among the first casualties of war. This would be another chapter in the complicated history of a church that, in the eyes of many *campesinos*, had never come down off its high horse.

In Ayacucho, the growth of Evangelismo occurred against the backdrop of a historically conservative Catholic Church.[10] Catholic priests had been closely associated with the *hacendados* (large landowners) who comprised the regional elites.[11] However, with the Agrarian Reform of the 1960s, the hacienda system—already in decline economically—further crumbled. The decay of the hacienda system in turn weakened the presence and authority of the Catholic Church in rural areas.[12] With the internal armed conflict, the Catholic Church further retrenched to the cities, leaving a spiritual and ritual void in rural areas.

Huamanga, the capital city of Ayacucho, boasts thirty-three Catholic churches, colonial structures so impressive they have become tourist attractions. The city is famous for its glorious celebration of Semana Santa, the crowds compressed shoulder to shoulder to celebrate the last week of Christ's life and his resurrection. Ornate religious images are paraded through the streets, suspended on wooden beams hoisted in the air by the faithful. When Jeffrey Klaiber wrote his history of the rise of the conservative Peruvian Catholic Church, he turned toward Ayacucho and a "living church [that] looked as though it had not changed much since colonial times," just as impervious to the passing of the centuries as those thirty-three steadfast structures.

Yet this is only one facet of the Catholic Church. At the national level, the progressive wing of the Catholic Church was heavily influenced by liberation theology and vocally denounced both armed and structural violence. The Peruvian priest Gustavo Gutiérrez of the Dominican order is widely considered the founder of liberation theology and one of its most eloquent proponents. In 1986, against the backdrop of indiscriminate repression, an escalating death toll, and the abuse of human rights—particularly those of the rural poor—Father Gutiérrez wrote:

> How do we make theology during Ayacucho? How do we speak of the God of life when people are cruelly and massively assassinated in the "Corner of the Dead"? How can we announce the love of God in the midst of such profound contempt for human life? How can we proclaim the resurrection of *El Señor* where death reigns, especially the death of children, women, the poor and the indigenous—the death of the "*insignificantes*" of our society?[13]

Unfortunately for Ayacucho, the man "making theology" during the worst years of the violence in the region was Monseñor Juan Luis Cipriani.[14] A representative of Opus Dei, Cipriani denounced human rights as a cloak for "terrorist organizations" and a form of "imperialism," going so far as to post a sign on the door of the archbishopric: "*No se aceptan reclamos sobre Derechos Humanos*" ("Human rights complaints not accepted here").[15] He also marginalized the more progressive Jesuits and Dominicans, insisting the church should focus on mass and prayer and leave the social and political work to others. Cipriani was such an obstacle to human rights work and to progressive clergy and laypeople that he warranted individual criticism in the PTRC's Final Report. Following a detailed chronology of the important role the Catholic Church played in accompanying and protecting people who were besieged by the violence of both the state and Shining Path, they turn to the grave exception of Monseñor Cipriani, "who repeatedly issued statements condemning the work of the Coordinadora Nacional and other organizations who worked in the defense of human rights."[16] Thus the Catholic Church presented meager competition for the Evangélicos in the *alturas* of Huanta, where the conversions were massive.

I was interested in hearing more about those conversions and Vidal's perspective on the rise of Sendero Luminoso, which he had experienced firsthand.

"Oh, it must have been '82 or '83 because the subversives had started in Ayacucho. I was walking, forming churches in the *selva* when the subversives started. I was working with my son Isaías. Oh, the Senderistas were watching everything I did! Baptizing, marrying people—everything. One time this young man, a Senderista, was watching me, all curious. I could tell I was making him think, no? He asked me afterward to sell him a Bible! I just gave him one. That young man, he'd been formed by the *curas de esos Senderistas* [the priests of those Senderistas]."

"The Senderistas had priests?" I asked, perplexed.

He nodded. "Of course."

I did not press him on this question, but from other conversations I had with Vidal it became clear he was referring to the Senderista ideologues. Just as a priest teaches his congregation, so did the Senderista cadres inculcate "Pensamiento Gonzalo" in their followers.[17] Indeed, one term villagers used to refer to Senderista sympathizers was *iñirusqaku*—the "convinced ones" or "the believers."

"I never talked against them," he continued, referring to the Senderistas. "I talked well about them so they wouldn't mistreat me."

"Were you ever threatened?"

He rolled his eyes and nodded in response to my question. "*Bueno*, once I was in the *selva* and the Senderistas had sent a message to Hatun Rumi—it's in the *selva*. The Senderistas had held their assemblies and drawn up Actas saying that I was a spy for the gringos and they needed to get rid of me," dragging his index finger across his neck.

I gasped. "The Senderistas said this?"

"Yes, the Senderistas had their Actas. But some people in Hatun Rumi heard about this so they warned me. But I thought, 'What did I do so they'd want to kill me?' So if they kill me—well, I just kept going. Then there was another warning saying they were coming. I said, 'Good. Let them come.' Then a third time, the older people had a meeting and they said, '*Hermano*, please, if those men enter, how will we be free if they kill you? It's better for you to leave.' Only the older people knew anything."

"How did they know?"

"At night we all met, the old people, my son, and me—we talked, but the other members of the church didn't know anything. The Senderistas sent someone with a message for us. So we started to leave at night. It was spring," he remembered, "three days of walking."

"So people tried to protect you?"

"Yes, yes."

"And what was that about 'how will we be free if they kill you?' What did they mean?"

"I baptized people, I married them," he explained. "That way, if they were killed they'd be free."

I got it, struck that Vidal had been preparing people for God's judgment in the afterlife. This resonated with something several *ronderos* had said: they converted to Evangelismo during the violence, concerned that they would have to answer to God for what they were doing. Even while they were killing, they were thinking ahead to how they would someday atone for their actions.

"I was able to free many of them. I was thinking they'd all be killed," shaking his head as he remembered.

"But did the Senderistas ever ask you what you were doing?"

"No, never," he replied emphatically. "But from a distance they challenged me. They knew I was working there, they knew I'd formed each church and that I was preaching. They'd listened to me. So they didn't need to ask me anything—they knew me."

"Of course. *Hermano* Vidal, what did people say when they delivered themselves to God? What made them decide to do it?

"It was from watching the films, from the message. It was to find their salvation with El Señor Jesucristo. There were so many massacres, so many people were dying. But later they formed the *defensa civil* [*rondas campesinas*]. They started going after the Senderistas and killing a lot of them."

"What do you think of the *ronderos*?"

Vidal shrugged. "*Bueno*, they knew me. But one time when I left for Rosario, they wanted to kill me. The *defensa civil* asked to see my documents [*libreta electoral*]. They had a building with a second floor, heavily guarded. I heard someone say, 'Kill him.' Well, my son Isaías went up to the second floor and asked for my documents. Isaías saw the president—he was a *hermano*. He asked him, 'Don't you recognize my father?' The president was frightened when he realized who I was, and he gave me back my documents. If not for my son, they would've killed me. But it wasn't my time yet. I still had work to do, work for El Señor."

"You've had a lot of close calls. Senderistas, *ronderos*, Catholics—everyone was after you!"

Vidal smiled, and agreed that he had escaped death many times, thanks to El Señor. "It just wasn't my time yet, *hermana*."

"What do you think about the way they organized in *rondas*? I wonder, did it help or did it make things worse inside of the communities?"

"*Bueno*, they weren't evangelicals anymore. In that hour, they weren't evangelicals. They would just kill anybody. They just grabbed them and killed them. That's how it was. But with the *ronderos*, the Senderistas started to dwindle, things calmed down. It wasn't easy for us either. With the authorities we had to get—what do you call it? A pass. We also had to have one with the military. With these passes, they let us by. Without it, you were dead. Everything was controlled, *hermana*. Men, women, children—it didn't matter."

"But you kept visiting all these communities in spite of the violence?"

He nodded. "Yes, except for the worst part of it. I had to stop for a while. But once there were fewer Senderistas, I started working again. But in the *selva*," he paused, shaking his head, "with all the killing, there were microbes. I'm not sure just what kind, but all sorts of illnesses started appearing."

"More illnesses?"

He nodded. "Oh, there were so many dead who weren't buried. They were just left hanging in the trees, dumped in the river. There were so many flies. Well, lots of dead who weren't buried."

At the sound of the door scraping the floor, we both looked up. A tall slender man with high cheekbones walked up the aisle toward us. He smiled and greeted his father. It was Isaías, the son Pastor Vidal had mentioned many times during our conversation. We introduced ourselves and realized we had seen each other before on the road from Huanta to the highlands.

Isaías pulled up a chair to join us around the table. "I'll be heading up to Carhuahurán later this month for the Fiesta Espiritual."

"Then we'll see each other. You know, I was talking with your father about his experiences, and how during the war the churches were full. But now some people have said the church is *enfriándose* [cooling off]. What do you think is happening?"

"The problem is when there was violence there was more work. The pastor from one church would visit another church and so the *hermanos* were encouraging each other. But when the problems passed, this enthusiasm also decreased," replied Isaías.

I nodded. "How old were you when you started traveling with your father?"

"I was twelve years old. I always went with my father, and I liked it. Since I was fifteen, I've continually preached. Now I'm contracted by the association," referring to Llaqtanchikta Qatarichisun (LQ), an organization that spun off from World Vision.

"What are you doing with LQ?"

"We've been filling out questionnaires. In Carhuahurán we worked with widows. There are orphans, too. We've met so many widows who lost their husbands during the violence and orphans who lost their parents. We've also seen what happened to the harvest. With everyone we asked how much they plant, how much they harvest. We started to wonder how they could survive. They told us that sometimes they live with relatives—uncles or distant relatives who give them food. That's how they live. Sometimes they tell us, 'If my father had lived, if only my husband had lived—we wouldn't be working, we'd be eating well, we'd have animals.'"

"What do people want when you talk to them? Revenge? Fines?"

He shook his head. "They don't talk about revenge. They ask for economic help. They say, 'If I hadn't lost my husband—before the violence we had fifteen bulls, eighty cows, eighty sheep, and other animals too.' And when we ask them how many they have now, they have two, three sheep."

"This is what I've been told, too. People lost so much during the violence."

Isaías nodded. "Before they would help us out so we could travel, preach—now they ask us for money."

"I'm still thinking about the widows, the orphans. Do you address the theme of repentance, reconciliation when you preach?"

"Repentance yes, but not reconciliation. We don't spend enough time. We're only there one or two days. But the *hermanos* want to talk about this."

"And how do you talk about repentance? What does it mean in the evangelical church, *hermano* Isaías?"

"In the evangelical church, repentance is how we talk about the violence. We think, as flesh and blood, as humans, that we are—if something would happen, we would seek revenge. So repentance—sometimes you think, 'I'm going to get my revenge with such a person.' Well, you're already sinning. Repenting is saying to God, 'I have thought of doing this but I won't do it.' You leave it to the will of God because God says 'revenge is mine.'"

"And when you talk about this with the *hermanos* in the churches, are there people that can't accept someone's repentance? I mean, those who don't resign themselves to having lost husbands? When you visit the communities, is there really a willingness to repent?"

"Yes, yes. They understand, until tears flow. But there could be exceptional cases—the *hermanos* in the communities would know this. There could be people who're resentful," he acknowledged.

"Hmm. Your father said so many interesting things. He talked about opening up the heart so the Holy Spirit can enter. What is conversion for you?"

"It's the conversion to Christ, the conversion has to be born in the heart. You have to feel it inside. There are some people who have come to our church to deliver themselves but it wasn't from the heart but just for aid, for gifts."[18]

"Oh, the blankets and *calaminas*."

He shrugged. "It happens. But there are some that from the heart think, feel the presence of the Holy Spirit in their hearts and continue to, even now."

"So some have a deep faith?"

"Yes, I've seen it. Profound faith looks for a way to survive. They listen to the radio, they get encouragement through the radio," emphasized Isaías.

"Absolutely—many people have mentioned Radio Amauta. They tell me they always listened, even during the violence."

Indeed, Radio Amauta had been an important source of information for people in the *campo*. Amauta broadcast messages between family members, letting worried loved ones know someone had safely arrived in Huanta, making it past the military checkpoints and Shining Path sweeps throughout the countryside. The broadcasters also provided news updates, frequently lending a biblical spin to world events. It was Radio Amauta, turned down to a bare whisper, that accompanied people on cold nights in the caves, allowing them to imagine a caring international community of Evangélicos who prayed for them and assured them they were not forgotten.

But I had forgotten the time and how long we had been talking. I began thanking both Vidal and Isaías for their generosity. Rising to his feet, Vidal extended an invitation to me. "*Hermana*, let me show you where the martyrs died."

Vidal led me out the front door of the church and around to the back. Chickens scattered to avoid our footsteps as we entered a small corral. Pointing to a wooden plaque hung on the side of the church's outer wall, he explained that this was where the *marinos* (navy) had killed the six *hermanos* in August 1984.

"I am so sorry—I've heard about this. Were you here when it happened?"

"No. I was in the *selva*. But one day we woke up and were listening to Radio Amauta. They started to talk about Callqui, about how the *marinos* had killed six *hermanos*."

"August first?"

He nodded. "There was no shortage of enemies. The *hermanos* were in *culto* (service) with a gaslight. Back then there wasn't electricity here. The *marinos* entered and cornered them—they couldn't escape. They had a list of names and started calling people by name: 'You, outside. You too.' So they went outside. The *marinos* made the rest of them blow out the light and keep singing. They told them to sing as loud as they could. And then dynamite exploded."

"Right here?"

"In my house. The *hermanos* couldn't hear because they were singing. We heard the news—my family died there. Two young men I'd educated died. It was as though I were walking in my sleep. An old Presbyterian *hermano* told me the Senderistas had sent the *marinos*. The church of Callqui is known around the world because of that."

"What happened when you got back here?"

"When I arrived here and they'd killed the *hermanos*, we started a legal case [*juicio*]. The *marinos* didn't respect anyone—not women, not men, not children. They just killed until they were tired. Their captain was Camión—there in the stadium," Vidal recalled, pointing down the hill. "He escaped to the United States."

"Did the North American *hermanos* stay here during all this?"

"No, they went to Cuzco, some returned to the United States. They left. But there was the National Council, and they helped start the *juicio*. And World Vision also helped us."[19]

"Was there ever justice in the case?" I asked, knowing my question was rhetorical.

He shook his head. "That Captain Camión made them do it. He escaped to Quito, Ecuador, and from there they say he was kidnaped. But we know he escaped to the United States. The case is still open—it hasn't ended, even now. It wasn't even the Senderistas who did it. It was the *marinos*. Instead of protecting us, they killed us."

"What happened to the relatives of the people who died?

"They're still here."

"And what is life like for them? I wonder what it's like living with this?"

"Very difficult," he replied, shaking his head. "The people who killed—well, they did so in ignorance, not knowing anything, like a baby."

I was surprised by his word choice. "Ignorant?"

"Yes, ignorant. Sometimes the leaders made people kill, obligated them. They killed because that Captain Camión made them do it."

"So the men who came here that night were obeying authority?"

"Yes. One man came here and said their boss had made them do this. He asked us for forgiveness, to pardon him."

"When did that happen?"

"When a *marino* came here, one of those from that night, he came here and said, 'We killed. I participated in it but now I'm a Christian and I want to ask for forgiveness.' So all the relatives came here. With tears he asked them for forgiveness."

"As *hermanos*, there's an emphasis on reconciliation in the church, no?"

"Yes," he insisted. "We always talk about that."

"And the relatives, weren't they resentful?"

"Yes, some were, some weren't. One *hermana*, she'd lost her husband and that resentment [*rencor*] didn't go away. She said, 'Those animals killed my husband, they have to answer for that. They have to do something—they've destroyed me.' Even though we try to understand, it's difficult. Even now she's resentful. But some of the *hermanos* are forgiving from their hearts. She says, 'You can forgive because you lost sons. I lost my husband.'"

"Is it worse to lose a husband?"

"Yes, a husband is worth more—it's a greater loss. One *hermana* lost two sons and she forgave. She said, 'What am I going to do? I can't live like her— can't live hating.'" He shrugged his shoulders.

I nodded and followed him back out to the front of the church. We said our good-byes and I thanked him again before heading down the dirt road and past the stadium, where the shouts of the soccer fans echoed against the walls.

Reel Life

> When I watched the evangelical films, I began to imagine. I imagined that life really must be that way.
>
> —Juan, twenty-five years old, Canrao

Although individual conversion was frequently the result of revelation, in the *alturas* of Huanta—where the conversions were massive—the growth of Evangelismo had both individualizing and "collectivizing" aspects. Armed communities of faith were forged, and the Evangélicos would prove to be one of the most tenacious enemies the Shining Path militants would confront. Listening to Evangelical friends confirmed that the struggle between Evangelismo and Senderismo was a struggle of biblical proportions—an apocalyptic battle waged at the end of time.[20] How this happened becomes clearer once we go to the movies.

A few weeks after we crossed paths in Callqui, Pastor Isaías Trujillano arrived in Carhuahurán en route to the *selva*. He was talking up the Fiesta Espiritual that would take place the following month. He went door-to-door during the day, visiting the Evangélicos. As darkness fell, he enlisted the help of several villagers to prepare for showing the Bible movies he had brought with him. Just as his father before him, Isaías traveled with films and a generator as he made his way up and over the mountains.

After much debate it was decided the best place to show the films was on the side of Feliciano's two-story house. Several of the *ronderos* helped him hang a large white sheet with nails they hammered into his wall, and this rippling screen provided the background for the images projected that night.

Other men brought piles of *ichu* (straw) to soften the ground. Women began to arrive with their children, nestling into the *ichu* in a semicircle in front of the white sheet. Farther back, long planks of wood were dragged to the field and set atop adobe bricks to form benches. I sat down on one of the planks, Efraín, Shintaca, and Yolanda crowding together beneath my poncho. The cold fluctuated with the cloud cover, rolling in and out on the wind.

Feliciano opened the padlock on his door and called Simeón and Satú over to help him carry out a rickety table and set it up on the far side of the field. The table legs were uneven and after trying several rocks, Feliciano slipped a large flat one beneath one of the legs and the table finally stopped wobbling. An extension cord ran the length of the field, hooked up to the big truck battery that sat in Feliciano's store.

Isaías pulled two enormous reels from his backpack and opened a worn cardboard box. He had brought along a projector, the sort we used in grammar school when Mrs. Hauser threaded the thick brown coils into the machine and we took flight. He set his generator up on the table as far away as possible so the noise would not drown out the film. The crowd grew as the motor began and the white sheet came alive with Bible scenes.

I did not catch the title of the first film. I had run up to our room to bring down a pocketful of Sublimes—chocolate squares loaded with almonds. By the time we settled into my poncho again, the Virgin Mary was already pregnant. There were lengthy scenes of Joseph and Mary heading across the desert on a mule, prompting several people in the audience to remember how they had been forced to flee their homes with only the clothes on their backs. They, too, had walked for days on aching feet only to have people refuse them shelter, shouting, "Filthy *chutos* [savages]! Get off my land before you dirty it."

Mary's eyes were cast downward for virtually the entire film, thick eyelashes resting piously upon milky white skin. On the few occasions when she did look up, it was to heed the voice of God speaking to her from heaven. The films were worn, and the generator was not working at full force. Manuco suggested it was suffering from *sorroche* (altitude sickness) and thus the films were slow, as though a tired arm was turning a handle at too slow a pace. The soundtrack was garbled and the speed lowered all of the voices to the baritone-bass range. It was a bit of a shock to hear the Virgin Mary respond to God in the same thundering bass voice He used with her. I heard laughter coming from behind us. A group of men were standing at the back, the *ronderos* with both guns and blankets thrown over their shoulders.

In a few turns of the reel, the Assyrians appeared in chain metal gear, enormous men outfitted for war. As night fell upon the battlefield, two spies sneaked up outside a tent to eavesdrop and learned the following day's battle plans. The Spanish dubbing was virtually inaudible, and most of the villagers were Quechua speakers anyway. So it was the audience that provided the script. The spies were just like the *ronderos*, and spying was part of *vigilancia* to see what the Senderistas had planned. Film viewing was improvisational theater.

When the first film garbled to a close, Isaías gave a thirty-minute lecture on family and community life. The main theme was simple: he exhorted the women to stay home and fulfill their roles, leaving the men to go out and work hard. While he preached, Feliciano carried over a can of gasoline to stir the generator out of its *sorroche*.

The crowd was eager for more, and Isaías threaded Heinz Fussle's *My Brother's Keeper* into the projector. The opening scene consists of three little gringos shoplifting in a large department store, gleefully stuffing merchandise inside their jackets. The boys run up and down the aisles on a spree. However, as they turn up the fateful final aisle, three security guards close in on them. As the guards tower over the boys and begin to lecture them on the sins of shoplifting, the sneakiest little gringo breaks loose and manages to escape on his newly acquired skateboard. The next scene shows the same mini shoplifter, defiantly eating an orange as he swaggers down a blind alley.

In the alley, juicy orange in hand and mouth, he encounters a tall black man. Racist stereotypes dictate his role: he is dressed in tight polyester pants, and his lunar-sized afro is straight out of *Shaft*. People in the audience began pointing: they recognized this man from the department store, where he had watched the scuffle between the boys and the security guards. He begins by praising the boy for his clever escape, suggesting he consider the benefits of a life of crime. Fade out to evil chuckles.

The little brother's keeper appears in the next scene. He is the boy's older brother, a former crime buddy of the tall black man. Big brother was recently released from prison, where he found Jesus Christ and was born again. He now raises white doves on the rooftop of their high-rise apartment building. He is determined to save his little brother, a task requiring prayers and preaching, sin and salvation.

The images of hell are terrifying. Human faces melt away in Satan's flames, skeletal remains and teeth dropping in a damned heap. The worms and snakes eat their way through brains, slithering out of mangled ears and wailing mouths that only now—too late—proclaim the error of their ways. I looked around and every single face was transfixed, staring unblinkingly at the white sheet of hell.

Suddenly the sheet went blank. All heads turned toward the back, and we could see Isaías peering over the side of the field. The generator had gone the way of many soccer balls—it had fallen over the steep drop to the river below. We gathered around as two boys went running down the hill to retrieve what was left of the generator. Manuco shook his head and, inspired by the bottle of *trago* he kept tucked inside his jacket, proclaimed: "It must have been the Catholics. A Catholic must have given it a push!" Even Isaías managed a weak smile as we kept peering over the cliff.

The images that evening had awakened in the *hermanos* and *hermanas* gathered in Carhuahurán a sense of shared experiences with the actors who appeared on the screen, despite the radically different context. The audience was not passively consuming this visual feast but rather, as Michel De Certeau suggests, they were elaborating their own secondary productions.[21] These secondary productions allowed them to imagine a Christian community that erased centuries as well as cultural and national differences and to script a world in which they as well as the Israelites traverse the same landscape— a landscape of exodus, struggle, and return.[22] Arjun Appadurai has written that today the imagination plays a more important role than ever before in social life: "The new power of the imagination in the fabrication of social lives is inescapably tied up with images, ideas and opportunities that come from elsewhere, often moved around by the vehicles of the mass media."[23] Both the Bible films and Radio Amauta have been key players in the collective memories people have about the *sasachakuy tiempo*. I sat in an audience that ranged from *wawakuna* wrapped in shawls around their mothers' backs to elderly men and women who had first watched these films when the Virgin Mary was still a soprano. Where do the images come from that we use to construct our memories? Can "reel images" become the stuff of "real" life?

My understanding of these questions is greatly influenced by Gauri Viswanathan.[24] She suggests that religion is in part an epistemology, a way in which people both construct and interact with the real. If we understand conversion as not only a religious act but also a communicational act, an interpretive act, a way of restructuring relationships, then we can see religion as very much a thing-of-this-world. We come closer to the experiential and phenomenological aspects of conversion to Evangelismo. The familiar stories of grinding poverty, rural-to-urban migration, anomie, social mobility, and fostering collective identity are all plausible motives for conversion, but clearly they do not exhaust the motives people have for becoming an Evangélico or the legacies of that conversion. These motives and their legacies are innumerable and shape every chapter of this book. For now, we turn to a holy triad.

Bodies of Faith

What is it about the Evangelical message that resonates so profoundly with the experience of displacement? The exodus figures prominently in the testimonies I have heard, and forced migration was one product of the internal armed conflict. However, displacement occurs on several dimensions, not only in the spatial realm. Due to the political violence, many rural villagers were unable to reproduce their daily cultural practices: burying loved ones was frequently impossible, taking sacrifices to the mountains was dangerous, and fiestas and *ferias* were suspended at various junctures. Even for populations that remained in situ during the war, there was a cultural displacement that blocked the reproduction of individual and collective identity. As Akhil Gupta and James Ferguson suggest, even populations that remain on their land can experience changes so profound that the naturalness of a place is called into question.[25]

The Evangelical Christianity villagers practice contrasts with the "popular Catholicism" that characterized these communities for a span of several centuries.[26] Popular Catholicism—and its emphasis on the images of the saints—was constructed on the basis of the prehispanic Andean religion, in which faith was grounded in a sacred landscape of tutelary gods, via *huacas* and *wamanis*.[27] However, as Vidal has explained, Evangelical pastors urged people to burn the idols, arguing that the saints were just a "pile of rags" with painted *yeso* (plaster of paris) faces.

Pastor Pascual made the same argument in another conversation. It was a relentlessly rainy day and I was huddled inside my room in Carhuahurán, watching the dirt and straw mixture that held the doorframe in place slowly turn to mud, large gobs thudding to the ground. Amid this dreary scene of domestic decay, I heard a familiar voice outside my door. Pastor Pascual helped force open my door, strategically using it to shove the accumulated mud to one side of the room. He gave his striped poncho a few good shakes. His brown felt hat was also soaked, but he left it on. I never saw anyone take off their hat except in church or when singing the national anthem. I ladled up a cup of *miski yaku*, and we settled in for a chat. At some point I asked if the Evangélicos in Carhuahurán had destroyed their saints, and he began nodding mid-question.

"Our Señor forbids it. Before, people thought they had power. We believed in them. But they're just *yeso*. I also had fiestas and placed candles and flowers—kneeling I prayed to them," Pascual recalled, shaking his head. "But they're the work of the devil. You place flowers, candles, but nothing happens. But when you deliver yourself to the *evangelio*, you're with God and the devil hates you. The devil looks at you all bothered," he explained, making a diabolically bothered grimace. "He tries to make you fall however he can. The saints—they're made of *yeso*, dirt, rags! I could make one right now," he scoffed. "I could make a saint or a virgin! But they worship them. What power can these have?" He shook his head. "Those who trust in the saints are trusting in the devil—not in our Señor Jesucristo but in the devil himself. God doesn't permit that."

While the saints and tutelary gods anchored faith in icons and a defined sacred geography, Evangelismo is simultaneously "deterritorialized" *and* embodied. From the conversations I had with Evangélicos, it is clear the Evangelical body is occupied by either Satan or the Holy Spirit.[28] I think of this as "floating charisma": the transformative power of faith is no longer "fixed" in religious images or moored to the landscape. So where does it inhere? In the Bible and in the body.

I recall one evening in *culto* in Carhuahurán. The rain did not keep the faithful from climbing up the hill to the Evangelical church next door to Michael's corral. I was using my flashlight, a round ball of light bouncing along the path. I paused for a moment, remembering the curfew on flashlights that had been imposed at the Sunday *formación*. It was late 1999 and concerns that people were "walking again" (a reference to renewed Senderista activity) were fueled by sightings of flashlight beams in the hills. The *ronderos* had established a shoot-on-sight rule, but I checked my watch and it was only 7:30—the (flash)lights out began at 9:00 p.m.

I entered and took a place on one of the wooden slabs. After several hymns the pastor requested we stand to recite a passage from the Bible, and I noticed the women, each holding a tattered book in her hands. None of the women could read, but the formality of the book was important. That book appeared in many people's stories of the war. The Bible had literally saved lives.

Dionisia was one of the women in *culto* that evening. I was visiting her a few days later and offered to take her photograph. She was delighted by the idea and carefully sat under a bush in her yard, smoothing a few rebellious strands of hair with her hands. When I began to focus my camera, she told me to wait a moment because she had forgotten something important. Dionisia went into her house and I heard the sounds of a search. She came out with her Bible and told me to wait again. Flipping through her book, she finally came to the page she was looking for. She held the Bible up in front of her chest, opened to a blood-stained page 127: "This Bible saved me when the *malafekuna* attacked. The bullets were whizzing by my head and hitting houses. A bullet came straight at me—I saw the *terruco* take aim. But I held up my Bible and it stopped the bullet. God saved me that day."

Just as the Bible had the power to stop bullets, it also provided protection from the capricious mountain gods and the remains of the gentiles. In that same conversation with Pastor Pascual, I asked whether the *hermanos* should walk with their Bible in hand.

"Of course! You walk with your Bible because this is your weapon [*arma*]! It's our spiritual weapon," Pascual explained. "I don't trust in guns, and I don't carry one because my weapon is in Quechua, in Spanish. With the Bible, you follow God. If you carry this weapon, you aren't afraid. If you pass a spring that is evaporating—well, I've taken a drink from a spring as it evaporated. I've decided 'here I'm going to sit.' You aren't afraid because God is with you. You can sleep anywhere, you ask God, you say, 'I'm with God,' and you aren't afraid." Thus the Bible helped protect Evangélicos from many of the *males de campo*, including witchcraft and its potentially lethal effects.

In addition to charisma inhering in the Bible, it infuses the body. The Evangelical body is filled with, and testimony to, God's power. Conversion narratives were replete with revelations in which God operated with a surgeon's precision, removing illness and healing the body. This is a religion that ritualizes rupture and elaborates histories of discontinuity: the reborn Evangelical body testifies to the power of the Holy Spirit to effect dramatic change. The word is made body for the Evangélicos, whose testimonies underscore the felt presence of God at work in their bodies and in their lives. Numerous pastors assured me that Evangélicos who had been forced to flee carried their most important possession within them: their faith in El Señor Jesucristo.

Local Theologies

> There will be world war. The people will suffer until death, but without finding death. God will take death away from them. People will want to die. From the highest peak of the mountains people will throw themselves. They'll cut their own throats with knives, but they won't die. Now people try to escape death, but a time is coming when they will seek it. Nation against nation, the world war will come. Now they say they're preparing arms. I'm not sure—I think they say the arms are atomic. For the war between nations, a world war between governments. Between pueblos they'll terminate each other. The civil war we had here in the *campo*—their pueblos were peaceful then, not like us. We were in *sasachakuy tiempo*. But war will shake their pueblos, will leave their cities desolate. Everyone will flail themselves—this will be called the river of blood [*yawar mayu*]. Oh, for many kilometers people's blood will flow like a river! Their intestines will be like *guano* all over the ground. According to the word of God we are in the final days. It says in the Bible that nation will rise up against nation, kingdom against kingdom. All of this is happening. They talk about all of this on the radio.
>
> —Pastor Pascual Bautista, Assembly of God, Carhuahurán, 1999

As the violence increased throughout Ayacucho, city-based pastors—Vidal included—found it increasingly difficult to continue visiting rural communities such as Carhuahurán. Vidal stopped his traveling from 1984 to 1991 due to death threats from the Senderistas: he was not alone in being the target of their violence. As the PTRC discovered, Evangélicos were explicitly considered an ideological and organizational obstacle to the spread of Senderismo.[29] Where the Evangélicos reigned, people's hearts and minds were already committed, and it was Evangelicals in the Apurímac Valley who were among the first to organize *rondas campesinas* and take up arms against the "legions of the antichrist."[30] Local pastors exercised tremendous autonomy and began interpreting the Bible according to the daily realities of war and within a narrative tradition emphasizing the cataclysmic change of "*tiempos.*"

When contemplating what sort of interpretive language popular religions employ to characterize the past and imagine the future, we might think in terms of narrative sedimentation. Andean oral histories are replete with millenarian, messianic imagery, and this is the context in which local pastors began "pentecostalizing" their religious message and practices.[31] As Robbins has noted, Pentecostal Christianity has both world-breaking and world-making facets, which introduce their own cultural logics while being organizationally local and responsive to local concerns.[32] The Evangelical message was blended with Andean narrative traditions, with which it resonated. My earliest conversations in the *alturas* of Huanta included references to the time of the plague, to the clouds of locusts that had eaten crops and blocked out the sun, blackening the entire sky. This was a world of portents that were being interpreted and given meaning: local Evangelical pastors were key figures in providing a narrative structure in the midst of the chaos of war.[33] As it turns out, it was *not* only Monseñor Cipriani who was "making theology" in Ayacucho during the internal armed conflict.[34]

This was also a militant theology that allowed for arming (and subsequently disarming) these communities. There is, of course, nothing intrinsically peaceful about Evangelismo. Indeed, Christians have a bellicose track record on the world stage. In both the Apurímac valley and the *alturas* of Huanta, many *ronderos* saw themselves as Christian soldiers marching off to war.[35] The descriptions of the Senderistas focused on their monstrosity and their allegiance to the Antichrist. As Pastor Pascual recounted, "They were demons, worse than dogs. They did not care about life, about death. It was all the same to them. They weren't human." Within this framework, killing enemies was an act in the service of God. Here I part ways with Pastor Vidal, who insisted the *ronderos* were not Evangélicos in the moments in which they killed. To the contrary, these were Christian warriors doing God's work in the battle between good and evil, and some groups of *ronderos* sang hymns as they marched off to patrol.[36]

Yet killing also provoked ambivalent emotions for many men. Saving souls was a concern not only for pastors such as Vidal who baptized people in the midst of the armed conflict in preparation for what seemed a certain and untimely death. Individual *ronderos* also struggled to reconcile "Thou shall not kill" with their participation in the armed struggle. On first glance killing would seem incompatible with Evangelismo and the alleged sanctity of human life. However, the pentecostalized framing of the violence allowed the *ronderos* to religiously justify taking a life *and* anticipate standing before the "Tribunal of Christ" on judgment day. For many Evangélicos, they were preparing to atone for their acts even as they committed them.

Which leads us to the communities in the central-south that remained Shining Path strongholds. The massive conversions that characterized the *alturas* of Huanta occurred during the 1980s as these communities took a stance against Shining Path, formed their *rondas campesinas*, and became armed communities of faith. In the case of Carhuahurán, some six hundred families from surrounding communities formed a *centro poblado* for security purposes, and the Evangelical discourse was one resource mobilized to construct a common enemy and to suppress long-standing boundary conflicts and other rivalries. However, given the antagonistic relationship between two ideological projects—Evangelismo and Senderismo—what happened in Accomarca, Cayara, Hualla, and Tiquihua?

During the TRC, I began spending more time in these communities and was struck by a different Evangelical chronology. While people in the north were worried the church was *enfriándose* (cooling off) in the postwar period, in the central-south Evangelismo was heating up. New churches were being built, the number of Evangélicos was on the rise, and there was a shared discourse regarding who the new *hermanos* and *hermanas* were. In Accomarca, mama Aurelia whispered that they were "those who have a past." In Hualla, Moises sneered in disgust as he spoke about the former Shining Path militants who were now reborn: "Before they were beasts, savages. They walked around with their weapons. Now they walk around with their Bibles—now they want to be *runakuna*. God may pardon them, but I can't." One evening in the Assembly of God church in Tiquihua, Pastor David Ipurre began the service by holding up his Bible and telling his congregation, "If we had known these commandments, we would not have killed. We would not have killed among brothers, among cousins, among neighbors." I was not so sure; they may well have killed but with a different ideological reason for doing so.

In the context of a morally complex social world of guilt, defiance, remorse, and resentment; of losses for which there is no true redress; where determining accountability and thirsting for justice are ongoing and contentious processes; at a time when evangelical pastors are busy treating so many *heridas del alma* (wounds of the soul)—the role of Evangelismo in broader justice debates demands our attention.

Judgment Day

> [The] religious imagination about justice reflects the state's legal system back upon itself as an empty shell, decorated on the outside with the ceremonials of rule but devoid of the accountability that would make it just.
> —James Holston, "Alternative Modernities"

I ended the last chapter suggesting we look more closely at the role community-level faith-based actors play in transitional contexts. By now it should be clear that Evangelical Christians have had tremendous influence on the course of the violence and its aftermath. Robbins notes that the reorientation of people's moral fields is one of the most important aspects of Pentecostal Christianity's cultural transformation.[37] I agree, and stress that I am not equating the legal and the moral; the gap between the two is one productive space for Evangelismo.

Transitional justice imports many elements from the liberal justice and human rights traditions with their foundations in Enlightenment principles of individual freedom; the autonomous individual and the social contract; the public sphere of secular reason; the rule of law; and the centrality of retributive justice with its emphasis on punishment, particularly in the form of trials. Some have referred to this as the "liberal peace-building consensus" and acknowledge the many contributions this approach has made to postwar reconstruction.[38] However, when we look beyond conflict resolution or peace-building to the daily work of social repair, the limitations of secular justice to address profound moral injuries may in part explain people's faith in divine justice. Confronted with the burden of unpunished crime *and* the steadfast hope the *sasachakuy tiempo* never repeats itself, divine justice is not simply "peasant fatalism" but rather an alternative conception of justice and reckoning that lies outside the liberal approach to these issues. The invocation of Christian compassion *and* righteous wrath weaves throughout daily life in these communities—both north and central-south.

Doña Flora is a deaconess in the Pentecostal church and one of the first *hermanas* in Carhuahurán. She is a force to be reckoned with—someone who, as a young girl, had fought off the *hacendado* who tried to take advantage of her. She converted long before the *sasachakuy tiempo*, prompted by a revelation in which God operated on her leg and removed the black ooze that had spread up and down her thigh, itching incessantly like a hoard of angry ants. She spoke frequently about her faith, which caused her face to flush with what I can only call passion.

One afternoon I asked her about the final days and what would happen. Although at first Flora assured me she would need several days and nights to fully answer that question, she finally offered an abbreviated version of the end of time.

"In revelation I talk with Him. I fasted for six days, without water, without food, nothing. When I finished the week of fasting, El Señor appeared to me—with an apparatus as large as a recorder, shining, and He placed the apparatus in the pulpit. It was like a lantern but it was as big as a tower. It reached up to heaven, all white and I climbed up. There were many flowers—we don't see that sort of flower here on earth. There was just a big field. So I called out with my hand, 'Everyone who was created by God, come,' and my echo kept repeating. I called three times, and when I came back down there were so many people waiting. It's like sheep that we mix with other sheep, or like our sheep and goats that we can't mix. Everyone was separating—those who were with God on one side, and those who weren't with God on the other. To the left and to the right they were separating. When I sat down on that apparatus, Our Señor, He could see inside me. He could see inside all of our bodies, like He had cut them open."

"Were you dead, on the ground?"

"No, but opened up. You're not dead, but alive and you're seeing your heart. Our hearts were shining, as if water had entered. Everyone who believed in God, their hearts were shining, some so big, and some even bigger," using her hands to show their varying sizes. "The people who had fasted, there was a light shining in their hearts. I saw, like when we kill a sheep, it was like that. Opened up. And my heart, the right was white but the other side was still lacking—it's black even now! But other people who don't know God, their hearts were totally black. Those who know return with God."

"So, people are chosen?"

"Yes, and He doesn't make them go back."

"So God will judge—He will look into each of us?"

"Yes, and some will be saved."

"And what about the others—the ones with black hearts?"

"They're sent back. They'll be punished in the rain of fire."

While some would argue that justice deferred is justice denied, I want to complicate that maxim. There were multiple justice systems interacting during the internal armed conflict and its aftermath: those of Shining Path, the armed forces, human rights organizations, the *ronderos*, communal authorities, and the divine. Each of these actors holds different conceptions of justice and reckoning, of what constitutes the individual and collective good, and which takes precedence when they come in tension. These different understandings of justice reverberate throughout these communities and challenge the supremacy of liberal models of justice and the dichotomy they construct between retributive and restorative forms of justice—while favoring the former.

In complex moral situations, judging may be fraught with challenges. In conditions of sustained political violence and militarized states of emergency, many people will have behaved less admirably than they might have wished. Some will finger a neighbor in hopes of extra food or an end to torture; some will name names to settle old accounts; others may kill under threat of losing their own lives; still others will kill for the sheer pleasure of doing so. Reconstructing a moral community in the context of many bloodied hands calls for exploring these multiple conceptions of justice. For some people and groups, legal justice—criminal justice and punishment—will be the highest priority. For others, this may be what they demand for the leaders they hold responsible for their suffering yet have very different ideas of what should be done with the local-level perpetrators with whom they live. Trials may be demanded, and legally mandated, for the Taylors, Fujimoris, and Miloševićs, and people may want the most brutal local leaders thrown in jail. However, many people are more disturbed by the neighbor down the street or the fellow that smirks at them each week at the market. Justice takes many forms—both in its demands and in its application—and asking, "Who are the victims and whom do they hold responsible for their suffering? Who are the guilty and what should be done with them?" may lead to answers we could not have anticipated.

I was told repeatedly that we cannot see into another human being's heart, followed by the question, "So who are we to judge?" Some will find solace in leaving that task to God. This does not supplant demands for other forms of justice in this life, particularly redistributive justice, but it may provide a necessary complement to the always imperfect, always deferred ideal of earthly justice. I have been made achingly aware of the limits of secular forms of reckoning in the face of deep moral injuries—for addressing the *heridas del alma* that sent so many people searching in the Clinic of the Soul.

PART II

Common Sense, Gender, and War

Chapter 5

Speaking of Silences

Common sense is not what the mind cleared of cant spontaneously apprehends; it is what the mind filled with presuppositions . . . concludes.
   —Clifford Geertz, *Local Knowledge*

IN ACCOMARCA THEY told us about Eulogia, a young woman who died long before our arrival but who continues to appear in the memories of various women we spoke with. Eulogia was mute and lived during the time when the military base sat on the hill overlooking Accomarca.

The soldiers came down from the base at night, entering the house Eulogia shared with her grandmother. They stood in line to rape her, taking advantage of her inability to verbally express her pain. Her female neighbors told us, with a mixture of compassion and shame, that "We couldn't do anything. We were afraid they would visit us as well." So they listened to her at night, along with her grandmother who sat across the room, unable to protect her granddaughter.

Eulogia's muffled, guttural sounds still resonate in her neighbor's ears. "We knew by the sounds. We knew what the soldiers were doing, but we couldn't say a thing." The soldiers succeeded in depriving everyone of their capacity for speech.

There are two versions of how Eulogia died. Some told us she had fallen, walking down the steep cliffs toward Lloqllepampa. Others insisted she threw herself from those cliffs, unable to bear her pain.

Elaine Scarry has argued that pain and torture seek to "unmake the world" and to rob human beings of their capacity to speak and to make sense—a sense that one can share with other human beings.[1] Eulogia could not resort to language: she could not put words to her pain; she could not denounce injustice. She also appears in my memories: it is impossible to erase the image of a young woman screaming with all her might, unable to say a thing.

When people talk about rape, they talk a great deal about silences. What to do with these silences—how to listen to them, how to interpret them, how to determine when they are oppressive and when they may constitute a form of agency—is a subject of much concern and debate.[2] Clearly if there is a theme capable of imposing silence, it is rape. Women have many reasons to hide that they have been raped and, with justice a distant horizon, few reasons to speak about a stigmatizing, shameful experience.

My goal is this chapter is not redundancy. We know rape can be a strategy of war, and recent developments in international jurisprudence have recognized this.[3] I am averse to presenting graphic details that may resemble a pornography of violence and that may be yet another violation of the women with whom I have worked. Rather, I want to share some of the conversations that my research team and I have had, addressing a series of themes that left a deep impression upon us.

First, I explore the historicity of memory, discussing how certain victim categories become "narrative capital" within the context of a truth commission. Second, I turn to what women talked about and how their narratives are "thick description" in the best anthropological sense of the term. Drawing on their thick descriptions, I examine some assumptions about what constitutes a "gendered perspective" on armed conflict. In doing so, I discuss how women talked with us about rape and the emphasis they placed on how they had attempted to defend themselves and their family members. Third, I examine how women were coerced into "bartering" sex to save their lives and the lives of their loved ones. I then discuss how rape between men and women—and between men—was a form of establishing relations of power and "blood brothers." I conclude this chapter by considering some of the legacies of the massive sexual violence that characterized Peru's internal armed conflict, reflecting on the possibility of reparations in the aftermath of great harm.[4] But let's begin with some "common sense."

Commissioning Truth: A "Gendered Perspective"

One goal of truth commissions is writing new national narratives that are more inclusive of groups that have been historically marginalized within the nation-state. In her discussion of postconflict issues, Martha Minow writes: "The most distinctive element of truth commissions, in comparison with prosecution, is the focus on victims, including forgotten victims in forgotten places."[5] There is hope that democratizing history may exert a positive influence on the future and that truth commissions may be a better format for writing that inclusive history. In contrast to legal proceedings and the aggressive questioning that characterizes them, truth commissions are considered "victim centered" because they include empathic listening rather than an adversarial hermeneutics of suspicion.[6]

One group frequently included in the forgotten victims category is women. Indeed, the word "victim" conjures up a gendered set of images when the topic is war. However, although allegedly victim friendly, parallel with the rise of truth commissions in postconflict settings was the lament that "women don't talk." There are different reasons for this, but in her review of truth-seeking mechanisms, Priscilla Hayner determined that "Most truth commissions have not been active in seeking out, encouraging or facilitating testimony from women."[7] Additionally, the early commissions in Argentina and Chile assumed a gender-neutral approach to truth— an approach that has been criticized for overlooking the ways in which gender neutrality frequently defaults into a perspective that privileges men and their experiences.[8]

A concern for the lack of "women's voices" prompted the commissions in Guatemala and South Africa—and subsequently Peru—to actively seek out testimony from women. These more recent commissions have argued that truth itself is gendered and thus have sought to incorporate a "gendered perspective." In terms of sheer numbers, they were successful: in both South Africa and Peru women provided the majority of testimonies given to their respective commissions.[9] In all three commissions women described in detail the harm done to their family members and to their communities, testifying to the ways in which armed conflict affects every aspect of daily life, frequently exacerbating the underlying structural injustices of their societies. However, they overwhelmingly did not talk in the first person about rape. Thus the lament that "women don't talk" shifted to the concern that "women don't talk about themselves."

The concern that women do not talk about themselves but rather focus on the suffering and harm done to loved ones has prompted a variety of "gender-sensitive" strategies aiming to capture women's experience of violence—generally defined as rape and other forms of sexual violence. That women do not talk about rape is thus posed as the problem that a gender-sensitive approach is designed to resolve. From this perspective, the incitement to speech is well intentioned. The problem may be the sort of speech that commissions "commonsensically" seek.

The Peruvian TRC was given a gender-neutral mandate, but feminists were successful in insisting the commission think about the importance of gender in their work.[10] Drawing upon the earlier commissions in Guatemala and South Africa, they argued for proactive efforts to include women's voices in the truth-seeking process.[11] Thus the Peruvian TRC decided to include sexual crimes in its mandate because of the broad language used in the Supreme Decree, the importance of the topic, and "the need to recover the voices of women affected by such crimes."[12]

Additionally, the TRC's Linea de Género (Gender Program) persuaded the commission to adopt a broad definition of sexual violence that reflected changing international norms. Rather than strictly investigating rape, the commission used a broad definition of sexual violence in its work: "Sexual violence is a type of human rights violation, and includes forced prostitution, forced unions, sexual slavery, forced abortions, and forced nudity."[13]

In light of concerns that "Perhaps the most commonly underreported abuses are those suffered by women, especially sexual abuse and rape," there were efforts to encourage women to come forward.[14] As the head of the Gender Program wrote, "To encourage victims of sexual violence to participate in the [Peruvian] TRC's investigation, the PTRC developed a series of training documents that included communication strategies on how to conduct investigations in the country's rural areas and provided guidelines for the interviewers. The PTRC also organized a public hearing on women's human rights."[15] Thus "gender-sensitive" strategies were employed with the goal of soliciting women's testimonies about rape and other forms of sexual violence. The results?

Of the people who gave testimonies to the TRC, at the national level 54 percent were women and 46 percent men; in the department of Ayacucho, women provided 64 percent of the testimonies.[16] Women certainly did come forward: they spoke a great deal but not necessarily about sexual violence—at least not in the first person. The total number of reported cases of rape was 538, of which 527 were committed against women and eleven were crimes against men.[17] Of these cases, 83 percent were attributable to armed agents of the state.[18]

If legal standards of proof are the measure of success, these numbers are grim. Women overwhelmingly refused to speak about rape in the first person. However, a potential strength of truth commissions is their blurring of genres. While legal standards of proof might disallow "hearsay" or "anecdotal evidence," truth commissions can work with other evidentiary standards to establish "historical truths." This is what the preponderance of "third-person" testimonies permitted the Peruvian TRC to do. As they state in their Final Report, although the numbers do not show the magnitude of the problem, the testimonies allowed the commission to infer that sexual violence was a common practice during the internal armed conflict. Thus if indeed they could not quantitatively demonstrate the extent of sexual violations, the qualitative and tangential information collected allowed the commission to assert that sexual violations against women were a generalized practice during the internal armed conflict.[19] These findings are important, and the PTRC's Final Report is a tool in the struggle for gender justice.

But let's stay with those statistics. When discussing the underreporting of sexual violence, the primary factor cited is shame. As Julissa Mantilla has explained, "According to the PTRC, the number of cases of sexual violence against women was significantly less that the number of other human rights violations; however, the PTRC recognized the statistical under-representation of these cases. The same type of under-reporting occurred in Guatemala and South Africa due to the victim's feelings of guilt and shame."[20] She also notes that in Peru the idea persists that rape is not a human rights violation but rather a collateral damage of war. Additionally, acts of sexual violence frequently occurred within the context of other human rights violations—massacres, tortures, arbitrary detentions—and such violations overshadowed the reporting of sexual violence. For example, in many massacres the women and girls were separated out and raped first; however, the incident may only have been reported as a massacre.[21]

However, there was the "historical truth." I do not find it surprising that many women provided testimony about sexual violence in their capacity as witnesses rather than as victims. While shame is a factor that influenced this trend, it also reflects the gendered nature of memory specialization. Women narrate communal suffering and the quotidian impact of war: thus it is not so strange that they are the bearers of these collective memories as well. It is to women's memory work and the gendered dimensions of war that we now turn.

In her research on the South African TRC, Fiona Ross argues that the commission essentialized suffering and gender, focusing on harm as the violation of bodily integrity. Thus the "rape victim" narrative was constructed, and prized. In the Public Hearings, narratives of rape were elicited—extracted from broader testimonies—and became emblematic of "women's experience" of apartheid.[22] Yet as Ross poignantly demonstrates, women had much more to say.

Yes, the PTRC adopted a broad definition of sexual violence, including forms of abuse extending beyond rape. However, even a broad definition of sexual violence may result in a narrow definition of the gendered dimensions of war. In the thick description women provided, they narrated a broader set of truths about systemic injustice, the gross violations of their socioeconomic rights, and the futility of seeking justice from the legal systems that operated nationally and locally. When women talk about the suffering of family members and of their communities; when they recall the long walks to the river for water and the hours spent scrounging for bits of kindling; when they tearfully recall their children's gnawing hunger that they tried to calm with water and salt; when they remember with outrage how they were subjected to ethnic insults in the streets of the very cities in which they sought refuge—they *are* talking about themselves and the gendered dimensions of war. And, beyond the dangers that engulfed them, they have much to say about the actions they took in the face of those challenges. They also give us much to consider regarding commonsense notions of a gendered perspective on war.

Memory Projects

I suggested earlier that to talk about rape is to talk about silences. When I first started my research in northern Ayacucho, it was not just women who maintained silences regarding sexual violence. Communal authorities, all male, routinely denied that the women in their communities had been raped. I was unanimously informed that of course there had been *abusos*— but always somewhere else, an index finger pointing in the direction of some neighboring community. If we think a bit about militarized masculinity, for communal authorities to admit that rapes had occurred in their pueblos would mean admitting they had been unable to protect "their women." Shame thus cuts a broader swath.

However, in the context of the TRC something changed. There was a preponderance of witness testimony about rape and sexual violence. While much of this testimony came from women, men made up the other 46 percent of those who gave testimony to the commission. Moreover, communal authorities did talk about the sexual violence that had occurred in their own communities. Why the shift?

Within the context of the truth commission, communal authorities set about developing their own "memory projects." In every community, there were assemblies held to discuss what would be said to the TRC's mobile teams when they arrived to take testimonies. There was an effort to close narrative ranks, prompted by the many secrets people keep about a lengthy, fratricidal conflict as well as the expectations a commission generates. I attended numerous assemblies in which authorities reminded everyone what they had decided to talk about, reminding the women in particular not to start talking about "things that were not true."

Let me provide an example that addresses several of the issues with which we are concerned. The truth commission conducted focus groups—in addition to taking individual testimonies—as part of their work on regional histories (*estudios en profundidad*). In June 2002, the TRC team held two focus groups in the same community, one with men and women, and the other comprising only women. The transcripts from these focus groups provide an opportunity to situate truths within the dynamics of gender and to think about the gender and historicity of memory. As part of their work, truth commissions construct typologies of victims and of perpetrators. These categories inform the memory projects that people and communities develop.

There is much emphasis on the politics of memory and on memory as a cultural form. We must also consider the economics of memory. Among the conditions of possibility for the emergence of "new memories" are changing economic circumstances and motivations. Commissions generate expectations. It did not matter how many times people were told they would not necessarily receive reparations for giving their testimony: giving one's testimony was in part instrumental and it would be ingenuous to think otherwise. While giving testimony can be prompted by various factors, the hope of some economic relief was an important incentive. Memories were narrated with new possibilities and aspirations in mind.

The transcripts of the focus groups are lengthy, so I will summarize the main themes. I will not name the community, but it was located in the central-south of Ayacucho and had been one of Sendero's support bases. The groups were recorded and subsequently transcribed; I quote from the written transcriptions in the present tense to preserve people's statements.

The meeting with men and women begins with the two facilitators introducing themselves; they are subsequently addressed as "Señor Comisión de la Verdad" or "Señores de la Verdad." To prompt the conversation, one of them asks, "How was it here when your *paisanos* lived—before there was so much death?"

One of the men replies: "Here we were, peaceful, without fights, without hating each other. During fiestas we drank, we ate. When someone died we visited. When someone called, we answered. Then all of this [Sendero Luminoso] appeared. We've been innocent. They cut our throats because we were innocent."

The other men join in with details about when "Sendero arrived," talking animatedly about one of the teachers who had been a local *cabecilla* (SL leader). A series of killings are detailed, followed again by the insistence, "All of these things they did to us, to innocent people." Another man adds, "The children trembled with fear. So did the women."

What follows in the transcript is the first attempt to quiet one of the women who tries to speak. The men admonish her: "You shouldn't talk unless you know [the story] really well or we'll vary the information. This machine [tape recorder] will tell everything just the way it is in Lima." She falls silent.

There is more discussion about their innocence, and then the talk turns to a local massacre. Another woman tries to speak; she is told to be quiet.

In describing the army massacre, one of the men notes: "We decided the men should escape—they hated the men. We didn't think they'd do anything to the women."

They were wrong in that assessment, and what follows is a description of how the soldiers began raping and killing the women. A third woman tries to speak up and the men tell her to be quiet. Once again the men insist, "Our pueblo was innocent."

Finally, one of the women is allowed to speak about the killing and the raping. She recounts how each woman was hauled off by three soldiers and raped. When the soldiers finished, they dragged the women back to the clearing.

Another woman softly cries: "To the women—the things they did. To innocent children, to old women without guilt, to useless married women like me. What possible guilt could we have had?"

The men provide more details about the raping and horrific deaths of many people who were burned alive. One of the men explains: "There were killings, so we requested a military base to protect us. We petitioned for a military base. We men built the base."

Aware that the women had been systematically told to stop talking, the mobile team decided to meet with a group of women alone. Again, the transcript is lengthy; I summarize the conversation.

The facilitators welcome the women: "Here we are to have a conversation about different themes related to the war. The idea was to just get together as women. All of the information you give will be totally confidential and you don't need to worry . . . feel complete *confianza* [trust]." The TRC team explains they are interested in knowing how life was before and during the armed conflict. They begin by asking how the women are doing, and whether they are well organized.

One of the women replies, "Before, we were totally disorganized! But now, little by little we're getting organized because some of us know our rights. Before, we didn't even know what our rights were. We were in the dark. The men humiliated us—they said, 'Oh what do women know!' They even said—they still say—that we only go to meetings to sleep. But more or less, now we know our rights."

Another woman adds, "We were marginalized by the men. Even now, machismo shines bright! Now in assemblies we talk, more or less. Before, there was so much illiteracy. People asked why they should educate girls when all they were going to do was herd sheep, take care of the house. Now, we want our girls to go to school."

The facilitators pursue the topic of education, which brings the women around to lamenting their own interrupted studies. None of the women had finished primary school. Additionally, once Shining Path began to proselytize the curriculum changed drastically. The schoolteachers began to talk about *el movimiento* and how everyone could be useful to the revolution. Once the conversation turns to the theme of Sendero, two of the women assure the facilitators that they feel so much better when they forget. There is a wave of affirmative murmurs. One woman assures the PTRC team, "When I forget, I'm well. Remembering, even now, I just go crazy. I can hardly stand it. But I'm so-so when I forget. It's hard to answer your questions—so hard to go back and remember all that."

The facilitator is undeterred: "It's necessary and very important to remember so that this never happens again."

The women do go on to talk, almost always using the first person plural in their responses. They describe the key Senderista militant who took over the local school and the threats used to make them participate in SL. They explain that for lack of money—with so many children to care for—they had been unable to flee to the relative safety of Lima. They stayed behind when their men fled to the coast and when they tried to send their sons beyond harm's reach. Their children were always getting sick, particularly with *susto* because there was so much violence. Their children's illnesses were compounded by hunger: both the Senderistas and the army troops stole animals and destroyed crops. There was no food—at times nothing more than water flavored with salt.

At this point one of the facilitators asks the women how the soldiers had behaved.

The first list of grievances includes family members killed by the soldiers. The women who lost husbands describe the enduring impact of their loss. In addition to the emotional toll the conflict has had on them, they insist on how different life would be if only they had husbands by their side. They would not be so poor.

The women repeatedly come back to how difficult it was to care for crops, livestock, for children. They were always on the run, waiting for the sound of gunshots, helicopters, leather boots at the door. Animals died or were stolen.

The painful refrain.

"When the soldiers arrived here, we had to run and hide in the ravines. They would throw kerosene on the crops we'd stored. They would shit on the wheat or barley that we were storing—they mixed their shit up with the *cereales* so there'd be nothing to eat. So we had to carry our *cereales* with us when we ran. Oh, we had livestock! They even stole them in helicopters. That's why people here learned to drink. So much pain! So much fear!"

Once again a woman insists, "Remembering that life, we have such a sense of weight bearing down on us. We feel much better when we forget."

One of the facilitators interjects: "It's difficult to remember. It's sad. But it is so important to remember."

The women do continue, and their complaints about the soldiers are multiple. One woman adds, "Many of the young women were left with children."

And yet another: "They raped the young women. They stole from our houses. They took our animals in their helicopters."

"Oh, life completely changed."

Abruptly, one of the facilitators intervenes: "*Bueno.* Now we know we have rights. Back then some women participated in Sendero. Were there any women leaders [SL] here?"

One of the women responds: "Oh no. Women here didn't participate in Sendero—just women from other places. I saw some of them. Maybe they already knew they had rights and that's why they joined. But no women here—no."

"No, not here," adds another woman. "But there were some in other places. But not here."

Another woman speaks up. "Well, it's scary to talk. I personally am afraid to talk about this. They say that Sendero might start up again. Who knows—there might be some of them in this pueblo. What if they find out? I'm very afraid."

"Is there resentment among people in this pueblo? Do you want to talk about that?" the facilitator asks.

"No, there's no resentment. We just want to forget. We never talk about those things with lots of people. Just in a family group—then we remember, then we talk. Not in a group like this."

With that final line the focus group draws to a close. One of the facilitators thanks the women for their participation, reiterating what she and her colleague had said: "We know it's hard to talk about these things, but it's also important to do so. We hope we've helped you get a bit of relief by talking. Remembering all of this is hard for us, too, but it's not in vain—*it will bring something good.* So thank you all and remember that you should always talk. Don't be quiet. *You have to talk so these things never happen again.*"

These transcripts are noteworthy for many reasons. This was one of the communities with which my research team and I had been working, and I was interested in the sorts of memories narrated in these focus groups because the context in which testimonies are given and received is central to the forms those testimonies take.

Recall this community had been a support base for Sendero. However, the victim typology is important in terms of understanding the men's emphasis on innocence. The heroic *rondero* identity is not available to men in this region of Ayacucho; their armed participation was on the losing side of this war. Thus the victim categories are an important source of "narrative capital" vis-à-vis the TRC and, metonymically, the state. The innocent dead, the trembling children, and the raped women are important categories of potential redress. Thus women were alternately silenced while their suffering was appropriated for communal purposes.

Pressing demands as innocent victims plays with the dualism that informs the logic of law and these commissions charged with historical clarification. In the assemblies held in this community prior to the arrival of the TRC, it was decided that people should talk only about those who had died at the hands of the soldiers. The concern was twofold. When communal authorities convened the assemblies and began forging their memory projects, they told people that widows and orphans were groups of interest to the commission. As the president of this community described, "One of the orphans stood up and said he was ready to tell the commission about his father's death. 'I'll tell them how Antonio Sullqa and Clemente Gamboa killed him—how they slit his throat.' Well, there were Antonio and Clemente standing right there across from him! *We knew we couldn't talk about it like that or everyone would be killing each other again.*" Thus the authorities decided that only certain deaths—those that occurred at the hands of the armed forces—would be talked about with the TRC. They were also concerned that if people began talking about killings within the community, it would be taken as proof of Sendero's presence and their sympathies during the war. Thus the memory project focused on "innocent victims," and the women were consistently told to be quiet for fear they would "vary the information."

Additionally, as happened in many communities, authorities petitioned for the installation of a military base for "protection." This irony repeats in many pueblos: which was the greater fear, the soldiers or the neighbors? And once that decision was made, whose security and at what price?[23] Communal agreements implied certain sexual agreements, and "security" was a gendered good. The men in these communities built the bases that multiplied throughout Ayacucho during the violence: women and girls "serviced" the troops. In some communities, sex became commodified as women began selling sex. Far more common, however, was rape.

I want to juxtapose the first group with the second one held with only women. The storylines are distinct: the men narrate the battles and attacks while women tend to focus on the everyday aspects of life during war. Women's unpaid and frequently undervalued labor becomes even more burdensome during war. Women were involved in defending their communities; they also remained responsible for maintaining the home in the face of the dual challenges of political violence and the poverty that was sharply exacerbated by the war. Although survival may be "less dramatic" than armed struggle, an analysis of the domestic economy of war reveals the extent to which survival itself becomes a daily struggle. Living in caves for months, moving from one place to another on a daily basis, cooking and caring for children under harsh conditions—these women did not limit their protagonism to epic masculinist models.[24] All women struggled—and some were armed.

Additionally, the focus group was guided by commonsense assumptions about women and war. Convening a random group to talk "as women in total *confianza*" resonates with well-intentioned feminist and therapeutic impulses. The incitement to speech hinges on a belief that talking is intrinsically healing, and thus participating in the focus group would provide the women "some relief." This was at odds with the women's insistence on forgetting and certainly at odds with the woman who finally told the facilitators that she was "afraid to talk."

In the context of civil conflict, one can only assume the random assembly of a group of women is unproblematic if women are first defined as peripheral to the conflict. By defining women as noncombatants—by assuming women are a homogeneous group of apolitical bystanders or victims—one has the illusion of yielding a group with shared interests based upon their identity as women. This is a questionable assumption in many cases, and certainly in Peru where an estimated 40 percent of Shining Path militants were women.[25]

I mentioned that my research team and I worked with this community and learned the names of the women who participated in the focus group. One of the women is the wife of a local Shining Path (ex-)*cabecilla*, and we were assured she had been just as ruthless as he had been. Thus, instead of finding themselves in a therapeutic environment, several of the women sitting in the group were concerned about the consequences of anything they might say in front of someone they held responsible for lethal violence in their community.

Moreover, there is speech itself and the promise that talking "will bring something good." In addition to the crude deployment of psychoanalytic notions of "talking cures" and catharsis, there is an implicit theory of language at work in this incitement to speech. Language is conceived as merely referential rather than constituting powerful action in the world. In Quechua-speaking communities, there is another theory of language at work.

Language is understood to be a way of doing things; speech is performative and words are action. Many conversations ended abruptly with someone glancing nervously over their shoulders and wondering if the *apus* (mountain gods) had heard what they said. In other conversations people insisted that just talking about Shining Path would cause the guerrillas to reappear. Talking was dangerous, words were frequently weapons. Silence was protective and powerful.

I think back to the communal authorities who explained why they had forged their memory projects: "We realized that if we started to talk about that, we'd be killing each other again." Talking about violence within the community is understood to establish the conditions of possibility for its recurrence. Speech may provoke violence; words can be lethal. Yet the facilitators kept insisting, "*You have to talk so these things never happen again.*" The statement makes little sense for people who have assiduously sought to control the damage words can do. Talking does not necessarily lead to *nunca más* (never again): precisely the opposite.

In this same community many people had not provided their testimonies to the TRC because they were worried they would be subsequently summoned to the city to "*manifestar.*" *Manifestaciones* are the verbal testimonies given about disputes. Communal authorities occasionally asked to borrow my tape recorder so that someone could *manifestar* about a communal conflict or problem. These tapes would remain in the community, the words tied to the social context in which they were spoken. This is different from the tape recorder placed in the center of the focus group: "This machine will tell everything just the way it is in Lima."

Manifestar: to expose clearly; to place in view; to make known or to discover. The logic of exposure and transparency is at odds with a culture in which indirectness is valued.[26] The capacity to keep secrets was magnified by Shining Path's "Regla de Oro." The Golden Rule? Silence. Everyone is involved in this moral economy of speech and silence, including the anthropologist.[27]

I hope I have demonstrated the complexity of women's experiences and the multiple subject positions they assumed during the internal armed conflict. Women in the focus group insisted life had changed completely and referred to both the destructive and transformative consequences of political violence. As Elisabeth Rehn and Ellen Johnson Sirleaf note, "Conflict can change traditional gender roles. Women may acquire more mobility, resources and opportunities for leadership. But the additional responsibility comes without any diminution in the demands of their traditional roles. Thus, the momentary space in which women take on nontraditional roles and typically assume much greater responsibilities within the household and public arenas does not necessarily advance gender equality."[28] This paradox resonated throughout Ayacucho. Parallel to the losses and injustices they experienced, women also referred to the liberating aspects of the internal armed conflict and how the years of war had "opened up their eyes." And there was another set of parallel narratives: women's stories about rape.

The Other Heroes

In both South Africa and Peru, the truth commissions held public hearings, and women were invited to speak about violations of their human rights. Fiona Ross has demonstrated how the South African hearings focused on sexual violence and rape rather than the systemic injustice of apartheid or women's roles in resistance efforts.[29] In Peru's Public Audiences, several women talked about their experiences of rape, one introducing the audience to her six-year-old daughter, born as a result of the woman's gang rape in prison. For each viewer who squirmed in discomfort, there were others applauding the bravery of these women for talking publicly about "their rapes."

These are troubling displays.[30] By constructing these few women as courageous for speaking out, the implication is that only those women who choose a public forum to talk about rape are counted among the brave. Obscured are other forms of courage women practiced on a daily basis during the internal armed conflict and, importantly, other messages are also transmitted in the broadcasts of these public displays. The audience is told war stories replete with heroes and victims, a gendered dualism that is too familiar.

I foreground the protagonism of women confronted by sexual violence, motivated by a desire to question war stories that keep reproducing the heroism of men and the victimization of women. This dualism informed the work of the Peruvian TRC. For example, during the Public Audience with the *ronderos*—a group that has elaborated a collective identity as heroes of La Patria and key actors in the "defeat of subversion"—not a single woman was invited to give her testimony even though there are women who not only participated in the *rondas campesinas* but rose to leadership positions.[31] In the Public Audiences in which women did participate, they were included as victims: Las Lloronas in contrast to the heroes of La Patria. However, women participated in the defense of their communities, their families, and themselves. War stories influence the public policies implemented in the postconflict period: these histories are a form of political action. There are multiple forms of heroism, not all of which are "male."[32]

We turn now to the conversations my research team and I had with women who chose to talk with us about rape. We spent months living in these communities, which may explain why some women sought us out to talk about their own experiences of rape and sexual violence. We never asked a woman if she had been raped. The question seemed ethically unacceptable given that we were not in the position to offer these women any form of justice or sustained counseling. The conversations have a common format: "Come back tomorrow." Women needed time to prepare themselves to talk about this issue and to prepare an environment of complete privacy. None of these women had spoken before about having been raped, and each felt she had much to lose if her husband or children heard her.

In their narratives, women insisted on context: when women spoke about rape, they located that violation within broader social dynamics. They detailed the preconditions that structured vulnerability and emphasized their efforts to minimize harm to themselves and to the people they cared for. With their insistence on context, women situated their experience of sexual violence—those episodes of brutal victimization—within womanly narratives of heroism.

"I Armed Myself with Courage"

Elizabet was seated in the door of her aunt's house in Cayara. Several years earlier her aunt had placed her in charge of taking care of her home when she left for the relative safety of the coast. Leonor sat down with her to talk, noticing her face was bruised, her nose raw with scratches. Her left eye was covered over with a flap of skin, and Elizabet struggled to raise her eyelid against the weight of the stringy mucous that clouded her vision. Her voice sharpened with rage: "My eye—the soldiers did this to me. Those filthy dogs. They've ruined my life. They've done me harm, and now I can't see well. Sometimes in the darkness, I fall. The last time I was carrying two buckets full of water when I fell, and I scratched my face. The soldiers came to my house calling me 'terruca.' 'Terruca' they keep shouting while they beat me, abused me. Until one day—I armed myself with courage and grabbed one of them by the chest and hit him with a trunk of wood. I threw him out. From there I went to Ayacucho, leaving all my things abandoned. I had no husband to protect me, to take care of me, to make them respect me," her voice rising with each word. "When you have a man at your side, somehow there is more respect."[33]

As Elizabet made clear, the most vulnerable were the widows and single women—women without a man in the house to provide some form of symbolic protection. Several women told us they had married in order to have access to this protection. In contrast with long-standing patterns, women began to take younger partners due to the lack of mature men in their communities.

Elizabet was not alone in "arming herself with courage." Many women described how they had tried to defend themselves, with sticks, teeth, screams, and fists. However, they did not defend only themselves; many women fought to protect their loved ones. Other women padded their skirts with wadded up clothing, pretending to be pregnant in hopes of dissuading potential rapists.[34] Still others smeared blood on their underwear, hoping their bloodied state would dissuade the soldiers, while others resorted to "strategic pregnancies" to exercise some form of control over their bodies, as Maricela Tomayro did.

"Strategic Pregnancies"

> The soldiers dragged my husband out of the house, dragged him to the plaza. Then they disappeared him. I followed them to Canaria to look for him. I demanded they give him back to me. Those soldiers beat me—my chest still aches from how they beat me. They wanted to abuse me, but they couldn't.[35] After everything they did to me, I don't forgive them. It's their fault my children never went to school. Let them come here and at least fix my house! I have three children. After my husband disappeared—well, the soldiers wanted to abuse me. They tried to and I knew I didn't want to have a child from those devils. I decided it would be better to have the child of one of my *paisanos*. I had the child of a widower so I could make sure those miserable pigs didn't have that pleasure. They raped in groups—they raped in line. How could a woman tolerate so many men? Not even a dog could put up with it.
> —Señora Tomayro, Hualla, 2003

Señora Tomayro's words condense so much. It was overwhelmingly women who engaged in the search for the disappeared and the dead. That search took them to police stations, army bases, hospitals, and jails. For rural Quechua-speaking women the state was personified in the Spanish used to curse them, in the doors shut in their faces, and in the beatings and other forms of abuse they encountered as they searched for loved ones.

Additionally, access to reproductive health care and family planning was minimal prior to the war, and further reduced by the destruction of hundreds of rural health posts during the internal armed conflict. Rape frequently resulted in unwanted pregnancies, bringing further pain and stigma to the mother as well as to her child. Within a context of minimal choices—and even less recourse to contraception—women sought to exercise some control over their bodies, even if the range of control was reduced to strategically getting pregnant by a member of their community (a *comunero*) rather than by soldiers lined up for gang rape.

But there is more. Women were somehow trying to preserve "community," which confers both rights and obligations. Single mothers complain about the challenges of forcing the fathers of their children to recognize the child and provide the mother with some sort of financial assistance. This struggle plays out in every community. However, by giving birth to a *comunero*'s baby, women bring that child into a familial and communal network of reciprocity and obligation. Becoming pregnant by a *comunero* affords the woman some means of assuring she has someone against whom she can press her claims and those of her child.

Yet this is not just about material resources; it is also about the emotional toll. The faces of children conceived through rape will serve as reminders to their mothers of a painful past. These strategic pregnancies are protective *and* preventive. They are women's efforts to exert some control over the present as well as the future, over their bodies and the production of "future memories."[36] Women like Señora Tomayro were trying to make their fetuses *bearable*. I will say more about this when introducing a boy who was one of those painful reminders.

Finally, Señora Tomayro conveys the enduring economic impact of losing one's spouse. Within an agricultural economy, women need access to male labor to complement their own productive activities. It is also men who more commonly engage in seasonal migration, earning cash to supplement the household economy. In her demand—or perhaps accusation—that "It's their fault my children never went to school. Let them come here and at least fix my house," she conveys a vision of what might constitute reparation for all she has lost, and survived.

"Women like Me"

I have preserved the following conversation in its entirety, convinced this woman's experience is not unique, although she has lived with a profound sense of isolation because of what she endured. This is a story about one mother's defense of her young daughters.

Early one morning Dulia went out to walk the streets of Hualla, enjoying the silence that softened the edges of that conflictive town. As she reached the top of a hill, Prudencia Valenzuela Uscata called out, "*Señorita*, come here. I want to talk to you. *Llakiytam huillakuyta munayki* [I want to tell you about my *llakis*]." She grabbed Dulia's hand: "Come to my house tomorrow."

At sunrise the next morning Dulia went to Prudencia's house, only to find Prudencia surrounded by children. She gestured for Dulia to follow her through to the room behind her kitchen, telling her, "Wait here. We're going to talk without my children listening. I don't want anyone to hear us."

Another half hour passed before Prudencia came back from her kitchen and sat beside Dulia. Hurriedly she pulled out her bag of coca and began *chakchando* (chewing coca leaves). She acknowledged it was very early to begin *chakchando* but that she needed to do so in order to talk. With a sigh, she placed her hand on Dulia's: "Oh, *señorita*, my sadness is so great because I have to take care of all of this alone."

The two women were interrupted by steps and looked up to see one of Prudencia's little girls pushing open the door. Prudencia scolded her gently and closed the door, placing a rock against it to hold it shut. She sat again at Dulia's side and after several sighs and more coca, she began: "My daughter is traumatized because the *cabitos* [soldiers] entered my house. I lived with my son and my two daughters. The soldiers tried to take my older daughter when they entered my house. I had a little store. It was on the edge of the plaza, and the soldiers always bothered me because I was alone."

"Did you have a husband then, mama Prudencia?"

She nodded. "But my husband was already afraid. When they [the soldiers] took men to the base, they made them lie mouth down like animals and walked on top of them. They put hot iron on their genitals! They beat them on the head with the butt of their guns. That's why my husband left for Lima. 'They may do something to me,' he said. He left from one minute to the next—the father of my children never came back. It was October when they entered my house. I'd gone to my *chacra* to weed, so I came home tired. 'I'm going to sleep,' I said. I told my daughter, '*Mami*, go and close the door, close it tight. You're a big girl now.' She was eleven or twelve, the older one. But my daughter tied the door shut with a string, nothing more. She didn't close it tight."

Prudencia paused to add a bit more coca to the wad in her cheek. "They cut the string with a knife and entered. I was sleeping, but they shined the flashlight in my eyes. They'd opened the door. How were they able to open it? They shoved a gun against my chest and a knife against my throat. There were five soldiers in my house. 'Give me a pill, give me a Mejoral. There was a confrontation today and there are many casualties. Give me a Mejoral or I'll kill you, I'll blow off your head.' But I didn't want to. I said, 'No, I can't give you anything.' So one of them shouted at me, 'Where are the pills?' 'I don't know,' I said. So they kept shouting that they were going to kill me. They were grabbing me by the neck, and it hurt when they were grabbing me. My oldest daughter—they started to grab her to take her away."

Prudencia slowed her words down, each syllable loaded with defiance. "I told them, 'My daughter, no. Not my daughter, not even if you kill me.' My daughter was twelve and we'd heard about how the soldiers raped—people say they even raped dogs. I was so afraid, thinking that if they dragged her outside they could do just anything to her. I didn't want them to take her outside." Prudencia shook her head as she remembered that night. "Not my daughter! I was holding onto her so they couldn't take her. I was holding her tight." She paused to show Dulia how she had held onto her daughter with all of her strength even as the soldiers were beating her.

"That's how I was holding on to her, grabbing onto my bed frame with my other hand. The soldiers kept grabbing at her, trying to pull her away from me. So I put my daughter between my legs and covered her with my skirt, and the little one I grabbed with my free hand. My little boy was also in the bed, but they didn't pay any attention to him because he was a boy. My two little girls, I kept holding onto them and to the bed frame. I didn't let go of my daughters. My older daughter, they kept trying to grab her. My little one was still drowsy, so I pulled her hair hard to make her scream—I hoped someone would hear. One of the soldiers said, 'Damn it! What are you doing? Don't make noise!' Then he punched me in the face. But when I kept holding on, one of them said, 'Come on, come with me now or I'll kill you. Nothing's going to happen.' They were pulling at my hair, my clothes, my arms. But I didn't want to, not for anything. I'd heard people talk, saying that with all sorts of tricks they [the soldiers] try to get you outside so they can rape and kill you. That's why I didn't want to go outside."

This time it was Dulia who paused. She needed to breathe. Prudencia looked at her, waited a few moments as if to judge how much more her listener could take, and began again at full speed. "When I was holding on like that, they hit me really hard, several times. Then they took my daughters from me. They carried the oldest one to the corner while one of them was standing guard outside. Inside, two of them tied me to the bed and one of them grabbed my braids. The others were pointing a gun in my chest, making noise with the trigger. Another held his knife to my throat. Then my son cried out, 'Don't kill my mama. Here's the key.' So they used the key to open the store while the others held back my daughter and me. One of them started to rape me while the others pointed their guns at me. This nobody knows—not my father, not my mother, not my littlest children. No matter how much I tried I couldn't get them off of me. There were five of them, *señorita*. The five soldiers left their guns in the corner. Then with their knives they kept threatening me. My daughter screamed and ran toward me—there were my three children. For holding onto my older daughter, they raped me. They raped me because I wouldn't let them rape my daughter. That's why my daughter says, 'To save me, they raped you,' and that's why I suffer alone. My husband left me—because of this he left me [referring to her second husband]. He left me because people say that the women in Hualla are the soldiers' leftovers. There was a lot of gossip because the soldiers took the women away—married women, young women, they took them away to the base. Oh, God, what sorts of things did they do to them in the base!" The tape goes silent.

"That's how it was—and nobody knows about this. *Not even women like me know.* I'm afraid of what my family would say. And women like me—they would look at me in the street, saying all sorts of awful things. I don't say anything—not even to my husband. But that's why I didn't go to Lima."

With these words, she paused. Both women sat in silence, and the only sound one can hear on the tape is their breathing. Dulia finally touched Prudencia's shoulder gently and asked her, "Did you get pregnant from this?"

Prudencia shook her head. "No, I don't know why but I didn't get pregnant. I cried day and night. 'In shame I'll give birth to the baby of a soldier. Then everyone will talk, wondering who got me pregnant,' I kept saying to myself. I cried day and night. After all of this I was so afraid and had to move from my house. But the soldiers kept looking for me and insisting on doing that to me again. That's why the father of my little boy—I thought of him as family. So I had my son. When the soldiers would come for me, I'd go to his house. Sometimes, because he was my neighbor, I called him out of trust. That's how I had my son—so as not to please the soldiers, not to have the child of a soldier. I wasn't going to let those soldiers do that. After a while, my son's father had another family so we separated. Now I have another partner, but he doesn't know anything about what happened to me. If he knew, he'd beat me."[37]

In our research team we talked at length about rape and how raped women are repeatedly violated: first during the rape itself and afterward because of the stigma that marks them in their communities. As Señora Prudencia lamented, "women like me" have usually not confided in anyone—they have seen far too many examples of the price women have paid for talking. Not one woman with whom we spoke had achieved justice with respect to the man or men who had raped her, and this remains true today. Among the greatest injustices of this war are the stigma of the raped and the impunity of the rapists.

Moreover, there is the parallel narrative structure and the insistence on context. Señora Prudencia was relating more than her victimization. It was important to her that we know there were five soldiers pinning her down, armed with guns and a knife. She still fought, even though they punched her in the face and outnumbered her. Over and over again she returned to her resolve: they would not touch her daughters unless they killed her first. She may have been raped, but she succeeded in protecting her two daughters. In her subsequent actions, she outstrategized the soldiers, moving to her small house in the hills at night and ultimately deciding to get pregnant with her neighbor rather than by the soldiers. When we listen to what she foregrounds in her story, we hear pride in how hard she fought defending herself and her daughters. This cannot be tidily compacted into the victim category without forcing her—and other women like her—to silence their courage. It may well be that courage which allowed her to preserve some sense of her self despite both the initial violation and the injustice of the events that followed. We cannot change the past, but one goal of any reparations program should be changing the present in which "women like me" live with shame instead of recognition of their struggles and heroism.

"The Soldiers' Leftovers"

I now present two final conversations that allow us to appreciate how pervasive the sexual violence was and how it affects women's everyday lives and relationships. These conversations provide further evidence of the complex, diffuse nature of the harm women talked about, as well as the ways in which they have tried to minimize that harm. I begin in Hualla, known for having been a militant support base for Shining Path. When the soldiers arrived in Hualla, they came to *castigar el pueblo* (to punish the town).

In barrio San Cristóbal, there is a rundown house with one lone room opening out onto the street. Dulia was struck by the ramshackle house and knocked softly on the door. Serafina Ucharima Chocce peered out. She was thirty-eight, thick hair worn in braids, the black bundles contrasting with the cold-induced red of her cheeks. Dulia explained why the research team was there, and the woman told her to come back the following day when her husband would be gone.

When Dulia arrived the following day, she found Serafina washing plates. She invited Dulia to enter her house, which consisted of one room that served as both kitchen and bedroom. Dulia's eyes were soon watering uncontrollably from the smoke that filled the room. Once Serafina had finished her chores, she shook out a sheepskin for Dulia and told her that her husband had already left so they could go talk out back.

The fresh air of her small backyard was a relief, and both women settled onto sheepskins. Catching herself, Serafina called to one of her daughters: "Go outside and watch to be sure your papa doesn't come. If he shows up, tell me right away." Somewhat nervously, she commented that she didn't want him to know she had talked with anyone.

While they shelled fava beans, Serafina described how difficult life had been during the war, and as she spoke she became increasingly nervous and began rubbing her hands together. "Those troops killed people all the way to Cayara. When they arrived here, they abused us, too."

"What did they do here?"

"Here they entered homes, they raped women. They made women disappear."

"Were some women left with children?"

"Yes, my sister was left with a child when she was raped. But the baby died—it would've been a girl. She was three days old."

"What happened to your sister?"

"She told only me. She had a store and lived with her husband, but her husband died. The soldiers went house by house, entering the homes where women lived alone. Then they raped them."

When she began to think about what had happened to her sister, Serafina could barely control the shaking in her voice, and she began to cry. "Me, too, there in the mountain. My mother had left without her documents and I was worried they'd say she was a *terruca* because she had no papers. Carrying my son on my back, I went to our house in the hills [*estancia*] to take her documents to her. My mother was in the house when I arrived. 'Mama, here's your document,' I said. We were in our house. It was afternoon when three soldiers came. They raped me." Her voice cracked, and she sobbed. Dulia offered her tissue and the two women just sat for a few minutes.

"I don't know if you would like to talk some more?" she asked. Serafina nodded. Dulia hesitated, but asked her if she had given birth.

Serafina shook her head emphatically. "No, no, no. I didn't give birth. This was in 1989 in the afternoon. 'You're a *terruca*,' they said. When the base was here the soldiers did this to me. When they were told to look for *terrucos* in the mountains, they arrived at my house in the *puna*. When they arrived they yelled at my mama. 'Old *terruca*, you're lodging and feeding the *terrucos*, *terrucos* just like you.' But we said, 'We haven't seen them.' 'Oh, you're *terrucos*. That's what you are,' they said. 'No, no,' we insisted. When we said that, one of them pulled my mama outside. Inside they shoved a gun against me, by force they raped me." She was silent for a few minutes. "Three soldiers raped me. All three. They raped me."

"Were they sober? Drunk?"

"They were sober. That's what happened to me, what happened to women like us. Some got pregnant because they were raped." She continued to cry. "They raped me. 'Damn it! *Warminayahuachkan, terruca de mierda!* [You're making me want a woman, *terruca* of shit!].' That's what they said, damning me the whole time. 'If you don't let me, I'll kill you,' they said. They shoved the gun into my chest. 'I'm married, I have a husband,' I told them. But they didn't let me go. 'Shut up, damn it!' they shouted. They kept talking *groserías* [obscene words] while they threatened to kill me. After, they warned me not to tell anyone or they would kill me. Ever since, I've been afraid of the *cabitos* [soldiers]. Once they left my mama came in. I ran to her, embraced her. I cried, "*Mamay, imapapaqtaq warmita wacharihuaranki* [Mami, why did you give birth to a girl?].' She told me, 'Calm down now, they've left.' She held me and we cried together. She said, 'Those damned sons of the devil.' That's what happened to me."

"Serafina, does anyone else know what happened to you besides your mother?"

"No—only me, my mama, and my heart know. Who was I going to tell? People might talk, that's why I don't say anything. Here in this pueblo, this happened a lot. Some women gave birth to soldiers' babies. Those children are alive in our pueblo, some are here."

"What do people say about those children?" Dulia asked.

"Nothing, they aren't interested. They just say, 'She had a soldier's child.' They look at the women with scorn—they don't respect them. Some say, 'That's how women are.' There're a lot of problems. My sister is married again now. What was she going to do? Her husband knows she was raped."

"Does her husband say anything?"

"Yes. '*Soldadupa puchunta casarayki* [I married a soldier's leftovers].' Saying that, he beats her."

Dulia and Serafina had not finished talking when one of her daughters came running in breathlessly: "Mama, Papa is already coming!' Serafina became very anxious and worried about her red eyes. She asked Dulia to leave without her husband seeing her. Dulia wiggled her way out the back fence, but not before Serafina mouthed out the words "come back tomorrow."[38]

There are several common elements in the experiences these women shared with us. Most of the women indicated that their husbands had been away when they were raped. As Ana María Tamayo has observed, "For many women and girls, there is no safe way to escape war zones."[39] Men have greater mobility, and many of them left for provincial or coastal cities to save their lives—frequently at the insistence of their female partners or mothers. Thus many women were left alone with their young children and were at even greater risk of sexual violence. However illusory, the symbolic import of having a man in the home afforded women a greater degree of protection against predatory soldiers.

Additionally, Serafina headed out to the mountains to take her mother her identity documents. Anyone detained without his or her papers was at even greater risk of being considered a terrorist, and thus Serafina was motivated by a desire to protect her mother. As in many cases, women placed themselves at increased risk of sexual violence in an effort to protect those they cared for. While obvious, it is worth stating: In most cultures, gender socialization results in women being the primary caregivers, and that care giving may become dangerous during war. Women frequently found themselves confronted with sexual violence precisely in those moments when they were attempting to fulfill their gendered roles. Being a mother, a wife, a sister—those roles and responsibilities may confer added danger during armed conflict.

"Trading Their Bodies"

It was sunrise in Tiquihua when Señora Edilberta Choccña Sanchez invited Edith and me in, pulling out two sheepskins for us to sit on. She brought her *manta* (shawl) full of wheat and we began separating out the wheat from the pebbles while Edilberta recalled the *sasachakuy tiempo* and what had happened to so many women.

"It was 1987, so all of the soldiers came back newly commissioned. The assholes—they abused the women indiscriminately, all of the women, even the married ones."

"So there were rapes here?"

Señora Edilberta threw her head back in disgust. "There was so much rape. They carried off a woman and this woman came back totally abused, dragging herself along. They say the boss went first, and then all of the soldiers had their turn with her. That's how they raped her—raped her until she couldn't even stand up. Lots of soldiers raped her. Oh, in case it was just one, just two? No! Her legs couldn't even hold her up afterward. There was so much fear! That's why women started getting together with younger men. They abused us so much, equally—not only the communism [Sendero], not only from within this pueblo, but equally. *Ay, Señor* [God]! The courage these women had! Oh the courage—how these women defended their character!"

I was struck by the expression "defended their character." As Edilberta made clear, these women not only tried to defend themselves and their loved ones from physical harm but also fought to preserve a sense of themselves that would not be sullied by rape.

"I don't know," mama Edilberta continued, "but even the terrorists, those who were *pelotones* [commanders] abused the married women. For their husbands."

I looked a bit confused and she tried to explain. "When the *pelotones* said, 'Kill him,' the majority of women, the married women—well, they gave birth to the children of the *compañeros* [Senderistas]."

Edilberta was confirming what several other women had told us: women were forced to "barter sex" to save the lives of their loved ones.

"Are those men still here?" wondered Edith.

"Not now . . . well, Crisóstomo is still here. He's already reconciled, that's what he says if you ask. But Amador Pariona, no. They killed him because he was saying, 'From the field below up to Huillquipata, I'm raping all of the women.' So the men killed him. 'He's abusing our women,' the men said, so they killed him. See—now you're really seeing everything they did. Being *terrucos* they abused the women, they ruined the married ones. *Ay Señor!* So much abuse, from the soldiers and from the *terrucos*."

She paused and looked intently at both of us. "*Ay*, why did they abuse so many women? The soldiers even abused elderly women. They left children here. And my cousin—the soldiers took her brother, took him to the base. You, having such grief for your brother—you'd save him, no? You'd do anything, no? To save him, she surrendered her body. That's how she saved her brother. But she had a son with no father. A son from a filthy, slobbering soldier! Oh, how many children did those soldiers leave behind? A lot. That's why I'm telling you—the married women have never said anything."

"Are the children of the *terrucos* here, too?" I asked.

"Yes, but they're in the hills," pointing to the mountains surrounding us. "We don't see the *terrucos*' children."

Edilberta stood up to empty her *manta* full of cleaned wheat into a large basket in her kitchen. She came back with potatoes, still hot enough to burn our hands. She sat beside us again and kept talking.

"The soldiers—oh, there were so many of them. There was so much fear. It's because they raped married women, young girls—the soldiers raped the women. They abused us. You think they didn't?!" her voice rising to an indignant pitch. "It wasn't just the *compañeros*—the soldiers raped even more when they came here."

Both Edith and I nodded in agreement, thinking about the other women who had talked with us. It was clear the Senderistas raped: equally clear was a consensus the soldiers systematically raped as a weapon of war.

"Mama Edilberta, where did you live then?"

She pointed with her hand: "There in the plaza. It was a kindergarten—they [the Senderistas] made it into a school for women. There were a number of women here, their children were *compañeros*—the *compañeros* were their children. *Bueno*, before we were all *compañeros*—it wasn't just one or two people. Oh, now they say, 'Only he was a *terruco*. That man, he was a *terruco*.' But all of us were."

We waited to see if she wanted to say something more about her participation in Sendero, but she returned to the issue of rape. "Here they raped—those *sinvergüenzas* [without shame]! It was an awful life, even with the children—after giving birth, the husbands would ask, 'And I suppose this is mine?' They accused their wives of giving birth to the soldiers' babies. It was an awful life, beatings and abuse. The husbands were always becoming bitter. 'That filthy woman, left over from the soldiers,' they said. 'That woman, she's left over from the soldiers.' My cousin, her son is already grown. She left because her husband found out. How would he not find out? People here gossip—when it comes to gossiping, they're in first place for that."[40]

Forcing the women to *entregar sus cuerpos* (surrender or barter their bodies) was a widespread practice. In conversations with ex-soldiers, they explained how they took advantage of their power to force young women to "barter sex" to save their loved ones. When the troops arrived in a pueblo, they would decide which of the young women were the prettiest. Their fathers and brothers would be rounded up and carried off to the base, denounced as *terrucos*. The women—a euphemism given the age of some of the adolescents—would head up to the base in search of their fathers or brothers. There was a form of exchange: sex could save the life of their loved ones.

This sacrifice had a price. Women who "have been with soldiers" are negatively viewed. Whether by rape or other forms of coercion, having been with a soldier carries its own stigma. In addition, several women assured us that husbands beat the wives they scorn as "soldiers' leftovers." There has been a "domestication of violence" following the war. While dead bodies in the streets may be a thing of the past, angry men and increased alcohol consumption are a nasty mix.[41] One enduring impact of the militarization of daily life and the forging of militarized masculinities is an increase in domestic violence, a phenomenon noted in many postconflict settings.[42]

Thus I turn to the men, convinced that a gendered perspective on war should include an analysis of men and masculinity; "gender" is too frequently a code word for "women," leaving men as the unquestioned, unmarked category.[43] I discuss the rapists, arguing that gender-sensitive research should include studying the forms of masculinity forged during armed conflict as one component in reconstructing individual identities and collective existence in the aftermath of war.

Blood Brothers

> In explanations of atrocities, one particular form of social identity—masculinity—has frequently been ignored.
> —Dan Foster, "What Makes a Perpetrator?"

There is not just one explanation or motivation for sexual violence during armed conflict.[44] As with any sort of human action, the specificities matter. My aim here is to reflect upon several key themes that emerged in my research as well as in the testimonies given to the PTRC. There is a need for more research in Peru on sexual violence and gender ideologies and how these influence daily life in times of both peace and war. I begin with war.

In their research on sexual violence during the internal armed conflict in Peru, Carola Falconí and José Carlos Agüero found that in "almost every case, those responsible for committing rape were members of the armed forces, especially the army, and to a lesser degree the police and Sinchis."[45] Similarly, in my research it became clear that although the Senderistas and in some cases the *ronderos* raped, the systematic use of sexual violence was a practice deployed by the *fuerzas de orden* (agents of order). In short, where there were soldiers, there were rapes.

Also generalizable was gang rape. When women described their experiences with rape, it was never one soldier but several: "They raped the women until they could not stand up." The soldiers were mutilating women with their penises, and the women were bloodied. These were blood rituals.

When analyzing gang rape, we should think about why the men raped this way. An instrumentalist explanation would indicate the soldiers raped in groups in order to overpower a woman or so that one soldier could serve watch while the others raped. However, it would be a limited reading that attributes this practice to the necessity for pure force or standing watch. When a soldier pressed his machine gun into a woman's chest, he did not need more force. When the soldiers came down from the bases at night to rape, "privacy" was not their primary concern. They operated with impunity.

Clearly there is a ritualistic aspect to gang rape.[46] Many people insisted that after killing someone, the soldiers drank the blood of their victims or bathed their faces and chests with the blood. There were blood ties established between soldiers and bloodied wombs that birthed a lethal fraternity. These blood ties united the soldiers, and the bodies of raped women served as the medium for forging those ties.

In their analysis of rape during the 1992–94 Bosnian war, Bülent Diken and Carsten Bagge Lausten suggest that gang rape forges a "brotherhood of guilt" based in part upon the abjection of the victim.[47] For the authors, men's guilt is the key emotion: guilt unifies the perpetrators, and rape is a rite of initiation. Additionally, in tracing how women become "abjects," they argue that shame resists verbalization while guilt incites it: "whereas guilt can be verbalized and can perform as an element in the brotherhood of guilt, shame cannot, which is why it often results in trauma. War thus both creates and destroys communities [of the perpetrators and the victims, respectively]."[48]

I advocate shifting the focus from guilt to shame and shamelessness. Gang rape not only broke the moral codes that generally ordered social life: the practice also served to eradicate shame. Committing morally abhorrent acts in front of others not only forges bonds between the perpetrators but also forges *sinvergüenzas*—shameless people—capable of tremendous brutality. To lose the sense of shame—a regulatory emotion because shame implies an Other in front of whom one feels ashamed—creates men with a recalibrated capacity for atrocity. Guilt unifies; shame individuates. Acts that obliterate shame also obliterate a sense of self, lending themselves to processes aimed at subsuming the individual to create group cohesion and "selflessness" in the service of a collective. Additionally, there is a temporal aspect to understanding these acts and the men who engage in them—and to understanding why the solidarity of guilt may well give way to a deep sense of shame over time. In my research, I am struck by the fact that "men don't talk"—at least not in the first person about their participation in rape.

But they certainly do talk during the act itself. Women emphasize what the soldiers said while raping them: *Terruca de mierda* (terrorist of shit), *ahora aguanta India* (now take it, Indian), *carajo, terruca de mierda* (damn it, terrorist of shit), and *India de mierda* (Indian of shit). The soldiers were marking the women with physical and verbal assaults. For example, the soldiers brought women from neighboring communities to the military base in Hualla to rape them, returning them with their hair cut off as a sign of what had happened. In other conversations in Cayara and Tiquihua, people told us the women returned to their communities "scarred" after having been raped in the bases. The women's bodies were made to bear witness to the power and barbarism of the *fuerzas de orden*. Importantly, in both my conversations as well as the testimonies provided to the TRC, acts of sexual violence were almost always accompanied by ethnic and racial insults, prompting me to consider the ways in which gender, racial, and military hierarchies converged during the internal armed conflict.[49]

Racing Rape

> [S]exual privilege—and the lack of it—is so deeply inscribed in the history of race in the Andes as to make it impossible to talk about one without thinking about the other.
> —Mary Weismantel, *Cholas and Pishtacos*

I begin this section by briefly citing three testimonies that were given to the TRC. In the first, a former soldier recounted an occasion in which his platoon had detained two women: a female dentist and a young girl who was selling fruit juice in the street. The girl—a *chola*—was given to the troops for a *pichana* ("broom" in Quechua, referring to gang rape in which all the soldiers participate in turn). There were forty soldiers. The dentist—a *mestiza*—was reserved for the captain.[50]

In the second, a former army lieutenant recalled his time stationed at a military checkpoint, charged with examining the documents of everyone who was traveling along the road. He and his men stopped many young women from the coast, and the unfortunate ones who had no papers knew immediately what they must do: "We want to meet the captain. We don't want to be with the troops." As the former lieutenant explained, "Sometimes there were four or five of them. They were with us [the officials] on the condition we didn't turn them over to the troops. We kept them for ourselves and let them go the next day. But sometimes there were *cholitas*—we had to give them to the troops. They had to pass through all the soldiers because the troops demanded it."[51]

The third and final example. A rural Quechua-speaking woman recounted her experience of gang rape: the forced nudity, the number of soldiers, the excruciating pain, and her fear. She provided details but refused to repeat the words the soldiers had used to insult her. *Palabras soeces* (filthy words) was all she was willing to say. She could tolerate recounting the sexual violence, but she was not about to repeat the barrage of racial insults she had endured.

Officials and soldiers, *mestizas* and *cholas*, coastal women and rural "Indians," men and women. There are numerous identities at work in these testimonies, and each of them is located within a hierarchy of power and privilege. There is no way to discuss the internal armed conflict without addressing the issues of ethnic discrimination and racism.[52] This is poignantly true when we attempt to understand the uses and logics of rape. In the section of the Peruvian TRC's Final Report that addresses sexual violence, the commissioners state, "Many times, ethnic and racial differences—converted into criteria for naturalizing social inequalities—were invoked by the perpetrators to justify actions committed against those who were their victims."[53] The examples given above demonstrate this. Lighter-skinned women were reserved for the officials; the *cholas* and "Indians" were turned over to the troops. In cases in which both officials and foot soldiers were raping the same women, then it was rank that determined a man's place in line—and that rank would in turn reflect ethnic and racial stratification.[54] Who was entitled to inflict pain on another reflected gender and racial hierarchies; however, I am intrigued by the inverse, *by the ways in which the raping was used to produce those hierarchies.* Thus I consider "racing rape."

In thinking about the pervasive use of ethnic and racial insults during acts of gang rape, Mary Weismantel's book *Cholas and Pishtacos: Stories of Race and Sex in the Andes* was extremely helpful. In her analysis of the ways in which acts of sexualized violence confer racial identity, she provides insight into the ways in which racial and sexual identities are inscribed on bodies through rituals of domination and submission.

In part her analysis focuses on the *pishtaco*. This figure spans time and space, a remarkably resilient figure in Andean tales of racialized and gendered violence. The *pishtaco*—an aggressive male figure who sucks the body fat out of his Indian victims, slashing their throats and raping the women with his insatiable phallus—is always white. He has been, at different historical moments, a Spanish priest, a *hacendado*, a gringo anthropologist, a Peruvian engineer from an NGO, or a member of the community whose sudden wealth gives rise to rumors that he has somehow exploited his neighbors: the constant is the fusion of aggression, sexuality, and whiteness. As Weismantel argues, "In linking a man's propensity to sexual abuse to his race, *pishtaco* stories interrogate the long and often forgotten history of race and rape. 'Rape,' like 'woman,' or 'whiteness,' does not have a single trans-historical definition, but rather is produced through and defined within specific historical contexts."[55] Within these specific historical contexts, the *pishtaco* "is whitened by his sexual aggressivity, and masculinized by virtue of his whiteness."[56] Thus ethnic or racial identity is to some extent achieved, a structural position one body can assume relative to another.

This is what I wish to capture with "racing rape." Given the ethnically or racially based distribution of women for the purpose of raping, the troops—drawn from darker-skinned social strata because class has color in Peru—were raping women not unlike themselves. *La pichana* consisted of *cholos* raping *cholas*, and of *cholos* bombarding their victims with the same ethnic insults they had endured in their own lives. Raping, combined with the eth-nic insults, was a means by which these young men "whitened" themselves and transferred ethnic humiliation to their victims. As Judith Butler has argued with regard to gender, identity is performative. Rather than being "already there" waiting for its expression in language, identity may be the product of the "signifying acts of linguistic life."[57] To borrow the title of an influential article, "the women are more Indian"—and raping them cer-tainly made them so.[58]

However, even in the midst of so much sexual violence, there were men who did not want to participate in the raping. In my conversations with ex-soldiers and ex-sailors, they insisted participation in the rapes was obliga-tory. It is possible that this fiction is a balm for their conscience; some men, however, provided details about what happened to the soldiers and sailors who did not want to join in. A single example from a conversation with someone who served in La Marina in Ayacucho during the early 1980s is telling.

> Some of the recruits were really young. They were just adolescents. They didn't want to participate [in the rapes]. If someone refused, the rest of the men would take him aside and rape him. All of them would rape him, with the poor guy screaming. They said they were "chang-ing his voice"—with so much screaming, his voice would lower and he wouldn't be a woman anymore.

Again we see that raping was a means of establishing hierarchies: between armed groups and the population, and within the armed forces themselves.[59] It was common to force men in a community to watch as the soldiers raped their wives, daughters, and sisters. And it is striking that the soldiers raped according to rank, beginning with the officers and finishing up with the recruits. There were multiple audiences for this violent sexuality, and the performance was intended in part to impress other men with whom one jockeyed for status within the battalion. The erections achieved and placed to brutal purposes in the context of gang rape lead me to insist the men performed for one another.[60]

When we speak of militarization, we need to think beyond the stationing of soldiers in the bases. Militarization also implies changes in what it means to be a man or a woman: the hypermasculinity of the warrior is based upon erasing those characteristics considered "feminine."[61] This hypermasculinity is constructed by scorning the feminine, and one aspect of that scorn is feminizing other men by inflicting physical and symbolic violence.[62]

Narrating Heroism

Marcos caught my attention the first time I saw him in a communal assembly. He was a striking figure in khaki and black, his posture exaggeratedly erect. His black hair was cut short, and his black sweater alternated with his camouflage pants, finally ceding to his black leather boots. In the room he shared with his young wife, various pictures of Marcos with his machine gun and belts of ammunition were hanging by nails from the wall. He told me about those pictures one evening.

"I was in the army when *las papas quemaban* [the potatoes were burning, referring to the heat of battle]. One time we were out on patrol and we had a confrontation with the *terrucos* and killed six of them. We captured *una china* [a young girl]. We were a total of twenty-eight soldiers, and everyone raped that poor *china*. I didn't because she was fifteen and I was only seventeen—I felt like she was my sister. Afterward we let her go because she begged us. She said she'd been forced into Sendero in the jungle. The officers in the army allowed all of that. They even told us, "Those fucking *terrucos* rape your women. Is that all right? That's why they told us, 'I authorize you [to rape].' They also made us eat gunpowder for breakfast. We weren't afraid of anything."[63]

Not one man with whom I have spoken admitted to having participated in rape. Men told me about having killed, but in no conversation has a man ever talked about participating in rape.[64] The same men who have described in detail the last minutes and expressions of a dying victim—the struggle that gives way to resigned limbs, to silence, to unblinking, glassy eyes—have always insisted it was other men who were raping. It is difficult to narrate one's heroism when a man was one of twenty-eight soldiers standing in line to rape a young girl. I am not accusing Marcos but rather noting that each narrator screens the facts he presents to his interlocutor, and the representation of self is a continuous negotiation between what to hide and what to reveal. But listening to Marcos, I heard the echoes of those hoarse recruits.

Where are these former soldiers and sailors now? How do these men feel about what they have done? They must also carry the traces of the armed conflict and their participation in atrocities. When they caress their wives, when they look into the faces of their little girls, when they stare into a mirror—what do they see reflected there?[65] This is one legacy of the war that has not been studied, and obviously it would be methodologically challenging. However, I am compelled by the deep injustice of both rape and its narrative burden. It is, of course, women who are incited to speak about sexual violence; the silence of the gang rapists is left undisturbed. I have never heard anyone ask a man, "Did you have blood on your penis? Were you first in line, or tenth? Did you penetrate her vagina or her anus? Did you ejaculate? How many times?" I imagine we recoil just reading the questions, and yet women are routinely asked to narrate their experiences in an idiom of sexual vulnerability and degradation. What does it mean to be asked to narrate your life in an idiom that cannot possibly do you justice?

"The Soldiers' Gifts"

Among the legacies of the massive sexual violence that occurred during the internal armed conflict were unwanted pregnancies and, at times, unwanted children. Some of these children were sent to live with extended family members residing outside the community, while others were raised by their mothers amid the gossip. One communal authority bitterly complained about *los regalos de los soldados* (the soldiers' gifts) who were born in his pueblo. That community alone has more than fifty young people who carry only their mother's last name—their father's identity was never determined. The following examples illustrate some of the ways women dealt with "the soldier's gifts."

Over the years I have known several children who were the result of rape. Here I mention just one boy whose mother had been passed around by the soldiers in the base that had overlooked their community for almost fifteen years. I first noticed him because he was standoffish, never joining the growing group of children who made my room a lively place. I tried to speak with him a few times, but he had no interest in conversation. After months of living in the community, I finally had an opportunity to ask someone about him. It was late afternoon and I saw him heading down the steep hill toward home, his three goats and one llama kept together with an occasional slap of a slender stick. The woman sitting at my side knew him by name: Chiki. My face must have expressed my surprise because she whispered that his mother was "one of those women."

Chiki is a painful name for a young boy, who in turn was a painful child for his mother. *Chiki* means "danger" in Quechua and in daily usage refers to a warning that something bad is about to happen and should be averted. People recall the ways they learned to look for a sign that the enemy might attack. One such *chiki* was a strong wind that blew through the village, rattling the roofs and letting people know something evil was about to occur.

This boy was one of those "future memories," a perverse distortion of time. He could not be a warning; it was too late to avert this particular danger. Rather, he was the product of an evil event his mother had been unable to escape. His mere being extends his mother's memory both to the past and into the future. Her son is a living memory of the danger she survived, as well as a reminder that nothing good could possibly come from this Chiki she had failed to avoid.

Other women tried to abort with herbs, sometimes ridding their bodies of fetuses they could not bear. Still others resorted to infanticide. There is a long-standing practice of "letting die" those babies who are unwanted, perhaps because they are born with physical defects or are the product of rape. The idea is that *criaturas* do not suffer when they die; one can leave them sleeping "mouth down," gently drifting off to death. Recall the discussion in Chapter 2 of women's concerns about the transmission of *llakis* and *susto* from mother to baby, either in utero or via the "frightened breast." How could a baby born of such suffering and fear be normal? Most women were certain they could not. Letting them die reflected a desire to spare them the violence of memory.

Thus it is not surprising people also have theories regarding the impact of rape on pregnant women. In addition to possible congenital defects, these children faced a challenging process of socialization given their violent conception. In Cayara one woman explained it this way:

> There are lots of sick children here—some are already adolescents. My neighbor's son is already a young man. When his mother was pregnant, the soldiers abused her. The boy was mistreated even before he was born! He was born different. Halfway *sonso* [senseless]. He can't speak. It's like he's crazy. It's as though he lost his use of reason. He doesn't talk, he's different—*sonso*. He's not like a normal child.[66]

Recall the seven adolescents in Accomarca, those "children of the massacre" who were each born with some form of congenital birth defect. The number was surprising. In my experience, it is exceptional to find a child with birth defects in rural communities. How to explain these seven adolescents in just one community?

Guilt pervaded our conversations in Accomarca. A number of people lamented, "It's because of us the soldiers came here," referring indirectly to their participation in or tolerance of Sendero. "It's our fault." People also insisted on the innocence of those who died in the army massacre of August 14, 1985. They insisted "the guilty" had already escaped into the hills, leaving the sixty-nine innocent people who were burned alive. For the speakers, their survival implies a tainted past. Could it be the seven mothers of these children let their babies live as a form of atonement? Seeing these children each day—could it be they sought to pay their debt to the innocents who were raped, tortured, shot, and burned that horrible day in Lloqllepampa?

Debts unpaid, and justice painfully deferred. My mind wanders back to Eulogia, whose guttural expressions of pain continue to haunt the women of Accomarca. She is one of the few people in this book whose name I have left unchanged. I felt that no further harm could come to her at this point in time. Besides, I could not have invented any name more appropriate for this young woman than the one she had.

Eulogy: a speech or writing in praise of a person or thing; *a funeral oration for someone (or something) who has died.* Irony? Perhaps.

Over the years of living with her memory, I have come to think of Eulogia as symbolizing certain forms of community and compassion that are extinguished during brutal acts of violence in which no one responds. What died when her neighbors turned a deaf ear to her muffled cries? Was this really a failure of language or a failure to respond to the pleas of a young woman in need? For me Eulogia remains a powerful example of how the armed conflict signaled the death of relationships that are still awaiting the conditions for their rebirth.

*   *   *

I began this chapter by noting that truth commissions are considered "victim centered" in their approach to investigating the truth about periods of political violence and terror. This may be both a strength and a weakness. In their use of more flexible evidentiary standards, commissions are effective in offering alternative histories generally at odds with official versions of what happened—particularly when agents of the state were key perpetrators. However, their focus on categories of victimization, combined with the highly gendered nature of victim imagery, may unintentionally construct other silences. By foregrounding suffering, they may obscure other relationships women have with their pasts. There is a bit of irony; commissions are charged with investigating the truth, and yet the broader truths that women narrated were too frequently reduced to the sexual harm they had experienced.[67] "Gender crimes" are not only sexual. Rather, women spoke at length about multiple factors that structured vulnerability during the internal armed conflict. These factors tell us a great deal about underlying and enduring forms of inequality that remain intact during times of "peace."

Additionally, in the conversations my research team and I had with women, they insisted on giving meaning to and exercising some control over their suffering *and* their protagonism in the face of danger. If it is true that "A gendered understanding of conflict remains conspicuous by its absence," then commissions must move beyond their victim-driven logic to open up narrative space for women to provide testimony that is not limited to suffering and grief.[68] Thus "gender sensitivity" would focus less on strategies designed to make women talk about "their rapes" and more on developing new ways of listening to what women say about war—and how they say it.

And there is what they do not say. Given that women overwhelmingly refused to talk about rape in the first person, what might constitute reparations or redress? How does one attempt to "repair" the unspoken? The question is not rhetorical: designing reparations programs that address sexual violence against women is a challenge confronting many postconflict countries. I do not have the answer, but I am quite certain how *not* to go about it.

In his work on a consultancy with Sierra Leonean refugee women in northern Liberia, Mats Utas was surprised that every woman they interviewed readily declared she had been raped during the Sierra Leonean Civil War. As he soon realized, presenting themselves as victims was a means by which women established themselves as "legitimate recipients" of humanitarian aid.[69] Testimony about rape was a ticket to aid.

What about the ethics of this trade? What about the coercive elements of "tell me your story of sexual victimization and you'll receive a blanket and cans of food?" Or, in the context of a postwar reparations program, "provide graphic testimony about your rape and perhaps receive a stipend"? I cannot divorce methods from ethics: in this case, both are repugnant. There are questions that we do not have a right to ask and silences that must be respected.

Moreover, if being a subject implies telling a story, then perhaps many women choose not to narrate episodes of victimization as the core of who they are today—the core of the self they live with and present to their interlocutors. The word "recover" has many definitions, among them "to take back what has been lost; to re-cover." What if part of recovery is taking back some sense of the private, intimate sphere that was violated? In a woman's refusal to make rape the narrative core of her subjectivity, might we see an insistence on the right to opacity in this era of confessional obsession and the tyranny of transparency?

And yet many women did talk in great detail about the gendered dimensions of war—and some talked about rape. There is a tacit agreement in giving and receiving testimonies, an implicit promise that some form of justice is forthcoming. Women consistently expressed a desire for redistributive justice: scholarships for their children, decent housing, potable water, food in the house, and crops and livestock in their fields. This is what women repeatedly demanded—both the women who spoke about rape and the hundreds more who did not. We must work with this vision of redistributive justice and expand it to include shame. One thing that could be redistributed is the shame that has been unjustly apportioned to women; this shame should belong to the rapists, who have enjoyed total impunity. Antje Krog asks, how might maleness be reconstructed following periods of violence?[70] How might masculinity be demilitarized following war? In Peru, there has been scant discussion about the thousands of soldiers and sailors who raped during the internal armed conflict. The *sinvergüenzas* forged during bloody acts of gang rape are not discussed in public discourse in Peru. This is indeed a troubling silence.[71] Reparation should include the redistribution of goods and services; it should also include the redistribution of shame to those who earned it.[72]

Finally, when survivors of sexual violence speak about their experiences, they place a responsibility on their interlocutors to respond to what they have heard. There is a need—and an obligation—for the Peruvian state to implement a reparations program for survivors of rape, and this should include material and symbolic components. Within the symbolic reparations, I argue for public education programs about the massive sexual violence that occurred during the internal armed conflict. Among the themes that should be included in these educational programs, I advocate focusing on the injustice of placing blame on these women for what happened to them *a la fuerza*—under force. Then—maybe then—we could begin to rewrite the war stories to include the heroism of so many women. These women's narratives force us to rethink commonsense notions of women and war, and lead us back to the words of Señora Edilberta Choccña Sanchez: "Oh, such courage! These women defended themselves with so much courage."

Chapter 6

The Widows

FIELD NOTES, APRIL 6, 2000: We slept on quicksand mattresses that made getting up in the morning a slow process. When one limb was successfully extracted, another inevitably sunk back into the mattress, lost among the mounds of smelly blankets and soggy foam. I want to remember how everything looks in the *campo*. The *ichu* filling the space between the sticks in the roof, tiny patches of blue sky by day and starry sky by night glimpsed through the cracks. The beaten-down dirt of the floor, worn smooth by cracked plastic shoes and wild brush brooms. Blackened pots jumbled in the corner next to the rocks that serve as the fireplace for cooking. The wind rustles through the house, against the backdrop of dogs barking in the distance. Yesterday Yolanda, Shintaca, and *wawa* Gloria came up to the base to play, gathering in the room across the way and singing for hours. Yolanda had filled the brim of her hat with bright pink flowers and the shiny metallic lining from a pack of cigarettes. The moments of complete silence and expansive night skies, when stars crowd up against one another, tumbling until they hit the horizon and then wrap their way around to come up again from the other side. The *warmisapas* sitting outside my room, *chakchando* coca, pulling worn plastic bags from the folds of their skirts, sharing coca and *toqra*. The women's remaining teeth turning deep brown, wads of coca held between teeth and cheek. Small weathered hands with blackened nails, so frequently placed over mouths, audacious words uttered behind a screen of bony fingers. Callus-covered bare feet tucked beneath layers of embroidered skirts that tie at the waist with a woven *chumbi*. Acrylic sweaters in red, green, or black held closed by the same *chumbi* and a large safety pin with ribbons and shoelaces threaded through the keys to the padlocks hanging on their doors. The hours spent with *warmisapas*, remembering the days when meat was abundant, their men were respectful, and the young people obeyed.

Armed conflicts are undeniably destructive, and the burned-out villages scattered across the highlands of Ayacucho conveyed the materiality of that devastation. What was less clear at first were the generative aspects of the war. I simply could not see them amid the charred ruins of homes, schools, churches—the infrastructure of social life that lay in disarray. It was only with time that the productive consequences of the armed conflict became visible and audible, frequently emerging as contradictions in daily life.

In Chapter 2 I questioned the category of PTSD and the ways in which this diagnostic category "flattens" the complexity of postwar social worlds. We can think in similar ways of trauma narratives and the politics of victimhood that imbue postconflict struggles, as well as the implications of forcing political biographies and power dynamics into a "trauma narrative." And let's conjure up the images. The victim narrating trauma has an archetypal persona: The War Widow.

I routinely watched the widows, at times the most outspoken women in their villages, shrink into the role of "widowed victim of war" when state agencies and nongovernmental organizations came around. They assumed this diminished role literally, shoulders slumping into helpless defeat. This was impotent widowhood as a compulsory social performance, women's bodies incorporating the imperatives of the role.

I do not want to be misunderstood. The Peruvian government published a Census for Peace in 2001, in which it estimated there were twenty thousand widows as a result of the internal armed conflict.[1] One-third of all households in Ayacucho are headed by women, and these households are generally among the poorest.[2] Obviously widows have suffered, and their poverty serves as a constant reminder of all they have lost. However, gender fluctuates across social fields, and to cast these widows as only victims is to distort who they are and how they move within their communities. Widows, perhaps more than any other group, embody the contradictory effects of war.

The ambivalence of the widows is captured by the word *warmisapa*— Quechua for "widow." *Warmi* is "woman" and *sapa* is a suffix that can mean "much" or "alone." Thus *warmisapa* literally means "much woman" or "woman alone" (although my Quechua instructor insisted it could also mean *demasiado mujer*—too much woman; I think he was editorializing).

There are various ways to interpret this term. Within the complementarity framework that has informed many studies of gender in the Andes, this can be understood as implying a gender imbalance because the woman does not have a male counterpart.[3] This is one legitimate way of understanding the term, but it is only one.

At some point in my research, I decided to invert my questions. Rather than continuing to wonder why women rarely spoke out in communal assemblies, I began listening for where women were vocal participants in communal affairs. This inversion led to *quejas* (complaints brought before communal authorities) and *qarawi*. Women are insistent in presenting their *quejas*, even though justice remains elusive, administered largely by men. I recall how many of the widows spoke about themselves: "We are big mouths, we're demanding!" Indeed, *warmisapa*—"a lot of woman."

And there is *qarawi*, a narrative form in which widows are central. *Qarawi* has a long history in Peru and refers to ceremonial poems or ballads. José Varallanos describes *qarawi* as "the most authentic poetic and musical expression of the native people of Peru."[4] He continues: "Members of indigenous communities sing these songs in Quechua in the hour of affliction, of work and of pleasure. Thus in the candlelight wakes, in their religious fiestas, in the agricultural *faenas*, during *herranza* [when animals are marked with ribbons through their ears], one hears these songs in dialogue or sung in unison . . . and it is women, with their sharp voices, who play the best role."[5]

In my experience, it is only widows who sing *qarawi*, which is central to virtually every important event: weddings, funerals, crop planting and harvesting, the inauguration of a highway, or a visit from elected officials. *Qarawi* is a form of historicizing events while they are unfolding, and it is the *warmisapas* who do the historicizing.

While the style and tone are similar, the lyrics of each *qarawi* are improvised in the moment. This is why asking a woman to sing a *qarawi* just for the sake of recording it always resulted in an empty tape. Widows sing *qarawi* only in the context of important events or rites of passage, and the lyrics are composed "on the spot" with the women taking turns and then joining in on the lyrics that emerge as the refrain. The songs tend toward the burlesque, allowing both for commemorating as well as editorializing on these events. For instance, when former mayor Milton Cordova arrived from Huanta for the inauguration of the highway in Carhuahurán, at the front of the procession sent to greet him were three widows, singing in the high-pitched tones of *qarawi*:

> Señor Mayor, you are arriving on the Camino Real [the Royal Road],
> Welcome, Señor Mayor.
> We hope you've brought the documents.
> Arriving on the Camino Real,
> We hope you did not forget to bring the documents that you promised us.

The documents in question concerned the municipality's commitment of resources for various projects in the community; thus the widows were offering a lyrical reminder of the mayor's campaign promises.

Similarly, weddings were accompanied by praise for the institution of marriage, as well as a running critique of the groom, the bride, the quality and quantity of the food served—while the *qarawiyuqkuna* (the singers of *qarawi*) reminded the families when their glasses of *trago* threatened to run dry.

During the war this lyrical tradition was placed to new purposes. The *qarawiyuqkuna* were among those who stood watch for enemy attacks. In Huaychao villagers described how the elderly women would sing out, "Careful! There are three pigs entering your field!" when the guerrillas drew near. *Qarawi* became a tool in communal defense.

I also relished watching widows joke with men during *faenas*, teasing them in a way married or single women would not be inclined to do. They could joke about the men's (questionable) sexual prowess, their ability (or not) to dig a deep hole into the Pachamama and plant their fertile seeds—all comments that provoked fits of laughter. These exchanges worried many married women, who professed to know more than one man who had "lost himself with a *warmisapa*." When some widows did take a lover, at times to make economic ends meet, they insisted they would tolerate no physical abuse. As several widows exclaimed, "Who does he think I am, his wife?" Thus widows do have certain freedoms and are a destabilizing presence that calls into question the "naturalness" of male and female roles.

This liminality came up time and again. For instance, due to the demands of the political violence and the absence of their loved ones, widows and single women were forced to redefine their roles and assume new responsibilities with regard to defense activities. In the summer of 1995 I had a long conversation with President Modesta of Pampay, a village in the valley of Huanta. We spent an afternoon sitting on a grassy knoll as doña Modesta described how she came to be commander of the village's *ronda campesina* in 1988 and subsequently president of her community in 1994. As she told it, "We were left as widows here, many widows. So we were obliged to take up *cargos* [communal responsibilities]. Because we are widows and our sons left to work in other areas—want to or not, we had to do something."

I was curious about what it had been like for a woman to serve as commander of her community's *ronda campesina*. "And how did you patrol, with weapons?"

"Yes, with arms. Chewing our coca, that's how we took care of ourselves. We put ourselves in the position of a man," doña Modesta explained.

"Were you afraid?"

She nodded emphatically. "Oh, there was great fear. We were thinking they [Sendero] might arrive by day or by night and kill us all. But now when a dog so much as barks, we're already jumping! With all we've been through, we're experts."

The idea of putting oneself "in the position of a man" reflects the extent to which occupying public space and exercising visible forms of power are associated with militarized patriarchy.[6] In fact, the woman who was then serving as commander in Pampay told me, "We carry out the defense with arms, *qarichakuspanchik* [making ourselves macho, making ourselves men]."[7] The process of "making oneself macho" was not limited to the women of Pampay. In 1994 there were twenty-two women from different villages throughout the Huanta valley who attended coordinating meetings with the civil defense patrols in the military base in Castropampa.

Thus, when I first sat down to write something about widows, and postconflict gender relations more generally, I was utterly bewildered. For everything I wrote about widows, there was a list of counterexamples. I could not resolve the contradictions any more readily than could the men and women with whom I lived. In trying to understand my experiences in Ayacucho, Sherry Ortner's comments regarding the contradictions and multiplicity of logics operating in any given society resonated. She suggests we analyze these contradictions in terms of social transformation: "There is an ordering—a hegemony in the sense of a relative domination of some meanings and practices over others. It is both this ordering and its potential disordering that interest me."[8] What I want to preserve is the ambivalence of the *warmisapas*, both the term as well as the liminal space these women occupy in their communities.

In the following pages, I present various conversations with widows in order to explore these ambiguous, fascinating women. I begin by questioning a facile embrace of popular memory, arguing that "the popular" is a category rife with fragmentation and conflict. It is more productive to consider local struggles over memory as a way to examine the elusive nature of the "we" that narrates communal histories of war. Community is both ideology and practice, both a specific discursive incitement and a structure of feeling. Widows incorporate the fault lines, and in the contours of speech and silence they provide insights into the complex obligations people have to the dead and to the living, to the past and to the future. I then consider how the economies of war and reconstruction may exhaust social solidarity, pitting villagers against one another in a competition for scarce emotional and material resources. The influx of funding for postconflict reconstruction moves unevenly throughout these conflictive communities, both reflecting and at times exacerbating the gendered dimensions of postwar politics. In taking "community" as their unit of intervention, state agencies and nongovernmental organizations may overlook the ways in which the aid they provide can have unintended consequences. However, while at times those unintended consequences further marginalize the poorest sectors of these communities, people are tenacious in their efforts to improve their lives. In addition to material assistance, these organizations also introduce new lexicons that villagers appropriate in an effort to access goods and services. The language of rights is one such appropriation. Women in general, and widows particularly, have picked up on the language of rights to press a variety of claims. I conclude with some thoughts on how the accelerated changes of the war have resulted in certain openings regarding women's roles within their communities, particularly for the *warmisapas* whose losses bring them both pain and possibility.

"Popular Memory"

War and its aftermath serve as powerful motivators for the elaboration and transmission of individual, communal, and national histories. These histories both reflect *and* constitute human experience as they contour social memory and produce their truth effects, and they use the past in a creative manner, combining and recombining elements of that past in service to interests in the present.

In these communities, the narratives being elaborated about the internal armed conflict have a political intent and assume both an internal and an external audience. The deployment of war narratives contributes to forging new relations of power, ethnicity, and gender that are integral to the contemporary politics of the region. These new relations impact the construction of democratic practices and the model of citizenship being elaborated in the current context. In the *alturas* of Huanta it is the heroic war epic that has guided both the form and the content of these histories, compacting polyphonic memories into the dominant war story paradigm.[9] This epic style emphasizes masculine heroism and has been canonized not only in these communities but in the academic literature as well.[10]This masculine version of the war—of *ronderos* defending their villages, defeating Sendero Luminoso, and establishing new democratic practices and demands for citizenship—obscures the disjunctive and contradictory construction of citizenship in these villages. These disjunctions reflect the axes of differentiation—for example, gender and generation—that operate within these communities.

If indeed the war has permitted subaltern sectors of the rural population to seize the national stage in a slow and intermittent construction of citizenship, armed participation against Sendero Luminoso and the relationship the *rondas* formed with the armed forces have frequently reinforced patriarchal relations within these northern villages, resulting in an unequal exercise of rights and sense of belonging to that imagined community called the nation. National integration achieved via participation in an armed conflict influences the political culture that follows, contributing to what Teresa Caldeira and James Holston call "disjunctive democracy."

> By calling democracy disjunctive, we want to emphasize that it comprises processes in the institutionalization, practice, and meaning of citizenship that are never uniform or homogeneous. Rather, they are normally uneven, unbalanced, irregular, heterogeneous, arrhythmic, and indeed contradictory. The concept of disjunctive democracy stresses, therefore, that at any one moment citizenship may expand in one area of rights as it contracts in another. The concept also means that democracy's distribution and depth among a population of citizens in a given political space are uneven.[11]

That the distribution of democracy varies according to the axes of differentiation that riddle any given political space—be it the nation or a *campesino* community—explodes the notion that one can speak of the "subaltern" or the "popular" as a monolithic group whose interests flow "naturally" from members' marginalized position. A rigid dichotomy between "the official" and "the popular" obscures both the fluidity within such a dichotomy as well as the fragmentation that exists on each side of the great divide.

This same binary logic manifests in many texts on political repression, postwar processes, and memory. There is a repetitive analytic structure that informs both academic and activist approaches to these themes. On one side of the dichotomy is the category "official memory." This category appears cloaked in various names and adjectives: "State," "institutional," "dominant groups," "hegemonic memory"—in short, "bad or repressive memory." On the other side lies "popular memory." The bearers and adjectives are "subaltern groups," "the marginalized," "civil society," or "counterhegemonic memory"—in short, "good or emancipatory memory." Reflecting psychoanalytic influence on our thinking about memory, that which is repressed is imbued with "the truth"—somehow, the repressed holds the key to the *really real*. Thus, the implicit goal is to supplant "official memory" with "popular memory" as an intrinsically democratic project.

However, is it true that power and stratification do not operate within "the subaltern" or "the popular"? What happens to the axes of differentiation previously mentioned? To homogenize "the popular" is to erase the fact that it can be simultaneously oppositional and hegemonic in any given context. As Florencia Mallon argues:

> The question of complicity, hierarchy, and surveillance within subaltern communities and subaltern cultures is a thorny one indeed, one that cries out for nuanced and sympathetic treatment. On the one side, raising this question makes clear that no subaltern identity can be pure and transparent; most subalterns are both dominated and dominating subjects, depending on the circumstances or location in which we encounter them. . . . To see both sides at the same time, to mark the heroism and the treachery, is most certainly a challenge.[12]

Anyone who has spent time in a rural community knows that we are far from the romanticized image of the "Andean community" as an eternal and harmonious entity. "Community" is a strategic and constructed identity, and its maintenance involves processes that seek to perpetuate communal hegemony.[13] Although communal processes attempt to maintain "community" because villagers derive some benefit from belonging to a collective, this does not mean that all members of the collective feel the community offers equality or justice. Just as the power of speech—the authority to narrate the war years—has remained in the mouths of men, the administration of justice has remained in their hands.

In each community there is an official history for those who come around asking, and reciting that history is not limited to the occasional focus group. For example, former president Toledo visited a northern community in October 2002, and that same morning in the assembly the mayor had reminded all of the men gathered that "journalists will come today. You don't have to talk with them. If they ask us anything, we're going to say we don't know the truth." The men nodded in agreement. The mayor then glanced toward a group of widows sitting along the edge of the field. "And watch it—we don't want any of the women saying things that aren't certain."

The authorities in this community, as in others, closed narrative ranks with respect to the war and their participation in the conflict. However, people who are marginal to the working of power, particularly narrative power, have other perspectives regarding the histories of their pueblos. These alternative histories are not necessarily "more true," but neither is "popular memory" complete without including this polyphony. It was only time that allowed me to hear the silences that shaped communal histories and to understand how much people have invested in the collective history those silences construct.[14]

Pallqa, July 1995

It was my first summer in Ayacucho, and the staff at World Vision was generous with me. They were virtually the only nongovernmental organization known in the highlands of Huanta. The regional director of World Vision, Victor Bellezza, had played a key role in negotiating the return of these communities to their land. For communities that had been forcibly displaced, returning to rebuild involved petitioning for permission to do so from the military officials at Castropampa. Victor had been an ally in these efforts, and at that point World Vision enjoyed tremendous legitimacy throughout Huanta. It was early in the rebuilding efforts, and villagers were not yet disenchanted with the proliferating NGOs and their seemingly endless needs assessments. They did not yet suffer from testimony fatigue.

I was eager to visit communities in the highlands of Huanta, and the safest way to do so was to hike the mountains with World Vision. It was still dangerous for unknown people to walk those roads. The *rondas* patrolled every night, as well as during the day in villages located farther inland toward the jungle.

Early on a July morning, Marilú Calderón and I set out for the highland communities with which World Vision worked. We took the truck almost to the end of its line some four hours uphill from Huanta. The driver lurched to a stop as we banged on the roof of the truck cab to let him know we wanted off at Pallqa. We eased ourselves over the edge of the truck bed, and other passengers began handing us our dusty backpacks.

From the one-lane dirt highway, Pallqa was a quick walk down the side of a sharp cliff. The community interested me because widows headed 40 percent of the fifty-three households in the village. Pallqa was technically a "returning community"; people had picked up what possessions they could and relocated during the worst years of the war. We were arriving not long after villagers had returned to their land to rebuild. The challenge was sobering. The village had been burned down several times, and blackened ruins lined the soccer field and staggered up the other side of the ravine. Makeshift roofs sat at precarious angles, barely clutching the uneven slopes of the remaining charred walls.

People began to shout out greetings as we crossed the soccer field, and several women came out to welcome us. Within minutes one of the women handed us a bowl of boiled potatoes and a bag of salt. Marilú and I pulled out the big bag of bread we had brought with us, and soon we were joined by a group of children whose shyness was no match for a *chapla*.

We spent that first morning stretched out on a corner of the soccer field, talking with the widows. I was excited to be starting my research, tape recorder in my backpack and a list of questions running through my mind. It was still a novelty to be a North American in rural Ayacucho, and the women were patient in answering my questions. We explained that I was learning Quechua, and they agreed that I could tape our conversation; the irony of my methods would occur to me later. At the time, I only saw "war widows" and was indeed conversing with the public, unified face of communal suffering.

I was interested in knowing what life had been like during the *sasa-chakuy tiempo*, and the women related that history with gestures animating their speech. They held their backs; they wrapped their arms around their stomachs; they clasped their hands to their hearts; they wiped away tears that refused to cease. What they said verbally was complementary, at times secondary, to the body language they used: what made me *feel* their words were their gestures. My body would serve as one of my "key informants."[15]

It was striking that every woman spoke in the first person plural—*ñoqa-yku*. All statements were uttered in the register of "we."[16] When I sat down later to write up the conversation, I was unable to individualize responses. During those first years in Ayacucho, conversations had a Greek chorus quality to them. There was scant public space for divergent memories; the risks were too high. At different points in our conversation that day, one of the women would get up to chase a child, squat to one side to pee, or check on something in her house. The other women would wait for her to return: "We can't answer because not all of us are here."

In response to a question regarding when the violence began, the women insisted that Sendero had attacked Pallqa "four times because we refused to accept them."

"How did they first arrive?"

"With a list of names. They came looking for people. They killed sixteen men."

When villagers refused to accept Shining Path, the Senderistas burned their village over and over again. Under the threat of constant attack, villagers sought refuge: "For two years we slept in the caves, always fleeing."

Life in the caves was unbearable, and people began relocating. Most of the widows moved farther downhill to Chaka, which would eventually become a multicommunal refuge or "resistant community." Many of the men went to Huanta, settling on the fringes of the city in the rapidly growing barrios.

"What was it like living in Chaka?"

"Ay, in Chaka we had nothing but water to drink."

"Didn't people there help you?"

"Not at all. They didn't give us anything! They accused us of using their water and dirtying their pueblo!"

The distance had also been a hardship. The women slept in Chaka, returning during the day to work in their fields. This gave them only a few hours a day to work because the walk on foot was so long and it was danger-ous to be out walking in the dark.

"Even our animals died from hunger," they recalled.

"I wonder—who suffered more, men or women?"

The response came without hesitation. "Women. Women suffered more—the men could escape. We had to carry our children." Once again, weathered hands were pressed against backs, stomachs, and hearts. When the danger subsided in the early 1990s, villagers began discussing the pos-sibility of returning to their community. Pallqa had originally consisted of two haciendas; however, to return they needed a sufficient demographic base. After a series of assemblies in Huanta, people joined forces to return together as one community in September 1994.

"What was it like to come back and see everything like this?"

"Too sad! We remembered everything we had before Sendero."

Remembering was shot through with fear. Since January 1995, all the single women and widows had been participating in the peasant patrol, sit-ting up at night in the towers positioned at strategic corners of the com-munity. Each village had its *torreones*: tall rock structures where the *ron-deros* spent the night, standing watch against possible attacks. The humid rock and cut-away windows were no match for the biting wind, and the men insisted *trago* was the only way they could withstand the cold.

"Do you have guns?"

"The men stand watch with guns. We have whistles."

Another woman added, "The big problem is that we have no weapons. We just have to run."

The *warmisapas* kept stressing how weak and tired they were. "This is a dog's life. Living alone, it's like a dog's life."

"With rain and without rain they killed us. We're always remembering, even in our dreams."

"We've suffered in our pueblo because it's *our* pueblo. *We bear the suffer-ing because we were born here*," explained another widow.

"We've cried so much—we look, but we don't see."

"We can't forget everything that happened. Our fear we can't forget, *and until now we don't want to forget our pain*."

"I wonder, what's going to happen to Pallqa?"

A chorus of sighs. "We're just women—all women! We can't build. We'll have to go somewhere else and work for other people. Just women? How can we possibly rebuild?"

Marilú gave them a pep talk, assuring them they could rebuild and that World Vision would help them. She reminded them that even though they had lost so much, they had also learned a great deal during the *sasachakuy tiempo*. There was a murmured acknowledgment that life had changed, and not only for the worse.

"Now we speak up in the assemblies. Before, we didn't even come to the assemblies. We lived spread out and hardly ever came to the pueblo. Now we live *agrupados* [grouped together]."

"Oh, if a neighbor farts you know it right away!" We all laughed. Thin walls might not make for such good neighbors.

"I'm curious—how did you select Eucebio as your president?"

"He was chosen because he has eyes," they explained. "We women, we're illiterate. We look, but our eyes don't see. We're blind."

The conversation wound down as the women noted it was time to begin their cooking fires. As happened in every village I visited during those early years, the women asked for pills—any kind, any color, any size. They ached, their heads throbbed, they felt weak. All Marilú and I had were a few cold tablets, which we distributed to outstretched hands.

Early the next morning people began gathering at one end of the soccer field, in response to Marilú's request for a communal assembly to find out how the rebuilding was coming along and what supplies people needed. After the initial greetings, the men sat to one side of the field and the women clustered on the other. Eucebio tried to call the meeting to order, asking everyone to come near. The men began calling to the women, telling them to get up and come on over so the meeting could begin. After some rustling of skirts, one of the women replied, "Ah, let the pueblo come over to us!"

The men laughed in response to this challenge, and not a single one of them moved. Finally one of the men cried out, "The minority rules. Come over here!"

My head pivoted back to the right, eager to see what the women would volley back. Mama Juliana nonchalantly pulled the thick vein out of a coca leaf, placed the leaf in her mouth and looked straight at the men: "*Manam!* The majority rules here."

Evidently they did, at least in this case. A few awkward moments passed and slowly the men began to stand up. One by one they brushed off their dusty jeans in an effort to shore up their dwindling dignity. They slunk over to where the women were seated. Eucebio shook his head and glanced our way. He winced, and the assembly began.

The following week I met up with Eucebio in the World Vision office in Huamanga. He was rail thin, his jeans hanging on his belt rather than his waist. He lamented, "Can you see how difficult it is for me? The women—oh, they're just a bunch of sleepy, illiterate women! They're lazy! What am I supposed to do?"

Skinny Eucebio felt sorely put upon, in part because he was the laughingstock of all the surrounding communities. When the widows became too unruly in Carhuahurán, it was common for some man to call out, "Why don't they get themselves over to Pallqa where women wear the pants?" With equal frequency another man would add, "Ah, in Pallqa there are lots of widows waiting for their *yapa*" (literally the second helping of food, in this case referring to a second spouse). This exchange inevitably had people doubled over in laughter, and thus Eucebio complained to anyone who stood still long enough to listen.

He continued to complain about the women, adding that his son was not certain he wanted to come back to Pallqa. "He's of two minds now, one from the *campo* and one from the city." Eucebio shrugged. "Besides, he says he likes the girls in the city more. They're cleaner, prettier—you know ...," his voice trailing off.

I just smiled and asked him to explain what was involved in the return process.

"*Bueno*, we had to obtain authorization from the military base at Castropampa. We had to document the attacks we suffered—the confrontations we had with Sendero—and hold assemblies to come to an agreement and sign an Act of Return. I have copies of it here," showing me a slender binder he had slipped under his arm.

We sat down, and Eucebio slid a sheet of paper across the table. "This is our 'Historial de Ataques' [History of Attacks]."

"Would you mind if I copy it down so I don't forget?"

He gave me the go-ahead with a nod.

HISTORY OF ATTACKS

1984: First attack, four dead.
1984: Second attack, burned everything.
1985: Third attack, assassinated families, 42 dead.
1986: Fourth attack.
1986: Fifth attack, killed the men.
1989: Sixth attack, relocated to Huanta.

I thanked him for sharing the document and asked if there was anything else they had to do in order to secure permission to return.

"Well, we had to give them a list of everyone in the community who was going to return, and we had to nominate a Junta Directiva for the *ronda*."

"So you had to make sure you had a *ronda campesina* in order to return?" I asked, thinking about the widows and single women with their whistles sitting in Pallqa's drafty watchtowers at night.

He nodded.

I leaned forward. "Tell me, what made you want to go back to Pallqa?"

"Well, *la vida alto-andina* is very difficult. But we want our pueblo to progress. In our community, we have land and at least we can eat."

At that moment, Victor Bellezza's secretary gestured toward Eucebio, letting him know it was time for his meeting.

I want to piece together my conversation with the women, the "History of Attacks," and all that I would learn about Pallqa over the years. While I ultimately focused on Carhuahurán, Huaychao, and Uchuraccay, the constant movement of people and talk between communities meant that I heard a great deal about Pallqa, and I would visit the community several times.

No matter what sort of math one uses, the numbers and the dates do not add up. The women insisted Sendero Luminoso killed sixteen men when they first attacked because they had refused to accept the guerrillas. However, the "History" indicated four people died during that first attack. This is not about number crunching; it is about memory projects, the politics of mourning, and private transcripts.[17]

In 1995, villagers told me Sendero had been the enemy and that they had suffered terribly for refusing to embrace the insurgents. The "History of Attacks" followed that story line, and the attacks appear in tidy, albeit lethal, chronological order. Given that the "History" had to be approved by the military officials in the base at Castropampa, certain deaths at certain hands were enumerated. Others were silenced—or at least reassigned to the "appropriate" perpetrators.

As I would learn, however, Pallqa had been quite sympathetic to Sendero. According to testimonies given to the PTRC by villagers in surrounding communities, Sendero openly held assemblies in Pallqa until 1985.[18] That year, the army entered and killed a number of men. I do not know how many, but forty-two sounds like a massacre: no massacre was ever reported. While Shining Path did kill members of the community when they met with some initial resistance, it was the army that had widowed most of the women, killing their husbands as alleged Shining Path sympathizers or militants. Thus some widows mourn the community's fallen heroes, while others serve as physical reminders of the guilty dead.[19] Perhaps that helped explain the social divisions than ran as deep as the ravine that enveloped the village.

It may also explain the body language that shadowed our conversation that day in Pallqa. Which widows were legitimized in that "History of Attacks"? Those few who had lost their husbands to the guerrillas. The other deaths appear in the numbers, but their stories were subsumed under the aggregate statistics that allocated blame to Shining Path and thus made it possible for villagers to petition for the right to return to their land. The collective good is frequently paid for with individual sacrifice.

"We can't forget everything that happened. Our fear we can't forget, *and until now we don't want to forget our pain.*" What is that obstinate memory about—that refusal to forget one's pain? The hands that were pressed to aching backs and stomachs; eyes that could look but not see; where does grief settle when it cannot find a home in language?[20] How do women live with losses that are denied, even by members of the communities in which they live? Linda Green, drawing upon her work with war widows in Guatemala, has suggested that bodily symptoms may authorize alternative histories: "The body, as a last resort, has become a repository of both history and memories, much as ancestral land had been before. In this way, the body is an oppositional space, a space of resistance."[21] Communities forge and reforge their memory projects, and these political mythologies seek to govern narrative space and bodily experience. Some widows incorporate the deep differences submerged in the Greek Chorus, tenaciously preserving their pain because aching bodies may be the only permissible testimony to people they loved.

Ñoqayku—the collective voice. This "we" is rife with internal divisions, illustrating the ways in which narratives of violence and narratives of community may be mutually constitutive, both in terms of what is said and what is silenced. Collective memory plays a normative role even within the space of a peasant community, and the widow's bodies are a corporeal index of contradictory orders and levels of obligation. These widows are (counter) memory specialists.[22] In their obstinate memories, they disrupt communal histories and narratives of continuity such as that presented in the "History of Attacks." A seamless history of loss at the hands of the Senderistas is at odds with what the widows know and with the losses many of them privately grieve. Alliances changed along with political conditions; some deaths were commemorated, others relegated not so much to oblivion as to the interior space of the widow's bodies.

Women's Words

I remember sitting around a table in the TRC office in Ayacucho when the commission had recently begun. We were discussing the widows and how they fell into two groups: those who had lost their husbands to the armed forces, and those whose husbands died at the hands of the Senderistas— both narrated as lethal, external forces. As we went through examples from different communities with which we worked, Pallqa among them, the consensus was that the legitimized loss was that which could be attributed to Sendero because there was public space to speak about those deaths. That was true, to a certain extent. I now realize these categories were far too general and static. What counts as "legitimate grief" changes as national and communal histories are revised, underscoring how politically charged public displays of grief can be. There is also another category of widow that is overlooked in the two groups mentioned above: women who watched other members of their communities kill their husbands. There is no anonymity in these deaths. The perpetrators did not arrive; they lived next door, or perhaps just down the path.

The Widow in the Cave

> The population's rejection of widows must be understood symbolically. Their presence
> is the palpable image of a violent, cruel, painful past that they express by their mere
> existence.
> —PTRC, Final Report, 2003

Felícitas is one of the most isolated widows in Uchuraccay, marginal in terms of communal decisions but central as the target of gossip and concern.[23] Other community members killed her husband the same day they killed the journalists and their guide, accusing him of being Sendero's designated *responsable* (representative) in Uchuraccay. Although she had remained publicly silent for some twenty years, it is clear the story she shared with us was one she had repeated throughout the years to her two surviving sons. It was within the context of the truth commission that Señora Felícitas extended her audience beyond the family cooking fire, relating her version of those bloody events in January 1983.

She was tenacious in remembering, recounting the details of that day as though they were replaying before her eyes and down her spine. "Oh, they've told me over and over that I should forget what happened. They've ordered me to forget! They've even threatened to kill me if I talked. They still threaten me." These comments served as the introduction to the first of many conversations we had, always on the same topic: how villagers had killed her husband and their subsequent efforts to silence her.

On that particular afternoon, Edith and I piled onto her bed, tucking her musty blankets around us. Her sons Nerio and Walter—young men of twenty-eight and twenty-three years, respectively—sat across the room. Nerio and Walter had heard this story many times, and yet they listened attentively as their mother began. Perhaps they listened in the hope that if they heard the story enough times, they might finally understand how people who had known their father his entire life had killed him with their bare hands.

January 26, 1983: the day eight journalists and their guide made their way on foot to Uchuraccay, en route to Huaychao to investigate the death of seven Senderistas. Villagers reacted within the logic of war, convinced the visitors were a group of guerrillas coming to attack. When the villagers closed in around the journalists and their guide, it was Felícitas's husband, Segundo Quispe, who tried to intervene. He insisted it would be better to turn the journalists in to the police in Huanta. His intervention led the other *campesinos* to deduce that Segundo was also a *terruco*. He kept trying to convince his fellow villagers they were mistaken, but they did not believe him and insisted Segundo had accompanied the *terrucos* as they arrived in Uchurraccay.[24] They deliberated, and decided to kill him along with the others.

"Mama Felícitas, how many . . . how many people participated?" I struggled to find some delicate way of asking a horrible question. I kept moving my hands as though somehow I could convey the question without having to say the words—coax out a response without verbally asking something so painful. I finally placed my hands firmly on my thighs. "I mean, how many people here killed your husband?"

"Oh, it must have been thirty people. It was as though I was sleepwalking. I didn't realize what they were saying, doing. It was like I was in a dream. My husband was already dead—he was a cadaver. His eyes were hanging out, his blood was running everywhere across the ground. They killed him. They used rocks, rocks that looked like hatchets. They smashed his head with those rocks. His intestines were falling out, his insides were falling out."

She was speaking quickly, her words one step ahead of her tears. Felícitas kept clutching her skirt in her hands, rubbing her face, drying her eyes. She took a deep breath, and then another. "What were they killing him with? I asked myself. I didn't realize what was happening because I had *susto*. It seemed as though they were hanging him. So I went below, but my *comadre* told me, 'Get out of here. They're going to kill you.' I thought I should stay— if they killed me, so they killed me." Doña Felícitas shrugged her shoulders and wept softly. "But they killed my husband," she added.

Edith and I hesitated. "Do you mind telling us how they killed him?"

She nodded. "That Juan—they tied him [her husband] behind his mule. So the mule dragged him all over the ground. But when he didn't die they stuck him with a knife. Here in his stomach," holding her hand to her abdomen. "His intestines came falling out, his eyes came out to here," gesturing with her hand held several inches from her face. "That's how I found him. There was so much blood. Seeing all that, *hukmanmi karqani* [I was of another form]. They kept asking me, 'Where are you going to complain? Who are you going to complain to? Which one of us are you going to denounce?' Asking me that over and over, they cornered me. They had hatchets in their hands, rope in their hands, knives in their hands. 'You're going to die, too,' they shouted."

Felícitas suddenly sat upright, dropping her skirt around her. She spat out the words: "'So you're going to kill me! Go ahead—kill me! Two of my children are with their uncle, here are three more at my side. Get all my children together, and kill us all at once. Kill me with all of my children!' I kept asking them, 'Who will care for my children? Where will my children live? Kill me together with all of my children!'" Felícitas shook her head and clutched her hands to her chest. "Oh, I was sobbing when I said that. 'Kill us all together. If we must die, then we'll all die together!' I kept shouting that over and over again." She fell silent, looking at her sons.

"Oh mama Felícitas, I'm so sorry. What did you do then?" I asked.

Mama Felícitas took another deep breath and wound the folds of her skirt tightly around the fingers of her left hand. "Well, there was a woman there while all of this was happening, my aunt Teodosia. So she spoke up, 'Why are you killing everyone like this—killing them as though they were worms? All of you, at least pardon this woman! What guilt does this woman have? The man, he's the guilty one. He's the one who was talking about who knows what with these visitors [the journalists]. Not the woman! Who's going to take care of these children? If you kill her, then you'll have to kill them all. If they have to die, then you'll have to kill them all!' That's what Teodosia said. So then they all started talking. 'Should we pardon her?' they asked. Some people answered, 'Let's pardon her,' but others said, 'No, we can't pardon her. We need to kill her.' Oh, my children were trembling. They went crazy. It was as though I was in a dream, just thinking, so I'm going to die. But then they said, 'We're going to pardon you. But you'll never talk. You'll go nowhere. You'll always stay here with all of us watching you. If you ever go to any authority to denounce us, we'll kill you. You'll end up like your husband—dead.' I was so afraid that I escaped to the *puna*. The Argumedos [the family of the guide who was killed] looked for me. 'Where is Segundo Quispe's widow?' they asked. Oh they were looking for me. But I was nowhere. I escaped to the *puna* with my children, carrying my littlest ones. I was there—chewing coca, living on water—we had no food. No one came. They burned down my house, just the walls were left. Sometimes at night I would come back down to cook, but the children wouldn't eat. Only the tiniest ones could eat," gesturing toward Nerio and Walter, who nodded without saying a word. "The rest of us, we couldn't eat. Oh, it was like I was in a dream. I wasn't *runa* [a human being] anymore."

It was not only doña Felícitas who saw her husband's cadaver but her children as well. "Because of the *llakis* we had when my husband died, from crying so much, my children went crazy. My children saw how they killed their father. So ever since then, it was as though they were sleepwalking [*muspaypi qina*], and they cried. With *llakis*, they had no appetite."

"So they died from *llakis*?" asked Edith.

She nodded. "*Llakis*. One of them also died from *susto* because the soldiers chased us, firing their guns. We were also afraid of the *puriqkuna* [the Senderistas, literally 'those who walk']. So three of my children died." She struggled to dry the tears that were rolling down her face.

"They all died?"

She nodded. "They became sickly and died. They went crazy. Surely God took them so they wouldn't suffer anymore. They were so sick with *llakis*! They didn't eat and finally my children died. So young to die!"

We were all silent for what seemed like several minutes. The only sound was the wind rattling the *calaminas*. When she was ready, mama Felícitas began again.

"They didn't want me to denounce them. I never said anything because they kept telling me, 'If you talk, you're going to die. Just like your husband—if you denounce any of us, you'll die.' So I never said anything, not even when people came looking for me. When the helicopter came for the cadavers, they all told me, 'Get lost! Hide yourself!' They made me hide in the mountains, in a cave. They made me stay in the cave, with just my children. I was sure they'd kill me. I kept asking them, 'But who'll take care of my children?' With my children sobbing, we had to escape to the mountains, hide in the cave. I lived in that cave. I never denounced anyone. I never said a word. Finally, when my children were grown up," pointing to Nerio and Walter, "they asked me outright, 'Mama, why did you never talk? Why didn't you denounce them? Why didn't you go with the soldiers? Look at us—we're poor, we never went to school, maybe you could've got a *garantía* [a guarantee, issued to ensure one's safety]. Then we could have gone anywhere and gone to school.' I've thought about it so many times! Maybe I could have gone in the helicopter with my children. They could have taken me—oh, just anywhere. I think maybe then my children would have studied. I think of this now and it weighs down so heavily on me."

Felícitas slumped again into the layers of her tattered skirts. She just stared at her two sons as her tears kept falling. Edith and I searched our pockets; we simply had to come up with some concrete form of solace. I finally grabbed my backpack and found a roll of Suave. I handed mama Felícitas a wad of bright blue toilet paper, but she just stared at the wad in her hand. Finally she blinked, and lifted the paper to her face to dry her tears.

Whenever I think of mama Felícitas, I imagine her shut away in that cave, enclosed in a private realm of hurt and rage. Her words were so dangerous that she was hidden from view when people came asking about what had happened that bloody day in 1983. The boundaries of the speakable were literally enforced, and Felícitas was confronted with irreconcilable social imperatives. How was she to honor her conflicting obligations—to the memory of her dead husband, to the community that was both the source of her suffering as well as her livelihood, and to her two surviving sons? In short, whom would she betray and with what consequences?

Felícitas's husband was killed and buried like an animal in a shallow hole rather than within the community's cemetery. He was indeed a member of Shining Path, and the villagers of Uchuraccay had taken a collective stance against the guerrillas. Had Felícitas made her way to the police station in Huanta she might have succeeded in setting into motion an investigation into Segundo's murder—or he might well have been considered just one more dead peasant, and a "guilty one" at that. If the police had inquired into his death, the community would have responded in the collective voice, as they did regarding the dead journalists. The community as a whole assumed responsibility for the killing, carried out because they thought the journalists were *terrucos* arriving to attack them. Moreover, when peasants in the neighboring community of Huaychao killed seven Senderistas, the Peruvian president had praised the villagers for their bravery in defense of La Patria. Could Segundo's widow have denounced his killers while still narrating some sort of honorable death for him? What narrative options did she have? Should she look to the past and speak, or to the future and remain silent? Was she foremost a widow or a mother? Surviving in such circumstances required the capacity to turn the truth inward, consuming her grief rather than allowing it to consume her.

Arthur Kleinman asks, "When there is real uncertainty about what to do and when the level of danger is high enough to threaten what really matters to us, what kinds of decisions do we make?"[25] Mama Felícitas had lived with her decision for twenty years. When she described how heavily that decision had weighed on her, I hoped her sons would assure their mother that she had done the right thing. They did not. I cannot deny the anger I felt looking at them, grown men safely standing across the room in disapproving judgment of their mother's "failure" to denounce the people who had killed their father. She had already buried a husband and three other children. For Felícitas, remaining in the community and betraying a sense of duty to her dead husband was an attempt to assure a viable future for her two surviving sons. They would be able to work the family's land and participate as *comuneros* in communal life. "Mama, why did you never talk? Why didn't you denounce them?" That her sons were alive to pose those questions was all she had to show for twenty years of emotional labor. With her silence the widow in the cave had fulfilled her maternal obligations the best way she knew how.

Economies of War and Reconstruction

> The internal armed conflict Peru experienced between 1980 and 2000 was the longest, most intense and, in human and economic terms, the costliest episode of violence in the entire history of the Republic.
> —PTRC, Final Report, 2004

In the section of the PTRC's Final Report on the impact of the internal armed conflict, the staggering consequences of the violence register on every level. The testimonies given to the commission lament the loss of life, labor power, infrastructure, and social solidarity.[26] Of the deaths and disappearances reported to the TRC, the majority were men between the ages of eighteen and thirty-four.[27] The lack of male labor power reverberated throughout the rural economy; in many conversations with women, they recalled the *sasa-chakuy tiempo* as a period of "great sacrifice, at times becoming both man and woman, father and mother." Between the death toll and the estimated six hundred thousand people internally displaced from the primary conflict zones, hundreds of peasant communities lay in ruins. The image of *pueb-los fantasmas* (ghost towns) appears repeatedly in villagers' descriptions of their communities.

These profound economic changes have material and affective consequences. Kay Warren has suggested that "High theory aside, class is not a separable domain but rather a multidimensional form of stratification that is in practice often gendered, racialized, and saturated with cultural difference. For instance, as a result of the genocidal civil war in Guatemala, impoverished rural widows became a distinctive political-economic class—the result of Mayan family structure, agrarian sexual division of labor, and the violent repression that killed their husbands and left these women without a subsistence base."[28] In Ayacucho, *warmisapas* do constitute one of the poorest sectors in these communities, and widows also lament the loneliness that weighs down on them. I recall elderly women in Cayara and Tiqui-hua, drunk and passed out in the street, their skirts rank with urine. It was Saturnina who sobbed, "There is no one in my house. I don't want to eat when there's no one there. Sometimes I don't eat because when I'm alone, I remember the people who used to be at my side and how I would serve them my soup." So while exploring the ambivalence of the *warmisapas*, I want to hold present the bitter poverty and loneliness that is one facet of their lives, and how the increased poverty produced by the war has restricted forms of compassion that previously served as a cushion for vulnerable members of these communities.[29]

"Old Women with No Strength"

Izcarceta is one of many widows in Carhuahurán. Her husband died shortly after they returned from a stay in Lima. Her daughter had insisted her parents leave Carhuahurán during the war and come to stay with her in the capital. "The *terrucos* had burned everything here—they burned our house. My daughter insisted we come to Lima." Izcarceta shook her head. "I couldn't get used to Lima. Besides we'd left our harvest here, so we came back. But when we got here, my husband's stomach swelled up—he died two or three days later. He told me, 'Once you've buried me, you can't stay here. Go to Lima where our children can take care of you.' When I finished a year [of mourning] my daughter tried to get me to come to Lima again. I told her it was too hot! So she decided to rent a house in Huamanga."

Izcarceta spent two months in Huamanga with her daughter. This time it wasn't the heat that drove her back: she just wanted to be home. But home was difficult, too. "I live like I'm in the street, with nothing. We're like *forasteros* [strangers] here, like you're not really in your village."

I just looked at her, thinking of how she slowly made her way up the steep slope from the river each day, buckets of water pulling at her weary arms.

"Mama, do people help the widows here?"

"*Manam*! No. Oh, people here are totally different," she lamented.

"Did people help *warmisapas* before?"

Izcarceta nodded, "Before people had *caridad* [charity, compassion]. They cared about the women with many children—they worked for them. They would carry wood, on their animals they would bring wood. Now, the young people—they loathe old women with no strength."

"Why did people change? What happened?"

Izcarceta shrugged. "They say they don't have time. 'We're too busy,' they say. We have to pay ten *soles* a day for someone to work our land.[30] Where is a *warmisapa* going to get that sort of money? When all you have to drink are your tears, how can you pay that?"

The theme of *caridad* and how little there was left figured heavily in our conversation. Izcarceta veered between sadness and indignation. I wanted to hear more, so I posed a question in the rhetorical register. "Mama Izcarceta, do the older women participate in the work here?"

She sat upright. "*Awriki*. Of course! Look at the school," she pointed. "Look at that wall," pointing again with a skinny finger. "We've always helped. We didn't say, 'Oh, we're women so we're just going to sit down right here!'" We had a good laugh at the thought of the women lounging around in a lazy heap.

The midday sun beamed across the room as she described how things used to be. "People always used to help. At the end of the day they would help on our land."

This reminded me of a conversation I'd had with a professor at the University of Huamanga. Fredy Ferrua had told me about certain practices that disappeared during the war, and one he had mentioned was *miskipay*. "Mama, I've heard there was something called '*miskipay*.' What is *miskipay*?"

Izcarceta nodded, recognizing the word. She explained that during the workday, the men take breaks and chew coca while they rest. "You need to feel the taste [of the coca]. In the afternoon you chew [coca], during the day another and in the early morning another. This is how they work, chewing coca." The wads of coca chewed at different times of the day mark shifts in work, and *miskipay* was the wad of coca chewed after the last break to give the men a bit of extra energy to put in some time on the widow's land. *Miskipay* was one form of *caridad* the wartime economy had snuffed out.

Every sentiment has a history, and *caridad* certainly does.[31] Everything was scarce following the war; only suffering was abundant. People had "hardened their hearts" to withstand that suffering, and hardening one's heart also implied constricting the compassion one could feel for others. Emotions, morality, and concepts of justice are not atemporal, outside the historical, political, and economic contexts in which people live. In a restricted economy, compassion is also limited.[32]

Additionally, social relationships were increasingly monetized and women, particularly *warmisapas*, had less access to wage-paying labor. Such labor was generally reserved for men and traditionally included seasonal migration either to the coca plantations of the *selva* or to the coastal cities between planting and harvesting seasons in the highlands. Women, charged with caring for children, had less mobility. This pattern was accentuated by various construction projects that followed the war, for example, building the highway or the schoolhouse. Men were paid ten *soles* a day for working on the highway project; on the schoolhouse project, they received food. Women were not considered suitable for either one.

The projects that did arrive for women in the early postwar years included garden crops and small animals such as guinea pigs and chickens. Oh, the death toll of those little creatures was staggering! Somehow the organizations selected animals that died quickly in the highlands, but not before women had tried in vain to save them—and the local animals they infected before they died. We were never certain what went so wrong so frequently; when in a joking mood, women attributed the little animals' untimely demise to *sorroche* (altitude sickness).

It was a conversation with the widow Margarita that captured these tensions and illustrated the fallacy of assuming that postconflict reconstruction assistance is fairly distributed among the presumed beneficiaries.[33] Aid frequently resulted in increased social stratification as certain "natural leaders" of the community were routinely selected to participate in trainings, elaborate project priorities, and speak on behalf of their villages. These "natural leaders" were adept to begin with and consolidated their local standing by skillfully managing resources. These men—and their wives, whose names were the first ones mentioned when state entities or NGOs wanted to ensure that "women" were represented—were important brokers, distributing aid via local patronage systems. Most *warmisapas* were peripheral to this distribution, as mama Margarita explained.

"Not Equal to a Man"

Margarita Maulle would often come by around midday, drawn by the promise of a bowl of soup or tuna with noodles. She was one of the poorest widows in Carhuahurán because she had no immediate family. She had come from Huaychao as an in-marrying daughter-in-law years before. Her clothes were always tattered and I could count her remaining teeth on the fingers of my two hands.

"How did your husband die, mama Margarita?"

"The *puriqkuna* killed him. So I was left alone here. He was still young when they killed him. I just have my little grandson now."

"How many children do you have?"

"None." As she explained, her little grandson was the son of one of her cousins. Margarita had been given the boy to raise, a common practice in Andean communities.[34]

"Why did the *puriqkuna* kill your husband?"

"They said he was an authority so they killed him. He was a hardworking man, not like some of those who don't do anything. But he wasn't an authority. They came for him at night. We were both sick and didn't hear a thing. Well, right there at the head of our bed we heard them yell, '*Compañero!*' We had a fierce dog but it didn't even bark!'"

"Were the *puriqkuna* already hated here?"

"Not yet, but people were already talking. We didn't know what to believe."

"What were people saying?"

"'*Terrucos* are going to come here,' they said. What's a *terruco*, we wondered? We thought it was all a bunch of lies. They said *terrucos* would arrive in great numbers to kill us. But we thought, *how could people who are like us kill us*?" Margarita laughed as she remembered how she and her husband had doubted what they heard. I thought of her fierce dog that did not make a sound that night.

"So that's what happened. When we were sick in bed they came for my husband. 'We're going to have an assembly here in the pueblo,' they said. They came around to round up all of the neighbors. They'd brought them from all around. I was so sick, but I grabbed my cane and my niece and we followed behind them. Ay! There was no pueblo left—all of the houses had been burned down!"

"So the *puriqkuna* already hated this pueblo?"

"I guess so. They must have. As a woman, I didn't know anything. I never really came to the pueblo. I was just in my *chacra*. Women—we didn't come to the pueblo, just the men."

"Why didn't the women come to the assemblies?"

Margarita shrugged. "We were with our animals, we had so much cooking to do. Just the men went to assemblies."

"Ok—so what if the men stay with the animals and the women go to assemblies?"

Margarita held her hands over her mouth and laughed. "I don't think that would be very good. How are we women going to talk? We can't talk like the men. If we talk, they wouldn't believe what we say. They say we talk like crazy people!"

"Is it true?"

"Well, sometimes some women talk and they don't get it right. They talk as though they're asleep! They leave the themes to one side and forget all about them."

"Hmmm. I wonder—do you ever dream about your husband?"

A smile brightened her face. "Of course. Dreaming with him is good."

"Do the two of you talk in your dreams?"

She nodded. "We talk. He'll say, 'We're going to work in the *chacra*, so you need to look for some workers so they can help us.' He talks to me like that."

"Do you miss him?"

"Yes, especially in work. He was so hardworking. They killed him for no reason at all."

"In your dreams, does he warn you if something bad might happen?" I wondered.

She nodded. "Of course. I'm always dreaming with him."

"When do you remember him most—think about him the most?"

"In work. Or when someone invites me to eat, or to come over and cook together. Also when the work is hard. Like now—I was planting alone and it was so hard."

"Did no one offer to help you?"

"*Manam*, mama. It was just like when I needed to re-roof my house; I couldn't find anyone to help me. They don't even want to give me *calaminas*!"

"But why?"

"They only divide them up between the men and because I can't work like a man—they tell me, 'You aren't equal to a man.'"

"But don't the *warmisapas* help with community projects?"

"*Bueno*, I go. The *warmisapas*, we go to help. It just happened to me again yesterday. I went to work because they said there'd be food. I thought maybe they might give me some, so I went to help. I brought some of my *ichu*. I even left my *ichu* when they told me I couldn't work like a man. So I went home."

"So they tell you that you aren't filling your husband's place, not doing the work like he would have?"

Margarita nodded. "They say, 'Señora, the food is only for those with strength.'"

"Is life always so hard for a *warmisapa*, mama Margarita?"

"Oh, it's difficult! We cry sometimes. You don't have any wood, you don't have any food, you've run out of salt, all the money you have fits in the palm of your hand. It's only the men—when they work, they bring back money."

"This is so unfair! And before the violence, did you have to pay for workers?"

"*Manam*—it was *ayni* [reciprocal labor exchange]. Now everything is money. Oh, this life is changing."

"Is it because of the *sasachakuy tiempo* that everything is changing?"

"Why would it be? I suppose so. They say that everything that's happening, it's because Dios Tayta is angry."

"Yes, I've heard people say that. Tell me, I know it's difficult being a *warmisapa*, but is it only difficult? I mean, are there times when you can be calmer—not arguing with a husband like so many of the women complain about?"

"Oh yes," Margarita nodded emphatically. "You can be *tranquila*—like now you can just sit and talk because if you have a husband you can't even sit down! Plus, without a husband you can go visit your family, your friends. You can take your time being with them. You can also laugh, *chakchar* [chew] coca."

"If married women walked around joking and laughing, what would happen?"

"Oh, they could just start saying anything about you. They would sure start to talk! They'd say you're flirtatious."

"So sometimes being a widow is not such a bad thing?"

Margarita shrugged. "Yeah. Mostly it's difficult with work. You just can't do it. And when *warmisapas* work, the production isn't the same. Men can dig deeper with the *chakitaklla* [foot hoe] while women just use a *lampita* [handheld hoe]. We don't plant as deeply so the roots are shallow and don't grow as well."

"I've also heard some people say the earth is a woman—Pachamama. They told me that Pachamama likes it better when the men work."[35]

"Oh yes, it's Pachamama that conceives. When a woman works, it's not the same. Because the earth is mother, when a woman works—when a *warmisapa* works—the earth can't conceive."

How often I heard the expression "old women with no strength." Reconstruction efforts tended to focus on infrastructure, perhaps with good reason given the level of physical destruction. However, in focusing on infrastructure and assuming that the communal counterpart to donated materials would be manual labor, these projects excluded the *warmisapas*. These interventions seemed to operate on a "trickle-down" approach that assumed providing aid to communities would benefit all members of the collective, failing to consider how the type of assistance provided might exclude the most marginal members of these communities.[36]

Rebuilding was associated with strength, defined as physical, masculine strength. This was explicitly juxtaposed with the lack of strength attributed to the widows. *Warmisapas* were relegated to the "unproductive" category and thus peripheral to the benefits that were one result of the role the northern communities had played in defeating Sendero. Women's labor was undervalued in the best of times; these were not the best of times. Many people saw the widows, together with the orphans, as burdens—particularly widows and orphans who were reminders of shifting allegiances and occult histories of the war.

However, I return to the contradictory effects of the violence. If you, the reader, see only tragedy in the iconic figure of The War Widow, then I have failed to adequately depict these women. Reflecting on her work in India, Veena Das has written, "But to be vulnerable is not the same as to be a victim, and those who are inclined to assume that social norms or expectations of widowhood are automatically translated into oppression need to pay attention to the gap between a norm and its actualization."[37] I heartily agree. There is much more to say about the *warmisapas*.

Changing Times

> In my time, parents didn't permit their girls to go to school. They always said, "If you want to go, then take your animals with you." Before and even now, girls work more in the family, washing clothes, cooking, caring for animals, gathering wood. Before it was even worse because people thought life was going to stay the same. But that's not how it is. After, we realized this and realized that today and in the future, life is for the *ñawiyuqkuna* [those who have eyes/vision/education]. This difference came after *los accidentes* [the war]. Now both girls and boys study, they even finish primary school. Now they have us as examples of ignorance, of how they should not be.
> —Teodora Huamán, twenty-six years old, Macabamba (a returning community in the highlands of Huanta), 1999

"In my time," uttered as though an elderly grandmother were recounting tales from some distant past. Jarring words when spoken by a twenty-six-year-old woman. People frequently insisted time had accelerated, particularly for those who had been internally displaced to the cities and subsequently returned to their communities. If "returning community" invokes a sense of returning to "how things were before," then the term is misleading. Returning meant going back to one's land but with new ideas of how life should be.

A recurring theme in the highlands of Huanta was "Now we are going to live as civilized people." This phrase reflected both an internalization of racism on behalf of the rural population as well as a desire to partake of the sorts of services that previously existed only in urban settings. Spatial practices changed drastically during the violence as people began living in nucleated settlements for security purposes. While challenging in terms of increased social proximity and flatulent neighbors, living in more populated centers made the provision of services more feasible. Communal authorities worked with engineers to draw up their "urbanistic plans," which inevitably included a central park, straight streets, a schoolhouse, potable water, electricity, and a highway—always a highway, symbol of movement and modernity. Throughout the highlands villagers clamored for "the progress and development of our village." This language of civilization and modernity is a demand for material equality and change.[38] New spatial practices, increased migratory experience, the arrival of domestic and international NGOs, an increased state presence following the internal armed conflict, new roles assumed during the violence: yes, times had changed, as had certain assumptions about gender.

"Ancient Time"

Mama Dionisia came by for late afternoon *miski yaku*, a welcome heat source during the freezing month of June.[39] I was delighted to hear Dionisia calling from the doorway because she was always lively and up for a chat.

I had been trying to make sense of the widows and it was puzzling. I wondered what Dionisia thought. I remember how surprised I had been to learn she had a husband: I never saw him and she rarely mentioned him. She was far more interested in talking about God. But that afternoon, I was intent on trying to understand what seemed to be an utter lack of support for Carhuahurán's *warmisapas*.

"Mama Dionisia, there are lots of widows here, no?"

"Oh, lots of them."

"Why don't the authorities help the *warmisapas*?"

She shrugged. "I don't know. They have to look for workers, pay them to work."

"Should the authorities help them?"

"Of course they should. They've suffered so much, especially the widows who have no family members here."

I nodded in agreement. "I've also noticed that in the Sunday *formaciones*, hardly any married women attend. Why don't they go?"

"Well, here some women live far away from their *chacras* and so they can't get together for the meetings. But whenever there is a call from Huanta or something, there we are. You know, some of us are just *conformistas*—some women don't think about things and don't realize how much has changed. There are new laws now and they don't even realize it and just go on living like we did in *antiguo tiempo* [ancient time, in this case referring to the period before the violence]. That's why they just go to their *chacras*. And when some women attend the *formaciones*, other women start talking about them. For them, their whole life is just living here in the pueblo and they don't think about anything else. So they criticize those of us who go."

"So some of the married women want to go to the *formaciones*?"

Her eyebrows arched sharply upward. "Of course! I always want to go. On Sundays they talk about everything and we want to hear, to listen. Then we know what's happening in reality. But some of the women, the sun isn't even up and they're already in their *chacras*," she scoffed. "They don't know about anything. They live like they did in *antiguo tiempo*."

"So some of you keep up on what's happening?"

Dionisia nodded. "When we get together in the Mother's Club, we just keep giving our opinion! We tell the other women that we should participate in the *formaciones* because we aren't living in the *antiguo tiempo* anymore. After all that terror everyone needs to participate, both the men and the women. We should all work together, turning night into day. Maybe then we can get ahead."

"Do you still worry about the violence—that it could come back?"

"Of course! We're always on alert. In the *tiempo de peligro* [time of danger] we were always on the alert."

"What would you do if the *tiempo de peligro* returns?"

"We'll be crying—so much crying! But that's why I say we all need to learn how to use a rifle. *This is not like in antiguo tiempo—everything is changing, just like the time.*"

Using *antiguo tiempo* to refer to the prewar years is a powerful index for gauging the experiential dimension of these many changes. I am not constructing a "before and after story"; however, many villagers do because that best captures how it feels to have lived through massive change. Dionisia had moved with her husband from Pera to Carhuahurán during the violence for security purposes, as had many of the other villagers living in Carhuahurán. Although this meant a long walk to their *chacras*, it also meant being centrally located. These new spatial configurations made it more possible for women to participate in communal assemblies, although not all of them were interested in doing so. Indeed, the *conformistas* did not attend and criticized the women who did. However, although most married women could and did opt out of attending the assemblies, this was not the case with the *warmisapas*. As the recognized heads of household who represent their families in communal affairs, widows are required to attend. While some sat quietly to the side, some did not. Mama Asunta was proud to be one of those who did not.

"With Our Words"

Two *colectivos* (minivans) arrived with passengers returning from Huanta.[40] The children who lived around the large field came running, interested in knowing who and what arrived. Mama Benedicta also drew near and kept shaking her head.

"What is it?" I asked.

"I've lived to see cars arriving in Carhuahurán. I never thought I'd see this—never believed I would see such a thing," she replied. Mama Benedicta walked over to the edge of the field to sit down, contemplating what her own eyes could scarcely believe.

Several schoolteachers stepped out from one of the *colectivos*. They had headed down to Huanta to pick up their checks, turning payday into their standard one-week escape from classes. A truck also arrived with the school breakfasts provided by the government. Another truck pulled in not long thereafter, chartered by "Project Women" from the NGO Llaqtanchikta Qatarichisun. The personnel climbed out of the truck, bringing sixty guinea pigs and some alfalfa with them. "Project Women" was geared toward workshops about the collective raising of chickens and guinea pigs, and included sessions on women's rights.

Asunta, a *warmisapa*, watched it all and told me what she thought about the workshops. "Participating in these workshops, you learn many things. The men should listen to women, between the two they need to talk. Sometimes, the men really beat their wives. Me, now I go to the assemblies and I speak up. I complain about how the authorities are spending money! That's the good thing about us, the *warmisapas*. Even if we must sacrifice, they're always having us participate in the meetings, in the *faenas*. We learn about what the men are doing and we have a chance to participate—to participate with our words. But the married women, they're always in their houses or with their animals. Ha, when we go to these trainings, the men say we're just going to learn to complain. They say, '*Carajo*—go ahead and complain. Just see what they can do to me!' The men talk, saying the women must be getting advice. That's why some of the women can't talk to their husbands about their rights—they don't believe in them. That's why it would be good if they trained the men, too, about women's rights so they can understand. But I don't ask for this. Let some of them with husbands ask."

As Asunta illustrates, the *warmisapas* participate in communal spaces where married women are usually absent. They listen to the debates in the assemblies, the *formaciones*, and, at times, they "participate with words." They hear the debates in the flesh rather than receiving a summary or interpretation from a husband. While they do not participate on equal footing with the men, they do weigh in with their opinions. At times this weighing in occurs on the margins as the widows marshal public opinion via a complex network of gossip.

A recurring figure in weavings and ceramics sold throughout Ayacucho is Las Chismosas (The Gossiping Women). Three women are depicted sitting in a circle, with their faces either turned away from the viewer or hidden beneath their hats as they bow their heads and murmur among themselves. Las Chismosas are omnipresent in this artwork, just as gossip is omnipresent in these communities.

The term for gossip in Quechua is *simi apaykachay*—*simi* is "mouth" and *apaykachay* is a verb meaning "to lead, to conduct, to transport something from here to there." Gossip refers to using one's mouth to move something—to direct something or someone—from one place or condition to another. Women, particularly widows, are key figures in both the artistic representations and daily practice of gossip. Oh, how communal authorities worried about controlling the *warmisapas* and the words they murmured about everyone and everything. Recall the mayor who looked over at the widows sitting on the sidelines during the communal assembly held in preparation for former President Toledo's visit. As he insisted, "Watch it—we don't want any of the women saying things that aren't certain." Perhaps an even greater concern was that they might say something that was "certain"—but censored. From the assembly in Pallqa and the "majority that rules," to the nervous authorities trying to control the women seated on the sidelines, to the focus group in which the men told the women to shut up—with their words, *las chismosas* threaten to shake things up.

Asunta also spoke about rights, another realm in which gender relations are unsettled. The theme of women's rights and organizing spread in rural Ayacucho during the violence, one component of the broader discourse of human rights. Women went searching for missing loved ones and in the process began socializing individual losses. Confronted with the dual challenges of armed conflict and increased poverty, women began organizing and "politicizing motherhood." As the members of the Mother's Club in Purus explained, "We were so sad because we couldn't feed our children well. Our children cried for food, and it's the mother who must do something." And they did.

Isabel Coral has analyzed the important roles women played in civic organizations that addressed survival needs during the internal armed conflict. From the Mother's Clubs and "soup kitchens" to the glass-of-milk committees, rural women and women on the urban peripheries entered new social spaces in an effort to access resources and fulfill their gendered obligations under conditions of extreme duress. While these organizations were founded in response to state-sponsored social welfare programs that were paternalistic in nature, they provided rural women with an apprenticeship in organizing to access state resources and services.[41] For many rural women, this interaction with the state was a novelty. For instance, one afternoon mama Juanita in Huaychao described how she saw the government.

"*Bueno*, I look at it like my parents. When we need something—any sort of thing—we can go to our parents if they're living, saying, 'Papa, Mama, I don't have anything to eat! I don't have any money. Give me something please.' Saying something like that, no?"

"And with the government, what was it like before the violence?"

She thought for a moment and shrugged. "How would it have been? I don't really know about that. Was there a government back then? I couldn't really say for sure if there was or not."

In addition to making the state present in women's lives, these collective spaces provided human rights and feminist organizations with a "ready-made" channel for introducing the theme of women's rights. This discourse can be one resource for expressing grievances and pressing claims, particularly for "unruly" widows who had no man at home telling them to stay there. It was another conversation with mama Juanita that powerfully illustrated these themes.

This morning the sun forgot to rise over Huaychao.[42] It was always a pleasure to feel the heat of the sun against one's face or back after a night of intense cold. We cranked up our gas stove to boil water and recaffeinate ourselves into an upright position.

Verticality achieved, Edith and I headed off to talk with Juanita Cabezas, one of our favorite people. She lived just the other side of the small creek that runs through Huaychao, and the muddy planks of wood that served as a footbridge let us off just a few feet from her house. We knocked on the door and her smiling face greeted us. She took each of us by the hand, inviting us to sit next to the warmth of her cooking fire.

Juanita is a youthful widow, probably around thirty-five years old. She is known for being active in community affairs and for her *don de hablar* (gift for speaking). On this particular morning she began complaining about the inability of the village authorities to resolve problems. We were eager to hear more about the resolution of conflicts. "When there are problems here, what do the authorities do?"

She snorted. "When we notify the authorities they don't say anything, even when I was hit. A woman yelled at me, 'You shit, who do you think you are? Right now we're going to kill you, you shit.' Three women had joined up and the other grabbed me when I tried to answer. The other kicked me and knocked me to the ground."

We were shocked. "Why? What did they say?"

Juanita stopped peeling potatoes long enough to throw her hands up in disgust. "Just nonsense! That woman has a cousin. So she must have said, 'Ooooooh, that Juanita is trying to take him.' That's what she must have thought. She thought, 'That shit, the damn pain in the neck. I'm gonna grab her and beat her, that slut!' Juanita stopped waving her knife around and returned to peeling potatoes. "*Mami*, if your brother were talking to someone, would you try to stop him? If you had a cousin, when he talked to someone, would you try to stop him?"

"No, mama Juanita." I knew better than to disagree with someone holding a knife in her hand.

"Of course not! If I had a cousin and he talked to someone, I wouldn't stop him. But that's why they hit me when we were in this party. They said, 'You shit! Bitch, I'm going to beat you right now.' So I went to complain to the authorities, because authority is not a game. Authorities are to respect. But when I said let's go to the authorities, she yelled back, "Shut up! Damn, what a shit you are! You're all old, walking around all tired out. Pretending to be young—you keep trying to walk well.' That's how it is. When you walk by, they look at you to see if you're walking well or walking sick. God knows our lives, knows how we are. With our body we walk, even dirty. When we have time to bathe, we bathe—but if you don't have time, you can't."

"Plus it's so cold," added Edith.

"Of course! Too cold! But those with husbands don't know the lives of the widows. Them, they make their husbands work. Those married women just wash, cook, and afterward they sit in their houses taking care of their children—with their children they just sit around. But for us *warmisapas*— Ha! There's never enough time to even bathe. We have to work. We don't have wood, we don't have food. So our time isn't the same as theirs, and theirs isn't the same as ours. Married women have one time, and the *warmisapas* have another time that is totally different. Our lives are different."

"And what would help you?" I asked.

Juanita thought for a moment. "Well, that's why I wonder how to meet up with the truth commission. I'd say that we *warmisapas* want to live in our rights. The women who spend their lives married, they have rights, and us with our lives as widows, we want to have rights. But with respect because if there isn't respect then just anyone can hit you—younger or older people can hit you. But with our rights we can make them respect us. Now, even the trees each have their names, whether it's eucalyptus, alder, or cypress— that's how they're in their rights. So we widows want to be in our rights, too."

Mama Juanita demonstrates how a global discourse, in this case human rights, can be reworked in locally meaningful language. A proliferation of NGOs began working in rural Ayacucho during the second half of the 1990s, and "women's rights are human rights" was one of their messages. This language was picked up by many women in their ongoing efforts to protest inequality and abuses at the communal level. The discourse of human rights had "extra-local" resonance, and the "extra-local" had traditionally been used by men to bolster their prestige. I think of this as "traveling power" because communal authorities were often said to "walk for the good of their communities," referring to their efforts to secure projects and services from different state and nongovernmental entities in the city. For women to invoke a language that "came from elsewhere" was an attempt to move beyond the indifference of local authorities to gendered complaints and demands for justice.

Sally Merry has called this local reworking "vernacularization."[43] For Juanita, human rights were vernacularized in an arboreal idiom. Just as "tree" is a category encompassing great diversity, with each type of tree bearing its own characteristics, ecological niche, and name, so is "woman" a category that must be disaggregated to understand the diversity of women's lives. Juanita provided powerful examples of the different needs women have following armed conflicts and how these needs may place them at odds with one another. Able-bodied men were in short supply, and the women who beat Juanita were not about to let her make off with their male cousin. She was a rival for his manual labor, which was probably more threatening than any claim she might make on his amorous attention. Juanita knew she was being sized up by other women, accused of being old and weak yet trying to pass herself off as a healthy, vigorous woman looking to snare a younger man in the scarcity of a postwar gender economy. Her insistence: only God can judge.

There is great eloquence in noting that widows and married women have "different times." Time in agricultural communities is frequently measured by work cycles: the time of harvesting and of planting; the rainy and the dry seasons; and certain fiestas that are tied to the agricultural calendar. There is a rhythm to life in these communities, and for the *warmisapas* the beat has become very fast indeed.

Anomalies

This chapter concludes by thinking about the *warmisapas* and the ambivalence they personify, which in turn conjures up the word "anomaly": "The state or fact of being out of place, out of true or out of a normal or expected position; deviation from the common rule; something out of keeping with established or accepted notions of fitness or order." In their *qarawis*, and in certain liberties they do have, widows exercise forms of power that permit them to move in liminal spaces within their communities. They question normal or expected gender positions; they may revel in deviating from the common rules; they may subvert accepted notions of fitness or order; they may embody silences that punctuate the spoken and the unspoken.

With these two chapters exploring The Rape Victim and The War Widow, I have tried to open space for anomalies. This has meant unpacking the categories, just as Juanita did when she spoke about trees and their diversity. Although these categories imply a shared set of experiences and concerns that seemingly emanate from one's anatomy, any claims to homogeneity rest on the spurious assumption that such categories encompass rather than elide the heterogeneity that characterizes the lived reality of millions of women and girls. What should be included among "women's issues" during periods of conflict and postconflict? How do we ensure that the global agenda reflects the local and regional priorities of socially, culturally, and historically situated women? Perhaps considering the anomalies is one place to begin.

PART III

Looking North

Chapter 7

Intimate Enemies

JUANITA WAS ONE of the people who made me think more about how villagers began killing each other and how they stopped. She was talking about the *sasachakuy tiempo* one day, and recalled how the women had participated in the *ronda campesina*. Juanita had played a leadership role within the female ranks and grew nostalgic as she remembered those times. Standing soldier-straight, she began marching around her house, shouting out orders to the imaginary *ronderas* falling into step at her side. She took a few triumphant turns around her small house before sitting back down with a loud sigh. "There was so much order back then! Not like it is now."

She had warmed up to the topic and began to describe the attacks, her memories veering between acts of bravery and the mutilated bodies of the dead. Then in passing, as though it were a minor detail, she recalled that the authorities from Huaychao and several neighboring communities began to hold assemblies in the large fields that lay between their pueblos.

I was surprised. "Juanita, you mean, in the midst of the killing, you started holding assemblies with other communities? Right in the midst of the violence?"

She nodded, adding that communal authorities called everyone together to begin talking about what they were doing to each other. Hundreds of people showed up.

I was impressed by the initiative. "How did you all decide to do that?"

She shrugged and thought for a moment. "Well, at some point we realized that if we just kept slashing each other's throats for the hell of it, there wasn't going to be anyone left alive around here."

*   *   *

At some point in reading accounts of mass violence, there is usually a moment in which the reader sets down the text, shakes his or her head, and wonders, "How in the world did this happen?" How did family members, friends, neighbors turn on one another? How did individuals become "kill-able"? And it may not be just the reader who is disturbed by these questions: survivors of violence are frequently looking for answers as well. Part 3 of this book attempts to answer some of those questions and to pose a few more. In the context of sustained lethal violence, what are the resources individuals and collectives use to bring the killing to a halt? And, once the killing stops, what happens next?

We know a great deal about how "ordinary people" can be socialized into committing horrific acts of violence, and there is an abundant interdisciplinary literature focused on the socialization of torturers and killers (who did not necessarily start out being "monsters").[1] We will see aspects of various explanatory models in villagers' accounts of the war, and I am not convinced there is anything unprecedented to be said about the ways in which people can slaughter their friends and neighbors. History is replete with examples. However, understanding how people make *and* unmake lethal violence in a particular place and time is crucial to disassembling the structures of violence and engaging in social reconstruction. As Martha Minow concludes in her examination of collective violence, "Saying that context matters is not the end of the analysis. Rather, it is the beginning."[2]

We begin by considering how war shaped moral life, challenging notions of acceptable conduct and the meaning of living in a *human* community. Taking a genealogical approach to the construction and deconstruction of "the enemy" in these villages allows us to grasp the militarization and demilitarization of daily life and moral reasoning. Militarizing and demilitarizing these communities was not limited to purchasing weapons and stationing soldiers throughout the countryside. Militarization also involved the re-formation of *conciencia*—an important conflation of conscience and consciousness—and subjectivities.

One component of a genealogical approach involves local moral idioms—the ways in which people discuss and evaluate issues of accountability, justice, punishment, and reconciliation in the vernacular. In his writing on moral experience, Arthur Kleinman has argued that moral engagements are practical engagements and that they may be deeply disturbing. Indeed, he cautions that *moral* is not synonymous with *good* in an ethical sense: "The moral experience that people share could be far from good, even malign. The values that we express and enact can be inhuman."[3] In the context of intersubjective worlds in which victims, perpetrators, witnesses, and beneficiaries are intermingled, tracing shifts in moral reasoning and conduct is imperative. As we shall see, it was not only the enemy who "fell out of humanity." Rather, part of what must be reconciled is suffering endured *and* inflicted. How do people rebuild a moral order that permits the rehumanization of former enemies as well as themselves? How do people attempt to remoralize their world? What are the resources people mobilize in an effort to reconstruct social life?

Many studies of peace processes and reconciliation remain at the macrolevel, and these studies are important. However, frequently "transitions to democracy" and "national reconciliation" are simply the reworking of elite pacts of governance or domination.[4] To date there has been scant ethnographic research on the points of disjuncture between popular notions of justice, pardon, and reconciliation and the ways in which these concepts are deployed by transitional and successor regimes. For example, in his study of the South African TRC, Richard Wilson argues, "The inability to translate the national reconciliation project into local reconciliation resulted from the lack of any dispute-resolution mechanisms within the TRC framework to negotiate the return of former 'pariahs' to the community. In the main areas of conflict, the TRC became a ritualized performance with little accompanying organization on the ground to actually implement its grand vision of reconciliation."[5] Indeed, ethnographers of reconciliation processes have underscored the contradictory logics at work when introducing a "politics of scale" into one's analysis.[6] Although the literature on transitional justice has focused almost exclusively on the international and national spheres, transitional justice is not the monopoly of international tribunals or states: individuals and collectives also mobilize the ritual and symbolic elements of these transitional processes to deal with the deep cleavages left—or accentuated—by civil conflicts. Introducing a politics of scale allows academics and practitioners to capture locally and regionally salient definitions of justice, reparations, and reconciliation. In addition to allowing policymakers to design more relevant and effective interventions, these studies emphasize that transitions in the political realm must be accompanied by transformations at the subjective and interpersonal levels. In offering an ethnography of the making and unmaking of lethal violence in these communities, the next four chapters move beyond transcendent concepts—justice, forgiveness, redemption—to explore how they are lived and practiced.

First we consider the use of violence before the *sasachakuy tiempo*, which serves as a reminder that violence both destroys and constructs communities. Conflicts were constant within and between villages, and ritualized battles figured among the conflict management mechanisms practiced throughout Ayacucho. However, although the battles were widespread, the exercise of lethal violence was rare. Something changed during the *sasachakuy tiempo* as villagers "learned to kill our brothers." We consider some of the ways this "learning" took place, exploring the local dynamics of making enemies and the demographics of who those enemies were. There were similarities between the regions in terms of how people discuss the killing. However, there were also important differences, which I will foreshadow in this part before shifting our focus to the southern communities that served as important support bases for Shining Path. Although Ayacucho was the "birthplace" of Sendero Luminoso, there were local patterns to the violence and its consequences—within and between communities, and between these communities and the Peruvian state.

In the highlands of Huanta, external agents lit the revolutionary spark, which spread as members of these communities initially embraced the militants' promise to eradicate the wealthy as part of their class-based analysis of injustice. In contrast, in the southern communities, the initial spark was internally lit. There the militants, and many of the *cabecillas*, were *lugareños*—sons and daughters of the same communities in which they waged war. Thus, although a common cultural logic was the "exteriorization" of Shining Path and the construction of social distance in the midst of uncomfortable proximity, there were distinct regional trajectories to the killing and its consequences. Over the next four chapters, I focus on the highlands of Huanta, where villagers ultimately rejected Shining Path and began forming the famed *rondas campesinas*. Here *comuneros* "cleansed" their communities of guerrilla sympathizers and subsequently purged their communal histories of guerrilla sympathies.

But this is a tale not only of killing but of its aftermath. A key concept in local moral idioms is *caridad* (charity or compassion). A chronology of *caridad* leads us to the ways in which people began to rebuild social life and to how and why villagers began converting former Senderistas into *runakuna* again. We hear from people who granted the gift of pardon to the repentant (*arrepentidos*), as well as those who remain beholden to that gift. The rehabilitation of former enemies drew upon the *propias prácticas*—the mechanisms of communal justice—implemented to convert former guerrilla members into redeemable subjects and *comuneros*. These processes of "microreconciliation" occurred throughout the *alturas* of Huanta and drew upon an incitement to memory as well as social rituals designed to remind people what they had promised to forget. In that complicated alchemy lie some of the most enduring legacies of lethal violence among intimate enemies.

Punish But Do Not Kill

> The ethnographic reconstruction of violence must write from and toward a ground that few existing moralities can account for. Writing violence becomes the exploration of moralities that have not yet arrived but that are busy being born in amoral acts.
> —Allen Feldman, "Ethnographic States of Emergency"

Juanjo, Edith, and I attended a *toro pukllay* (bullfight, but literally *pukllay* is "play") in Uchuraccay in October 2002. We chose a spot atop the remnants of a stone wall, swapping participant observer status for distant spectator once we caught sight of the bulls. We sat beside the harpist's wife, who had been to Uchuraccay several times. She told us that before the war villagers had contracted her husband to provide music for their fiestas, and she had accompanied him. On one trip she was present for a ritual fight, and the memory of it had her clutching her chest. "Oh such ferocity! They were grabbing rocks. Over there, in front," pointing to the open field across from us, "women, even children were grabbing rocks, throwing them. I had to escape above. Oh, they were ferocious!"

I might have chalked her comments up to a *mestizo* tendency to delight in discussing the "exotically violent peasants" had I not heard (and read) so much about these "collective and violent games."[7] Throughout Ayacucho, people described the battles that preceded the internal armed conflict. Villagers would head out with rocks and slingshots, fighting until they drew blood. The *peleas* (fights)—or "battles" as they called them in Tiquihua and Hualla—tended to coincide with fiestas and drunkenness and could last for several days.[8]

Villagers in Uchuraccay had much to say about the *peleas*. There were fights not only between families within the village but with members of neighboring communities. Similarly, several people in Tiquihua and Hualla spoke longingly about the "battles of years past." Don Mauro Quispe related with enthusiasm, "We would all go out with ash mixed with garlic, slingshots, rocks, sticks. We fought with all of that. Everyone went. People came out hurt, their heads broken, bloody—but there were no deaths." On this last point he was insistent, as were many others. The goal of these battles did not include killing. In fact, in Uchuraccay people remember one year when a family exceeded the limits of the fight, killing an adolescent boy by smashing his head with a rock. Communal authorities rounded up the guilty and delivered them to the police station in Huanta.

There have been conflicts in these communities since the "time of the grandparents," and these ritualized battles were a form of conflict management that allowed for both the expression and the social containment of retributive emotions. These ceremonial battles offered a space to channel and express accumulated resentments within certain parameters and reflected a cultural emphasis on reciprocity—in this case, reciprocal violence aimed at the release of socially disruptive emotions such as envy. With regard to envy and resentment, I think of the eternal conflicts over communal boundaries and the great economic gaps in these communities. While 65 to 75 percent of the population in Ayacucho lives at the poverty level, macroeconomic indicators can obscure important regional differences, as well as the stratification within communities. For example, in Uchuraccay prior to the political violence, the gap between rich and poor families was enormous. The *gente humilde* (little people) had an average of eight to twelve heads of livestock, in contrast with the *gente grande* (big people), who had an average of one hundred to one hundred and fifty.[9] Resources were channeled by families and marriage patterns, tempting me to use the word "dynasty" to refer to the management of wealth in these communities.

Thus the questions: Prior to the armed conflict, *when* was it acceptable to kill, and to kill *whom*? According to oral and archival sources, killing was exceptional prior to the *sasachakuy tiempo*. Communal justice was characterized by a long-standing proscription against taking human life. The justice repertoire consisted of corporal punishment, economic sanctions, and, in extreme cases, the infliction of "social death" via expulsion of the guilty party. The use of the death penalty, however, was virtually unheard of. Peruvian anthropologist Carlos Iván Degregori explained this rarity with an expression he heard frequently in rural Peru: *castigar pero no matar* (punish but do not kill).[10]

Similarly, in his study of communal justice in Peru, Antonio Peña Jumpa found a long-standing reluctance to take human life, using expulsion instead as punishment for those who refuse to reform. Peña Jumpa argues that the "ultimate sanction" was to deprive the transgressor of *la condición de comunero* (membership status in the village).[11] Such individuals could be required to forfeit their land in addition to leaving the community, thereby impeding family members from laying claim to those lands, which were generally requisitioned for communal purposes.

However, although killing was rare prior to the armed conflict, there were a few cases in which villagers applied the death penalty. The decision to do so was discussed in communal assemblies and imposed in the name of the community. These were measured decisions, not individual acts of vengeance. For instance, in Carhuahurán in 1975 or 1976, the "community" killed a family of cattle rustlers who had ignored the authorities' multiple warnings to stop robbing livestock and to move elsewhere. Following the usual procedure, on three occasions the authorities had given the perpetrators both punishments and opportunities to "correct their errors" prior to taking this fatal step. When the former president of the community related the story of the Quispe family, he was still puzzled: "How is it they didn't listen, being intelligent people?"

With time I learned there was another long-standing way of killing: witchcraft. In each of these communities there were, and are, witches whose services are sought out to direct misfortune and settle accounts.

Intermediaries

The anthropological interest in witchcraft is almost as old as the discipline itself. The topic has been approached in myriad ways, including research into rationality and systems of thought, explanations of misfortune, language and performativity, conflict generation and resolution, and cognitive psychology and specialized perception.[12] Each of these approaches has informed my thinking; however, my experience living in a world with witches also informs this analysis. How could it be any other way given the omnipresent concerns about witchcraft that permeated daily life in these communities? Understanding the role of these intermediaries in the deployment of lethal violence prior to the *sasachakuy tiempo* is vital to a genealogy of moral reasoning.

Examples are abundant, but I offer just one from Accomarca, where people anxiously described the most powerful witch they knew.[13] When José Carlos, Edith, and I went around to people's houses to explain our project, several people referred to Cele Gomez, the most feared man in the pueblo. Mama María lives one block away from the witch and told us, "I've seen him for years and he always looks the same. His wife's already old, but he never ages. He changes his skin like a serpent, that's why he never ages." Her voice dropped to a whisper. "He knows everything we're talking about right now." Even the privacy of her large garden did not offer us a place beyond the reach of Cele Gomez.

Mama María was one of several women who informed us, in hushed tones, how Cele Gomez had killed their husbands: "Cele Gomez killed my husband using witchcraft, all because of envy. His whole body swelled up, all of it, and he died—the poor man."

When we subsequently reviewed the log of *quejas* (complaints) registered in Accomarca, we confirmed that numerous women had denounced Cele Gomez to the communal authorities for having killed their husbands, citing "envy" as the motive behind those who had contracted his services. As we learned, in each of these communities the authorities had taken measures to control the witches at work in their pueblos.

The long-standing practice of witchcraft is important. The practice of harming another person (sometimes fatally) by means of an intermediary was not foreign to people's experience prior to the armed conflict. Considering the omnipresence of *envidia* and *odio* (hatred) in people's explanations regarding the origins of the war, it appears that new social actors provided both a continuation of this form of violence and a break with the witches' monopoly on its implementation. Indicating to the Senderista cadres or to the soldiers who was on the other side—even if the finger-pointing was based on hatred or revenge rather than any real alliance with an armed group— was a means of inflicting harm in an anonymous, indirect manner. This was "mediated" or "distanced" violence and was in keeping with tradition.

However, something else changed during the *sasachakuy tiempo*. Time and again we were told that witchcraft activity had decreased during the war, and not only because there were other intermediaries on the scene.[14] Rather, their services had been rendered increasingly superfluous as *campesinos* began settling accounts themselves, using rocks, knives, and guns. This was not violence by proxy or the "banality of evil" conducted at a bureaucratized remove. The killing was up close and hands on.[15] I was interested in understanding how people shifted from mediated to direct violence—compelled to understand how family members and neighbors were resignified as enemies and made "killable." Part of the answer lies in the influence of the Shining Path cadres' "moralization campaigns."

*   *   *

It was in the late 1970s and early 1980s that Senderista cadres began visiting rural villages in the highlands of Huanta to mobilize peasants for the revolution. The first visit in Carhuahurán occurred in 1979, when a group of university students arrived from Huanta. Feliciano Rimachi, president and subsequently mayor of Carhuahurán, was still an adolescent when the guerrillas appeared. He had invited Efraín and me to come by and talk, although he was evasive about doing so. Feliciano liked his power, and seeking him out for an interview was a frustrating courtship. He knew he could keep us waiting, and he almost always did.

Efraín and I decided to take a bottle of rum up to Feliciano's house. We had all danced in the same *comparsa* (group of performers) for Carnival the month before, beating out the other *comparsas* for first prize. I thought he might feel more inclined to speak with us after the evenings we had spent practicing for the competition.

He was in a good mood and invited us in, offering us chairs around a table rather than the sheepskins we were accustomed to. His house had three rooms, enormous when compared to other houses in the community. His wife, Raida, was in the kitchen, cooking on a large gas stove Feliciano had brought up from Huanta. She brought us a cup for the rum before disappearing into the back of the house.

We spent some time catching up on community news, particularly the construction of the highway that would run from Carhuahurán to Huanta. This project was the culmination of years of insistence on the part of the villagers. A few more dynamite blasts and days of working from four in the morning until sunset would wind the dirt road into the open field at the center of Carhuahurán. Just as the road wound around, so did our conversation, until it became clear he was in the mood to talk.

"Don Feliciano," I began, "maybe you could tell us about the history of Sendero in Carhuahurán?" Efraín poured a glass of rum and held it out to him. He took a drink before responding.

"When they first came here, they said they were students and that we shouldn't vote for Belaúnde [a presidential candidate]. That's all they said, but they also had these books by Lenin."

"Did they arrive armed? Did they have weapons?"

"No, not at first," he replied. "With the authorities they tried to make friends—they even spent Carnivales here. I got to know them during Carnivales." He paused and looked at me intently. "They passed Carnivales here, just like the two of you. They drank, danced, played music. They played soccer and just talked with people. At first they said we were all going to live as equals, that everyone was going to have a car and that there would be no rich or poor."

Efraín nodded and leaned forward in his chair, resting his elbows on his knees. "Feliciano, what did people think about that idea?"

"When they began saying that, the authorities realized they might take *our* things and try to make everyone equal. The *varayoqs* [civil-religious community leaders] spoke with them and told them not to come back here. But they would come back during fiestas. They would *concientizar* ['consciousness raise'] people, and they started identifying as the Left."

I thought about his comments later—both the comments about Sendero as well as the veiled commentary on Efraín and me. We had already been made aware that introducing oneself as a university student in rural Ayacucho was not conducive to building trust. Feliciano was always watching us, along with the other *comuneros* who remembered those *universitarios* and where their visits had led.

I was also struck by how *campesinos* perceived the *concientización*. Evidently the language of equality was appealing in terms of leveling relations between the rich and the poor to the extent these two groups were mapped onto urban and rural areas. The notion of equalizing everyone *within* the communities was a less popular idea. Marcos Rafaelo, then lieutenant governor of Carhuahurán, had also been a young man when the Senderistas came around with flyers explaining the Ley de Común (Law of Commons). As he recalled, "They told us everyone was going to live as equals once the state was overthrown. All of our agricultural products were going to be placed in a large storehouse and distributed equally to each *comunero* according to need. They also told us they would kill the elderly because they're useless." The revolutionary discourse was becoming less persuasive.

As *comuneros* weighed what they were hearing, Senderista militants increased pressure upon the communities to organize and join their ranks. Don Feliciano explained how the visits began to change. "'We're a political party,' they said. But people here knew they were Sendero and started grabbing them. My father was governor then. They whipped him and made him pay a fine for telling them to leave. They made people give them llamas and they left. But they left their book behind and I read it."

Sendero Luminoso operated on several fronts, referring not only to their geographic offensive but to their political and ideological agenda as well. One component of their revolutionary project was *campañas moralizadoras* (moralizing campaigns). Nelson Manrique has described these campaigns as the "other line" of Senderista activity, which consisted of "compulsively moralizing, drastically repressing infractions committed against a very strict code of ethics, which include[d] sanctions against crimes such as drug use, theft, adultery, etcetera."[16]

This "compulsive moralizing" had a widespread trajectory. Billie Jean Isbell in Chuschi and Ronald Berg in Andahuaylas found that during the initial *campañas moralizadoras*, Sendero targeted cattle rustlers, adulterers, greedy shopkeepers—the "usual suspects" that peasants held in contempt for violating cultural norms.[17] These transgressors were a chronic problem in any community. Thus in Chuschi support for executions and public whippings was almost universal.[18] In the initial moralizing campaign and *juicio popular* ("people's trial"), the guerrillas publicly castigated two men, one an adulterer and the other a wifebeater. These *juicios* animated several women to subsequently denounce their husbands to the Senderistas in hopes of equal outcomes.[19] The search for justice is an eternal lament in the rural countryside, particularly for women who are central to legal disputes but not to their adjudication.

However, the Senderistas did not stop with the groups that were universally reviled. Increasingly the *juicios populares* became a means of silencing communal authorities who represented obstacles to Sendero's revolutionary project, as well as *campesinos* whom they suspected of serving as *soplones* (army informants). What the guerrillas replicated was a double standard that was all too familiar to *campesinos*: the powerful dictate what sort of justice and for whom.

At times villagers also denounced one another, using the Senderistas to settle old scores. Such was the case in Carhuahurán in 1983 when an angry villager who had been punished by local authorities for theft informed on the men, denouncing them as *soplones*. This was Carhuahurán's first experience with a *juicio popular* directed against *gente inocente*. It was a determining moment when the guerrillas rounded up eight communal authorities and a random group of villagers whose names they read from a list written on the back of a matchbook.

They forced the *comuneros* to accompany them to Huaychao for a *juicio popular*. Each person's hands were tied tightly behind their back, they were blindfolded, and they were forced to their knees. One survivor, Manuco, decided to argue with them because he had done nothing wrong: "I told them what had happened, that the thief just wanted revenge. But they wouldn't listen to anything I said." Everyone was found guilty as charged and the guerrillas began shooting each person through the back of the head. Manuco remembered, "They killed them like birds with a slingshot. They died instantly, their heads blown apart."

Manuco survived thanks to God's grace. At the precise moment in which a Senderista cocked a rifle and pressed the cold steel against his neck, the sound of an army helicopter sliced the air. The guerrillas began shouting to one another to run, dispersing into the hills. Although some villagers insisted the sound was made by shots from another *juicio popular* in a neighboring village, Manuco just shook his head: "There was no helicopter, there were no shots. It was God."

Although the Senderistas ran that day, it was not long before they came back. Feliciano remembered it all as we sat drinking rum.

"Later they came back, with weapons. They threatened the authorities. They told us to start organizing and form a Comité Responsable. The person in charge here was Agabito Cayetano. He was illiterate, but he had family that had worked for those guys. They were students, Huantinos [from Huanta] and the Cayetanos had worked on their land. So they had *confianza* with him."

"Did they hold meetings here?"

Feliciano nodded. "They started having *asambleas populares*. They called all the young people. They had people grouped by ages for the *asambleas*. They served food. They began obligating people, 'Let's go to this place or that place.' They made people go to Qano, Uchuraccay, Chaca. But I didn't like it. I didn't go. I told them I didn't have time. They told me the first time they would pardon me, the second time they would pardon me, but the third time they wouldn't pardon me again. So I joined as a combatant, but I just wanted to escape. They just robbed. Straight out they told us we were going to go out and get clothes for free. They robbed *transportistas* who were headed for the jungle and merchants. They told us we would finish all those people off and keep their things. I didn't like this. There are so many *burgueses* [bourgeois]—how were we going to finish them all off? We were going to kill soldiers, *guardia civiles*—they can't be finished off. And they wanted to kill innocent people, they talked about this in the meetings. But if we said anything against it, they called us *yanauma* ['black heads,' referring to the woolen balaclavas or ski masks the soldiers wore for warmth and anonymity]. They forced people and made them assault people."

"Killing innocent people." This phrase came up many times, cited as one reason *campesinos* began to reject Shining Path and realign their sympathies and allegiance. Who those "innocent people" were becomes clearer with the following example and illustrates how the term was used in reference to killing that exceeded even the recalibrated limits on lethal violence.

Paulino Figueroa is diminutive in stature but well respected as a charismatic leader in Uchuraccay. One day World Vision arrived to distribute T-shirts to the children enrolled in their Patrocinio Program (Child Sponsorship Program). Paulino tried one on and it fit him perfectly. From that day, the nickname Patrocinio stuck.

We visited Uchuraccay several times during the truth commission process, and I admired Patrocinio's outspokenness. He is one of a new generation of *campesino* authorities who has nothing of the "humble peasant" in his bearing. He was willing to stand up—politely and with dignity—to various city and state officials who arrived in his community, accustomed to making village authorities do their bidding with a few orders and a snap of their fingers.

During one trip, Patrocinio called Juanjo and me aside to tell us what had happened in Uchuraccay. He insisted, "We have our own truth" and began by telling us "how it all started."

"People let themselves be tricked [*engañados*]. The *terrucos* came here and made everyone meet. There was an authority here, Alejandro Huamán.[20] They grabbed him and a member of his family. They brought him tied up like a thief and made everyone gather. Then, like a warning, they killed them in front of everyone. After that people reacted, young and old.

They were saying, 'This isn't what we thought. This is no good. We'll end up killing each other and finishing ourselves off.'"

"Why did they kill them?"

"They killed him [Alejandro Huamán] because he was walking in the *chacras*. As an authority, he walked for the good of his community.[21] Well, some people felt he was working for the good of the community. As an authority, he needed to work for everyone. But he was becoming egotistical. Because he was an authority, he thought he was better than everyone else, and he wanted to take advantage of people. He was becoming greedy, and people were beginning to be humiliated. So there were people against him because he'd done some bad things. That's why they killed him. But then people here reacted because Uchuraccay didn't want to receive those *puriqkuna*."

"Why *did* people start opposing the *puriqkuna*?"

"Because they began killing their *prójimos*—killing innocent people. That's why Uchuraccay reacted. We had a meeting and reached an agreement. We realized what was happening and asked the military to install a base here. We were saying, 'If this keeps up, there won't be anyone left.'"

As Paulino illustrates, the communal assessment of Alejandro Huamán was mixed. Although some people felt he was fulfilling his responsibilities and working for the good of his community, others felt he had become abusive and was acting out of greed and self-interest. His behavior transgressed practices of reciprocity, thereby violating an important aspect of local norms. From ritual battles and the exchange of violence, to *ayni* and the exchange of labor services, reciprocity is an animating force in daily life. Reciprocity establishes a nuanced network of expectations and indebtedness, maintaining both economic asymmetries *and* respectful social interactions. For the members of the community who "fingered" Alejandro Huamán to the Senderista militants, his blatant display of greed invited *envidia*—and its consequences. His murder fell within the range of acceptability. In contrast, when the militants moved beyond abusive authorities to killing *comuneros*—and when *comuneros* realized their actions were leading to the indiscriminate use of lethal violence—there was a reassessment of where the unchecked expression of *envidia* was headed. There would be no one left.

It is important to understand the role of violence in the historical project of Senderismo. In this authoritarian movement, violence ceased to be instrumental, becoming an end in itself. As Carlos Iván Degregori argues, "Blood and death must be familiar to those who have decided to 'convert the word into armed actions.' The evangelical allusion to the Redeemer—'the word made flesh'—is not gratuitous. It announces Guzmán's and *Sendero*'s attitude towards violence. She is the Redeemer. She is not the midwife of history, she is the Mother of History."[22] Abimael Guzmán insisted that each village would be required to pay its "quota of blood" and that a million lives would be the price of the war Sendero waged. For many villagers, the quota was far too high.

The revolutionaries failed to consider central tenets in the communal conception and administration of justice, in which death was reserved for the most extreme cases and rarely applied. The brutal and seemingly indiscriminate violence of the Senderista cadres was a key factor in alienating the *campesinos*.

Added to their disproportionate use of lethal violence was economic exploitation. Most adults could remember the *hacendados* who had been ousted by the Agrarian Reform of 1968–70. To have thrown off one form of extraction only to take up another? The guerrillas misread rural peasants in thinking they would passively accept a change in masters. In the *alturas* of Huanta, economic injustice was a constant theme in the stories people told about the war. In contrast to the southern region, where Shining Path cadres began their political work a decade prior to the armed phase of the revolution, in the northern communities an explicit discussion of Sendero's political ideology was rare. Rather, the *terrucos*' thieving ways was a major theme. The following conversations with don Domingo and mama Manuela help us understand how many people perceived the militants' conduct.

Don Domingo Santiago was the oldest person in Carhuahurán. He was tiny, his frayed jacket hanging down past his knees and the cracks in his black plastic shoes filled with *ichu* to ward off the cold. I had greeted him in passing as we walked up the steep hill for water on frigid mornings, the air an iced shard of glass cutting into my lungs. I was eager to move beyond our morning exchange of "Llumpay chirin, manachu?" ("It is so cold, isn't it?") shouted over the running water shooting out of the plastic tubing and bouncing off the sides of our buckets. I began passing by his house, but the lock was always slipped through the wire hanger, and neighbors told me he had already left for his *chacra*.

After many passes, I walked by his house late one afternoon and found the door partially open and a large mound of freshly unearthed potatoes piled right outside. He had returned early from working in his *chacra* and was seated in a sliver of light just inside the door of his one-room house, an enormous book opened across his legs. His Bible had survived the Senderistas, who had burned the Catholic church and smashed the saints, discounting all of it as reactionary nonsense.

I leaned in, not wanting to startle him. I failed. I did not realize he was quite deaf, and my efforts at a polite greeting were inaudible. I stepped back apologetically, but he recognized me from our early morning chores as well as the reports his neighbors had given him of the gringa who kept coming by peering through the crack in his door. I explained why I had come by so many times: "Don Domingo, you know the history of this place better than anyone. I was hoping you could come over for coffee and tell us about the history of Carhuahurán and the *sasachakuy tiempo*."

Don Domingo nodded, "There aren't many old people left these days." He closed his Bible, slowly rose from the sheepskin he had been sitting on, and we walked around the corner to my room next to the crumbling watchtower.

Efraín had coffee and a bag of *chancay* waiting for us. *Chancay* is the only bread sold at small stores in the villages, and they have an impressive shelf life. I called them *pan de otro siglo* (bread from another century) and asked villagers if they had included *chancay* with the rocks they threw at the Senderistas during the war. We spent many hours dunking *chancay* into our cups of coffee, softening it to a chewable consistency.

"Don Domingo, what was it like when you were little?" I asked him.

He explained that his father had come to Carhuahurán from the hacienda at Huaynachancha, thrown out after refusing to work any longer for the owner, Germán Dedoya. "Dedoya and his *caporal* [overseer] insulted people. '*Chutos* [savages],' they yelled. It was very hard working on the haciendas, living *waqcha qina* [like a poor person, like an orphan]. My father refused."

"I can see why he wanted to come here," I commiserated. "Was Carhuahurán already a community when your father arrived?"

"Yes, it'd been a community for a very long time." This led him into a lengthy description of the decisive role his grandfather and father had played in the War of Independence in 1824 and the Salt Tax Protests of 1896. Domingo's fluid chronology moved back and forth across the 1800s and

1900s, and occasionally to the Incan empire of Tawantinsuyo that he had learned about as a child in school. He contrasted the *allín gobiernu* (good government) of the Incans with the abusive *hacendados* and the beatings his father had received. Nonlinear narrative conventions allowed for tremendous movement between *tiempos*, mingling past and present.

We served ourselves another round of *miski yaku* and asked if he knew something about the history of attacks upon Carhuahurán.

"Yes," he replied forcefully. "There have been many attacks. The Spaniards came in search of gold. They only wanted gold. But the Senderistas wanted everything we had—they even took the green poncho that I always wore! They burned our houses and took everything they could find. They were *suakuna* [thieves] and nothing more." Thus centuries of exploitation were condensed, and the injustice of dispossession still rankled. The image of the guerrillas as common thieves driven by bloodlust and greed was one of the dominant themes in the *alturas* of Huanta, and the women in particular could provide a detailed list of how much they had lost.

One day I headed up the hill to Manuela Condorcay's house, one thin wall away from the Evangelical church.[23] She was busy shelling *habas* (fava beans) while her sons Ruben and John played with the new baby pigs in the family's corral. John was a toddler, but Ruben was six: if the family had owned more than one lone sow and her close-eyed newborns, Ruben would have been out pasturing them rather than rubbing their little snouts with his finger.

We had spoken before, but that day I asked if she had lived in the village during any of the attacks. Manuela abruptly sucked in her breath. Yes, she had. She did not know the date, only that the attack occurred when villagers had already begun living in the damp, cold caves, coming out during daylight hours to pasture their animals or tend their fields. "It was no longer life. We lived and died like dogs." One day the Senderistas found them and rounded everyone up.

"What did you do? What did they do?" I asked, feeling the fear in her voice.

"They still didn't have guns, just knives. They killed people with knives. They had a list and began calling names. We were singing hymns, both men and women. They began cutting people's throats and we were crying. They made us watch. Then the women [Senderistas] yelled at us, 'What are you crying about? If you keep crying, we'll cut off all of your heads!' Those women were smiling while we cried. Oh, we had such fear! *We forgot we had been people.*"

Manuela sucked in her breath several more times as she spoke, insisting she still saw all of this clearly even when her eyes were closed. "They stole our animals. They took twenty cows, fifty llamas, and all of their *crias* [babies]. And they killed others even though we begged them not to. 'What guilt could our little cows possibly have?' we begged. But they killed them anyway."

These affronts to the material and moral economy that informed daily life drove *campesinos* in the *alturas* of Huanta to take action.[24] Florencia Mallon, in her study of peasant nationalism during postcolonial Mexico and Peru, has suggested "[a] political history from a subaltern perspective must also take seriously the intellectual history of peasant action."[25] Throughout the highlands of Huanta, villagers were listening to the radio, reading the military flyers that were distributed en masse, holding communal assemblies, and communicating with family members in Lima. They were gathering information and making decisions. A decisive break with Shining Path figured among those decisions.

It was in January 1983 that villagers in Huaychao killed seven Senderistas and quickly reported their actions to the police station in Huanta. *Comuneros* in Carhuahurán and Uchuraccay were watching, waiting to see what sort of reprisal was in store for Huaychao. As Feliciano and Marcos told it, they realized the Senderistas could be killed, particularly if villagers forged alliances with the military that had entered Ayacucho in December 1982 to begin the counterinsurgency campaign. This new armed actor was yet another element to consider. Marcos recalled: "The Senderistas told us we would fight with slingshots and rocks." He shook his head. "What were they thinking? The soldiers had long-distance rifles and helicopters—how were we going to win with slingshots?"

The cadres also wanted to impose their own community-level *responsables* and threatened communal authorities who got in their way. While villagers may have supported killing abusive leaders, cattle rustlers, and other thieves, killing conscientious authorities was a key factor in alienating people. For example, I had a lengthy conversation with Narciso Rimachi in Huaychao in 2003 in which he explained what led villagers in his community to kill those seven Senderistas. The following is an abbreviated version of what he said about this pivotal event and its consequences.

*   *   *

"They started visiting here, saying, 'We're fighting against poverty. We want everyone to be equal, both the rich and the poor.' They also told us that anyone who committed an error would be punished. But then they started talking about the *teniente gobernador* (lieutenant governor) and our other authorities. They said they were members of the government, that they were dogs who licked [former Peruvian president] Belaúnde's plate. Just like they said they would make the rich disappear, they said they would do the same thing to our authorities."

The military entered the zone in late 1982, and the presence of soldiers also informed the intellectual history of peasant action in the highlands of Huanta. As Narciso recalled, "They kept asking us about the *militares qara-chaki* [the soldiers with leather feet, referring to their heavy boots]. They told us we needed to tell them about the *qarachaki* or they would punish us." Narciso's voice mimicked the threatening tone of the Senderistas, who had told the villagers, "You're going to die if you don't tell us what they're doing!"

Confronted by these threats, people began to discuss what they were going to do if the soldiers came to Huaychao. They decided that if the soldiers arrived, they should kill the Senderistas and keep their weapons, then let the military know what they had done.

"So those *guerrilleros* were always coming here. And we were thinking—the authorities were talking about it. They kept saying, 'This is no good for us. Here we are, living in our pueblo doing nothing to anyone. We eat from our *chacras*, we have food, clothes. We're *tranquilos* in our pueblo. We shouldn't trust the people who are doing these things. If they come here again, we need to respond to them. We'll ask them to leave.' That was the agreement. Well, they came again and people here were waiting for them. By then our neighbors were realizing that when those *guerrilleros* arrived, well if there were any contradictions here . . . ," Narciso paused. "Some people here were telling them, 'So and so did this, so and so did that, that person is my enemy.' The *odio* had started to spread. So people started listening, and thinking that in these circumstances we weren't going to do well. 'If we keep this up, who knows where it will lead?' So we decided to receive those *guerrilleros* in a friendly manner, but telling them no."

There was, however, a backup plan in case "telling them no" was not persuasive.

"We decided, "If they respond well to us, then we'll answer nicely. If they don't answer us nicely, then we'll be bad too. That was the idea. Well, the fifteenth of January they arrived and starting saying, '*Ya compañeros*, we're coming here to speak with you. Pass the word to everyone!' They said they wanted to have a meeting with everyone. They said they wanted to make an agreement to fight against poverty. So they started calling people to come and meet. They started talking and people here said they didn't want to accept all that. So the *guerrilleros* said, 'If you act like this with us, then just like ashes you're going to disappear!' People here were thinking, 'What are we going to do? This can't be good.' People told them, 'We don't agree with your words and you can't force us.' That's what the authorities said. Well, those people said, 'Why can't you accept our words? You are a bunch of *yanaumas*, *miserables*! They kept saying this, with all their weapons, too. '*Carajo*, the *miserables* of Huaychao! We'll leave you in ashes! We're like the grains of sand in the river, too numerous to count! We'll turn you into dust, *miserables*!' Narciso shook his head. "Here we were, we didn't even know about weapons, about ammunition—nothing. And there they were with their arms, carrying weapons. They shouted, '*Carajo*, we need to kill them!' You see, they had also made an agreement that if we didn't accept them, they would kill us. Well, people here thought that before they do something to us, we'd better grab them. We argued with the *guerrilleros*. Those people from the party started to curse Huaychao—we were such an enemy! From the adults to the children, from the young people to the old—we were their enemy. When we started thinking about it, they made mistakes. They made a mistake in killing innocent people, worse yet when they were talking against the government. They were wrong there. We started thinking they weren't good people. How could it be? Killing people from the government, people who guarded the government, *teniente gobernadores* here in our pueblos? We knew that couldn't be right, so we rejected them."

Not long after the seven Senderistas were killed, President Belaúnde himself appeared on television praising the villagers of Huaychao for their patriotic actions in defense of the state and urging other communities to take similar actions to rid the country of "criminal terrorists."[26] Narciso described how neighboring communities reacted to the news. "Right after that, people came here to find out what had happened. They came from all sides [listing the neighboring communities]. All of us had a meeting and debated everything. 'Such and such is happening, why are these things happening?' We kept talking about it, and people decided that all of this could only turn out badly for us. We all decided it was time to rise up like one single hand, like one single person. It was time to stand up. All the authorities made an agreement and all fifteen communities signed an *acta*. They all agreed that these *guerrilleros* were not good people. For us, people of the *alturas*, they did not come here as good people. Worse—they were our enemy."

Once a decision was made about what to do with the Senderista militants, the focus of the discussions shifted inward to potential sympathizers within the villages. What should be done with them? Narciso's response was calm and direct: "The soldiers said that anyone who was with the *guerrilleros* would be killed. So we started cleaning [*limpiaykuta*] our communities. We cleaned them—all of the people who'd been with those *guerrilleros*. We started cleaning our communities."

Along with "cleaning" their communities, authorities petitioned for the installation of military bases in case there were reprisals. One petition led to the establishment of the military base in Carhuahurán in 1984. Thus began a tense, conflictive, but strategic relationship between the villagers and the armed forces.

For security purposes, villagers began to live in nucleated settlements (*centros poblados*). In the case of Carhuahurán, the *centro poblado* consisted of the *comunidad madre* of Carhuahurán and its eleven annexes. These *centros poblados* were a new form of collective life, a product of the internal armed conflict. At this juncture, the challenge was to submerge old conflicts, and new tensions regarding allegiances, in the name of constructing "community" as a strategic identity in the service of survival. Producing a communal structure of feeling would draw upon Evangelismo, history, and death.

*   *   *

Mario Quispe was the president of Carhuahurán during the worst years of the violence, and most villagers remember him as a "great man." He was also an Evangelical pastor and played a central role in taking in the "refugees" who arrived under a cloud of suspicion from outlying settlements. To be a refugee was to be suspect; the military routinely rounded people up on the grounds they were terrorists. Don Mario took these people in, giving them land to work and safe haven.

Civil-military relations were tense, and villagers' complaints about the soldiers were abundant. One complaint was how the soldiers "harassed" the women and girls. There were many rapes in Carhuahurán and babies who were left to sleep facedown so they would silently drift into death. Mario finally decided to speak with the commander of the military base, demanding the soldiers respect the women and leave them alone.

Several nights after his visit to the base, two soldiers came to Mario's door while his wife was at church. They insisted he accompany them to the base, with his five-year-old boy trailing along behind them. Mario was never seen again, his son left to cry his way down the hill in search of his mother. People shook their heads in remembrance: "We never found his body. We didn't dare protest to the officials in Huanta [where the main military base was located]. The soldiers threatened to leave if we complained, leave us to be killed by the *terrucos*. We couldn't say anything."

I arrived too late to know don Quispe, but his presence infused the written records of the assemblies held during those years, and I spent much time speaking with the current mayor, who fashioned himself in Mario's mold. Feliciano Rimachi was recognized by many as a hero of the war, his body testifying to that heroism. His hands end in scarred stumps, the result of a Senderista grenade that exploded in his hands when he tore down a red flag planted in the *puna* above Carhuahurán. Mayor Rimachi used his status as a war hero to construct an authoritative voice in forging communal history and identity. Echoes of Mario Quispe resonated in don Rimachi's leadership at *asambleas comunales*, as well as in his addresses to the *ronderos* during the *formaciones*.

The *asambleas* and the *formaciones* are both a model *of* and a model *for* "community." In these meetings a sense of community is created and reproduced. During the worst years of the war, general assemblies were regularly held as Carhuahurán began its transformation into a multicommunal *comunidad resistente*—a resistant community, the term used for pueblos that stayed in situ during the *sasachakuy tiempo*, formed their *rondas campesinas*, and participated in the war against Sendero Luminoso. Communal authorities in Carhuahurán wear the title "*comunidad resistente*" with pride, and their famous *ronda* allowed many of those same authorities to "clean up" their own pasts after they renounced their early participation in Shining Path. The proud *rondero* identity has been useful and strategic.

For example, during *fiestas patrias* (Independence Day celebrations) in the community of Carhuahurán in 1998, the mayor addressed all of the *ronderos* present during the flag-raising ceremony. In this salute to the Peruvian flag—a practice carried out every Sunday in rural villages throughout

Ayacucho—Mayor Rimachi spoke to the crowd of men that had formed in rows and columns, rifles slung over their shoulders:

> Today is the anniversary of our country, and all of us as Peruvians should celebrate with pride, affection and respect. It was on a day such as today that we freed ourselves from Spanish domination, just as we fought against Sendero to defend what it means to be Peruvian. This feeling of having fought should be present in us so that we feel proud and remember that the struggle has not ended but could start anew at any time. For this we must be ready for the task and not lose the fervor that we have had.

The glorious history of struggle that Mayor Rimachi related wove together two centuries of resistance in the name of La Patria. This appropriation of the past was even more striking in the history he wrote as part of an NGO-sponsored competition in 1997. The contest was directed toward community presidents so that they would write the history of their communities during the war, with a prize to be awarded for the "best history."

In "The Problem of the Resisters: A History That Repeats Itself After 182 Years," Mayor Rimachi traces the villagers' role in the War of Independence, the Salt Tax Rebellion, and the "war against subversion." He chronicles the principle Senderista attacks the community of Carhuahurán and its annexes endured, the number of deaths that resulted, and how the "rebellious *campesinos*" overthrew the guerrillas. He finishes his history stating that, "One can say the best *campesino* is the Peruvian one for his resistance, capacity for recuperation and adaptation to inclemency, disasters and civil problems that have endured for the fourteen years of the war against the subversives and how he demonstrated before history his capacity and recuperation from bad elements."

This glorious history of *una genta rebelde* (a rebellious people) constructs an imagined identity that spans two centuries and revindicates a population long marginalized as mere *chutos* of the highlands. In seizing the public space of the flag raising, they reinscribe this nationalist act with their own meaning as not only members of the nation but heroes of La Patria. In Feliciano's written history and the rallying speeches addressed to the villagers on any given Sunday, he uses the history of *una gente rebelde*. This is historicity, the conscious production of historical narrative, as an empowering mode of social action.[27]

This appeal to a glorious past characterized the war years as well as the tenuous present. In the general assemblies, communal authorities reminded villagers where their allegiance should lie: with the state. Don Domingo recalled the meetings: "People here rebelled against Sendero because we were subjects of the state. We were in the hands of the state, we wanted to be faithful." Villagers closed ranks in the interest of a coercive unity.

While historical narratives played a role in producing communal senti- ment and suppressing internal divisions, words were also central to com- mitting acts of lethal violence. There were Senderista sympathizers in Car- huahurán and its annexes—sympathizers who were not swayed by appeals to patriotism or the recounting of a glorious history. Other words would prompt other actions, illustrating David Apter's insistence that "To do vio- lence to others, we must do violence to language." It was not just Huaychao that started "cleaning up."

"How We Learned to Kill Our Brothers"

> We knew the Cayetanos had been giving food and lodging to the *terrucos* [Senderistas]. In their house up on the *puna*, they let the *terrucos* spend the night. We knew what the soldiers would do if they found out. We knew we had to stop that. So we rounded up the family one night, all but the youngest child, and took them down to the river. We hung them all that night and dumped their bodies in the river. That's how we learned to kill our *prójimo* [fellow creature, brother].
> —Anonymous community, *alturas* of Huanta, 1998

I begin with this "emblematic memory," to borrow a term from the histo- rian Steve Stern.[28] "Emblematic memory" refers to collective memories that condense important cultural themes and take on a certain uniformity as they are retold within a social group. The killing of the Cayetanos is also a foundational memory. In each village, people recall "when it all started," which refers to killing *within* the village, carried out by members of that par- ticular community or with their participation. These foundational murders marked both an ending of one *tiempo* and moral code and the beginning of another.

The decision to kill Senderistas and their suspected sympathizers was discussed at length in general assemblies prior to taking action. To quote again from David Apter, "When people do try to take control, and by means of interpretive action, then the iconography of violence, the choreography of confrontational events, the planning of actions based on interpretation and interpretations deriving from actions becomes a process. The process enables one to shuttle back and forth between violent acts and moral binaries."[29] In the context of these rural villages in Huanta—where Evangelismo spread rapidly during the 1980s—the moral binaries consisted of constructing the Senderistas as radically, dangerously Other.

It is crucial to grasp the demographics of the Senderistas—and how these varied over time—and between the north and south. In both regions the early cadres were schoolteachers and university students; however, while they were "outsiders" in the *alturas* of Huanta, they were family members (frequently sons and daughters) from the communities in the south. In *both* regions the rank and file was composed of *campesinos.*[30] Some peasants participated by choice, particularly in the early years before the Senderista cadres became increasingly repressive. Many others were forced to join, either by Sendero or due to the perverse military logic. It was common for villagers not to have identity documents; in some instances the guerrillas burned them, in others peasants had never considered such documents of any importance. It was not until the war began that mobility became drastically dependent on identity cards. To be undocumented was to be considered a "terrorist" by the police and military, frequently with lethal consequences.

When the soldiers swept through the countryside, undocumented young men were understandably nervous. Many villagers know someone who was unfortunate enough to have been out on the roads when the military set up random checkpoints. Young men ran into the hills to escape them and, once there, found themselves considered suspect by the guerrillas as well. As several now grown men recalled, "We decided it was better to join them so that someone would protect us."

When neutrality becomes dangerous, people find themselves selecting a side or being assigned one. Certainly *campesinos* did ally themselves, and in the early years of the war many sided with the Senderistas. At times the guerrillas played on long-standing antagonisms, intensifying them and often giving them a lethal dimension they had not had before. However, as Sendero became increasingly unpopular in the *alturas* of Huanta and the military presence increased dramatically, the guerrillas' use of forced recruits became more common. As don Feliciano told us, Sendero rounded up villagers and forced them to participate in attacks on neighboring communities. The columns that arrived in the depth of night were increasingly composed of other peasants rather than *universitarios*.

This was not a sanitized war in which buttons were pushed and bombs delivered. The fighting was carried out with knives, rocks, slingshots, *tirachas* (homemade guns), and only later with purchased rifles. So how do people smash open the heads and slit the bellies of intimate enemies?

Another Life

When Quechua speakers talk about the *sasachakuy tiempo*, certain terms reappear throughout their narratives. Two of these are *huk vida* (another life) and *chay punta vida* (that life before, that first life). These temporal markers reflect a historical consciousness in which *tiempos*—distinct times—are used to "periodize" history.[31] For example, recall the conversation with Jesús Romero, who spoke about different times: the time of the grandparents, eternal time, and the time of the Son of God. He emphasized that times change and so do the people who live within those different periods. He also explained that traditions change, as do the laws governing a particular *tiempo*. This is a historical consciousness characterized by rupture; a sense of before, during, and after; of people *now* not necessarily being who they were *then*. This has tremendous resonance with Evangelical rituals of rupture: people may confess, repent, atone, and emerge as *musaq runakuna* (new people) who leave their old identities behind.

The issue of identities is fascinating. In his work on community-level violence in India, Deepak Mehta notes that face-to-face relations are fraught with potential conflict and that shifting contexts have the potential to efface the concreteness of relationships and replace them with imagined identities.[32] The *sasachakuy tiempo* was a time of profound upheaval and the bewildering loss of context.[33] Identities were no longer certain. Many people were considered two-faced (*iskay uyukuna*) and untrustworthy, and people even doubted themselves. In the words of one man, "We never knew who we were dealing with. I couldn't talk—not with my mother, not with my brother, not with my neighbor. We were all two-faced."[34]

Many were two-faced, while some were faceless. Just as *envidia* is present in the majority of conversations, so are the *mascarayuqkuna* (the masked ones). The insistence that "they were masked" is coupled with the rhetorical question "where could they have come from?" These phrases speak volumes about how people understand and psychologically manage the violence they have inflicted as well as the violence they have suffered. Given the perpetrators who live in these communities, both the "masked ones" and the rhetorical question "where could they have come from?" serve to maintain something of distance and anonymity where little of the two exist.

Additionally, people lived in a time of hallucinatory realities when the line between the real and the surreal blurred. What could be more surreal than seeing a soldier grab a chainsaw to butcher someone? How not to doubt one's own eyes when watching a *terruco* cut out an elderly woman's tongue because she dared cry for help? In Hualla, Señora Rufina recalled the war years: "Ay, in that time only pigs walked the streets. Only the dogs barked, only cats crossed the streets. There were no people. Only two or three of us remained. The majority left for other places because they didn't want to die." Hualla was a ghost town, the animals displacing—and eating the cadavers of—human beings. Even nature itself was altered. In Tiquihua, don Moises' eyes shone as he told us, "When I remember, it makes me want to cry. What could this pueblo have done to make such things happen? I'm not lying, but the sun didn't shine normally. It shined a different color. It was like a punishment."

Confronted by an altered world, even that which one saw with his or her own eyes was in doubt. In his work on "terror systems," Marcelo Suárez-Orozco draws upon his research on the Argentine military dictatorship to develop the idea of "percepticide": "Terror produced a widespread 'percepticide' in Argentina: the perceptual organs, too, soon became a casualty of the engulfing terror."[35] What one saw, what one heard—how to believe one's own senses? Perhaps one could not. Another omnipresent term is *Hukmanmi karqani* (I was of another form). The sensation of not recognizing one's own body or trusting one's perceptions reflects extreme experiences that surpassed the frames of reference that defined life. One was faced with others, and oneself, engaged in activities that challenged the norms that had given meaning to human life, a state summed up by many *campesinos* who lament, "We were no longer people" and "It was no longer life." I have purposely chosen the words "to be faced with oneself": there is a form of distancing or disassociation conveyed by these terms. Another time, another life, another self.

Just as people perceived nature itself to be altered, so were people's *conciencia* and their hearts. The *sasachakuy tiempo* provoked perceptual and moral recalibrations, as doña Victoria explained during one of our visits to Cayara.[36] We had been trying to figure out how people understood the violence committed within and between communities. It was common for men and women to shake their heads and assure us they were still trying to understand what people had done to each other. Doña Victoria was one of those who still wondered what had happened.

"Why would it be that people of our own race converted into heartless men? They say they took drugs, *pues*, in the form of pills. That's what they say. Then they would convert into another person. They had no sense, they were crazy. They say they took drugs."

"And who told you this, mama Victoria?"

"The people who know, *pues*. That's why their hearts went crazy. They weren't people anymore. They were not people. They took drugs—pills. Then they had no fear, no respect."

"So the *terrucos* took drugs so they could kill?"

She nodded. "They say they took drugs. Those pills they took—and with the young people they robbed their hearts. They taught them their ideology and then gave them pills. After they took the pills, those young people would accept everything they did. Their hearts converted into something else. Crazy. Like an animal behaves. It was like someone made them so bitter, converted them into enemies of other people. That's how it was. That's why their hearts aren't tranquil anymore."[37]

Similarly, and in this case speaking about his own actions, an ex-*cabecilla* in Tiquihua contemplated his past: "Was it the water we drank or maybe the blood that flows through our bodies? Maybe that's what made us so bad, made us such devils." People also attribute the atrocities they and others committed to an "altered state" or loss of *conciencia*, be it due to drugs, the devil, or—quite simply—the envy and hatred that overflowed with lethal results.

The *sasachakuy tiempo* also signified enormous changes within these communities in both regions. In many cases, communal authorities were assassinated, "beheading" the communities. In the south, local authorities were frequently committed Senderistas, imposing their own order and eliminating those who opposed them. Internal order was massively disrupted, and latent conflicts were exacerbated as the mechanisms of constraint and conflict management that had crafted local moral worlds were destroyed. The absence of communal institutions capable of resolving conflicts and administering justice was a constant throughout Ayacucho, as Hipólito Cayetano explained in Huaychao:

In those years, all of the older men had died. You can see—we're all young. That's why we're so backward. They killed off the old men, the ones with experience. They killed our *umasapas* [literally big heads, referring to those with knowledge]. There was no one left to orient us. We don't know how to walk [*caminar*]—we don't know how to negotiate [*gestionar*] things. Now that it's just us young guys who're authorities, no one obeys at all. Ever since then, we're in bad shape. We live with so much tension.[38]

Magnifying the chaos within these pueblos was the absence of state institutions that might have intervened non-lethally to reestablish order. Aside from the soldiers stationed throughout the countryside, the state was absent. Faced with abandonment by the state and the elimination of many communal authorities, alternatives were limited. In the words of many villagers, "Who were we going to complain to? Where were we going to look for help? There was no one."

Amid this upheaval, two lethal ideologies were influencing the scenario. Communal justice, which emphasizes conciliation between parties to a conflict, ceded to ideologies that eliminated the "gray zone" of communal jurisprudence.[39] Both the Senderistas' ideology as well as that of the armed forces emphasized eradicating the enemy, obliterating the gray zone in favor of a reading in black and white. Particularly in the southern communities, villagers cite the Senderistas' indoctrination as a key factor in the brutality they practiced among themselves. The Senderista doctrine introduced not only new justifications for killing but also new forms of killing that were intentionally "spectacular."

Although allegiances were frequently shifting and blurred, for the military there was no middle ground. This thinking was made clear to me in 1998 in an interview with Lieutenant Valka, who had been stationed in Ayacucho for ten years during the "war against subversion." His rotation brought him once again to Carhuahurán before heading into the *selva* to search for the guerrillas. He was pleased to regale me with his war stories, told without a tear, "Because I am a gypsy [*gitano*] and gypsies never cry." He insisted that even after all those years, some of Carhuahurán's annexes were still collaborating with Sendero, and he was just waiting until he had enough information to prove it. "You need to know, there is no middle ground in this war. These people are either with us or they're with Sendero." I did not tell him that indeed there was a liminal space for those who wanted nothing to do with the fighting or for that growing percentage of *comuneros* who were war-weary. By 1998 many people wanted nothing more fervently than the assurance that the *sasachakuy tiempo* would never return. It had been a long, arduous time since those first militants arrived with their promises and villagers had begun "cleaning" their communities and making enemies.

Making Enemies

We begin in Huanta, where constructions of the "enemy" drew upon psychocultural themes as well as Evangelismo. Different narrative conventions pertain to different realms of experience, and they do so in a dialectical manner. Although I am uncomfortable constructing the sacred and the secular in opposition, for heuristic purposes I do so at this point. Parallel to the secular "event" history that villagers recount about the state and the military during the war, there is a sacred emplotment strategy that was and is equally true. Different histories explain different things, and it is only the tyranny of scholastic logic that wants to pin people down to one version of experience—to one seamlessly coherent narrative. As Hayden White suggests, it is only an imaginary narrative that can offer us a history that is perfectly coherent, without contradictions, without multiple logics.[40] The multiple logics allow for the complexities of contradictory consciousness, the coexistence in individual minds of two seemingly incompatible conceptions of the world. Thus people could see their relatives and neighbors in the guerrilla columns that attacked them while also insisting the Senderistas were not really human at all.

When narrating the war in the *alturas* of Huanta, people used various terms to speak about the guerrillas: *terrucos, malafekuna, tuta puriq, puriqkuna,* and *anticristos.* Each term reflects the condensation of concerns regarding evil and monstrosity, also captured by the many villagers who insist the Senderistas had "fallen out of humanity."[41]

Terrucos is a derivative of terrorists and was borrowed from the military discourse regarding the Senderistas. The Peruvian armed forces conducted a classic counterinsurgency war during the early 1980s, and the notion of communist subversion as a cancer afflicting the national body was common. National Security Doctrine—that genocidal product of the cold war and its bipolar cartography—worked via a double vision. The "communist menace" came from without, spread via the domino theory, yet there was also a lurking internal contagion that justified repressing domestic dissent. This discourse was picked up by villagers and reelaborated: the cancerous legions of the Left appear as the *plagakuna* (the people of the plague).

Externality drew upon state policies and discourse as well. At one point president Fernando Belaúnde (1980–85) insisted Sendero Luminoso was externally financed, although this proved to be incorrect.[42] However, the army promoted the idea of foreign intervention as part of its psychological warfare. Flyers were dropped throughout the countryside, warning villagers of the insidious threat of subversion. One flyer depicted peasants fleeing, cowering as they pointed to an enormous beast with claws, while a soldier appears in the background to rescue them. Framing the graphic are the words "¡*Ayacuchano*! The subversive criminal is a foreigner that has come to destroy you—Reject him!"[43]

Both *malafekuna* (the people of bad faith/bad conscience) and *anticristos* draw upon the idea of "godless communists," as well as the biblical interpretations villagers elaborated about the war. With *malafekuna*, what is also implied is that the Senderistas lacked any conscience, being people who "were only born to kill. " Additionally, given the centrality of the "social covenant" in the establishment and reproduction of community—a theme discussed at length in the next chapter—the image of Senderistas as people of bad faith speaks to a key concern. How does one "recovenant"—how does one negotiate—in good faith with people who have none?

Also common is the term *tuta puriqkuna* (those who walk at night), which stems from long-standing fears of the condemned (*jarjachas*) who walk this earth, inflicting their vengeance on the living. The *jarjachas* are humans who take on animal form as part of their divine punishment. Children can describe in great detail the glowing eyes, hideous teeth, and bloodthirsty ways of the *jarjachas* who inhabit the wild space of the *puna*. I asked many of them how they knew the *jarjachas* were out there, and the answer struck them as obvious: "We *know* they are there because our parents tell us so." Stories that circulate long enough can have a veracity that "personal experience" may not.

And there is the *puna*, where the wild things are. In classic studies of the Peruvian Andes, social scientists have argued that the savage *puna* is constructed in contrast to the civilized space of the village.[44] It is the home of *jarjachas*, as well as the setting for sexual trysts among young people eager to avoid a parental eye. I was told the Senderistas always attacked from the *puna*, frequently arriving undetected on the wind.

Also common is *puriqkuna*, a symbolically rich term. *Puriqkuna* are people who walk and never stay in one place—transgressive people who are out of place, belonging nowhere. This shares a certain logic with the assertion that the Senderistas were *piojosos* (covered with lice). In addition to illustrating concerns with categorical purity, there is something else being referenced by this imagery.[45]

I recall many sunny afternoons in the villages, when long black braids were unwound and washed. Family members would sit on sheepskins, picking the lice out of one another's hair. These are intimate moments. Mothers work through their children's and their husband's hair, and the children gather a younger sibling in their lap, thick black hair giving way to busy fingernails. The idea that the guerrillas walked endlessly and had heads covered with lice suggests something fundamental about their lack of connection both to place and to other people. Humans live in families: What must those *piojos* imply about the status of the Senderistas?

Perhaps not imply but confirm. In an almost mocking fashion, villagers described how the *terrucos* forbid the use of kinship terms; everyone was *compañero* or *compañera* (comrade). This attempt at revolutionizing the affective realm of the family would become a key site of resistance. In his work with former guerrillas from three Senderista bases in the Ayacucho and the Ene River Valley, Ponciano Del Pino argues that "family and culture [were] factors that came to weigh against the discourse of the Senderistas to the extent that human needs subverted Shining Path's artificial order."[46] Recall don Domingo's description of life on the haciendas living *waqcha qina*—like the poor, the orphaned. To live without family is to live in material and affective destitution.

Villagers also insisted the Senderistas "were gringos . . . they came from other countries." Indeed, when I had recently arrived, many villagers were terrified of me. As I was told, "The Senderistas were tall, Kimberly, like you. They also had green eyes. They looked just like you." It was disconcerting to know that my very appearance was frightening.

For the children, such images inspired the same sort of fear as the *jarjachas*. Yolanda and Edith described the tall white men with long beards who ride along the *puna* on horseback. Yolanda grimaced, "They are *llumpay hatun* [very big] and covered in hair."

Edith pulled at my arm, "They smell bad, too."

Yolanda's eyes grew large. "They ride white horses with big tails that can whip around and cut off your head." Their hands went up to cover their faces; just talking about the tall white men was frightening.

Green-eyed, white-skinned, fat-sucking *pishtacos* have a long history in the Andes, as we saw in our discussion of sexual violence.[47] These supernatural beings kill people by stealing the fat from their bodies. The resilience of this figure throughout Andean history has been interpreted as a statement on the exploitation that has characterized relations between indigenous communities and "outsiders."[48]

Similarly, in her study of vampire stories in Africa, Luise White argues that many analyses of body-snatching, blood-sucking fears "seek to explain belief and the imaginary to the observer; they explain why someone might believe what is to most authors make-believe. I am trying to do something different, looking not so much for the reasons behind make-believe as for what such beliefs articulate in a given time and place."[49] So what do these beliefs articulate in a given time and place—in this case, the highlands of Huanta during the internal armed conflict?

In this region, the *universitarios* were outsiders, arriving from the cities. However, these *universitarios* were largely children of *campesinos* who had managed to migrate to the cities and study at the university in Huamanga. While they wore "city clothes," many of them spoke Quechua and shared a similar background with the peasants they were sent out to *concientizar*. They were not white or particularly tall; they did not have green eyes and they were not sucking body fat. The villagers' statements are not true, but that is not the interesting aspect of their assertions.

When villagers insist on the whiteness, tallness, green-eyedness of the guerrillas, they are giving biological force to their fears—loading political categories with somatic force. They draw upon a history of racialized violence in the Andes and a history of abusive relationships between their communities and the broader society in which they move.[50] Being treated as *chutos* is psychologically wounding. Although social scientists have deconstructed race to demonstrate it is a social fiction, these *campesinos* are insisting on the metanarrative of race rather than its deconstruction. Talk about race is a proxy for talk about exploitation and social injustice.

As I would learn during the TRC, in each community the figure of a gringo appeared when villagers gave their testimonies about the war. At times these gringos were Senderistas, in other instances they were mercenaries sent by the Peruvian government. However, in every case these gringos arrived to kill, and to kill brutally. A history of racialized violence is condensed in these bloodthirsty gringos that appear so frequently in *campesinos'* stories about the war. To inscribe this history in a bodily form permits the condensations of disperse forces—racist ideologies, discriminatory treatment, systemic injustices—into a concrete enemy, a physical form capable of being eradicated.

Many scholars have noted that Shining Path did not offer an analysis of ethnic domination in Peru, locating injustice within a critique of class.[51] However, just as watching Bible movies was not a passive activity, neither was listening to the Shining Path cadres. Recall the insistence on "innocent people": "The Senderistas said we were going to kill the rich. But that's not how it was. They began to kill innocent people, *campesinos*. They started to kill people of our own race." "The rich" and "the innocent" appear as antonyms that resonate beyond class. If indeed for the Senderista ideologues everything could be reduced to class, for peasants class was imbued with ethnic differences. At times, these differences invoked a biological imaginary, constructing differences that were supposedly physical, indeed "racial."

However, sometimes racial difference and "foreignness" were not distancing enough. The Senderistas were also described as (literally) otherworldly. Jesús Romero had lived through several attacks. As he recalled, "We killed them and saw their bodies. It was so difficult to kill them—they didn't want to die. They had to shoot them several times to kill them. Some of them were women. One time, I saw the bodies. They had three belly buttons and their *sexo* [genitals] were in another part of their body." Similarly, in Carhuahurán and Huaychao several villagers stated that the female Senderistas had long belly buttons that stuck out, while the males had *waqokuna* (tusks) like pigs. People insisted they could always tell if someone was a Senderista by examining his or her body. People were killed, bodies were seen, corpses were examined.[52]

Why the belly buttons, the tusks, and the out-of-place genitals? The rich elaboration of corporeal difference was central to the moral binaries characteristic of a wartime code of conduct. These villagers are phenotypically homogeneous. Certainly there is social stratification, but there are no categorical physical differences. Thus, people constructed them. Identities were in flux and it was difficult to know if anyone was what they seemed. Enrique Mayer has written, "Sendero slogans painted on walls proclaim that the 'party has a thousand eyes and ears.' Security employees, narcotraffickers, arms dealers, grave robbers and police all operate underground. Terrorists dress up as police, while police don *Sendero* guise to carry out acts of unauthorized violence."[53] One could not trust superficial appearances—they could be cast on and off far too easily. And appearance could not be taken at "face value" either. Villagers insist the Senderistas and their sympathizers were "two-faced" (*iskay uyakuna*). At a time when crucial diacritics of identity were blurred, bodies would be divined to produce truth.

The focus on genitals "out of place" also warrants our attention. In addition to conveying a sense of monstrosity, it also reflects abnormal reproduction, be it blocked or gone mad. For villagers, rituals central to social and cultural reproduction were casualties of war. During the worst years of the war in the highlands of Huanta, villagers sought refuge in caves, and a measles epidemic broke out with devastating consequences. Adults recalled that "we buried three to five children a day," adding to the hellish images of life in those bat-infested caves.

I have also spoken with men and women who stopped having sex during the *sasachakuy tiempo* rather than bring more children into this world. Faced with the suffering of the war, they decided it was best not to give birth to babies destined for so much sadness. Some of the children undoubtedly overheard the adults. When I asked the children I spent so much time with in Carhuahurán how many children *they* wanted to have when they grew up, the uniformity of their responses reflected battle strategy: "Just two. If the *terrucos* arrive, how can you escape if you have more than two children to carry?" In many regions the Senderistas carried children off to work as members of the "masses" that were supposed to keep the combatants fed. Many parents feared their children would be kidnaped and they might never see them again. Magnifying the villagers' worries was the Senderistas' slogan, "The leadership [*mando*] never dies." While peasants' reproduction— in every sense of the word—was threatened, the guerrillas insisted, "We multiply like the grains of sand."

These deformed bodies also drew upon the Bible, a key semiotic resource in the north. Monstrosity is a recurrent theme in Bible stories, and evil is frequently inscribed visibly on the body. Demonic figures appeared repeatedly in the northern narratives, and power is always ambiguous. These images dehumanize while also invoking superhuman powers: "They had to shoot her three times because she didn't want to die."

And the belly buttons—at times three, at times protruding grotesquely out of the abdomen. Our belly button establishes our first connection with another human being: our mother. This is our primordial connection, allowing one human to nourish another. In exploring the terms villagers in the north used to refer to the Senderistas, I found that several implied the *terrucos* had no family ties. One extreme form of this was captured in another expression used to describe the Senderistas: *Supaypa wawan*—son or daughter of the Devil. Those deformed belly buttons graphically capture that image, as well as another: "They were not of a woman born."[54]

In addition to these terms and the images they invoke, there is another element that reappeared in many conversations: the Senderistas bore a mark on their arm. Mama Marcelina had lived in Carhuahurán during the years of the war. She described the attacks she had lived through and the knife that had been pressed against her throat. And she knew something else: "The *malafekuna* had a mark seared deep into the flesh of their forearms. They all had the mark." She was one of many people who assured me they could always determine a real Senderista by that mark.

What might the mark be? Villagers have long practiced what is called "popular Catholicism," referring to a mixture of Catholic theology and indigenous cosmologies. This Catholicism shares many features with the Pentecostalized Evangelismo that was widely adopted during the war. This was a potent blend of revelations, miracles, faith healing, and the imminent arrival of the Antichrist: "And ye shall know him by his mark—666."

But the mark was about something more than the beast. The lament "among *prójimos* we were killing" still echoes—the original fratricide resonates. When Cain, tiller of the soil, and his brother Abel, a shepherd, each brought an offering from the fruit of their toils to God, Abel's offer was accepted while God rejected Cain's. Ignoring a divine warning on the pitfalls of sin, Cain murdered Abel out of envy. When God asked him where Abel was, Cain responded with a question of his own: "Am I my brother's keeper?" God then condemned him to wander the earth, bearing a mark that would last for seven generations.

In her genealogy of the mark of Cain, Ruth Mellinkoff notes, "Popular, customary, present-day ideas about the mark of Cain see it as a brand or stigma, a means to identify, humiliate and punish criminal Cain, yet such notions have no basis in the biblical text."[55] She suggests it is precisely the ambiguity of the mark that has made it "so good to think."

The mark of the Senderistas was their condemnation made visible, proof they had "fallen out of humanity." Erving Goffman argues that stigma is a language of bodily difference in which the difference informs the "moral career" of the person marked, in part because the individual is perceived as not quite human, as disqualified from full social acceptance. He also notes that visibility of the stigma is a crucial factor, as is the "decoding ability" of the audience.[56] Examining the bodies of the Senderistas was a form of divination, of reading the truth of their inner evil on the surface of their bodies.

This calls to mind the evidential or divinatory paradigm Carlo Ginzburg explores in *Clues, Myths and the Historical Method*. Drawing upon a shared "medical semiotics" or reading of bodily signs, this epistemological model allows the trained eye—be it medical or criminological—to decipher and interpret observable signs and marks to construct a complex narrative that can be directed toward the past, present, or future: "For the future, there was divination in the strict sense; for the past, the present, and the future, there was medical semiotics in its twofold aspect, diagnostic and prognostic; for the past, there was jurisprudence."[57] Thus the truth of the body could be projected back in time or serve as a presage of the future, both components in constructing accountable people.

People of bad faith, transgressive wanderers who were only born to kill, the people of the plague—the mark burned into their flesh produced bodies of evidence, blending juridical and religious methods of moral indictment. Thus political categories were naturalized and enemies were made. People began to kill among *prójimos*, and for a time such killing was central to constructing "community." This was made clear in a conversation with someone who had helped bury the bodies.

It was early morning in Carhuahurán when Chuko came by, reeling drunk with his Mauser (rifle) tossed over his shoulder. He was a member of Los Tigres, a special self-defense unit the village had started in addition to their *ronda campesina*. It was 1997 and there had been a series of Senderista incursions in outlying villages an hour or two away on foot. In response to the increased security threats, the community voted to pay a monthly wage to a group of young men. Los Tigres patrolled during the day, in addition to the obligatory night watch carried out in turn by all adult men in the *ronda campesina*.

Chuko knew he should not be drinking while on duty but insisted it was the only way to tolerate the freezing cold. We offered him a cup of coffee; it helped thaw his hands, but caffeine alone was not going to sober Chuko up anytime soon. He rose to his feet, waving the rifle around as he tried to catch his balance. The nozzle was aimed in whirlwind fashion around the room—and at our heads. He registered the concern that raised our eyebrows. "I should not have this gun right now—I'm too drunk," he told us, somewhat chagrined. He took the bullets out and handed them to Efraín before passing me the Mauser. "Can you hide my gun under your bed? Don't tell anyone—just keep it for me until I feel better." We were relieved to have him hand us the rifle, and I buried it beneath my blankets. He stumbled out, thanking us as he left.

He did sober up later that day and came back with a bag of *olluco* (a tuber) as thanks for concealing the weapon until it was safe for him to have it. He stayed for a while, telling us about the battles he had fought in during the war. He told us he had killed Senderistas and that the villagers had buried many dead guerrillas down below Carhuahurán, on the steep slope leading down to the river. "You know, before the houses here were always sliding down the hill. We kept trying to prop them up, but the cliff is too steep. But once we buried the *terrucos* down there, the ground stopped sliding and our houses stayed put." Evidently, burying Senderistas down below bolstered the community, figuratively and literally.

Regimes of Truth

> The question whether objective truth can be attributed to human thinking is not a question of theory but a *practical* question. Man must prove the truth, i.e. the reality and power, the this-sideness of his thinking in practice. The dispute over the reality or non-reality of thinking that is isolated from practice is a purely *scholastic* question.
> —Karl Marx, *The German Ideology*

So what are we to make of these "Senderista stories?" Michel Foucault famously wrote, "Now I believe the problem does not consist in drawing the line between that in a discourse which comes under the category of scientificity of truth, and that which comes under some other category, but in seeing historically how effects of truth are produced within discourses which in themselves are neither true nor false."[58] In villagers' accounts of the Senderistas, their actions and their bodies, we are confronted with discourses that have had powerful truth effects even if they do not unfold according to the truth tests of scientific logic or evidence.

There are several ways to approach this question, one of which is to locate these stories within the realm of practical logic. Pierre Bourdieu has contrasted scholastic logic with the logic of practice, a mode of knowledge that is the basis of our ordinary experience in the world and that rests in part on having a "feel for things."[59] Bourdieu cautions against an overly schematic logic that demands coherence where it does not exist. This is an important caution, particularly for anthropologists tracing the logic of war and moral sensibilities.

I am persuaded by Bourdieu's work on the body and belief, which in turn helps us understand the experiential aspects of moral life. In *The Logic of Practice*, he writes that "practical belief is not a 'state of mind,' still less a kind of arbitrary adherence to a set of instituted dogmas and doctrines ('beliefs'), but rather a state of the body."[60] He discusses the construction of our taken-for-granted reality, which leads him to explore the genesis of belief that is central to the "naturalness" of the world. He grounds the acquisition of belief in our bodies: "The body believes in what it plays at: it weeps if it mimes grief. It does not represent what it performs, it does not memorize the past, it *enacts* the past, bringing it back to life. What is 'learned by the body' is not something that one has, like knowledge that can be brandished, but something that one is."[61] The Senderista stories are *felt* to be true, and my fieldwork convinces me that saying something is so powerful that the enunciation can make it so. In many conversations, people hesitated to name the Senderistas for fear that speaking their name would make them appear. To state the *terrucos* had marks on their bodies may be constative, but performing the utterance sets the context for its veracity. The war stories thus have a double aspect: the constative meaning and the performative force that creates the truth conditions necessary for them to be effective. The performative aspect of the stories points to the poetics of these moral chronologies. In the poetics we capture the shape and the feel of these histories and the materiality of moral reasoning.

In rereading the transcripts from my interviews and field notes, there is a repetitive sentence structure—*se dice* in Spanish, which is marked by suffixes in Quechua that indicate a third person, either singular or plural.[62] "It is said," "they say"—these phrases are remarkable only in their abundance. This verb declension is paired with that other phrase which figured prominently in the stories people told about the war years: *Hukmanmi karqani* (I was of another form). The sense of self-alienation expressed when people spoke about their experiences during the *sasachakuy tiempo* is crucial to understanding why "hearsay" may be more convincing than personal experience. "I was of another form" indicates that first-person experience was not necessarily trustworthy. The stories "they tell" make sense of the inchoate nature of personal experience in times of war, when one has felt strange to oneself. The narrative force of *se dice* signals the death of the author—the truthfulness of the story does not depend on the individual speaker. Rather, the narrative force of the statement draws upon a broader regime of truth that erases the tracks of its own ontology. One is *disposed* to belief.

I return to Luise White's research on vampire stories and her concern with local notions of credibility and proof.

> A simple premise undergirds my interpretation of vampire stories in this book: people do not speak with truth, with a concept of the accurate description of what they saw, to say what they mean, but they construct and repeat stories that carry the values and meanings that most forcibly get their points across. People do not always speak from experience—even when that is considered the most accurate kind of information—but speak with stories that circulate to explain what happened.[63]

Senderista stories convey values and meanings; they construct a new moral order born in the commission of amoral acts. These are moral chronologies: the situatedness of the good is forged both in the moment of the act as well as in the subsequent narration. I am arguing for a phenomenology of morality—for a recognition of the felt sense of the good, the just, and of evil. These Senderista stories are not received with a hermeneutics of suspicion; rather, these moral chronologies "feel right," and to speak with these stories is to speak within the regime of truth that was the *sasachakuy tiempo*.

Chapter 8

The Micropolitics of Reconciliation

I WOULD LIKE to present myself as the quick and insightful anthropologist, but I am averse to lying. When villagers first referred to who had been human and who had not, I assumed these were interesting metaphors, idiomatic expressions. One of the first times someone used this sort of language was in passing. The conversation was so casual that I cannot even remember the context. I can only recall passing Michael one day when he was still in Los Tigres. Maybe I asked if everything was "*tranquilo*," perhaps where he was headed on patrol. I truly cannot remember what inconsequential comment I made. But when I look back on my field notes from that day, I see that I wrote down a phrase: *Montipi hapimuspan runayachirqaniku*—"We grabbed them [Senderistas] in the mountains to convert them into people." There is just that line. Nothing more. It was only later when I had heard these sorts of comments from a variety of people that I began to realize these were very real conversions—concrete practices of communal justice that villagers utilized in "making people."

Performing Justice

Eucebio's big flatbed truck pulled into the field in Carhuahurán, honking to let people know a truck would be leaving that day for Huanta. I ran down the hill to let him know Efraín and I would be traveling and that we just needed some time to get our things ready. He nodded, telling me he would wait. I walked back up the hill to the base and we packed up our things, locking the room behind us. We said our good-byes to people on the walk down, letting them know we'd be back the following week.

Efraín and I climbed into the truck cab to stake out seats. But an hour into going nowhere, I leaned out the window to ask Eucebio if something was wrong. He shook his head, "*Manam.*" I looked back over my shoulder and saw the truck was loaded with villagers and their *costales* (burlap sacks, in this case, full of goods), but we still didn't move. It was ten in the morning and we were still in Carhuahurán. The trip to Huanta took about six hours, longer still if passengers with many *costales* could persuade the driver to drop each of them in front of their final destinations, winding through the dirt streets on the outskirts of the town.

Eucebio finally came around to the driver's side and got in, looking a bit uncomfortable. "We need to wait for don Teofilo," he told me.

"Oh, El Piki is coming with us?" I asked.

"No, don Teofilo Chumayco from the Asociación Pro-Obras Hijos de Carhuahurán—él que mueve los documentos en Lima [Association Pro-Public Works Sons of Carhuahurán—he who moves the documents in Lima]." I nodded. Don Teofilo Chumayco Lunasco was an important visitor indeed. He was the head of the migrants' association in Lima, composed of people who had migrated from Carhuahurán and served as important resources in the capital. As Eucebio said, don Lunasco facilitated the community's paperwork in Lima. The Asociación Pro-Obras Hijos de Carhuahurán helped bring public works to the community, serving as a mediator between the villagers and the state bureaucracy. The truck was certainly going to wait for him.

Another thirty minutes passed before he appeared, recovering from the previous night's send-off. His baseball cap was pulled down low on his forehead, and white stubble Velcroed his scarf to his chin. Efraín and I fused our hips, making room for don Lunasco and letting him know how pleased we were to be meeting someone who had done so much for his pueblo.

Don Lunasco was seventy-five years old and had been one of the founders of the association. "The only original member left is *él que habla*—he who is speaking." As Eucebio maneuvered the sharp turn leading up out of the community, I asked don Lunasco when he had left for Lima.

"Before the *peligro* [danger]," he responded. He had remained in Lima and tried to send aid when possible.

"Oh, there's a lot more aid now, isn't there? The road, the school," my voice drifting off.

Don Lunasco acknowledged this. "El Chino [President Fujimori] has done some good things. But he's selling the country to Japan! There won't be anything left by the time he's done." Don Lunasco shook his head in disgust. "And besides, El Chino is earning $50,000 a month! Congressmen earn $1,000 a month! This is ridiculous."

I nodded. "There is a lot of corruption in politics, no?"

He threw his head back—"Yes, too much."

As we descended the slope at Pukaqasa, both Eucebio and don Lunasco pointed to sites where there had been Senderista attacks. The landscape was mapped with battle scenes. Eucebio pointed to several mountains, indicating where he had barely escaped with his life when the *rondas* had pursued the *terrucos*. Don Lunasco shook his head: "So many *campesinos* died here." We sat silently for a while, looking at the desolate fields.

As we pulled into Chaka, several villagers called out for Eucebio to stop. I bought a round of soda crackers for everyone at the *tienda* and climbed back in the cab. It was late 1999 and I wanted to hear a bit more about don Lunasco's opinion of El Chino. The brand-new school on the hillside provided a seamless segue. "Fujimori has funded lots of *obras* [public works], hasn't he?"

He nodded half-heartedly. "Yes, but he steals too much. And there's also that Ley de Amistad [Friendship Law] that he passed." Don Lunasco snorted and rolled his eyes. It took me a few moments to follow. As he kept speaking, I slowly realized don Lunasco was talking about the Ley de Amnistía (Amnesty Law) that Fujimori had passed in 1995 amid mass protest. This was a sweeping amnesty law extended to all members of the armed forces and the police, and worked both retroactively and proactively. Amnesty was granted back to 1980 and forward to an undefined date when the country would be deemed "pacified."

"What do you think of this Ley de Amistad?" I asked.

Don Lunasco thought for a moment. "Well, *it's a whole Catholic model.*" His voice raised into a dismissive lilt. "Oh, you're not supposed to punish anyone anymore. Oh, you just have to forgive everybody. It's not worth it anymore to denounce people or file a complaint." He shrugged and looked out the window.

I waited a bit before asking him, "What do you think? Is this a good thing or a bad thing?"

"Well, I guess it's all right." He shook his head again. "Ley de Amistad. In these communities, they have their *propias prácticas* [own practices]."

A bit of explanation. As with all of the *campesinos* with whom I worked, don Lunasco's first language was Quechua. Although he spoke Spanish as a result of his many years in Lima, it was conversational Spanish. I am certain he was functionally literate in Spanish—*él que mueve los documentos*—but there is a large gap between functional literacy and understanding the arcane language of law.

The vast majority of people obtained their news via the radio, which leaves much room for interpretation. It was common to have a group of people seated around the radio, scrap-wire antennae poking out at various angles in search of the airwaves. There was usually a designated translator who provided a synopsis of the news in Quechua. Although there were two Quechua-language stations in the *campo*, listening to Spanish stations was an important source of information and prestige. The ability to access extra-local sources of information in the national language was a form of power. The translator was an information gatekeeper, and he gave the news his own personal spin. New words—amnesty, refugees, privatization—were heard in a way that "made sense" to both the gatekeeper and his audience. Hence *amnistía* could become *amistad*, capturing familiar sounds as well as offering a critique of the idea.

Don Lunasco's disdainful assessment of the "whole Catholic model" is striking. Perhaps we can understand this disdain by thinking of it as "half a Catholic model," emphasizing forgiveness and friendship without integrating other aspects of the Judeo-Christian legacy: retribution and settling accounts. As Susan Jacoby has argued, "Retribution as a requirement for reconciliation is a pillar of the fundamental covenants governing both Judaism and Christianity—a fact of religious history that has frequently been ignored by Christian theologians intent on proving the superiority of Christian mercy to Judaic vengeance."[1]

Exploring the *propias prácticas* of these communities offers a way to understand subaltern concepts and practices of justice. Studies of legal pluralism have focused on the construction of customary law as a colonial and postcolonial category, arguing that customary law is an example of a hybrid legal system that is forged in dialogue between communal and national legal practices—a dialogue between unequal parties.[2] The communal administration of justice is a complex choreography of maintaining autonomy while accessing state and religious forms of adjudication and power.

One conceit of the modern state is its secularity, and the rule of law is the hallmark of modernity. However, the theology of law and politics reveals common origins, shared practices, and symbols. For example, in tracing the evolution of Latin American criminal justice systems, Mauricio Duce and Rogelio Pérez Perdomo found that Latin American codes of criminal procedure, although adopted by most of the countries in the second half of the nineteenth century (after the reform in Europe), remained linked to the previous inquisitorial tradition.[3] This shared Catholic origin speaks to Sally Falk Moore's critique of "articulation models" that imply that "elements that originated in one system remain in it even when the general context has changed. Inherent in the very idea of articulation is a presumption of continuing distinctness and separateness of the original system. The retrospective bias can create intellectual obstacles for the analysis of integrated combinants."[4] Moore's critique is applicable to Peru and to an analysis of the *propias prácticas* don Teofilo referred to. Communal justice deploys many elements of the state's symbolic repertoire, illustrating that autonomy is not synonymous with isolation.

In this chapter, I am interested in legal pluralism not only as the blending of "indigenous" and national legal systems but also in terms of the multiple legal strategies people practice in an elusive, ongoing search for justice. Legal pluralism works in a way similar to medical pluralism; certain forms of adjudication are considered appropriate to different sorts of problems. Thus legal pluralism refers not only to multiple legal systems but to multiple legal strategies and consciousness as well. Communal justice is deeply pluralistic, blending theology, politics, economics, and law in a synthesis that resembles Marcel Mauss's "system of total services."[5]

The blending of strategies draws upon both Christian *caridad* and righteous wrath. In her book *Between Vengeance and Forgiveness*, Martha Minow discusses the concept of restorative justice, suggesting it is based upon Christian notions of forgiveness and the reclaiming of humanity.[6] Rather than suggesting this as a model to be applied in all times and places, she notes that restorative justice presumes the presence of a community and of relationships worthy of repair. Her arguments have tremendous resonance with the processes of *arrepentimiento* (repentance) and reconciliation practiced in rural villages in Ayacucho. I will extend her argument by examining how villagers administer both retributive and restorative justice, illustrating Hannah Arendt's maxim that man cannot forgive what he cannot punish (and cannot punish certain acts because they defy proportionality).[7]

While the themes of security and defense were open topics—there were general assemblies several times a week to discuss these issues—the processes of confession, repentance, and reconciliation were not "public transcripts."

These juridico-religious practices aimed at the reincorporation of the ex-guerrillas into communal life were not openly discussed and formed part of the "hidden transcript" of demilitarization that evaded the watchful eyes of the soldiers stationed in the military bases or other state representatives who made their way to these rural villages. Concerns that the military would denounce their villages as *zonas rojas* ("red zones"—sympathetic to the guerrilla) kept these processes occult.[8]

The gap between private and public transcripts points to the ambiguous attitudes *campesinos* have toward the state. In her study in the southern Peruvian Andes, Penelope Harvey found that for rural villagers, "the state is both a source of progress and of oppression."[9] For people who inhabit "the margins of the state," looking to the state for justice may not be their first inclination.[10] Whereas analyses informed by Foucauldian governmentality interrogate the state in its rational-bureaucratic mode, what is obscured is the state in its other registers. As Begoña Aretxaga argues, the state materializes not only through "rules and bureaucratic routines, but also through a world of fantasy thoroughly narrativized, and imbued with affect, fear, and desire, that make it, in fact, a plausible reality."[11] The capricious, horrific, at times benevolent, at times malignant state forces villagers to combine various routes to seeking justice, determining what the state and its representatives are and are not "good for."[12] Thus popular legal consciousness includes an awareness of the state as both protector and aggressor, which in turn shapes the communal use of local conflict-dispute mechanisms that both access and limit the full force of the law.

(Christian) Compassion and (Righteous) Wrath

We woke up slowly that morning in Carhuahurán, still recuperating from the long truck ride the day before. There was a trade-off when riding in the trucks that bounced their way up to the villages. One option was to wake up at three in the morning and commiserate with the skinny dogs scavenging in the street. We would walk a few blocks to the park in Huanta and negotiate for seats in the cab. It was a luxury to sit in the cab, roll up the windows, and watch our breath creep across the windshield. To get the prized seats we had to outmaneuver schoolteachers, personnel from the NGOs, and the occasional *campesino* who was willing to pay the extra two *soles* for the comfort and the status of riding up front.

The other alternative was sleeping in until five and settling for a slender space in the open truck bed, surfing on *costales* stuffed full of goods being transported to the villages in the highlands. The wooden pole running down the middle of the truck bed provided some ballast, but the frigid morning air froze our fingers as we gripped the pole. The women tried to find some flat area on the *costales* to sit down as it was difficult to stand with a baby swinging back and forth in a shawl tied around their shoulders. The drivers made several rounds through the streets of Huanta, calling out their destinations in hopes of drumming up a few more passengers.

We had exercised the 3:00 a.m. option the day before, so waking up happened slowly that morning in Carhuahurán. We replied to early morning visitors from the warmth of our sleeping bags. Guilt that I was being a bad anthropologist forced me to extract my body, one reluctant extremity at a time. I cranked on our gas burner and placed a pot of water on to boil. Peering out the door, I saw that the sun was drying up the moisture the fog had laid down the night before. I made a thermos of coffee and handed a cup to Efraín. "I'll wait for you outside. I'm gonna make like a cat." I needed to stretch out my back in the sun and hear the bones crack their way back into line. We were living in a room in the ex–military base overlooking Carhuahurán, sleeping on Styrofoam mattresses stacked up on the dirt floor. The base was slowly disintegrating, the adobe blocks losing their angles and sliding formlessly back into mud. The painted blue aluminum doors that had guarded the entrance to the base now hung on their few remaining nails, the image of the skull and crossbones lying on its side.

Efraín and I decided to walk across the gorge to Cercán and see who might be home. We headed down the steep hill from the base. Decorum had prompted the soldiers to line each side of the footpath with whitewashed rocks; they remained, paint peeling back like cheap nail polish. Halfway down the slope we saw mama Benita sitting in her doorway, her spindle growing fat with bright red acrylic yarn her son Marcos had bought at the last *feria*. She asked us where we were headed. "Just to Cercán, mama," I replied.

"Hmmm," Benita nodded, wool spinning through her nimble fingers. She liked to keep track of who was doing what, where, and with whom.

We jumped off the four-foot ledge of dirt a tractor had piled up on each side of its route and landed on the crust of dirt covering the muddy field that hosted the weekly *feria*. Another steep descent dropped us in front of the four houses directly across from the cemetery. All of the padlocks were closed and only a few children who were too young to pasture animals were outside playing with sticks, drawing in the dirt.

As we rounded the curve in front of Miguel Quispe's house, we saw someone coming up the steep footpath, moving slowly under the weight of a large plastic bucket. The figure came into focus, sharpening into an elderly woman struggling up the hill. Efraín and I exchanged glances and walked down the slope to offer her help. Efraín slipped his hand through the white plastic handle and we turned around and headed back up. "Mamacita linda, papacito, gracias," the elderly woman repeated in the high lilting tones women use when greeting or thanking people. We arrived in front of a large wooden door and the woman unclasped the safety pin that held her keys to her sweater, unlocked the padlock, and propped the door open with a rock. Efraín crossed the room and set the bucket down in front of the blackened stones in the corner that served as her stove.

"*Imataq sutiyki*, mama?" I asked as she kept thanking us.

"My name is Marcelina," she replied, inviting us to follow her next door to the room that doubled as her bedroom and store.

One wall was taken up by her bed, an elevated mattress sitting on a wood frame, piled high with blankets. Clothes hung from the rafters overhead, a jumble of handspun wool and cheap polyester from the city. High-pitched yelps rang out in rapid succession, and out from under her bed came a round tummy on four paws. Pichi (Pee-pee), her little puppy, half walked and half rolled over to Marcelina's feet before squatting to demonstrate the appropriateness of his name.

Marcelina searched through the pile on her bed and pulled out a *manta* and a *pellejo* (sheepskin) for us to sit on. The two wooden planks that warehoused Marcelina's store were lined with blue and green Bolivar soaps, big waxy rectangles that we used for washing hair, clothes, skin, and pots. The rest of the shelves were stacked with sheer plastic bags full of the white food groups that villagers crave: sugar, noodles, and rice. Her daughter in Huamanga had brought big bags of sugar and rice up to Marcelina so that she could divide up the contents and sell a little something to generate cash.

Marcelina was amazingly candid with us from the first moment we met. She explained that her deceased husband had appeared in her dreams the night before, indicating that a gringa would be coming to see her. He assured her that even though most gringos are dangerous, I was not. She smiled and patted my knee. "He appears in my dreams a lot. It's like he's alive. They are good dreams. When I dream about him, something good always happens.

I sell something and I'm happy because I've dreamed about him. I think to myself, certainly God is going to send me something."

Marcelina was a *warmisapa* and had *el don de hablar* in abundance. She did not merely tell her stories; she performed them. When the subject turned to the war, Senderista attacks were mapped out on the dirt floor of her house with a stick. Spindles became knives, held to the throat to demonstrate how the *puriqkuna* had threatened her. She wrapped my scarf tightly around my head to show me how the guerrillas had hidden their faces with masks, leaving only their evil, squinting eyes shining out from the depths. *Hacendados* who had left the zone after the Agrarian Reform of 1968 were resuscitated, screeching, "*Indios, indios!*" in an imperious tone. History came alive in her store.

As with so many other *warmisapas*, mama Marcelina contrasted the *antiguo tiempo* and the *caridad* people had with the indifference that made life so difficult now. She lamented the demise of *miskipay* and the other forms of compassion that had been part of life in her community before the war. The loss, and recuperation, of *caridad* was a leitmotif that echoed throughout my field notes.

Marcelina returned to this repeatedly, telling us she still felt pain for those who had died. "You have *llakis* when you remember your fellow creatures. You remain perplexed, even now. You say to yourself, 'They did this to our fellow creatures [*prójimos*]? If they hadn't killed them, they would still be alive. They were good people.' This is what you say and you have *llakis*. If they had lived we would have many more [people] in this village. Now that they're not living, we always have *llakis* for our fellow creatures." She wiped her eyes again, adding, "When you have *llakis* and your tears flow, you ruin your vision. Crying so much means you can't see right."

It was both *llakis* and *caridad* that worked in interesting ways during the violence. As with other villagers, Marcelina spoke of her hatred for the *malafekuna* and her pain for villagers who had been killed, as well as her sympathy for the guerrillas who came around to Carhuahurán, begging to be *runakuna* (people) again. These strands of thinking and feeling ran parallel, reflecting the deep ambivalence those intimate enemies still provoke.

Marcelina was the first person I encountered who spoke openly about the *arrepentidos*—the repentant ones, literally the ex-Senderistas. I was familiar with the Repentance Law (Ley de Arrepentimiento) that former president Alberto Fujimori had passed in 1992 in an effort to eradicate the Shining Path.[13] Members of the guerrilla were given the opportunity to "repent," turn themselves in, and receive lighter sentences if they "named names." This counterinsurgency strategy resulted in some 6,630 combatants coming forth. However, the process of denouncing alleged Senderistas resulted in the detention of many innocent people who were falsely accused and imprisoned. Some have suggested this process allowed the guerrillas to "take out" long-standing enemies who had resisted the revolution.

References to *arrepentidos* are also found in letters sent from military commanders to the minister of state and prefect in Ayacucho shortly after the War of Independence when villagers in the "Iquichano territories" continued fighting in alliance with the Spanish Crown.[14] After the pacification campaign carried out to "conquer this marginal region of the nation," Coronel Vidal wrote a reassuring letter indicating "The Indians are reunited with us, repentant of the trickery they suffered from the caudillos, for which I believe they will be peaceful forever."[15]

The term *arrepentido* also appears in early legal codes, predating the use of repentance as a counterinsurgency tool. For example, in the *Diccionario razonado de legislación y jurisprudencia*, written by Joaquin Escriche in the mid-1800s, repentance is defined in such a way as to blur distinctions between the legal and the religious connotations of the word: "*Arrepentimiento*—In spite of having done something, the desire to annul, rescind, revoke or remedy what one feels he has done."[16] Escriche notes that in terms of crime, to repent diminishes the degree of criminality, which should subsequently diminish the punishment. However, to produce this effect repentance must be voluntary, opportune, and manifested in external acts. Thus the language of repentance has a lengthy history, both at the national and local level and in its religious and legal registers.

Marcelina told us about the *malafekuna* who had found their way to Carhuahurán: "They repented for the suffering they endured there in the mountains. Oh, how much they suffered, day and night, in the rain, they just kept walking. So they came to the villages. They would start to think about coming down from the hills. 'I'll go and present myself,' they said. 'Surely the villagers won't kill me,' they thought."

"And what happened when they came here?" I asked.

"They would arrive telling us they had been *engañados* [tricked], forced to kill, always walking. 'Pardon me' [*perdonaykuwaychiq*], they would plead. 'Pardon me,' they would beg the community."

We were there for several hours as Marcelina described in detail how the *arrepentidos* were received.

"They asked, 'Are you going to stop being like that?' If they were going to stop, we accepted them [*chaskiqku*]. 'But be careful you don't let them [the Senderistas] in.'" We would ask them over and over, 'Are you going to let the Senderistas in?' They would promise not to. We asked them if they could forget that they had learned to kill. They promised they could. Questioning and questioning, they accepted them. So *runayaruspanku* [they would become people], they were peaceful and weren't going back to that [Senderismo]. They were watched. They were watched night and day for where they might go. And if they didn't go back, then they were like *común runa igualña*—like common people, like us."

I thought about the *quejas* (legal cases) I had witnessed in the villages. "Were they punished when they came to repent?"

Marcelina nodded. "Oh, yes, the authorities whipped them in public. They were whipped with *chicotes* [braided leather whips with flayed ends] warning them what would happen if they decided to go back. Whipping them, they were received here."

At this point I was becoming confused about pronouns. There seemed to be one "we," but "they" was referring to Senderistas at one point and some other group as well. In carefully listening to the taped interview, it became clear who the second "they" were: the village authorities. While "we" included the *comuneros* and *comuneras* present, "they" referred to the authorities, an important distinction I will return to later.

I was also trying to get some sense of the chronology. No woman I spoke with used dates when talking about their lives, the war; dates simply did not enter into their narratives. I frequently struggled to understand if we were talking about an attack in 1980, 1985, or just last year. So I asked about soldiers, since their sustained presence in the base began in 1985. Marcelina replied, "The soldiers were ready to kill them. They killed them. That's why they [the *arrepentidos*] asked the community not to tell the soldiers. 'Please don't tell them, they'll kill me.' That's how they begged us. Oh, they begged a lot, crying. So they didn't tell the soldiers. Only later, the soldiers didn't kill them—later the soldiers found out but didn't kill them. That was later. Before, they killed even the children, the women, the men. They grabbed them, brought them here, and killed them."

Efraín leaned forward, "They killed them here?"

Marcelina nodded emphatically. "Oh, they killed many of them. They would grab them." She pointed toward the river that ran below Carhuahurán. "Below in the gorge they buried a lot of them. To kill them, the soldiers had them dig a hole. Sometimes they dug a hole with people from the community, and once they killed them they buried them there. When the bullet exploded, we'd say, 'There, it's done. They killed the *pobre* [poor person].'"

I wanted to follow how the decisions were made. "When did the community kill the *arrepentidos* and when did they accept them?"

Marcelina explained, "When they repented, then they accepted them. When they didn't want to repent, they turned them over to the soldiers. When they begged, crying, crying, they would whip them with a *chicote*, and people here understood them. They couldn't kill them. *Comun runakuna* [common people of the community] couldn't kill them."

"Did they only accept *arrepentidos* from here or from other places, too?" I asked.

Marcelina shifted her legs, complaining of the stiffness that made it hard for her to walk up the steep hills each day. "From other places, *pues*," her use of "*pues*" making it clear the answer struck her as obvious. "When they repented they stayed as though they were from here. *Qinan llaqtayarun* [becoming like fellow villagers], they stayed here and didn't go off to any other place. So they remained, right up until now, without going to the jungle, to Huanta, not anywhere. Like they were from this pueblo. They remained here. So we lived together, if they were peaceful. *Runayarunkuña* [becoming people already], not Senderistas anymore. They said, 'If I was walking with them, it was because they took me with a knife, with bullets, with threats.' Fearing for their lives, they remained here. Oh, how much they suffered, walking at night, with rain and without rain, eating or not eating. They escaped the *terrucukuna* and delivered themselves [*entregar*] to this village."

"When they delivered themselves, were they alone?"

Marcelina shook her head. "The men presented themselves, with their wives, with their children. That's how they lived. They always escaped man-woman. When a man alone presented himself, he would then go back to bring his wife and children. He would talk to the authorities so he could bring his family."

"Mama Marcelina, did anyone ever escape alone?"

"Yes, but when they came alone the soldiers grabbed them and killed them. Or sometimes they took them to Castro [Castropampa, the military base in Huanta]. But those who came with their wives and children, no. They didn't allow just one lone person because they said maybe they're here to educate themselves so they can attack our village. There was much more distrust."

The reasoning was complex, and I tried to understand as best I could. Marcelina repeated herself: "They would confess. They would come, asking to bring their families. They always escaped as couples, man and woman. If they came alone, we turned them over to the soldiers. If they came alone [single], there was more distrust. 'What if they're just here to plan how to attack us,' we thought. When they came as families, we had more trust. They could be *runakuna* [people] again."

I wanted to confirm something I'd been told by others. "Mama Marcelina, before the violence, did people here kill?"

Her reply was emphatic. "*Manam.* We were *tranquilos*! They only fought when they were drunk."

"But there were fights between communities, right? For land?"

She insisted there were not.[17] "No, we were *tranquilos*. We didn't go into other lands. We just worked our *chacras*. The *antiguo señorkuna* [former authorities] were strict and told us we could only work our own lands and not pass over into our neighbor's. There was much respect. *Tranquilos* is how we lived. Now, in this time of young people—they are *lisos* [bad, conniving], envious. It didn't use to be like this. Now there is so much more *envidia*, even toward widows like me. There is no *caridad*. They tell us '*mana valiq vieja*'—old worthless woman."

Repentance was not limited to Carhuahurán. In Huaychao and Uchuraccay people also spoke about *arrepentimiento*, making it clear this practice was both widespread as well as long-standing. Although the Evangelical influence, which grew dramatically in the highlands of Huanta during the 1980s, emphasized repentance and forgiveness, these communal practices preceded the internal armed conflict. The following example from Uchuraccay further demonstrates how these long-standing practices were employed during the *sasachakuy tiempo*.

"Patrocinio" (Paulino) and Elías Ccente were among the first to return to Uchuraccay; all they found were *zorzales*—an Andean bird—singing on the remaining walls of their burned-out houses. The road was so overgrown they had to clear it just to make their way in to see the ruins. I was deeply moved by the description both men gave of October 10, 1993, when they held a general assembly of villagers who had gathered to organize a return to their land.

Present at the meeting were members of eighty-seven families who had sought refuge during the violence in Huanta, Tambo, Carhuapampa, Huaychao, and the valley of Apurímac. Many of those who arrived were relatives who had not seen one another for almost ten years and had assumed their loved ones were dead. They met one another in tears, many crying out, "We have been reborn!"[18]

The young *ronderos* who accompanied the delegations from Qano and Carhuapampa had left Uchuraccay as children. They were now returning as adolescents who did not recognize their village and the other Uchuraccaínos present. The older women approached them, scanning their faces with their eyes. Recognition moved from visual to vocal as the women began calling the young people by their names: "Oh, you are the child of Ignacio Ricra, my cousin." Many tears were shed that day.

Don Elías, then president of Uchuraccay, addressed the communal assembly: "We have suffered these years like Adam and Eve when Jehovah expelled them from Eden. We haven't seen each other for so long, but now we're seeing each other once again and we must work together and reconcile among ourselves with the love of our Lord. In this way our Lord will bless us, in double He will give us His blessing. When Job lost everything, God blessed him by the thousands, and so we will also receive double His blessings." This assembly in the village of Uchuraccay can be understood as a quasi-biblical act of refounding communal life.

We all spent a great deal of time talking with Patrocinio about the history of his community during our work with the TRC. One conversation occurred following an *asamblea comunal* when Juanjo invited Patrocinio to come by for some hot coffee.

"How are things in your pueblo now?" prompted Juanjo.

"No, *hermano*," waving off the question with his hand. Patrocinio clearly had other topics on his mind. "I'm going to tell you about how it was before the violence—how the violence started. I'm going to tell you about when the *maldición de Dios* [curse from God] arrived here. There were about eight people, young people. They were *engañados* [tricked, duped] while they were still in school, and they tried to convince the older people. But the reaction against Sendero—that was from the very start."

I was struck by his comment when we subsequently listened to the tape. Villagers "cleaned" their communities as well as their communal histories. National politics shaped the narration of the past, and the erasure of any sympathies with Shining Past was a constant in the *alturas*

of Huanta as people constructed a collective identity as faithful citizens and defenders of the Peruvian state. However, glimpses of a messier history of allegiances did slip through: as Paulino made clear, the decision to turn against Shining Path was not spontaneous. *Comuneros* held meetings, discussed what was happening, and made decisions. Huaychao was not unique.

"There was a *terruco*, Martín. He came here and had everyone meet. But he wanted the meetings to be at night, and we couldn't understand why it had to be at night. If we're going to fight, let's fight openly. Well, they told us we shouldn't be talking like that—we were demoralizing people. But I wasn't afraid. So Martín said, 'We want to meet with all of the women thirteen years and older.'[19] Well, those young people who were *engañados*—by that time, they already had *allín pensamiento* [good thinking]. Two of them already had wives and they told the authorities, '*Tío*, this isn't right. They tricked us—this is no good. Don't let them meet with the women. They must be thinking something. Maybe they want to pick out the young women and carry them off.' Once they said that, the authorities met—very carefully so the *terrucos* wouldn't notice. They called together the *umasapas* to ask what we needed to do. Well, the day the *terrucos* arrived, everyone—men and women—was waiting for them. They say there were about fifteen *terrucos* that arrived. Everyone was ready and thinking, 'We're going to throw them all out. If they give us trouble, we'll kill some of them. If we need to, we'll grab some of them and kill them.' Don Paulino's voice was indignant, as though he was reliving those moments.

"So they argued with the Senderos. While they were waiting, some of them arrived, with their *jefe* Martín—plus the eight that were from here. But three of them didn't support them anymore—three of the *milicias*, the young people. So the *puriqkuna* arrived and said, 'We want to meet with the women and not the men.' People here were already on alert and they grabbed them and got ropes ready to tie them up. One of them pulled out a gun but he couldn't shoot because they'd already grabbed him. They took their guns and their knives. They started hitting them, kicking them. Well the *puriqkuna* started begging, 'Please don't kill me. I'll leave.' People here told them, 'Get out of here! We don't want you tricking people. We could get involved in something bad and the pueblo doesn't want that.' People were chanting, euphoric, chanting, 'Let's kill them!'

"Don Paulino, what were the *milicias* doing—the eight young people they'd tricked?"

"Oh, they surrendered. The rest of the people were saying they were going to turn everyone in to the soldiers, take them in as prisoners. But the *puriqkuna* kept begging them, 'Don't kill us. We'll leave and never come back again.' That's what they kept saying. Well, people here chased them, kicking them all the way, right up to the mountains. Some of them were from neighboring communities—they also let them go when they kept begging and begging. From then on, the Senderistas called people here the conquerors [*conquistadores*] because we threw them out."

"What did they do with the *milicias engañados* from Uchuraccay?"

"They made each one of them give their statement, and then they gave them a warning. 'From here on out, are you going to keep following them?' They promised they wouldn't. Well, as soon as they drove out Martín, immediately they held an assembly. People still hadn't let the young people go. 'Tomorrow we'll take them to the base in Huanta,' they were saying. But their families begged, and each one of them confessed about how they'd been tricked. Then each one signed an agreement: 'From here forward, we will do what we are ordered to do, or we'll leave for somewhere else.' So they repented. They had to repent in front of everyone if they wanted to stay here as *comuneros*. The young people from here—well, they hadn't done so much wrong. They hadn't been in it for too long, but they had committed errors that they needed to correct. Plus they repented, so they let them stay. It was maybe four months later that the eight journalists arrived."

In each of my conversations about these *propias prácticas*—what some villagers referred to as *nuestra justicia interna* (our internal justice)—confession and repentance figure as key components of communal justice. Maintaining one's status as a *comunero* or *comunera* required submitting to the norms of the community via public rituals steeped in confessional reasoning. When analyzing this material, I found myself returning to the work of Talal Asad. As he argues, "In much nineteenth-century evolutionary thought, religion was considered to be an early human condition from which modern law, science, and politics emerged and became detached."[20] This detachment allowed for a particular way of constructing religion as both an object of study and practice.

In *Genealogies of Religion*, Asad examines how in modern industrial society—and the social sciences—religion has been reduced to an internalized state of belief rather than a constituting activity in the world. He chronicles how religion has become marginal in modern industrial societies as a site for producing knowledge and personal discipline.[21] Significant to my argument is that positing religion as a separate, transcendental yet interiorized sphere has a particular history. When villagers are engaged in the administration of justice—in these rites of confession, punishment, and, at times, pardon—they do not see themselves as "acting religiously" as distinct from how they act in other contexts. Forcing a sharp distinction between the legal, the religious, and the political hinders an analysis of the administration of justice in these communities.

Constructing theology, politics, and law as separate spheres is one conceit of modernity. However, in discussing the role of confession, atonement, punishment, and "recovenanting" in these villages, I want to be clear that I am not constructing a contrast between (religious, read premodern) "them" and (secular, read modern) "us." Villagers enact juridico-religious practices that are coeval with procedures of the modern state and draw upon a shared symbolic system.

In his analysis of confession in law and literature, Peter Brooks argues, "The confessional model is so powerful in Western culture, I believe, that even those whose religion or nonreligion has no place for the Roman Catholic practice of confession are nonetheless deeply influenced by the model. Indeed, it permeates our culture, including our educational practices and our law."[22] Moreover, "Confession of wrongdoing is considered fundamental to morality because it constitutes a verbal act of self-recognition as wrongdoer and hence provides the basis of rehabilitation. It is the precondition of the end to ostracism, reentry into one's desired place in the human community. To refuse confession is to be obdurate, hard of heart, resistant to amendment."[23] In short, to be a moral outcast.

In these public rituals, "The *process* is often as important as the final result and constitutes a corrective space, a form of mediation and a moral sanction in itself."[24] And that process has certain formulaic aspects, which has led me to think in terms of moral scripts, performativity, and the law. The confessions are remarkably similar, and it is not only the person who is judged but how well they perform the moral script. The performance must be convincing.

Indeed, to enact the moral script requires more than memorizing the lines: as villagers insist, "The words must come from the heart and not just from the mouth outward." The performative aspects of justice were crucial and the performance itself judged. Confessing, atoning, sobbing, apologizing, begging, promising—sincerity would depend on both words and action.

At times, words and action meld. In his work on the sociology of apologies, Nicholas Tavuchis argues, "An apology is first and foremost a speech act" and that apologies are "concerned with the fundamental sociological question of the grounds for membership in a designated moral community."[25] In these particular moral communities, biblical narratives inform public apologies. People did not refer to the Bible to explain what happened—villagers did not speak *about* religion but rather spoke *with* religion. Biblical narrative conventions reflected and contoured individual and communal histories and the moral scripts that infuse popular justice. And these moral scripts reflect both strands of Christianity: restoration and retribution (which in these communities generally includes the infliction of some form of physical pain). While I am no apologist for corporal punishment, I do recognize that it is intrinsic to the administration of justice in these villages and to people's conceptions of (and desire for) order.

During the early years of my research I was repeatedly told, "Hay que imponer orden acá" ("Someone needs to impose order here"). This was a multidimensional lament. Given the precarious nature of life, the disruption of rituals, and the tense social context, systems of referents had been displaced. Villagers were expressing a desire to "fix" meanings and to know that some meanings were shared and stable. Villagers were also demanding that communal authorities resume their duties and restore some semblance of order to daily life. Orin Starn has noted that a new generation of scholars, influenced by a Foucauldian approach to the themes of discipline and order, tend to categorize both as inevitably negative. As he writes, "Such a position may apply to fascist police states, or perhaps to the prisons, mental health clinics, and other modern institutions that Foucault accused of subjecting us to control and surveillance in the name of reason and progress. At the same time, it is a mistake to ignore the multiplicity of meaning and motives that can attach to the will to create order."[26] Chaos may be fascinating theoretically, but it is exhausting experientially. Sometimes people would like to wake up in their beds and count on returning to them at the end of the day.

I think here of Huaychao: the village was in shambles following the war, and the disorder extended beyond the lack of infrastructure. A constant complaint was the lack of authorities who could command respect and resolve conflicts. Mama Juanita was unable to summon an authority to sanction the women who beat her. Hipólito Rimachi complained they had lost all of their *umasapas*, leaving the community with young men who did not know how to manage communal affairs. Beyond the borders of Huaychao, both Dionisia and Marcelina remembered how the *antiguo señorkuna* in Carhuahurán were strict and made people respect their word.

The chaos of war and its aftermath dispose people to forfeit certain liberties in their search for order. This exchange operates at the national level, where a typical post-authoritarian move is to generate fear of chaos in an effort to provoke demands for order and security from the government. The *mano dura* (iron fist) approach to crime following armed conflicts responds in part to fear (real or manufactured) that the violent past may recur. Similar processes occur at the communal level as many people made clear when they spoke with longing for the *antiguo tiempo* when "authorities knew how to make people show respect." A vivid example of this was conveyed in Huaychao when a group of children playfully told me to wrap my arms around Juez Rumi—Judge Rock.

Juez Rumi stands to one side of the large soccer field that runs through the center of Huaychao.[27] It was brought in by one of the *hacendados*, but no one could remember exactly when. It is too large to wrap my arms around and stands about five feet tall. Juez Rumi has a series of concentric rings, marking the various heights at which people were tied to the rock by their neck, hands, and waist. This is where "the guilty" were questioned and whipped, and where they confessed.

I asked my *compadre* Leandro about Juez Rumi, and he had me follow him to his house. He reached below his bed and pulled out a cardboard box. Inside was a carefully folded sheet of paper.

"Kimberly, take a look. I drew this."

He handed me a drawing of Juez Rumi with a *varayoq* standing to one side. Below the rock, in bold black letters, were the words "Huaychao Renace: Justicia Comunal" (Huaychao Reborn: Communal Justice). Leandro had drawn the picture, and in a communal assembly the *comuneros* and *comuneras* had chosen the drawing as the image that would represent Huaychao in the civil registry (*registro civil*, responsible for birth, marriage, and death certificates).

The *varayoq* was an elderly man in a brown poncho with the slender green and white stripes that characterized the region, and his brightly colored *chullo* was topped off by his felt hat. Several people, including Leandro, told me the *varayoq* was don Inocencio, an elderly man who lived up the slope above the cemetery. I visited him several times, but he stuck to the line he and the other elderly people had been assigned when Huaychao prepared for the truth commission: "I'm too old to remember anything that happened here."[28]

I was curious about this new logo, and Leandro explained what Juez Rumi meant and why villagers had overwhelmingly voted to have Judge Rock symbolize their community in the civil registry.

"I drew that *juez rumi* because for us it's like a hero. That's how I think of it. I drew it because that rock is very important. From the time of our grandparents, and the time of our own fathers and mothers—that rock was very respected! So in that sense I drew it to show communal justice and for the *varayoq* that is standing next to it. That's a tradition from a long time before. The *varayoq* was always ordering things so that there were sanctions, according to the error [*qocha*] the person had."

"What sorts of errors, Leandro?"

He thought for a moment. "Well, here's an example. The *campesina* people—the *varayoqs* overlooked everything. We defended ourselves, that's why we put it as a symbol. The *teniente gobernador* sent out the *varayoq* to make sure everyone was doing what they were supposed to. When a person committed adultery, the *teniente gobernador* sent the *varayoqs* to bring them here. They made sure the person came to the dispatch. First they interrogated them, and if they didn't want to talk they told them, 'If you don't want to go to Juez Rumi, you have to talk.' And if they still didn't talk—making themselves really tough—then they took them to that rock. They would tie the person by the waist, and if they kept being stubborn, they would tie their neck to the rock if they wouldn't talk. That's why the rock is like a hero here. It's the size of a person, maybe even a little bigger. That's where people easily began talking about any sin or crime [*qocha*] they had. After tying them to the rock, then they would make them go back to the dispatch and make an arrangement [*arreglo*]. That's why that rock represents respect, respect for the authorities. That's why we honor the rock so much. That rock is a hero here in Huaychao."

"So Juez Rumi was used to judge thieves and adulterers?"

Leandro nodded and went on to describe the role of Juez Rumi during the war.

"During the *sasachakuy tiempo*, Juez Rumi served us. That's where the bad people—the people who were walking with that '*política*' or who came here—that's where they were judged. That's where the *varayoqs* made people talk. They said, 'We're going to finish off the Senderos, and if you don't want that you have to repent. Those who are *cabezas*—the most responsible—bring them here and we'll take their statement. Depending on what they say, we'll make an arrangement.' So the soldiers made them come from Carhua-hurán and then they [the *varayoqs*] interrogated them here, tied to the rock. They declared, one after another. 'Those are the ones—they came, we aren't guilty. Forgive us!' That's what they said. Yeah—Juez Rumi deserves to be called a hero."

"What happened to people who were tied to Juez Rumi—what if they talked?"

"That's how many people were pardoned—they repented. But the rest—the people with the *mayor delito* [greater guilt or crime]—they killed them. That's what Juez Rumi was good for. Those who repented were set free. Of course the *varayoqs* were there with their *chicotes*—they respectfully whipped them, taking their declarations."

In these villages, *comuneros* combine the religious tradition of confession—the cure of souls and the reaffirmation of community—with the legal confession's need for a process of judgment and punishment. In these legal-religious practices, both retributive and restorative forms of justice are administered. As Susan Jacoby notes, "Remorse may wipe the slate clean with the gods, but men and women generally demand a more tangible penance."[29]

The moral scripts performed are both the model for and product of the "call and response" that characterized these rituals of questioning, confession, and repentance. Richard Terdiman suggests that "Confession is a quintessential form of mnemonic performance.... The practices of avowal [seek] individual or social purification."[30] These practices also rewrite the penitent's history and are key in the production of the redeemed, and redeemable, subject. Recall that the *arrepentidos* had to promise what they would remember as well as what they would forget in order to rejoin the community. There is a theory of memory at work in these rituals, based on an understanding of memory as both redemptive *and* dangerous. What is forged in these rituals are socially acceptable truths that involve a mnemonic readjustment both for those who confess and repent and for their audience.

I think here of arguments about punishment and deterrence. It may well be that punishment does not deter the criminal contemplating robbery or murder; however, perhaps retribution has a deterrence effect on those who have been wronged. Retribution helps stay the hand of vengeance. Hannah Arendt suggested that it is retribution and forgiveness that break the endless cycle of violence.[31] The administration of both retributive and restorative justice may permit the reclaiming of those who had haunted the *puna*, cast out of the community of humankind.

Making People

> Legal space is, before all else, not a tangible physical space; rather, before all else, it is a psychological construction.
> —Jean Carbonnier, *Sociología jurídica* (author's translation)

When I had recently arrived in Carhuahurán, I explained to people my interest in the history of the villages during the war. People nodded, silently. If I persisted, they inevitably referred me to don Feliciano: "He knows all the history. He's already written it." Indeed he had, and Feliciano handed me a neatly printed copy upon request. It was that "best history" he had written for the NGO competition.

I was eager for other written sources, and few remained. The Senderistas had burned the village several times and many documents had been destroyed. I wondered if any of the Actas Comunales had survived. I had asked don Feliciano on various occasions and he insisted they had all been burned. Control over the village's history was a source of power—and, at times, security—and Feliciano did see me as a rival, despite my efforts to avoid that role.

Thus it was a tremendous surprise when Michael came by our room with a large, worn book, asking Efraín and me to assist him in preparing a request for funds from the municipality in Huanta. The thick brown covers were frayed and water stains had formed wrinkled suns on the front and back. He opened the book to the page on which villagers had voted in favor of the request and noted the necessary details that we should include in the letter. We wrote the request and Michael left, forgetting to take the book with him.

There were some two hundred pages of minutes, a chronicle of meetings held throughout the mid-1980s through 1995. Handwritten pages were stamped with the village authorities' seals, signed by the villagers who could write and thumbprinted by those who could not. I looked first for Mario Quispe's name. People had told me so much about him—I looked for him on those pages. There he appeared in 1986 as the *teniente gobernador*. The

Actas traced his rise to president, and then his signature disappears just as he did in 1990. I added to the water stains. It was awful reading those minutes, knowing what would happen to him. In horror movies there is inevitably a moment when you want to scream out a warning to the people on the screen. You know what is behind the door or lurking in the long, dark hallway. You can see the blade being raised, casting back a thin stream of light. You know they should be careful, but you can't do a thing.

I went for a walk to clear my head and then sat down to take notes. On the first page: "Act of the Assembly carried out on this day the 18th of February of the year 1986 in the campesina community of the village of Carhuahurán of the jurisdiction of the province of Huanta and the Department of Ayacucho." Among the items listed on the agenda were: discuss the abandoned lands without owners (*sin dueños*); give the land to the *recogiados y otros*; and the need to seek a loan from the Ministry of Agriculture to purchase fortified seeds.

I did not know how to understand the first two agenda items. As anyone who has worked in Latin America knows, land is one of the key resources people fight over. Yet here land was being given to *recogiados y otros*. Who were those people?

Spanish speakers will have noted that *recogiados* is not really a word. However, as *amistad* is to *amnistía*, so is *recogiados* to *refugiados* (refugees). Prior to the political violence, there were no refugees in the highlands. People certainly moved around and not always of their own choosing. However, the category "refugee" was a product of the war; the term figured in the state's discourse, that of the soldiers, and on the radio stations. *Refugiados* became *recogiados*, thus making sense. The verb *recoger* means "to take back; to gather; to collect; to receive, to protect, to shelter." *Recogiados y otros* were those who came from outlying hamlets seeking refuge; they were also those unnamed people who came in search of redemption.

February 18, 1986. The entry begins with a listing of abandoned lands in Carhuahurán and its annexes. Some people had been killed, and others had migrated to the cities for safety. Where relatives remained, the land passed to them. However, some land was reserved for communal purposes, leaving those parcels that were given to *personas recogiadas y otros*. These parcels were referred to as *volto aroyo*, meaning they ran along the river below the village. Recall that the gorge below was where the dead Senderistas were buried. The *arrepentidos* would be kept close, and those bodies would remind them that they had been spared a similar fate.[32]

The Power of the Gift

> A gift that does nothing to enhance solidarity is a contradiction.
> —Marcel Mauss, *The Gift*

"One must repent in front of others," villagers insisted. Indeed, repentance took place in front of the community, in an *asamblea comunal* in which village authorities, *comuneros*, and *comuneras* were present. I return to Marcelina's narrative, in which she shifts registers from "we" to "they," providing insight into the coercive force of the *asamblea comunal*—both for the repentant as well as those receiving them.

"They"—the village authorities—ultimately have the power to make decisions in the name of preserving communal hegemony. While the "call and response" involved villagers, the decision regarding pardon rested with the authorities, and all of the authorities were men. As we examine these subaltern practices, we want to hold present the working of power within these villages and the ways in which gender and generation construct hierarchies.

The question of power is central in the administration of (Christian) justice. Rather than reflect an incitement to meekly "turn the other cheek," power and coercion figure squarely within the exchange of confession, penance, and pardon.[33] Tavuchis has written, "As I shall try to show, the production of a satisfactory apology is a delicate and precarious transaction."[34] His attentiveness to the transactional nature of apologies is useful: the transgressor offers an apology and may or may not be given the gift of pardon. *Per donare* (pardon) refers to "giving with all one's heart" and obeys the logic of the gift and the relations of power that gifts establish.[35] To receive a pardon is to be beholden: *my* power or authority to pardon *you* does not mean we are equals. The *arrepentidos* would be reminded of this.

Mama Benita was a widow; her husband was one of the authorities marched to Huaychao and shot in the head by the Senderistas in 1983. She was complaining one day that the *arrepentidos* are now authorities, something that rankled her. "Look at them," she said, "they have houses, land, animals. Me? What do I have?" She angrily shook her head.

"What do you think of this?" I asked, already sensing her response.

"We remind them sometimes that if it weren't for us, they'd be dead. They're only alive because people here allowed it." She spit her tired wad of coca on the ground in disgust.

Chronology of Compassion

In trying to understand the complex dynamics of the *sasachakuy tiempo*, I began to think of the changes in power and justice in terms of a chronology of compassion, underscoring the temporal construction of morality. If indeed at one point people began to kill each other, at another they began to remember their shared humanity and act on the basis of those remembrances. *Comuneros* and *comuneras* adapted forms of communal justice to "convert the *puriqkuna* into people again."

Who was spared—and who was not—was informed by this chronology of compassion. Some guerrillas were turned over to the soldiers; not everyone, even those who repented, was allowed to return. There was the Cayetano family, that emblematic killing of *nuestros prójimos*, during which all were hung save for the youngest child. Thus my insistence on a chronology of *caridad* and an awareness of the historical aspects of emotion and morality.

Various factors contributed to this chronology. Decisions regarding what to do with the Senderistas reflected the perceived degree of danger. During the earliest years of the war (1980–84) when danger was great and alliances in constant flux, communal boundaries rigidified in an effort to define "us" and "them"—and to keep "them" at a distance. This was the height of the killing within and between the communities; indeed, villagers referred to this phase of the violence as the war of the *sallqakuna*—people of the highlands.

However, the government installed military bases throughout the department of Ayacucho, and one of those bases was constructed in Carhuahurán in 1984. Villagers from the outlying annexes were resettled in the "mother community." Concerns that certain annexes remained Senderista sympathizers meant there was a great deal of internal surveillance. Even though civil-military relations were tense and frequently exploitive, villagers cite the installation of the base as a key factor in reducing the level of fear. Both the *rondas* and the soldiers were patrolling, and the Senderista militants no longer had unarmed villagers to prey upon.

Another decisive moment in this chronology of compassion in the highlands of Huanta—and also in the Apurímac and Ene River Valley region (VRAE) of Ayacucho—was the founding of the *rondas campesinas*. People mention that the presence of the *rondas* allowed them to live with a "bit more tranquility." The *rondas* performed a dual role: they patrolled for the

Senderistas in the *puna* and provided internal surveillance within the communities. This was a crucial factor: the *rondas* allowed people to feel less threatened by those in the *puna* and those who lived next door.

I am not denying the human rights violations committed by the *rondas campesinas*. They most certainly straddle the victim-perpetrator categories. However time and again I was told that serving in the *ronda* was a key step in the rehabilitation of former Senderistas, and that the presence of the *rondas* contributed to changing the constellation of power in rural areas.[36] Additionally, participation in the *ronda* was a way of demonstrating loyalty to the community and, by extension, to the Peruvian state.

Thus talk about forgiving and reconciling is talk about power. At the height of the danger, the community could not afford to be patrolling both the perimeters and the interior, and mercy was severely restricted. However, as "community" was reconfigured and strengthened, the long-standing emphasis on the rehabilitation rather than the execution of transgressors influenced the response villagers had to the Senderistas who claimed they had been forced to kill. There would be a shift in moral discourse and practice, as well as rituals to deal with those liminal people.

As we have seen, the administration of justice involved both punishment and restoration. To have people pay for what they have done is not just a figure of speech; this accounting approach to penance has a lengthy history. Compensatory concepts of justice figure strongly in these villages, with payment consisting of fines, labor, and pain. These retributive practices are aimed at punishing transgressors and staying the hand of vengeance among those they have wronged.

Robert Nozick's distinction between revenge and retribution is helpful in understanding the deterrence effect. As he suggests, retribution is meted out for wrongdoing, whereas revenge may be nothing more than a personal vendetta based on a perceived slight. Additionally, whereas revenge may know no limits, retribution has parameters and some measure of proportionality with the crime committed. Revenge can be motivated by personal grudges, whereas retribution is authorized by a third party. Nozick also suggests that revenge involves pleasure at seeing the other's pain, whereas retribution does not; rather, the satisfaction is found in justice being done. Finally, revenge is based on serial particularities rather than general principles applied to crime and punishment.[37] While the line between the two may blur, the distinction is nonetheless important.

When presenting my research in academic settings, I have been asked about revenge killings. I have been working with these villages since 1995 and no one has picked up a rifle to kill someone in anger. Certainly there are fights and threats, particularly when people have been drinking. However, I know of no one who has been killed in either a sober or a drunken fit of vengeful rage. This is striking given the charged social landscape.

In the rituals that Marcelina and others describe, justice has the reconciliation of the parties and the social containment of vengeance at its objective. The *arrepentidos* were whipped, but one senses they chose the violence of the community rather than the violence of the state. The infliction of pain is coupled with an emphasis on how much the repentant ones had already suffered—walking, always walking, with rain and without rain. The redemptive notion of suffering operates in these villages, perhaps a reflection of the "missionary justice" that provided the spiritual veneer for colonialist domination.[38]

And so people delivered themselves to the community, pleading with the villagers not to tell the soldiers in the base. The begging, the questioning, and the promises: There is a contractual morality established in this "call and response." However, contractual has a cold, legal ring to it: I prefer the term "recovenanting" because there is a sacramental aspect to the administration of communal justice. The *terrucukuna* are said to have "delivered themselves" (*entregarse*) to the community. The same term is used for those who have entered *el Evangelio* or have delivered themselves to the Lord.

Chapter 9

Deliverance

BY NOW WE have a good sense of why people who "wanted out" of Shining Path delivered themselves to the community. However, given that deliverance was transactional, we must consider what counted as a good reason to accept the *terrucukuna* and to reconcile with people previously considered *anticristos*. I do not use "forgiving" and "reconciliation" synonymously, and neither do villagers in Ayacucho. Although the language of these rituals is that of pardon and forgiveness, groups cannot dictate forgiveness. That right inheres to the individual or individuals who have been wronged. However, reconciliation can be, simply, coexistence—which in some contexts would be an ambitious goal indeed.[1]

As we have seen, it is not only violence suffered but violence inflicted that requires reckoning in the aftermath of war. In communities in which "hands-on" killing was rare prior to the internal armed conflict, one can imagine that killing generated ambivalent feelings for many of the people involved. Parallel to the communal (male) history of bravery in combat against Sendero were quieter and less heroic versions of the *sasachakuy tiempo*.

I realized early on that there were some topics men did not want to speak about in front of a woman. It does not matter how tactful or sensitive the woman may be—some conversations take place *entre hombres* (between men). One topic that fell within this category was the ambivalence that killing provoked. One afternoon we readied Efraín's *bolsa de vicios* (bag of vices) so that he could visit some of the men. It was a joke between us that he needed that *bolsa de vicios* when he set out—a bag of rum, cigarettes, and coca leaves. Although there were settings in which men and women drank together—wakes, *faenas*, and fiestas—there were also separate spaces for socializing around a few bottles of *trago*.

That afternoon Efraín found Clemente Condorcai alone at home. His wife was out pasturing their animals and had taken their little children with her. The conversation Efraín had with Clemente contains elements of the epic—and the ambivalent.

Clemente had moved to Carhuahurán during the *sasachakuy tiempo* because his uncle lived there. It had been difficult at first because villagers resented the refugees who were arriving from outlying hamlets, viewing them as both Senderista sympathizers *and* competition for increasingly scarce resources. However, it was not just resentment that made life difficult. "Not everyone stayed. The people here, some of them got tired of the soldiers screwing with them."

"How did the soldiers screw with people?" asked Efraín.

"They punished people. If you were late for *formación* or if you weren't in your right place during the *vigilancia* [armed watch], they would make you run up and down the mountain as fast as you could. If you didn't run fast enough they hit you. Or they would make you strip and force you to take a bath at night in the river."

Efraín commiserated. He knew just how cold the river was. "Did people protest, did they say anything to the soldiers?"

Clemente can be heard making a disgusted sound: "No. No one said anything. If you protested, the soldiers threatened to kill you."

He and other people from Anqas wanted to return to their village, but the possibility of future Senderista attacks kept them from doing so. "Some people tried to go back in '97, but the *tucos* [*terrucos*] grabbed them."

"What happened to the people who were stopped?"

"There were seven people. They [the *tucos*] didn't kill anyone, but they asked them lots of questions."

"So that's why you can't go back to Anqas?"

"Yeah. If it weren't for the *tucos*, we would've gone back already. We still think about going back someday, but there're so few of us." He paused before adding, "We used to have llamas, sheep, cows, horses. The cows escaped and the soldiers shot them all and ate them."

Efraín and Clemente kept passing the glass of *trago* back and forth. Efraín asked Clemente if he had stayed in Carhuahurán during the violence.

He nodded. "We were here." Clemente had been one of thirty men in his patrol, armed with rifles. "We stayed here, we fought. We defended the plaza and many people died. We went out to pick up the pieces of the bodies. We took *costales*, but we only found parts of their bodies. The *tucos* attached grenades to people and blew them up."

Clemente went on to explain that initially the women helped in the defense, but there were not enough rifles for the men, let alone the women. The military presence also shifted duties. "The soldiers told us the women shouldn't practice using rifles, only the men. The women were supposed to dedicate themselves to the kids. In case of an attack, they were supposed to carry the kids somewhere safe and take care of them."

Efraín asked Clemente to tell him more about the attacks and whether the *tucos* arrived with women and children.

"Yeah. One day when we were out on patrol, we found them. The women ran, but they were easier to catch than the men."

"Were the women armed?"

"Ah, with revolvers, rifles, and grenades. There were kids, too—the kids ran around with knives. We captured them. They told us how they'd suffered. They lived on nothing but water and hunted wild animals to eat. They told us the commanders wouldn't let them go, and they got used to robbing trucks to get their clothing. The *tucos* fooled people [*engañar*] in other villages. They said that soldiers and rich people would be killed, that *campesinos* weren't going to die."

Something began to shift in Clemente's voice. "We don't forget everything that happened. We are fighters and I've been fighting against the *tucos* since I was twelve. My father fought before me, and I replaced him. We've fought, the bullets passing by our heads. You have to be very brave to have done all this. The *vigilancia* was day and night. Each family had to *vigilar* three nights each week. You had to be brave. We've defended the state, we fought in the name of the president." His voice began to waver: "You know, the *tucos* said *campesinos* weren't going to die. But those people we killed, those *tucos*? They were poor *campesinos* just like us."

There is a Peruvian saying: *Los niños y los borrachos hablan la verdad* (Children and drunks speak the truth). Certainly drunkenness opened up something. In a number of Efraín's conversations *entre hombres*, the men can be heard encouraging one another to cry. "It will make you feel better if you cry," and a glass of *trago* accompanied the encouragement.[2] Indeed, one word for *trago* in Quechua is *waqay* (to cry). The only time I ever saw men cry was when they were drunk. If the public space of mourning is a "feminine" space because of the gendered division of emotional labor, then it is drunkenness that allows the men to express their pain. It was with the rounds of *waqay* that the epic battle stories could cede to the pain of having killed one's *prójimo*. For the men who painfully straddle the divide between victim and perpetrator, alcohol may lead them down another memory path, and their tears accompany them.

I have mulled over this conversation with Clemente, listening to him trace a lifetime of warring, replacing his father who had fought before him. Yet he also speaks of having killed "poor *campesinos* just like us." The contradictory consciousness that allowed people to insist the Senderistas were not human and yet recognize a family member or neighbor in the columns coming to attack them does not neatly partition these two versions of the *sasachakuy tiempo*. Faces rise and fall from *conciencia*, that important conflation of conscience and consciousness.

There is also an implicit understanding that poor people—people with relatively less power than others—may experience more constraint than freedom. With pressure from both the armed forces and the Senderistas, some people did things they did not want to do—or lived to deeply regret having done. It was common to hear that "we all make mistakes," emphasizing fallibility as a trait everyone shares, with *qocha* (sin or crime) being part of the human condition.

Additionally, in conversations about the *arrepentidos*, villagers lamented, "We're not innocent, but yes, we *are* innocent." Many people have blood on their hands; all adult males were required to participate in the *rondas campesinas* in addition to other armed actions in which they may have engaged. Danger was great, and everyone knows someone who was killed. Several people told me the *arrepentidos* were pardoned for the mere fact they were alive "in spite of everything."

There were also pragmatic issues. This was made clear in the highlands of Huanta as well as in the VRAE, also located in the department of Ayacucho. I had lengthy conversations with two leaders in the VRAE who explained why and how they decided to "recuperate" the Senderistas.

The first conversation took place in Llochegua, a bustling city struggling with both the benefits and the dangers of the drug trade. The mayor, Vicente Kitazono, is a large, outgoing man.[3] He had come to Llochegua on business during the internal armed conflict and was rounded up by the army. The price of his freedom was participation in the DECAS (as the peasant patrols in the VRAE were originally known).[4]

We spoke in his office, Peruvian flag draped from a pole standing to one side of his desk. It was 2005 and I had recently begun research on anti-drug policies, thus my questions were directed toward exploring how local officials viewed the U.S.–sponsored "war on drugs." However, the mayor was so open that I found myself drawn to my earlier set of questions. I tentatively asked whether there might be any former Senderistas around, and he broke into a big smile. We both laughed, and I could only marvel at how the passing of time changed the sorts of questions that did or did not bring conversations to an abrupt halt.

Our conversation that day was lengthy. He had lived in the VRAE for twenty years and had many stories to tell. He described how the DECAS had operated, taking a different approach than did the soldiers: "We would go out on patrol, and sometimes we'd come upon an encampment. The Senderistas would have already moved on, but we knew they'd be back. So we left notes under the doors of the huts."

"You left what?" I asked, stunned by the idea.

He laughed. "We left notes letting them know their families were waiting for them. 'Come back, we won't kill you. You can come back and live with us. Your family is waiting for you.' That's what we wrote. So we left those notes under the doors."

"But did anyone take it seriously—I mean the notes you left?"

"Absolutely. You see, the Senderistas told people that if they ever tried to escape, they'd kill them. They also told them that if they did manage to escape, we'd kill them. Either way, they'd be dead. That's why we left those notes. So some of them did escape, and they were always sick and hungry when they got here. But as long as they were willing to leave all that behind them, they could live here."

"Amazing. You know, I interviewed some children who were in Sendero. Did you ever find children out there?"

He nodded. "Oh yeah. One of those encampments, well the Senderistas had already moved on, but they left a group of kids behind. There must have been six or seven of them, and we decided to bring them back. Oh, I'll never forget it. We brought them back—we carried them on our backs. Well, when the soldiers saw us they couldn't believe it. They just shook their heads.

'There you are, caring for the same beasts that will pluck out your eyes just as soon as they're old enough.' That's what the soldiers said."

"I imagine they just thought you should kill them?"

He nodded. "But we didn't. We brought them back and distributed them to different families. We told them they'd better take care of them and raise them as though they were family. They had to sign an *acta* promising to raise them right. Those kids are grown up now, and they live here just like the rest of us."

"What made you do that? The soldiers thought you were crazy, right?"

He laughed again. "Yeah, but we figured that at some point the killing had to stop."

Later that same month I met with Antonio Cárdenas, a famous founder of the DECAS in Pichihuillqa who has an almost mythical status.[5] I expected a wiry, muscular man with a rifle strapped over his shoulder. However, Mr. Cárdenas has a disability affecting the left side of his body; he walks with a pronounced limp and his arm is withered and permanently bent at the elbow. As I would learn, he was famous for his battle strategy rather than for his fighting prowess.

I arrived in Pichihuillqa with José Coronel, the former coordinator of the PTRC office in Ayacucho. People were wary when we arrived because not long before the police had sent out a team to search for signs of cocaine processing (either *pozos*, the holes in which the coca leaf is processed, or the chemicals used in extracting the substance from the leaves). The women had come out to greet the police with sticks and rocks, beating and detaining them. My gringa face worried people who thought I might be a U.S. counternarcotics agent.

We explained our visit, and José's presence made it possible to stay and talk. He was well-known even before the PTRC, but his work with the commission made him one of the most recognizable people in Ayacucho. We were escorted to a few tree trunks outside a small wooden house and told that Antonio should be coming back soon from his *chacra*. Our wait seemed shortened by the thick slices of pineapple we purchased from the woman next door.

An hour or so later, Antonio came walking up the dusty road, immediately recognizing José. Once again, I was unable to resist the opportunity to ask a few questions about the violence; there I was sitting with one of the most famous leaders of the peasant patrols.

Our conversation confirmed everything Vicente had said and added a few more details. As Antonio explained, "We realized that if we wanted to win the war, we had to *quitarle la masa a Sendero* [take the masses away from Sendero]. So we started figuring out ways to do that. This way we could have more people on our side. That's what we figured. We recuperated so many people—they wanted to escape from them but had been too afraid." Thus another crucial element: these processes were an effective counterinsurgency strategy, relying on "taking back the masses" rather than killing them.

The success of this approach was illustrated once again. A young man strolled by, greeting us as people always do in the *campo*. Once he was a few hundred feet up the dirt road, Antonio nudged me and pointed with the fingers of his good hand. "See that guy? He was one of them. We brought him back and look at him—he lives here like us, works like us. *Tranquilo*."

In addition to these compelling reasons for administering rehabilitation rather than meting out death, participation in Sendero served as an apprenticeship. Men and women learned to use firearms and gained organizational experience. I was told the ex-Senderistas "have more vision," which refers to political insight and "savvy." Time spent *adentro* (in the guerrilla) was one way of learning a radical political discourse and developing a class-based critique of poverty and marginality.

Among the village authorities throughout the *alturas* of Huanta were numerous *arrepentidos*. Certainly they never told me this: other people did, at times with resentment and at times as a matter of fact. One such individual was don Feliciano, the war hero and president of Carhuahurán. Although he said he had been forced to participate and tried to escape as soon as he could, that is only one version of his trajectory. Don Feliciano had been detained by the military and thrown in jail. His changing allegiance came early and saved his life. Had he not recanted, the soldiers would have killed him. By disavowing all sympathy for the guerrilla, he was able to return to the village and construct a new identity. His trajectory was impressive but not unique: from Senderista to *arrepentido* to *rondero*, then on to president and subsequently mayor of Carhuahurán. The most he ever revealed to me was his observation that "Sendero had good ideas but the implementation was wrong."

This awareness of a bigger political agenda came out in interesting ways. In conversations with village authorities, they criticized other *campesinos* for being *muy conformistas* (very conformist). "They don't think of anything more than planting their fields and pasturing their animals," they said dismissively. They also insisted the violence "woke these people up." The *arrepentidos* who achieved positions of authority in the villages did have a more critical reading of political affairs, and they tended to be the individuals that nongovernmental organizations sought out as "natural leaders of the community" for purposes of recruitment, training, and, at times, favoritism. The NGOs noticed the same qualities that caught the guerrilla's attention: they sought out the *muy hábil* (the skillful and quick).

If "recruiters" were interested in skill level, for villagers assessment of the *terrucukuna* depended in part upon the *grado de delito* (the seriousness of the crime).[6] People seeking to come back were referred to as *concientizados*, *rescatados*, *arrepentidos*, and *engañados*. The terms reference the degree of culpability, which involved the question of conscience and the awareness of what one was doing. This evaluation was part of a sophisticated assessment of agency, guilt, and moral responsibility.

In Chapter 2 I introduced two concepts that are important here: *uriway* and *uso de razón*. With the discussion of *uriway*, we saw that identity is understood to be fluid and mutable. Human status is achieved; thus it can be lost and regained. With *uso de razón* we encountered a term that cuts across religious, political, and legal fields and is fundamental to the assessment of accountability. Children are said to develop the *uso de razón* around the age of six or seven; this is also the age at which children acquire memory. Just as the *uso de razón* makes *criaturas* (infants and small children) more fully human, so does the accumulation of memory. People with *mucha memoria* are considered better people, more intelligent—and they have more *conciencia*.

The issue of *conciencia* is crucial to the evaluation of responsibility for one's actions. I heard, quite frequently, that although people had gone with the Senderistas, some had not realized what they were doing: *inconcientemente se fueron*—unconsciously they went, not fully aware of their actions. These people were also the *engañados*—tricked or duped by the guerrilla.

Engañado is a term that works both ways. "Outsiders" use it disparagingly when referring to *campesinos* as illiterate, ignorant, and prone to believing whatever they are told. Villagers realize the insulting connotation of the word; however, they use it strategically when it serves their purposes to be the "blameless dupes." It is a way of shifting responsibility and displacing agency, as well as indexing how power imbalances shape their interactions with representatives of the state and *criollo* (white) Peruvian society.

Concientizados were people who had been persuaded when the guerrilla came to *concientizar* villagers but did not willingly participate in combat. For instance, Feliciano insisted there were no *arrepentidos* in Carhuahurán, only people who had been *concientizados*. As he told me, "*Arrepentidos* are those who were combatants, or the masses that turned themselves in." Thus many of the people captured in the mountains were people who had collaborated, but were never, to borrow his term, *defensores conscientes de los terrucos* (conscious defenders of the *terrucos*). Thus bringing them back was rescuing them (*rescatar*).

If you are confused, that is precisely the point. Ambiguity is what allowed this to work. Unlike positive law that is based upon categories alleged to be mutually exclusive, these categories are permeable and fluid. There is a gray area in communal jurisprudence between causal determinism and moral agency that allows for great flexibility in judging the rights and wrongs of particular cases. Ambiguity is a resource: in these villages, *inconcientemente se fueron* (unconsciously they went). And if not, they could certainly claim that they did. The gray zone of jurisprudence allows for porous categories and for conversions, moral and otherwise. Those who had "fallen out of humanity" could convert into people again.

Converting into people is a moral conversion involving a "change of heart," and the notion of purgation figures prominently. Many villagers, both Evangelical and Catholic, insisted, "You must repent from the heart and not from the mouth outward. When we repent, we go forth with a clean heart." I was assured that "After repenting, we are *musaq runakuna* [new people]. We are not who we were before." Identity is highly relational and as social context and relations change, so does the person.

People We Work With

Let's return to Marcelina's store and to the day I described earlier. We had been talking for several hours when we heard a high voice calling out greetings, and mama Izcarceta appeared in the doorway. "Mamachallay, buenas tardes," she lilted, patting my shoulder. Marcelina invited her to share some Kola Real and pulled out another sheepskin. Izcarceta lived down below the cemetery where most of the refugees from the annexes lived. She had come from Bramadero during the violence, after the Senderistas had slit her husband's throat.

At first I was concerned that Marcelina would stop talking about sensitive themes; however, she and Izcarceta knew each other well and spoke openly in front of one another. The two women continued to tell us about the *arrepentidos* and how they were given land. They were the *recogiados y otros* referred to in the Actas Comunales.

"So they'd be able to work, the community divided up land. So they could build houses, they were given land and *chacras* to work," Marcelina explained. "They're still working, and just like us they're eating. They became *runa masinchik* [people we work with]," Marcelina added, as Izcarceta nodded in agreement.[7]

It was striking that a widow whose husband was murdered by the Senderistas could nod in agreement that *arrepentidos* could become *runa masinchik*. I have doubts, which will be explored a bit later.

The term *runa masinchik* reflects the dominant moral ideology that places great value on reciprocity, which is expressed in various forms of collective labor.[8] In her study of "customary law" in Peru, Ana María Tamayo Flores notes the importance of communal forms of work such as *faenas* and *ayni* in the highlands.[9] These types of labor arrangements establish interdependence among the villagers who participate in them, and they are practiced because of the harsh geography of the region, which makes the introduction of technology almost impossible. Recourse to communal labor is necessary for survival, requiring cooperation between families and villages.

However, to treat labor arrangements as strictly economic configurations would obscure their symbolic dimension. *Ayni*, which refers to reciprocal labor exchange, is also a moral concept; working together and establishing mutual obligations makes "good people."[10] Reciprocity builds social networks, although not without a hierarchical dimension.[11]

Izcarceta explained *ayni*: "We help each other. Without being family, if you don't have relatives, people help back and forth, like *ayni*. Everything is *ayni*. I do something, the other person does something back. Some of the children know how to love [*kuyapayanku*]. 'I am going to bring you some water, grandmother,' they say. They bring me water in the afternoon. I cook and offer them a bit of food. I save them some of what I cook, or I give them candies." In addition to involving *arrepentidos* in relations of mutual obligation and accountability, giving the *recogiados y otros* land speaks to another key component of being *runakuna*. Recall the terms used to describe the Senderistas, one of which was *puriqkuna*. Transgressive wanderers without ties to land or family are suspect. One way people are made is via "emplacement strategies"; thus land was distributed and worked, and there was internal surveillance to make certain people "stayed put." Being of a place is a central aspect of identity formation in the highlands.

Lest we lapse into reverie about the generosity of spirit behind this land distribution, we should add another layer to our understanding. Given how many people were killed or migrated to avoid such a fate, there was a short-age of able-bodied workers. Having a larger labor base served communal interests. When I spoke with people from Pera and Bramadero, villages that moved in their entirety to Carhuahurán during the war, they offered another way of interpreting this "largesse."

Their criticisms came up in the context of conversations about Mario Quispe, the *hatun qari* (big man) I introduced you to. The only negative comment I had previously heard about him came from Feliciano. He suggested that don Mario "had pardoned too many people." Certainly he saved many people from death by providing refuge and land, thereby shielding them from being labeled terrorists by the military. However, many refugees felt don Mario *made* them work on Carhuahurán's land, and they insisted their labor had benefited the community more than it did them. From their perspective, this labor strategy was a form of servitude or atonement.

Finally, there is the importance of family. On the path to becoming fully human, having a partner is a crucial step. Unmarried men and women are buried as children are, with singing, dancing, and celebrating. There is no sorrow for them: they die as do the *angelitos* (little children), and no tears are shed. Tears are reserved for fully formed adults, and fully formed adults have partners.

"Making family" was also a way of incorporating ex-guerrillas into the village, and there is a gendered distinction to the process. Most men arrived with their families; however, women tended to come alone. As Tomasa, an *arrepentida*, told me, when the *ronderos* came through in pursuit of the *ter-rucos*, single women and widows were terrified. "The *ronderos* committed many atrocities. Women left with the *terrucos* to avoid the *ronderos* who would arrive a bit later," she said, angrily. Single women and widows were at greater risk of rape and robbery; they "escaped" with the Senderistas to save themselves. Thus they tended to be *rescatada* (rescued), or to come and repent alone. What became of them?

The answer came up in a circuitous manner, compiled from conversations with Marcelina, Izcarceta, and another widow, Margarita. I was interested in the religious history of the villages and had spoken with Catholic priests and Evangelical pastors who had traveled throughout the villages prior to and, in some cases, during the war. I wanted to know how villagers viewed them. All three women remembered an earlier time when the *varayoqkuna* used to head down to Huanta to bring the priests up for fiestas, baptisms, mass, and marriages.

"We used to listen to the mass, before the *malafekuna* burned down the church. Even the children used to listen. Their parents would bring them. We no longer have mass. Now, we're the devil's people. Oh, we're already growing horns!" exclaimed Marcelina.

"Did you have lots of fiestas before?"

"Yes, and the priests came. Now we don't have our church. Those *malafekuna* burned it along with all of the saints," Marcelina replied.

"And you said there were marriages?"

The three women nodded. "The priests would make the single mothers get married. The *varayoqs* would bring all the women here—all of them. The authorities would make them wait for the priest. Before, they didn't accept single mothers. The *varayoqs* made them confess who the father was, who had taken advantage of them. They'd get the man and make him come here and the priest would marry them," Izcarceta explained.

Marcelina added, "But if the women wouldn't tell or the men refused, then the widowers and old men could choose them. So the men chose, saying, 'I want that woman.' The authorities would give the woman to the man who had chosen her. Now they don't do this. Now they're *moderna warmaña* [modern young people already]. The *antiguo señorkuna* didn't permit this. They brought them in and made them get married. They would give the woman to the man who chose her, even if he were *opa* [slow-witted, dumb]. And *curaña rantikuykun*—the priest sold them [the women]."

"So the priest sold the women?" I asked incredulously.[12]

"*Awriki*. He would make all the single mothers walk around the plaza and the men could pick the one they wanted," Marcelina insisted.

Margarita concurred. That was how she married her husband, a man many years her senior whom she had never even spoken to before. "I couldn't say no. If you said no, they talked badly about you."

"But even so, what if the woman refused?" I asked.

"Then the priest would take her to Huanta. *A la fuerza* [with force] they made her marry someone," Marcelina insisted.

"Tell me, when did they stop doing this?" I asked.

Marcelina continued, "When the *antiguo señorkuna* were finished. There are no more."

"No?" I asked.

"No. Well, only with the *arrepentidas*—with the repentant ones, that's all."

So the "market of women" had continued but only with women who were *rescatadas* or *arrepentidas*, like Tomasa. She had been married off to an elderly man, whom she said was "*opa*." She hated him but had nowhere else to go. She had been given a choice: marry him or be forced to leave. Thus one cost of coming back was being "made family," not necessarily under conditions of one's own choosing.

The afternoon sun was casting long shadows and Izcarceta needed to head home and cook. Before she left, I remembered the mark that identified the Senderistas. "What happened to the mark they had—the mark on their arms?"

"When they began to act like *runakuna*, the mark disappeared," said Izcarceta.

"Yes, it faded away when they became people again," added Marcelina.

And so the "moral stain" disappears. However, in his study of stigma, Goffman observed that the repair of stigma means passing from someone with stigma to someone who has corrected a particular stigma.[13] The mark disappears but not the memory of it. Hence the emphasis in so many conversations on the need to "to remember but without rancor." However, this does not imply equality for those who have "converted back" since villagers live in a world of difference and stratification. Coexistence, not equality, defined the common good.

Administering "the Communal"

> Reconcile: to restore to friendship, compatibility or harmony; to make consistent or congruous; *to cause to submit or to accept.*

For groups that are not allowed a voice in the administration of justice, how does one quell a desire for retribution? For whom does reconciliation sit like a lump in their stomach and a constant irritant of their heart? For women, especially the widows. The work of grief is "women's work," and women literally embody the suffering of their communities in this gendered division of emotional labor. Thus it is phenomeno*logical* that they would carry the memories of unaddressed wrongs in their nerves, the lower back, in the nape of their necks. A thwarted desire for justice becomes a *felt* grievance.

It was long conversations with women that demonstrated the need for a political economy of forgiveness and reconciliation. Without economic redistribution, asking people to feel "forgiving" is itself an immoral act. For the women (and the orphans) their poverty serves as a constant reminder of all they lost. Consensus-making mechanisms may stifle their voices but not their rage.

To be clear, I do not believe justice is gendered. Arguments positing a womanly "ethics of care" versus a manly "ethics of rights" are essentializing and do not help us understand how concepts of justice are forged in sensuous engagement with the world.[14] However, although justice is not gendered, its administration certainly is.

In her article on ethnographic refusal, Sherry Ortner critiques anthropologists for "thinning culture" by sanitizing politics and ignoring internal conflicts among "the subaltern." As she insists, "If we are to recognize that resistors are doing more than simply opposing domination, more than simply producing a virtually mechanical *re*-action, then we must go the whole way. They have their *own* politics—not just between chiefs and commoners or landlords and peasants but within all the local categories of friction and tension: men and women, parents and children, seniors and juniors . . . and on and on."[15] By overlooking these internal conflicts, we end up with a romanticized notion of the subaltern and of resistance. We also end up with romanticized visions of "community" as the repository of the best of human values. Raymond Williams offers a lengthy entry on "community" in his book *Keywords*, and it is instructive:

> *Community*: community of relations or feelings; a sense of common identity or characteristics; can be a warmly persuasive word to describe an existing set of relationships. What is most important, perhaps, is that unlike other terms of social organization (*state, nation, society*, etc.) it seems never to be used unfavourably, and never to be given any positive opposing or distinguishing term.[16]

A romance with "community" obscures the working of power. In these villages, there are various axes of differentiation, including gender and generation. It is to the groups marginalized from the adjudication of conflicts that we must look if we are to understand the limitations of mandating reconciliation.

In the juridical-legal rituals Marcelina described, there were two "theys": "they" who came asking for forgiveness, and "they" who determined who would be punished and pardoned. Who was the "they" that made these life or death decisions? Who spoke for "the community"?

Every village authority in these communities was an adult male. What is practiced in these villages is patriarchal justice, and conflict resolution is frequently addressed to the maintenance of "community" rather than the satisfaction of the individual plaintiffs. There is an interest in resolving a range of conflicts within the village. "City justice" is expensive and highly bureaucratic, and rarely do villagers actually achieve the resolution of their cases.[17] City justice has not been kind to rural villagers; this history of judicial indifference plus a desire to preserve autonomy leads to much adjudication within the villages themselves.

Their frustration with the national legal system, and with lawyers, comes out in many ways. One of my favorite examples occurred when sitting around with Salomé and her family one evening in Carhuahurán. Her son Carlos had just adopted a puppy and was showing me how adorable it was when it toddled. Carlos set the little fellow down in the center of the room, and the puppy followed its nose right on over to his owner's dinner. Just as it prepared to dunk its head into Carlos's soup, Salomé scooped him up and scolded him: "Abogadacha! Sua kachkanki!" ("Little lawyer! You're being a thief!")

There is also a "harmony ideology" that contours conflict resolution and, as Laura Nader argues, this may be a coercive way of forging consensus and silencing dissent.[18] Thus, while these communal practices are critically important to the reconstruction of social relationships at the local level—and they have played a determining role in staying the hand of vengeance—I do not want to create the impression that equality and democracy are the result. Casimira made that very clear.

Edith was washing our dishes in the river when two young women walked her way.[19] Reyna and Casimira asked her to come by and talk with them later that day, and Casimira added, "If I tell you my life, I'm going to cry remembering those things and in an entire day we still won't finish talking because so much happened. But if you'll cry with me, then I'll tell you."

Edith sought her out at home later that same day. She was cooking, with her two tiny daughters playing to one side. Casimira launched into her story immediately: she had been waiting for Edith to arrive.

"During the violence, the *terrucos* killed my papa, my uncle, my aunt. I think I was about seven, that's why I can remember. One afternoon we were here, and my papa was in the *chacra* up there," pointing to the steep mountains across the ravine from Huaychao. "They were preparing *pachamanca*. I think he must have seen the *terrucos* when they were arriving, and he invited them to eat some potatoes. When they approached, they grabbed him and killed him. My grandmother tried to stop them. 'What are you doing to my son? Stop it! He's a good man—he's never done anything to anyone!' They grabbed her, too, and they smashed her head with a rock. The person responsible is Mauro Urbano. He's the one who brought those *terrucos* here. It's his fault—he's guilty of my father's death because he told those *terrucos* my papa was against them. It's just that my papa knew how to think and never wanted to get involved in those things. Right up there, with his mama and his brother, they killed them all."

Her voice was quivering, with rage more than sadness. She kept accusing Mauro Urbano, until she began to cry. "We cried so they would let him go, but they made us lie down on our stomachs and not move. While we were watching they killed my papa. They stuck a knife in his chest. Blood came out, flowing all over. One of the *terrucos* lifted his hood and put his mouth against my papa's chest and began drinking his blood. I remember his face, covered in my papa's blood. Every time I remember those things I cry, but I can't do anything. We were left orphans. We only had our mama to raise us, escaping into the mountains with only the clothes we had on. It was cold! So much hunger. My mama would *chakchar* coca, and she started letting us *chakchar* too because we had nothing to eat. We went to the base in Carhuahurán and complained that the person responsible was Mauro Urbano. They went and got him and in front of us he accepted his guilt. He promised to support us. He promised to work on our land because he was guilty of making us orphans, but he's never fulfilled his obligation. Now those documents don't exist anymore—they were burned. The *terrucos* in Carhuahurán burned them all. Only a year later—a year after my papa's fifth day—Mauro Urbano brought us a sheep. He told us, 'Take this. It's my fault [*qocha*] your father died.' So what am I supposed to do? What would be punishment if the life of a man has no value?"

"And what do you think now? Do you feel you could ever forgive him for what he did?"

"No. Well, if he would apologize, I'd forgive him. But he's never apologized and he never fulfilled his obligation to us."

"Do you really think that if he apologized, you could forgive him from your heart?"

Casimira nodded. "Yes, because Jesus Christ forgave the people who killed him. I could also forgive him. But we don't know what he's going to do now because he's always causing problems for us. *Qari qinaña qinakan*—like he's still some big man. Oh, he's always offending us."

The widows, the orphans, the single mothers—their poverty serves as a constant reminder of all they lost. The concept of reparations is central to the legal consciousness that operates in these villages, and settling accounts is every bit as biblical as "turning the other cheek." Retribution, in its various forms, has a strong moral hold on people.

Thus I think in terms of a political economy of forgiveness and reconciliation. Enduring conditions of social and economic inequality are not conducive to the reconstruction of social life and sociability. In conditions of chronic scarcity, compassion is restricted. In my experience, it is precisely the poorest sectors of these communities that express the greatest rancor. As the *warmisapa* Benita complained, "How am I going to pardon that man when he lives *tranquilito* in his house while I have nothing—no clothes, no roof, not a thing." In a world of deprivation, it is unlikely that forgiveness can flourish. Rather, as people insisted in each community, "Our poverty makes us remember everything we have lost."

In her influential discussion of vengeance and forgiveness, Martha Minow focuses her analysis on three categories: victims, perpetrators, and bystanders.[20] Absent from her discussion is a group that was consistently cited as a source of hatred and resentment during my research: the beneficiaries. While one pacifist slogan insists that in war there are only losers, in fact some people became quite wealthy looting and killing their neighbors. Justice conceptualized in its redistributive register was a constant throughout Ayacucho.

Finally, *campesinos* insisted on the difference between "forgiveness" and "reconciliation." Many people in the highlands of Huanta stated, "To live reconciled, well, that's how we live. But forgiveness comes from the heart and not just the mouth outward." The perpetrator—in this case, the former Senderistas who repented—had to ask for forgiveness in a communal assembly. The *comuneros* in attendance would judge whether or not the apology came "from the heart." Forgiveness also must come from the heart, from one person to another. As villagers insisted, no one can force one person to forgive another: it is a subjective state.

In contrast, they defined reconciliation as coexistence. It consists of restoring sociability and reestablishing the trust necessary not only to tolerate the presence of the other but to be able to cooperate with others on collective projects. It is a social state that responds to the exigencies of daily life and the theory that, after repenting, the person is not who he or she was before. While local authorities may administer reconciliation, in keeping with the "harmony ideology" that characterizes these communities, no one can mandate forgiveness. Consensus-making mechanisms may stifle certain voices, but they do not eliminate resentment or appease rage. The communal assembly in Huaychao described in the next section illustrates this point and questions the work of memory in the complicated process of social repair.

Remembering to Forget

There is an equation that infuses the work of truth commissions: more memory = more truth = more healing = more reconciliation. I am not certain why we believe this, but it is the logic that guides these commissions and the politics of memory that characterize our historic époque.

I question the tyranny of total recall, an idea that has been converted into an article of faith within the discourse of human rights. My fieldwork makes me reflect on the complex alchemy of memory and forgetting that functions at the local level—on the role of forgetting (which can consist of remembering something else) in the reconstruction of coexistence after years of intimate violence.

One aspect of forgetting that operates in these pueblos is *pampachanakuy.* Literally this means "burying something between us" and refers to the practices I have studied in the northern communities. Before the communal authorities, the parties to a conflict present their complaints, talking and negotiating until they reach an agreement (*acta de conciliación*); this agreement means they have "buried" the complaint between them. This practice—and the importance of remembering to forget—was the topic of a communal assembly in Huaychao on February 23, 2003.

*   *   *

It was eight in the morning when we joined the men gathered outside the *cabildo*. The *cabildo* is where authorities now administer justice, questioning and at times hanging the accused by their arms in front of a large wooden cross until they confess. There was an important *asamblea communal* scheduled that day. The villagers of Huaychao would vote on which of the neighboring municipalities to join—Carhuahurán, Uchuraccay, or Pampallqa. The decision was contentious, but joining forces to secure a sufficient demographic base was crucial in terms of demanding services from the state.

The *comuneros* began arriving one by one, ponchos wrapped around their shoulders, insulating them from the penetrating cold. But it was not only the cold that accompanied the wait; the men were also complaining about how "relaxed" people had become. My *compadre* Leandro was particularly vocal, kicking the wall with his big black boots and asking no one in particular how Huaychao could ever progress if there was no order to anything anymore.

Hipólito shook his head: "During the violence, one blow of the whistle was all you needed to make people come running. And look at us now!" Visibly frustrated, Hipólito sent a young boy over to the ruins of the Catholic church, telling him to ring the bell. Bullet holes from the war had left zigzagged scars in the clay, but the bell still rang loudly, echoing off the steep cliffs around us.

A round of "Buenos días" caused me to look over my shoulder just as don Lucio, president of Huaychao, arrived. He looked around, taking in the scarce turnout and shaking his head in frustration. We walked over to him, asking if he expected more people to turn up.

"Yes, but you have to make them come. It's not like it was before."

We nodded and took advantage of the fact that don Lucio was actually standing still for a few minutes. "Don Lucio, I've been wondering about the assemblies during the *sasachakuy tiempo*. Did you ever have a *pampachanakuy*?" I asked.

He shook his head. This was surprising because other villagers had told us they signed an *acta de pampachanakuy* in 1987 with Carhuahurán and Uchuraccay.

"So you didn't have a *pampachanakuy* here, don Lucio?"

"Well . . . only in the church, each person did this with himself. But not here in the pueblo, not in front of everyone."

Edith explored the topic further. "What do you think? Would it be good or not to do this?"

Don Lucio waited a moment before answering. "Well, yeah, it'd be good to do this with everyone because up to now we haven't and we're always arguing."

"Yeah. So, it would be reconciliation between all of you?"

Don Lucio nodded.

"And with the government, how would that be?" I wondered.

He shrugged. "Nothing with them, if the base didn't do anything to us." Suddenly he threw his head back, remembering something. "One time they invited me to a workshop in Lima. From all of the pueblos, the authorities went. People from Vilcashuamán complained that the soldiers had killed them—killed women, children, everyone. So I said to them, 'How are they going to kill people for no good reason? Certainly you were *terrucos*. That's why they killed you. But us, we killed the enemy—we killed those Senderistas,'" don Lucio insisted proudly. "I told them that and they didn't say another word."

Don Lucio looked around and had someone blow the whistle again. Turning toward us he added, "There's another thing. With them [the Senderistas], how can we have a *pampachanakuy*? They're all dead. There's no one left in this pueblo." Edith and I shot each other a glance; clearly not everyone we had spoken with would agree with that claim.

"But would it be good to have a *pampachanakuy* with the communities that you've always been fighting with, even since before the war?" I asked.

He crossed his arms into the warmth of his poncho. "Sure, then we could support each other between communities and demand more help from the government, all of us together. But it would be good if they came here and together we could have a *pampachanakuy*. Then we could go there, to their communities. It's no good if only two people come. What good is it with just two people?" Don Lucio shrugged his slender shoulders. "It has to be the whole population, but since they're so many, it would be better with the authorities—the communal president, the lieutenant governor, president of the *ronda*, president of the Mother's Club, of the Association of Parents—all of the authorities. That way everyone would come and it would be good." He paused for a moment. "But someone would need to help, people like you. You already know how we live, how we suffer. Because if it's only between us, nobody pays attention—that wouldn't work." Almost as an afterthought he added, "When you're in Carhuahurán and Uchuraccay, talk with them like you're talking with us and we can send them a letter saying we want to have a *pampachanakuy*."

Our conversation ceded to the men filing past with desks and chairs they were carrying from the *cabildo* down to the field in front of the school. It was about 9:30 before twenty-five men and eleven women finally showed up, the men forming a circle in the chairs and the women sitting to the side with the children. The assembly would be an endurance test, lasting almost five hours, the morning chill giving way to the relentless midday sun.

Edith and I sat on the damp cement steps in front of the two-room schoolhouse while Juanjo responded to a wave of don Fortunato's hand. Juanjo was recruited as scribe, taking his place behind a small wooden desk with don Lucio.

The *asamblea comunal* finally began with don Fortunato Huamán presiding. He called for the names of all present to be recorded in the Acta Comunal, and Juanjo wrote as quickly as he could. Once the roll call was complete, a group of men began complaining about Señor Santos Huaylla.

A man I had never seen before stood and addressed the group. "Someone needs to speak with don Santos because in the *faena*, he said we needed to kick out the authorities." I leaned toward the man seated to my left, hoping he could fill me in. As he explained, while participating in the *faena* on the highway, Santos had accused Hipólito Quispe, the current mayor, of trying to make all the decisions for the community. "Santos shouldn't have talked like that," he whispered to me. "That's not how it should be. We need to make him show respect—an authority is not just for any old thing. An authority is for respect."

Don Hipólito stood up, adjusted his bright blue scarf, and addressed the crowd congregated in the field. "Señores, I'm not trying to make all of the decisions for the community. There was simply a lack of coordination. But we need to talk clearly and in front of the person, not behind their back." I was struck that both Señor Santos and don Hipólito addressed the community rather than one another when they spoke.

The murmuring kicked in again, prompting don Fortunato to intervene. He looked straight at don Santos, who was staring intently at his feet. "Don Santos, you're already old," he scolded, implying that someone his age should certainly know better. "These sorts of things shouldn't be done behind someone's back. This is an error that you need to recognize." Señor Santos never looked up. He simply nodded his head, replaced his hat, and sat down.

Don Fortunato took several steps forward into the circle, looking up to the sky before speaking. "Let me tell you, brothers and sisters—please listen to me. What happened in the past [*tiempos anteriores*], well, we just can't spend all of our time on that. Rancor, hatred—it isn't worth it because we aren't in those times anymore. We need to live in peace, without criticizing each other. It's God's grace that we aren't dead. We're what's left over from the war. We were spared. Dios Tayta didn't want all of us to die."

People lowered their heads. I looked toward the women. Many of them were rubbing their faces with their hands.

Don Fortunato raised his voice a bit louder and gestured around the circle. "Look around you—many of our brothers and sisters aren't here. They're gone. We should live respecting each other, obeying each other, loving each other," his voice lingering on each word. "When we have a problem here, when anything goes wrong, we shouldn't be looking at each other as though we're from other nations!" Laughter erupted at that point, and people looked my way. I just smiled and threw up my hands.

Don Fortunato waited for the laughter to subside. "You know, in anything—well, sometimes we make mistakes. Don't we all make mistakes?" he asked the crowd. People nodded and murmured again. "We need to forgive each other for those mistakes. No matter who we are, we can make a mistake. We aren't always right. We aren't always just. So recognizing that—recognizing each other—we should try to live well, brothers and sisters."

Even the children playing among their mother's skirts fell silent. I was struck by the silence that followed don Fortunato's words, spoken forcefully but with no trace of anger.

The few other men of don Fortunato's age nodded, and one of them stood up to speak. "*Ari*, we need to remember this if we want to live well." He looked over toward the children. "Some of us who were born more recently, well they don't know. They don't remember how it was. That's why they don't pay attention to the authorities."

Don Fortunato thanked his *patamasinkuna* (age mates) for their participation. "If we think like this, we can work together. We can move forward because we can't stay this way. Our pueblo would fall apart. Some things—well, we just need to forget. Let's reach an agreement for the days to come."

Slowly he moved across the crowd with his eyes. "How do we want to spend our lives?"

With this exchange, the assembly moved on to the central topic on the agenda: to which of the Consejos Menores (municipalities) would Huaychao belong. The mood around the field changed. This topic prompted people to begin talking about the war years and the relationship between communities. Several *comuneros* spoke about the benefits of belonging to Pampallqa, but not before the debate turned to the conflictive history between the communities. The conversation grew increasingly louder and agitated.

The authorities solicited the opinions of the *comuneros* who were against the idea of belonging to Pampallqa. Jesús Mansano looked around, asking mama Alejandra to speak up. No luck—she had headed out to her potato fields earlier that day. "Well, let me tell you what she said. Mama Alejandra was saying that people in Pampallqa—during the war—they didn't even give us food, even though we asked in tears." I noticed the women, nodding and angrily pulling at the tufts of grass they were seated on. "No one had compassion. She wonders how we're going to belong to Pampallqa?" Jesús sat back down. Several women began to speak at once, remembering the treatment they had received from Pampallqa during the violence.

Don Fortunato gestured to the women, asking them to speak up one at a time. Although this initially silenced them all, strong emotions ultimately prompted some of them to address the group. What followed was a bitter litany of the poor treatment they had endured from their neighboring communities. Mama Juana recalled that in Carhuahurán they had accused them of being terrorists! Mama Victoria reminded everyone that in Uchuraccay they had counted Huaychao's dead among their own—and look at all of the things El Chino gave them! Before long, it was rage and not the bright sun that tinged their faces red, as the memories of so many wrongs came back in full force.

Amid the heat and the blistering anger, Juan Santiago stood up. "*Bueno*, Señora Alejandra was saying how are we going to belong to Pampallqa when they treated us so bad—they didn't even give us water with salt." He shrugged, not denying the truthfulness of her words. "But enough, we need to forget those things. *Ismusqa qina kachkan* [that's already rotten]. We don't need to remember those things. We need to leave this behind us." Leaving things behind did not come easily, and the women continued to press their grievances.

I glanced over at Juanjo, who had given up his effort to keep noting what everyone said. The conversations were multiple, each one dominated by whoever spoke loudest. Don Fortunato shook his head patiently, wearily before standing up again. His voice was soft, almost beseeching—and yet people fell silent again. He drew a deep breath: "Brothers and sisters, listen to yourselves. We're always in a state of envy, of egoism. Those times are past. We need to forget. Didn't we say we were going to forget?" He unlatched his arms from behind his back, open palms inviting his listeners to heed his words. "We need to forgive each other. These things already happened. *Pampachanakasun ya*—let's bury it. Those things we've already forgotten— well, here you go remembering them again. Do I have to remind you all?" Pointing to the ground below him, don Fortunato continued, "In this very field we all signed an agreement. We signed it with the people from Carhua- hurán, Uchuraccay, Pampallqa. We signed an Acta agreeing that we would forget everything that had happened between us. Don't you remember?"

There is irony in reminding people what they had decided to forget. How- ever, as so many people emphasized, without some forgetting, "We would keep hating each other like we did before." Thus selective forgetting, which I think of as remembering something else, is reinforced with social rituals such as this assembly in Huaychao.

Once again we are confronted with the need to rethink the way in which forgetting is understood in "memory politics." The work of Elizabeth Jelin has been extremely helpful.

> The space of memory is thus a space of political struggle, and fre- quently this struggle is conceived in terms of the struggle "against silence": *remember in order not to repeat.* The catchwords can be mis- leading. "Memory against forgetting" or "against silence" hides what is in reality an opposition between different rival memories [each of these with their own forgetting]. It is, in truth, "memory against memory."[21]

Forgetting is not simply what remains when memory has melted away. If indeed the reproduction of memories requires an ongoing effort, it is equally certain that maintaining "forgetfulness" is also an endless task. Rituals such as *pampachanakuy* seek to replace the memories of fratricidal violence and a desire for revenge with other memories of the past that include coexistence within and between these communities. Forgetting is not simply a strategy of domination employed by the powerful against the weak. Rather, it may be a state that is fervently desired by those who suffer from the afflictions of memory and seek relief from the heavy weight of a painful past.

Chapter 10

Legacies: Bad Luck, Angry Gods, and the Stranger

Closure: the bringing to an end or conclusion; a feeling of finality or resolution, especially after a traumatic experience.
Legacy: something transmitted by or received from an ancestor, or predecessor, or from the past.

I THINK ABOUT don Fortunato, invoking the *tiempos anteriores*, and Juan Santiago exhorting people to leave the past behind because it had "already rotted" and now is the time to "move forward." Each man was attempting to construct a before and after, a sense of ending and of beginning. These efforts are complicated for people living in communities steeped in blood and memories, engaged in social reconstruction amid the living legacies of a civil conflict. The present is shot through with memories of the past and hopes for the future; at times memories weigh upon the living as a curse; at other times they may serve as a resource. Studies of postwar social worlds must include memories of unaddressed wrongs *and* of a time "before all of this began"; address the grievances that wartime alliances generate in the present; and explore the reconfiguration of power and local institutions, among them family and community.

In their study of communal violence and social repair, Laurel Fletcher and Harvey Weinstein critique the ways in which much of the transitional justice literature has appropriated a simplistic view of psychotherapy, and they caution against thinking one can move seamlessly from individual psychological processes to making claims about the collective consequences of traumatic events.[1] They also note that terms such as "healing," "working through," and "closure" are seductive—and deceptive. The use of these terms has contributed to the teleological nature of transitional justice, which implies a linear process starkly at odds with the legacies of violence in Ayacucho.

In this chapter we explore some of those legacies. Rather than working from the perspective of closure, I am persuaded by John Borneman's suggestion that anthropologists cultivate "practices of listening" to grasp how people construct "departures from violence" in the aftermath of armed conflicts.[2] These departures are not endpoints, and they are imbued with temporal logics at odds with the conflict/postconflict dichotomy. People who have lived through violent times may try to construct a sense of "pastness," and many fervently hope "those times never return." Their departures from violence will be repeated over and over again as the impress of the past manifests in myriad ways.

This chapter begins with the presidential election in 2000 and the politics of fear that characterized former president Alberto Fujimori's campaign for an unconstitutional third term. Manipulating the specter of Sendero Luminoso and collective memories of the violence, Fujimori attempted to delegitimize the opposition by insisting that the "ashes of terrorism" were rekindling across the country while magnifying his role in "pacifying" Peru. The politics of fear reverberated in the local sphere; we will explore the impact in the *alturas* of Huanta. We will hear from one *arrepentida* and her daughter, whose life chances have been shaped by a stigmatized past. Their stories illustrate the gendered and generational challenges confronting those who bore the mark and those who were born in its shadow.

We then turn to two funerals for what they convey about the reinvention of rituals and obligations to the dead. During the *sasachakuy tiempo*, many people died "bad deaths," which has repercussions in the world of the living.[3] The anxiety provoked by the restless dead can have surprising consequences; watching middle-aged adults try to remember how one buries a human body was one of those surprises. However, while there was uncertainty about how to properly bury the dead, people expressed no doubt about the fate of transgressors. Divine justice weaves its way through daily life as well as ritualized events; the stories told about the departed became parables designed to teach survivors about God's wisdom and His wrath.

We conclude with *caridad* and the stranger. Throughout this book I have traced a chronology of compassion, an emotion that was sharply constricted at certain junctures. The arrival in Carhuahurán of *la loca*—the "crazy woman"—marked an important shift in that chronology. Once again I found myself listening to a parable, one that reminded both young and old about human conduct in "the time before all this began."

Vigilant: The Politics of Fear

I was in Peru to monitor the presidential elections in March and April 2000. I spent most of my time in the city of Huamanga and the highlands of Huanta, regions in which the Fujimori administration had mobilized its vast patronage system as well as utilized threats to influence voting patterns.[4] The manipulation of fear was one cornerstone of Fujimori's authoritarian project. Some threats played on the residual distrust that characterizes postwar life, widening social fissures at the national and local levels. On visits to Chaka, Purus, and Carhuahurán, villagers told me representatives from various state agencies had warned them that if Fujimori lost the election, his opponent would cut off assistance to their communities and release the jailed terrorists so that they could return to Ayacucho and slit everyone's throat.

Voting is mandatory in Peru, and those who fail to vote can be fined. When election time rolls around, thousands of rural *campesinos* travel to Huamanga and Huanta to vote. Villages are largely depopulated; only children, adolescents, and the elderly are exempt from voting. Leaving their villages virtually empty and unarmed was an enormous concern. The trip to Huanta from villages such as Carhuahurán required villagers to leave one day, vote at sunrise the next, and return home later that afternoon. The concerns centered on the possibility of a Senderista attack while people were away voting. The fear was great. Widows told me that when everyone left to vote, they would spend the night together, *chakchando* coca to calm their frayed nerves.

On the way up to Carhuahurán, I stopped at the military base in Castropampa, located on the outskirts of Huanta. Castropampa was the base responsible for the highland region in which I had lived. Although there were smaller bases established in various villages, Castropampa served as the central military installation. When Marcelina spoke about the guerrillas who refused to repent, she mentioned that "Castro" was frequently their final destination. I wanted to talk with the commanding officer about his views on the presidential election, the issue of "pacification," and the general situation in the highlands. During the internal armed conflict, the guerrillas had frequently timed violent actions to interrupt elections, and Sendero Luminoso had launched the armed phase of the revolution on May 18, 1980, just as people headed to the ballot boxes to vote in a presidential election. During the early years of my research, I had heeded colleagues' advice to return to the city during elections for my own safety. By the year 2000, I thought it highly unlikely that Shining Path could pose a serious threat; however, I wondered how the politics of fear worked in communities in which the recent past was present.

I left Huanta in a *taxi cholo*—a bike taxi with a tiny motor that pulls a cart behind it. The taxi can seat two people, although I had seen entire households sardined into those seats. We pulled up to the gate: "Zona Militar: Prohibido Detenerse" (Military Zone: Loitering Forbidden). Three young *cachacos* (soldiers) were guarding the gate and I explained that I was there to see if the commander was available for an interview. They opened the gate as I stood there, letting one car exit and slowly maneuver the deep gashes in the road that moved the mud downward. The gate then swung closed. The *cachaco* with the machine gun asked for my documents and told me to wait while he determined whether the base commander would see me.

He came back a few minutes later having obtained permission to admit me. As we walked through the gates and past the walled perimeter of the base, the *cachaco* indicated with his machine gun that we were heading to the building on the right. He escorted me to a waiting room outside Comandante Juan Vásquez's office. After a short wait, another soldier appeared, letting me know the commander was ready to see me, and ushered me in.

A metal desk sat on a thin blue carpet and everything was impossibly clean. The military made an effort to look official amid the mud and the animals grazing outside the door. The effort was successful, placing my mud-splattered condition in high relief. Comandante Vásquez stood as I walked across the room to shake his hand, apologizing for my boots that were leaving size ten stains behind me. He assured me it was no problem at all and gestured toward a chair.

He was extremely polite. He looked about forty, and urban; although his skin color was no different than that of the *campesinos* with whom I worked, his uniform and education made him a *mestizo* on the fluid continuum of "racial" categories in Peru. Joining the military was one strategy of social whitening for young men from families with modest means. He was handsome: high cheekbones, large dark brown eyes with heavy lashes, full lips backed by a full set of teeth. I realized how much I noticed teeth; they said so much about where one was positioned on the fluid continuum.

I introduced myself, telling him I had lived and worked in the highlands of Huanta for several years and was now back visiting friends: "I'm heading out to the villages in which I lived, and I'd like your opinion of the current situation." He began nodding in a reassuring manner as I was still asking my question, prompting me to ask a more pointed one. "Do you consider the zone pacified?"

His manner shifted, and he shook his head. "How can we ever have peace? Since the time of the Conquest, they've been mutilating bodies, constantly fighting. This is natural. This comes from the Incas and the Spaniards, who were even more bellicose. How can we have peace with these Indios?"

I could not bring myself to nod in agreement so I threw out another question: "Then you think Fujimori has not succeeded in pacifying the country, in defeating Sendero?"

He shrugged. "You know what the Senderistas did? They would round up *la masa* [the masses] from Pampallqa and use them to attack Carhuahurán. Then they would round up people from Carhuahurán to attack another village. Then the terrorists would just leave the people there to work it out. The *campesinos* were duped [*engañados*] by Sendero."

"How do you think they did that?"

"The people are ignorant, and illiterate. But you know what? The violence woke these people up [*despertó a esta gente*]. Ayacucho has progressed tremendously because of all the attention this region received as a result of the violence. The state—these NGOs—they've achieved a degree of development the area would not have had if not for the war."

"Other people have also told me that." My mind filled with images of rural peasants slumbering until violence thrust them into the twentieth century.

"And how is the situation in the zone now, with the elections coming up?"

"Well," he began, sitting back in his chair, "authorities from Carhuahurán, Pampallqa, and Qellaqocha came down here last week. They asked me to station troops in their villages when they come to vote."

"What did you tell them?"

"I had to deny their request. I don't have sufficient troops to meet that demand." Then he began smiling. "They came back a few days later to claim the Senderistas had attacked Carhuahurán. They're very manipulative."

"What do you mean?"

"There was no attack. They just want soldiers stationed in their villages." Comandante Vásquez was convinced it was not just the Fujimori administration that was manipulating the specter of Shining Path.

I was perplexed. "But they still have the *rondas*. What will happen to the *rondas*? If there's no danger, what will happen with them?"

Comandante Vásquez then said something I had heard from several representatives of Fujimorismo. "They will be converted into Committees for Development, working to improve their villages."

"Will they be disarmed at some point?

"Oh, of course," he replied emphatically. "How can we permit them to continue to have guns given all of the conflicts they have? Cattle rustling, adultery, land struggles. You know, the festering violence in the zone, prompted by cattle rustling and adultery, that's what was being expressed during the war, with Sendero as its screen."

"Hmm. And what will happen with the weapons the communities purchased? They were very expensive, no?"

He shook his head. "The only weapons they have are the ones the government gave them. I could go tomorrow to Carhuahurán and collect them all."

Comandante Vásquez looked past me to the door. One of the soldiers was motioning that he was needed. I stood up, thanking him for his time. He escorted me to the door, assuring me he would be pleased to speak with me further some other time. "By the way," he added, "I will be sending some soldiers out to the villages." I just nodded, thanking him again.

Walking back out past the soldiers, I headed down to Huanta on foot. I kept mulling over his comments, especially his assertion that it was the *comuneros* themselves who had staged a Shining Path attack in an effort to make the army stand watch over their communities during the voting process. It was hard to know just who was trying to frighten whom and with what intentions. I decided to check in with some colleagues, and my first stop was the office of Llaqtanchikta Qatarichisun (LQ), an NGO that had spun off of World Vision. LQ worked throughout the highlands of Huanta, providing material assistance as well as training workshops. In the LQ office, I received a different version of the recent incursion in Carhuahurán.

Mauro was an agricultural engineer and had just returned from two weeks in the *campo*. He still had stubble on his chin and hat hair from the woolen *gorro* (knit cap) he had pulled down over his ears for warmth. He was in LQ's main office, talking to some coworkers about what he had been hearing in the villages. From his conversations he was convinced the soldiers had staged the attacks. I was surprised. "But the commander at the base just told me he thinks the villagers faked the attack."

Mauro shook his head. "I think the military wants to stir up fears and scare people. They staged the attack to remind them why they'd better vote for Fujimori. They've convened a meeting every week with the *rondas* at Castropampa. They're telling them to tighten security and that they'll have their weapons taken away if Toledo wins." His coworkers expressed their disgust and went on to talk more generally about the upcoming election and the predictions of electoral fraud.

I headed out early the next morning, arriving in Carhuahurán midday. It was wonderful to see people after almost a year. Despite my incredulity that children could grow on a diet consisting of virtually nothing but potatoes, some growth spurts had occurred.

I was given a room in the new preschool villagers had built with funds from the municipality. It had a wood floor and ceiling, and glass windows that kept the wind out. The preschool teacher, Hermelinda, had decorated the walls with students' drawings and bright cutouts, and a flock of little chairs were clustered in the corner of the room. As I was unpacking, Yolanda and Edith appeared in the doorway.

"Señorita Kimberly, where have you been?"

I explained that I had been in the United States, writing and seeing my family. They both nodded and began reminding me of each room I had ever had while living in Carhuahurán. Their topographical memories traced a connect-the-dots from my room in the extinct *consejo comunal* (so dark and humid that potato plants began growing out of the wall), to my room behind the crumbling watchtower (with the floor that heavy rain had formed into puddles of varying sizes), and up the steep path to a corner of the former military base. And now here I was sleeping in the preschool. I certainly had gotten around.

We pulled up some chairs and opened a sack of *chaplas*, and both girls began to tell me all about what had been happening in Carhuahurán. "They attacked just last week," Edith began, in between bites of her *chapla*.

"When was this?" I asked.

"Just last Sunday. No, wait. The Sunday before." She looked to Yolanda, who nodded, confirming the day. "I think they came from the jungle because we found banana and orange peels up there. When we went to Huaynacancha, we saw the peels. They were men with beards."

"Did these men with beards stay here? Did they just pass through?"

Yolanda answered this time, saying they had only passed through. Edith grabbed my arm. "I saw them. They spoke to my little brother. They told him, 'We're *terrucos*.' Then he came running and told my papa."

"What did your papa say when Jonny told him what he'd seen?"

Edith swallowed some of the Coca-Cola I offered her. "He said, 'They must be *terrucos*. And what if they saw my radio? We need to hide my radio.' And my mama started to pack our clothes."

I was perplexed. "Why didn't people detain them?"

"People didn't believe it, so they escaped. But in Huaynacancha they told people, 'We're *terrucos*.' They were *huk clase* [of a different sort, not like us]. *Manchakuypaq*! [inspiring fear]. We thought, 'We'd better go to Huanta.' My mama was packing our clothes."

The sound of short footsteps made us look toward the door. Jonny came trudging along in his mismatched rubber boots. As always his pants were at half-mast, little round butt defying the worn elastic. He came over and I gave him several squeezes and a *chapla*. Yolanda passed him the bottle of Coca-Cola and Edith continued, speaking in her breathless, rapid way.

"The soldiers weren't here. They just got here yesterday for the elections."

"But is the base still in Qellaqocha?" I asked.

She nodded. "Yes, in Qellaqocha and in Pampallqa. Ten soldiers came through here on their way to Pampallqa. In Qellaqocha there are twenty soldiers."

As always, I was struck by how much the children, in this case nine-year-old Edith, knew about security issues. Her father, Satu, was active in village politics and the *ronda*. However, Edith was not unusual in her grasp of the details.

It was already late afternoon and I was worried that I would not have a chance to see some of my other favorite people. I told the children that I would be back later in the evening if they wanted to come by, and I headed down the slope to look for mama Dionisia. I called out as I reached her corral and found her in the kitchen. She brought out a bowl of boiled potatoes and we sat, peeling off the skins, adding a pinch of salt, and catching up on life. She also told me about the attack and how concerned everyone was. I told her I'd come by the following day to talk some more, wanting to make certain I visited several other households so no one would think me rude.

I walked uphill to the health post, and it looked as though doors were open on several homes across from the cemetery. I crossed the soccer field, walked past the still dilapidated primary school, and headed to Marcelina's. She was home, and soon Izcarceta and Flora joined us. All three women were concerned about what was going to happen when the majority of the villagers left to vote. Marcelina explained, "Just last week the Senderistas entered right up there," pointing to the slope above the ex–military base, "and threw bombs, bullets."

Izcarceta and Flora both nodded and recalled how terrified people had been. "The children were screaming," added Izcarceta.

Marcelina continued. "They've asked the soldiers to come back. When I was sleeping, I heard bullets exploding, bombs being thrown. I woke up with *susto* and ran up behind my house. 'Oh, what am I going to do?' I was saying to myself. People [*ronderos*] from here went out, shooting back. That's how they went looking for them. They say there were several *terrucos*. They found bullet casings. With all this fear, we've asked the soldiers to come back again."

Flora shook her head and wondered out loud if the Senderistas would *ever* be finished off.

Although still uncertain who was responsible for the attacks, I was interested in the social tensions they generated within the villages. "What happened when the attack occurred? Did people here say that maybe the *arrepentidos* were informing the Senderistas?"

Marcelina shook her head. "No, we only thought . . ." She paused. "Well maybe it could be, we were saying. I can't deny it. I was wondering, too. Maybe some of those *plagakuna* could return to Senderismo. But they didn't. They defended the village just like everyone else."

"But I keep wondering. Well, for instance, when people get drunk, do they start remembering who repented, who was out walking with them?"

Izcarceta nodded. "Yes, they say that when they're drunk. They say, 'How are they going to forget those Senderistas? What if they continue being Senderistas?' People say that."

Marcelina interrupted, "Even me, I've said that. I'm not going to deny it. If they were that way, they could return to it. They could do just about anything to us. We say that. And they respond saying, 'It might have been that way before, but not now.'"

"Do people hit them?" I asked.

"No, no," Marcelina replied. "They just talk."

Just Talking

"They say"—that narrative convention that framed so many conversations. They say that Fortunita Huamán was a *terruca*. I had been told about her, in whispering, disapproving tones. "She's had so much bad luck [*mala suerte*]. I wonder why that is?" people asked, knowingly.

Fortunita and some of her children lived in a one-room house above the cemetery. I had not sought her out initially, reluctant to be one more person scrutinizing her. I met her daughter Rufina first, one day when I walked down to the river to wash my clothes. I thought I heard someone singing but could see no one. The singing was soft and plaintive, and seemed to be coming from the bushes themselves. I walked out onto one of the large rocks jutting out of the river and heard a few giggles.

A young girl emerged from among the leaves, her hat ringed in shiny cigarette wrappers and flowers. I waved her over. She didn't move at first, just watched me. I went back to washing clothes, looking up a bit later to see her crossing the old helicopter blade that villagers had made into a bridge. She sat with me, not saying a word, keeping an eye on her three goats grazing across the way. After that day she began visiting our room, still quiet. Sometimes she came alone; sometimes she brought her little sister Lara or brother Hector.

Madeleine and I decided we would visit her one morning. We walked over and found the door open. A woman, Fortunita, waved us in. We climbed over a pile of blankets in her doorway, surprised to find her infant son in one of the folds. We sat down in the tiny room, and I tried to imagine so many children in so few cubic feet. Three-year-old Lara, child of misfortune, kept throwing herself in my lap. Her black plastic shoes hid her burned left foot, toes melted together into an unyielding square of flesh. However, the deep scar that tilted her face could not be hidden. Lara had fallen down a steep slope one day and had the bad luck to land on an old tuna can at the bottom. The ragged edges of her scar bore the impress of that can, the puckered skin tracing the entire curve of her right cheek.

Fortunita's belly was still large beneath her skirts, and weariness tugged at the corners of her mouth and the slope of her shoulders. She was worried that morning. Rufina had left two days before, taking twenty *soles* with her. Fortunita did not know where she had gone. She seemed as worried about the twenty *soles* as she was about eleven-year-old Rufina. She sighed as she looked out the door at the hills, wondering why she had such bad luck. Several times in the course of our conversation, she wondered out loud if God was punishing her.

Fortunita had had numerous children with numerous men. Some villagers described her as *haylaka* (very liberal) and applied the term to her eldest daughter, Dalia, as well. At sixteen Dalia already had a child with one of the soldiers, who had left for the city. Other villagers called these women *wachapakoq. Wachay* means to breed or give birth, and it is a verb that can be used for animals.[5] *Wachapakoq* refers to a woman who "loans" herself out to numerous men—and subsequent pregnancies. During the *faenas*, the men talked about Fortunita, telling Efraín that she had charged the soldiers five *soles* a visit.

The room was so cramped I felt we were imposing. Madeleine and I suggested Fortunita come to our room and we could make *miski yaku*. She nodded and began readying the baby. She spoke with us as she was wrapping him in a cloth: "I wanted this one to die. I have too many of them and I wanted to smother him. I should've just done it." She went back to wrapping the cloth around his tiny body, hoisted him onto her back, and indicated she was ready to go.

We set off, Madeleine holding Lara's hand as we walked up to our room. We lived behind the watchtower at that point. As we rounded the corner, a group of children were playing in the decaying tower, which now served as a makeshift latrine. We stopped for a moment to watch Yolanda and Edith leading Edgar, Víctor, and Jonny into the tower, yelling at them. They pretended to close the door behind them, warning the boys what would happen if they tried to escape.

The girls saw us and laughed. "We're playing *recluto* [army recruitment]. We make them stay in there and eat *caca*—that's all they get to eat!"

"What will happen to them next?" I asked.

"We'll beat them, put them in a truck, and take them away," Yolanda replied gleefully.

"And then we'll beat them some more," added Edith.

I peered into the tower and wished the young conscripts good luck.

We cleared off one of the beds, inviting Fortunita to make herself comfortable. She preferred to sit on a dry island on our floor, José Javier on her back and Lara at her side. Cups of sweet coffee were passed around. Our conversation would be as murky as that *miski yaku*. Fortunita knew what "they said," and she started off insisting it was not true and that the Senderistas had forced her into their ranks.

"Where were you from originally?" Madeleine asked, knowing that Fortunita had come to Carhuahurán during the *sasachakuy tiempo*.

Fortunita jostled José Javier, who was fussing in her *manta*. "From a village named Pucará. That's our pueblo. We have no land here."

"So Sendero took you from Pucará?" I asked.

She nodded. As she told it, the Senderistas had kept Fortunita and her family on the move between the *puna* and the *selva*, the guerrilla's constant movement aimed at evading the soldiers as well as the famous *ronderos* of Carhuahurán. Their evasive efforts eventually failed when soldiers raided the cave in which Fortunita and others were hiding.

"The soldiers found us. They brought my children and me here. They helped us bring our things—animals, pigs, sheep, and llamas. But when we got here they divided everything up."

"The villagers or the soldiers?" I asked.

"The villagers," she said, in a tone that made clear how angry she still was.

"You mean they took *all* of your things?" Madeleine asked.

"Yes, everything," Fortunita replied bitterly. "They said we'd been living with the *terrucos* and so they took our animals, divided them up, and ate them." Again she insisted, "But they were wrong. We lived escaping from the *terrucos*. I just tried to care for my animals, and we slept in caves at night so the *terrucos* wouldn't see us."

"What else happened? How did they treat you here?"

"Oh! They said we were talking with the *terrucos* because we were *terrucos*. But I never even knew a *terruco*. They told us they were going to kill all of us, my husband, my mother, my father." Fortunita paused. "My family had given the list to them—that's why we lived escaping from one place to another."

I did not interrupt but made a mental note about the list that Fortunita's family had given to the Senderistas. I cannot tell how committed she was to the guerrillas, if at all; she had many reasons to minimize that aspect of her past. Indeed, later in our conversation she would insist she had spent "just one day" with the *terrucos*, as though truncated time also cut short any possible sympathies she might have had with Shining Path.[6] However, in providing a list of names to the guerrillas, her family's fate took a particular turn. Shining Path militants had always boasted that the party had "a thousand eyes and a thousand ears," those sensory organs vastly multiplied by encouraging community members to spy upon and denounce one another as army informants (*soplones*) or traitors (*traidores*). The names of alleged enemies of the revolution were entered on *la lista negra de Sendero* —the black list of people destined for an "exemplary punishment," which often proved fatal. As a result of preparing that list, even if they did so under coercion, Fortunita and her family found themselves escaping from villagers who felt they had been "fingered" for death.

"Is that how you escaped? Is that why you weren't killed?" I wondered aloud.

"Yes, every day we moved, sleeping in caves." She shook her head wearily. "They accused us for no reason at all. We didn't even know *terrucos*. It was just our neighbors who had taken us to another village. Our neighbors told us, 'For no reason at all you're going to Carhuahurán, to those *yanaumas*.' When the *terrucos* threatened to kill us, we began sleeping in caves."

In accusing Fortunita of going to Carhuahurán and the *yanaumas* her neighbors evidently believed that she and her family were providing information to the *ronderos* and, by extension, the military. Senderista militants had numerous insulting terms for the *ronderos*, one of which was *yanauma*, literally "black head" in Quechua. This referred to the black woolen balaclavas the *ronderos* wore when out on patrol, in part to ward off the bitter cold, in part to provide "plausible deniability" when they were attacking neighboring communities where people might recognize them. Clearly her neighbors were somehow involved with Sendero or they would not have leveled the accusation against Fortunita and her family, whom I strongly suspect provided the Senderistas with that list of names in an effort to prove they were not *soplones* themselves. The constant in Fortunita's story was hiding in caves; just whom they were hiding from, however, was not so cut and dried.

"I can only imagine how awful it was in those caves," I commiserated, prompting a nod of agreement on her part. "What did you eat?"

"We cooked *papas* and other things. That's why here they say we were taking care of the *terrucos*. Here they said we were *iskay uyakuna* [two-faced]."

"So that's how people were talking about you?"

"Yes, people talked. 'So that's how they were taking care of the *terrucos*,' they said. We were marked for death, but God didn't want it that way. My uncle spoke up. He said, 'She's only a daughter-in-law there.' My father and my husband also presented themselves. My children were just little then."

Her uncle's insistence that Fortunita was an in-marrying daughter-in-law in Pucará, while she had blood relatives in Carhuahurán, was striking. In reckoning kinship, blood trumps marriage and in-marrying spouses (of either sex) are often assumed to have less allegiance to a village and, when there are conflicts, to be at a disadvantage when pressing their claims. Her uncle's strategy played on these ideas: even if Pucará was full of Senderistas, he was asking people to consider how much of a guerrilla Fortunita *really* was given that she had only married in to the community. The strategy worked: Fortunita and her children were spared—her husband was not. She would not specify who had killed him.

"Fortunita, what else did people say when you came here?" asked Madeleine.

"Before, they used to call us *terrucos*. They talked about us. But the authorities forbid them to keep saying those sorts of things. But when they fight, they keep talking—even now, just yesterday at the *feria*, they were calling me a *terruca* again."

"What makes them say that, even after all these years?" I asked her.

She shrugged. "When they're drunk, they throw rocks at us. That's when they keep saying '*terruca*.'"

"Is it true what they say?"

"No. It's a lie," she insisted. "I was only with the *terrucos* one day. They just say that because they plant in the *chacras* where we used to live and they think everyone there was a *terruco*. But there were plenty of *terrucos* here," she added with a smirk.

"Really?"

"Oh yeah. They'd posted signs when the priest was giving mass in the church—where the health post is now," pointing downhill across the soccer field. "While the priest was giving mass, they were staking their flag. They planted their red flag right here! When we were passing by on our way to the jungle, we saw that flag outside the church, and the *terrucos* were seated everywhere, even on the pews. They just say these things to be hateful."

"You mentioned the authorities. When people spoke badly about you, you say the authorities told them to stop—forbid them to use those words?" I asked.

She nodded. "In the *formación*, the authorities told people that if they kept saying those things, they'd be fined. That stopped them for a while."

"Do you think about leaving?"

"No. Where would I go? My parents died. Where would I go?"

I was curious about something. "Why do you think the authorities were supporting you?"

She thought for a moment. "I don't know. But they said we shouldn't say these things because we live in *tiempo de peligro* [time of danger]. They said we should live like we were all children of one person."

"When was this, Fortunita?"

"It was before. There was so much danger then."

I thought back to something else I had read in the Actas Comunales and that Feliciano had invoked when people began denouncing me as a *gringa terruca*. In 1991, communal authorities had passed the Ley Contra Chismes (Law Against Gossip). Gossip had become so divisive that authorities outlawed the practice and imposed a fine on anyone who was caught "just talking." The law was recorded in the Actas, signed, fingerprinted, and inked with each authority's rubber stamp.

"Was this when the authorities imposed the fine for those who kept talking?"

She nodded. "Yes, during the same time. They talked about the people who'd been marked."

"Oh, so it was the time of the marked people?"

She nodded.

"Do they still talk about the marked people?"

"No, not anymore. Well, not so much."

"When all of this happened, what did you think?"

"I thought I have bad luck, that El Señor Divino didn't love me."

"Why would God punish you?"

"I don't know, but I've been punished," she assured us.

We just sat for a bit, and I offered her more *miski yaku* and *chancay*. It felt wrong to offer her soothing words, to assure her that she did not have *mala suerte*. Her life story, all "they" had said and kept saying, Lara's little wedge of a foot and lopsided face—it would have been a lie to say anything encouraging.

Alessandro Portelli has suggested that oral historians understand subjectivity as "the study of cultural forms and processes by which individuals express their sense of themselves in history." Thus "The organization of the narrative reveals a great deal of the speakers' relationships to their history."[7] Fortunita was trying to piece together a life, fragmented by mixed feelings and allegiances, full of seemingly irreconcilable moments. She tried to manage a spoiled identity, combining and recombining events in the hope of making them come out right—in the hope that some other end to her story might still be possible. However, there is no comfortable narrative space that Fortunita, and other women who bore the mark, may occupy: there is no untainted subject position available to her, prompting a narrative flight that mimics her constant movement during the war. Creating a life is an ongoing historical project, and some people are disadvantaged in terms of the elements they may combine. In these villages, gender influences one's "historical project," and the redemptive rise to authority status is not a female trajectory. While I knew many men who had been reintegrated into communal life and had gone on to assume leadership positions in their villages, that was not an option for the *arrepentidas* I knew. For the women, memories seemed to fade more slowly than the mark itself.[8]

While we sipped our coffee, I thought of something else I had read in the Actas Comunales. I recalled the *recogiados y otros*. "Fortunita, so you could live here—did they give you land to work, to build your house on?"

She nodded. "The old authorities gave us land to build on." She went on to explain that she had worked on other people's land, trying to make ends meet. That challenge had not subsided. "My son sends me money sometimes from the *selva* where he's working, and I work for other people when I can."

Both José Javier and Lara were restless. I took Lara and set her up with paper and crayons; Fortunita began nursing her baby and asked if we had any rice. We did, and I poured some into a worn plastic bag she had tucked in her skirt. I thought she might want to leave, but when she finished nursing José Javier she wrapped him up again in the *manta* on her back and kept sitting there.

"Fortunita, you mentioned the soldiers brought you to Carhuahurán. When the soldiers were here, did they behave well?" asked Madeleine.

She shook her head in disgust. "Oh no, they were terrible. They robbed livestock, potatoes, fava beans. They stole my goat, chickens—nothing escaped them."

"You know, in some communities the soldiers mistreated the women. Did they abuse any women here?" I asked, using the verb *abusay*. Quechua speakers used several verbs to refer to rape rather than the verb *violar*. The vagueness of terms such as "abuse" and "bother" (*fastidiar*) made context extremely important. It also allowed me to ask the question in a veiled, indirect manner.

"Yes."

I waited to see if she had more to say; she did not. "And the authorities said nothing?"

"When the authorities said something, they [the soldiers] came at night and grabbed them to kill them," she replied.

"Whom did they kill?"

"Mario Quispe. They killed him when he protested the abuses they committed."

"Did people here protest? Did they look for him?"

She shook her head. "The soldiers said they would leave and let the *terrucos* kill everyone if people said anything."

Although Fortunita spoke harshly about the soldiers, rumor had it that they had spent many evenings in her house.

"Where did you meet Lara's papa?" I asked.

"In my house. He was a soldier and he came to visit me. He told me he didn't have a wife. He was from Ayacucho and said he wanted to marry me. He said he would work on my land and that I wouldn't suffer anymore. So I accepted him." Fortunita almost laughed as she recalled his promises and her belief in them. "One day he said he was going to Ayacucho to visit his family. He never came back, leaving me pregnant with Lara." She began fingering the hem of her outer skirt, pulling at the worn embroidery. "I have no luck," she added, softly as though speaking only to herself.

"It's not easy being a single mother, is it?" I commented, not raising my voice at the end of the sentence to make something so obvious into a question. "It's really hard."

She nodded sadly. "When you're a single mother, you're always needing something. I got together with a man from here because I had nothing. But he went crazy and left for the *selva*. I don't know. Sometimes I think his family just says that because they didn't want him to be with me. They don't want to recognize his child [José Javier]. I think his family told him to go. I think they asked him, 'How are you going to be with this woman with so many children—this woman who's older than you?' I think they told him to leave me."

"Abandonment is a big problem, isn't it?"

Fortunita was emphatic: "*Demasiado, mami*—too much."

It was already late afternoon, and Fortunita needed to head home and start her cooking fire. I walked her back, and there was still no Rufina. "We'll come by tomorrow and see if she's come home," patting her arm and hoping her daughter would be all right.

Back in our room, we needed to sit and absorb it all. "Madeleine, do you think things were always like this? There couldn't have been so many single mothers," my voice drifting as I attempted a mental calculation of the women we knew.

She shook her head. "No, I think having the soldiers here changed things. There are so many *huérfanos de padre* [children with no fathers]. This has to be a big change."

The next day I was able to confirm this with don Feliciano. He did not have exact numbers from before the violence, but he knew the current figures. Of a total population of some 3,300 in Carhuahurán and its eleven annexes (*pagos*), there were 110 widows and over 500 orphans, which referred to children missing either one or both parents. When I expressed my amazement, he nodded. "This is an enormous burden on the community, on all of us. You know, 331 people were killed here." There was no coldness in his voice, just a reckoning of what those numbers meant for the living.

Later that day came word that Rufina was back. We gathered up some bread and headed to Fortunita's. Rufina was there, but I barely recognized her. There was nothing of the shy girl singing by the river or visiting our room with her younger siblings. She was furious, yelling at her mother.

We started to back away from the door, but Fortunita signaled for us to come in. The shouting stopped. I pulled the bag of *chaplas* from my backpack, suggesting we celebrate Rufina's safe return. We passed the bread around, and Rufina grabbed the bag, throwing a *chapla* at her mother and her sister Lara. Fortunita offered a bowl of boiled potatoes, and we silently peeled them. Rufina dropped one on the ground, kicking it toward her little sister. "Lara, that's for you," she sneered.

Madeleine and I exchanged glances, not knowing what we had walked into. We had never seen Rufina act this way. We made some excuse and left.

The following day, Rufina appeared alone at our door. Again, she seemed like a different person. There was none of the rebellious, angry girl throwing food at her mother and sister. That day she looked only eleven, her eyes and nose red from crying.

We had her come in, closed the door behind her, and secured it with a rock so we could have some privacy. She was wiping her face on the sleeve of her sweater and looking terribly sad. She needed no prompting to tell us what was wrong, and what followed was a three-hour conversation about her complicated family life.

"I went to harvest *oca* [a tuber]. I went to my aunt Antonia's *chacra*. They paid me and I brought back food with me. My mother said how much she would like to eat fresh *oca* soup," she blurted out, still sniffling. "There's never any food, never any money."

"Your mother said she lost twenty *soles*, no?" Madeleine asked.

"I don't know anything about the twenty *soles*. I went to work. I *told* her that."

I pulled out a roll of Suave and handed her some toilet paper to blow her nose. "Has it always been like this?" I asked.

"No, not when my papa was alive." Rufina was crying so hard she began coughing. Madeleine patted her back while I boiled water for hot chocolate.

Rufina kept speaking between sobs. "I cry when I remember my papa. I think if he were still alive, he would be working in the *chacra*. If he were alive, we wouldn't be like this. My mama remembers, too, and she cries."

"What happened to your papa?"

"He died from colic. He died in the *selva*. On Todos Santos [All Saints' Day], we can't even light a candle. If I knew where he was buried, I could light candles, take flowers."

Rufina needed to sit and sob with people who handed her Suave and *miski yaku*. She began to draw deep jagged breaths that rocked her entire body. We just sat with her, patting her back. Rufina cried herself out, subsiding back into sniffles.

Madeleine spoke first. "You went to your aunt Antonia's to help. It must be difficult in your house."

Rufina nodded with her entire torso. "We never have any money."

I asked something I'd been trying to figure out, only to find the numbers ricocheting in my mind. "Rufinacha, how many children are there in your family?"

"There're eight of us, but Sabino's in Huanta and has forgotten my mother."

"Is Sabino your big brother?"

Rufina nodded.

"And who is Lara's father? Do you know him?"

"No, I don't know who he is," Rufina scowled. Her next comment, however, made clear she did know him but wished she did not. "Lara's father is the one who took my brother to Huanta."

As Rufina explained, Lara's father was a soldier who had been stationed in Carhuahurán for several months. When Fortunita became pregnant, he left for Huanta with promises he would be back. He did make a short return trip to Carhuahurán, and Fortunita succeeded in persuading him to buy some clothes for the baby. However, his visit was brief. He talked Fortunita into letting him take Sabino with him to Huanta, telling her he would help her son find work. He had tried to convince her to send her daughter Nicolasa along as well, but Nicolasa put up a major fuss. That was the last the family saw of Lara's father or Sabino. "He tricked my mother. He took my brother and never came back. My mother cries, 'What if he sold my son? What happened to him?'" No one knew, but it was not unusual for rural children to end up as household labor in the cities.

"How did he meet your mother?"

"He came to the house for *trago*, the same way Dalia's husband did. He was a soldier, too. They met in my house because my mother sold *trago*. That's why they came."

"So that's how your mother and sister got together with soldiers?"

She nodded. "My mama sold *trago* and so the soldiers came to our house. When there was a fiesta, they would rob the trucks—sugar, bread, animals. They brought us food and my mama and Dalia prepared breakfast for them. They would come back drunk at night—they came every night for *trago*."

We stopped there. I didn't want Rufina to feel like she was being asked endless questions. However, at some point it became clear, as it had with other children, that she was pleased to have two adults sit and listen to her. This was not the ordinary conversational pattern in Andean families, where adults did most of the talking. Rufina had settled in, and she had much more to say.

"You had another stepfather, too?"

Rufina nodded.

"What was his name?"

"Hmm, he was José, Javier's father. His family asked him how he could be with such an old woman, a woman with children. He would come home and like a little child he would tell my mother everything people had said. 'Why didn't you talk back to them?' my mother asked him. 'Why didn't you tell them, "It's my choice. I'm with an old woman and what does it matter to you?" My mother told him to talk back to them."

"What happened to him?" I asked.

"He went *loco* during Carnivales. Who knows what they gave him. They must have put something in his *trago*. He left for the *selva*, he went crazy."

Madeleine asked, "How did your mother meet your stepfather?"

"Señora Izcarceta brought him over. They came by every day. They kept asking my mama over to their house. 'Let's go *chakchar* coca,' they said. They tricked my mama. My sister Dalia got mad at my mother. 'You, as though you need another husband! There you are running down there. You should *chakchar* your coca here at home.' Me, too, I told my mama she shouldn't go every time they called her. They tricked her."

"Your stepfather came to your house?"

"No. When they were in his house and it was late, they would tell my mama, 'Stay here. We're going to sleep here.' My mama didn't want to. 'My children are alone,' she said. 'They'll miss me if I stay here.' Epifania, Izcarceta—my mama says they always insisted she stay and sleep there. They kept calling my mother over to drink *trago*. Finally my sister Dalia went over to their house and yelled at them. 'You call my mama too much. What are you, family? You keep calling her every morning, every afternoon—are you family? When she ends up pregnant, are you going to take care of her? Are you going to feed her?' Dalia almost hit them. 'You call her every day and give her *trago*, like food to a starving person. Like a drunk! Until she's bringing you our food, *carajo*! You know, if she gets pregnant again, we don't want her coming home. Do whatever you want—she can live wherever she lives. She can get pregnant wherever she gets pregnant. We're not going to take care of her. You can do it. *Carajo*!' That's what my sister Dalia told them. My mama started to cry. Dalia said, 'If you get pregnant again, I'm leaving for the *selva*. I'm never coming back. Forget that I'm your daughter.' My mama told her, 'Go ahead. Just go ahead.'"

There was so much condensed in what Rufina was saying. José Javier's father had been much younger than Fortunita, and just what role his family had played in bringing them together or tearing them apart was difficult to discern. However, I knew other couples in which the woman was substantially older, and it generally involved widows with *chacras* and no man to work them. Izcarceta herself was an elderly widow. She lived with several female family members in one of the shabbiest huts in Carhuahurán, down a steep slope where people from outlying annexes had constructed makeshift shacks when they came to Carhuahurán for refuge during the *sasachakuy tiempo*. Her family was destitute. Fortunita may have had several children, but she also had untilled land in her deceased parents' community a few hours away. Additionally, the young man had some sort of mental disturbance, which followed the pattern of marrying the *arrepentidas* off, even after so many years, to less desirable men.

Rufina paused before adding, "I also insult my mama. I tell her, 'You're already a grown woman with children and you sleep with men who could be your children!' My mama doesn't say anything. She just stands there."

"Why do you think your mother was with these men?" I asked.

She shrugged her shoulders. "I don't know. They tricked her."

I decided to be blunt. "Do you think your mother sought these men out because she loved them or because they would work on her *chacra*—you know, out of necessity?"

"Well, my [paternal] grandmother said, 'It's only my husband who's working.' That's why my mama told her she was capable of getting another man who could work. My grandmother told us not to listen to anything our mama says—'In vain she's talking,' that's what my grandmother said. But my mama said she could find a man to work. When my mother got pregnant the last time, my grandfather whipped her with a *tres puntas* [three-pointed leather whip]. He told her, 'You're giving yourself to these men. Maybe I'm not providing for you? You think I'm not helping you? I give you food to eat. Why do you keep getting together with men? I'm sure you tell them you don't have food.' He whipped her and she said nothing. Afterward she told him, 'It's my fault, *papi*.'"

"What do you think, Rufina? What do you think about all this?"

"It's awful. I get really angry with people. With this last baby, people said, 'So Rufina will carry [*cargar*—literally carry on her back, but also implies taking care of] this baby, your eighth baby.' I answered them. I was angry! I said, 'I'm not foolish enough to be carrying this baby. I'm not carrying this one. I don't know how, but my mama will have to do it.' That's what I told people." Rufina's voice suddenly softened. "But now I look at him and I can't help it. I want to carry him. I want to just leave him, but I can't." She paused before adding, "If this one had been born a girl, my mama was going to kill it. She was going to smother the baby with a blanket."

"Your mama was going to kill the baby?"

"Yes, she was going to kill it. She was going to smother it with a blanket, but the lady from the health post came to cut his *ombligo* [literally belly button but referring to umbilical cord]. She's his godmother."

"Why did your mother want to kill the baby?"

"She said, 'If this one's a girl, we'll kill her. I have so many children. How will I dress this one? If your father were alive, then he would buy clothing for it. He would get food.' That's what my mama said. You know, it was the same with Lara. She wanted to bury her. She wanted to smother her with a blanket. I begged her not to kill Lara. I cried and cried. 'I'll carry her, I promise.' That's what I told my mama, and that's what I've done. Every morning, whether it was a good day or a bad day, I carried her. Because I loved her so much, I carried her."

"So your mother also wanted to kill Lara?"

Rufina nodded. "My mother didn't want her because we were little. Hector was still little, too. That's why she wanted to kill Lara. My grandmother asked mama, 'When Rufina starts school, are you going to take care of this baby? Why did you bring this poor innocent into the world?' I told my grandmother that mama wanted to kill Lara but I'd stopped her. My grandmother got angry. She asked me, 'Why did you stop her? Your mother should've killed her. Now your mother will take even longer before she can work in the *chacra*. So you go ahead and take care of her. You just go on to school carrying her.' That's what my grandmother said. So I told her, 'Somehow I'll take care of her.' I tore up my skirts for diapers and I dressed her. I carried her and that's why Lara loves me."

Rufina took a sip of her hot chocolate and seemed to savor thinking about Lara as much as she did the sweet taste of her drink.

"My mama would have killed this one [José Javier] if he hadn't been a boy. She said, 'At least a boy will work in the *chacra*.' But I told my mama, 'How can you kill a poor baby? Surely it will curse us if you do. This one's a boy and can work in the *chacra*.' I begged her—'Poor little angel. How can you kill it?' So my mama didn't kill it. She said, 'It's true, it could curse us. Anything could happen to us then,' my mama said."

Rufina paused for a moment before continuing. "There's so many of us in my family. I don't know who taught my mama how to kill, but I stopped her."

We all paused for a moment. Rufina kept sipping her hot chocolate, and I realized that just the tips of her toes reached the ground below the chair.

"And Lara's dad was a soldier you said?"

"Yes."

"Did the soldiers give your mama money?"

"Yes. Well, only some of them. Some of them were good, and others no."

"Why did they give your mama money?"

"They said, 'Take this to buy your salt.' Saying that, they gave her money."

"How much did they give her?"

"Some of them gave her twenty *soles* and others just two *soles*."

"So your mother was friends with the soldiers?"

"Yes, they'd give us food."

"And what do people here say, because you were friends with the soldiers?"

"People don't hate just my mother—they hate our whole family. They say, 'We've already warned you many times. And one of these days we're going to punish you.' That's what they say. *They hate our family. They hate all of us.*"

"Were other women also with soldiers?"

"Yes, several of them."

"Why do you think they chose soldiers?"

"I don't know," she shrugged. "Probably for their money."

"If your mother takes up with another man, what would you do?"

She was resolute. "I'd leave. My mama and I have already talked about it, and I told her this is the last time. 'Be careful, mama,' I told her, 'be careful that you get together with another one. Be careful if you have another baby. If you have another one, I'm leaving you. You'll be left here all by yourself.'"

"Yeah. I wonder, did you like your stepfather?"

"Which one?"

I realized I had forgotten to define which of the men I was referring to and went back to "Lara's dad."

"No. I wanted to hit him! If he'd been my father I would have said, 'Good morning.' I would have taken care of him. I *hated* my stepfather and only put up with him for my mama's sake. I didn't wash his clothes. I washed my mama's clothes, my little brother's and sister's clothes. But I *never* washed my stepfather's clothes," Rufina added defiantly, proud she had refused to perform this familial task for a man she despised.

I reached out and brushed away some hair that had escaped her hat and fallen over her eye, wondering to myself how an eleven-year-old girl could shoulder so much. "You have a lot to think about and take care of, Rufina."

She nodded in agreement. "I worry most about my little brother and sister. How are they going to have clothes? How will my mother care for them? And if she has more children?" Rufina exhaled loudly. "We already have *nothing* to eat."

I do not believe things were always like this: revolving step-parents; hundreds of orphans; children scolding their mothers for having too many sexual partners and unplanned pregnancies; older widows with untilled land and vastly younger suitors; and the commodification of sex that was one legacy of the sustained military presence throughout the region. The war left many social institutions severely altered, family and community among them. Death, migration, abandonment—and soldiers stationed throughout the highlands—left many people struggling to get by, materially and emotionally. Take Carhuahurán as an example. With so many people killed and some five hundred *huérfanos*, families are reconfigured in ways that leave some people vulnerable as resources are stretched beyond their capacity.

There is also much more remarriage than before the war, and talk about step-parents revealed deep ambivalence about them.

One day I was sitting outside at a wake, and a family member of the deceased brought me a bowl of soup with a large piece of meat bobbing to the oil-slick surface. This was an honor, and I recognized it as such. I took several sips before I heard little Shintaca calling out, "What about me, *hawamama* [stepmother]?" Everyone began laughing, and the women I was sitting with saw my puzzled expression. As they explained, because I had taken several sips without offering her any of my soup, I was behaving just like a stepmother.

Hawamama is a fascinating term. *Hawa* signifies exteriority, distance, or remove. For instance, one word for foreigners or strangers is *hawaruna*—a combination of the word "people" (*runa*) plus the emphasis on exteriority. The term *hawamama* is an unsettling mixture of the familiar *mama* rendered strange, reflecting the fact it is a relationship established by marriage (affinal) rather than by birth or blood.

Stepfathers also prompted many commentaries, and key themes were mistreatment and molestation. It went something like this. In the course of conversations with widows, I asked if they thought about taking another husband. Loud guffaws ensued, coupled with concerns that stepfathers would mistreat their children, in addition to *fastidiando* (bothering) their daughters.[9]

The debates on incest taboos are an anthropological version of the chicken-and-the-egg: which comes first—the desire to commit incest and thus the taboo, or the taboo that creates the desire? To what extent do villagers' concerns about step-parents—miserly, abusive, molesting, depending upon gender—reflect reality? What sorts of psychocultural themes are expressed in these stereotypes?

Kinship is key to survival and to inheritance in these villages. As we have seen, *waqcha* is the Quechua word for both "poor" and "without family." However, kinship is also a discourse on obligation and hierarchy, cloaked in the language of affect. Penelope Harvey has suggested that "Affinal relations express difference and work against the ordered hierarchical complementarity of kinship. Affinity is necessary for productive sociality yet it implies disorder, confrontation, instability. Affinal relations are not contained by principles of ordered hierarchy."[10] Harvey thus contrasts the "trusting hierarchy of kinship" with the achieved hierarchy of affinal relationships, in which the non-blood relation is always potentially disruptive.

The reconfiguration of family is intensely ambiguous. Bluntly, there is not enough of anything to go around. Land, food, affection—this is a restricted economy in every sense of the word. Although some villagers benefited from the political violence and the pillaging the *rondas* and the Senderistas carried out on their sweeps through the countryside, more often war exacerbated poverty. The competition for scarce resources works in the material, affective, and symbolic spheres. Anxious talk about step-parents is anxious talk about life and love in times of war and its aftermath.

Additionally, recall that part of children's emotional education includes learning how to make others love them, challenging notions that motherly love is innate and simply waiting for a baby upon which to fix.[11] Not all children are equally loved, even by their own mothers; women were candid in discussing which child they loved the most and which ones they did not. This gradation had a gendered dimension: I cannot recall one favorite child who was female. One thinks of Fortunita, who was more inclined to spare the life of a baby boy because "at least a boy will work in the *chacra*." In conversations, numerous mothers described different treatment for a sick daughter versus a sick son. For the boy, they were more likely to scrape together two *soles* and head to the health post. I also recall many meals and the protein hierarchy that left girls at the end of the familial food chain. Girls may have reason to worry when families begin shifting around.

This was powerfully conveyed when mama Juliana gave birth to a baby boy. She lived across from me and was Shintaca's mother. Shintaca's father (a soldier) had left shortly after his daughter was born, and he sent nothing to Juliana in the way of assistance.

Juliana and her new partner lived with her extended family, which included Vilma, Yolanda, Edith, Víctor, and Jonny—children ranging from four to eleven years old. Yolanda's situation was the most precarious. While the others girls had birth parents living within the extended household, Yolanda did not. Not long after the baby boy was born, the girls began asking me for *ñuñu*, literally "breast" but in this case "breastfeeding." They would arrive in my room and begin touching my breasts and pretending to suckle.

I was thrown off at first. I was not quite certain what to do as these little girls kept fondling me through my clothing and insisting on *ñuñu* whenever they came by. It was Yolanda—who was being raised by her maternal grandparents because her father had left before she was born and her mother had died while Yolanda was still an infant—who finally looked at me beseechingly and pleaded, "I'm dying of thirst for mother's milk."

Children hear the conversations about which of them are lovable, or not. This particular generation grew up hearing that it was no time to bring children into the world and, if you do, best not to have more than two. How could you carry more than two to safety in the event the enemy attacked? For the children who were listening, how to know whether you would be one of those carried to safety in a parent's arms or left to the vagaries of war and luck?

The transgenerational aspects of war and its legacies remain woefully understudied.[12] In a previous chapter I introduced Chiki, a young boy who was the result of his mother's rape. That is one form legacies may take. There are many others. What is it like to be the child of the formerly marked ones, given that memory may be more indelible than the mark itself, the imprint kept fresh by people "just talking"? Eleven-year-old Rufina provides insights into that life history, illustrating the challenges as well as her resolve to improve her life and that of her younger siblings. I could provide abundant examples from other communities where one knows which children will play the "bad guys" in school plays; it is always the same small pool that is cast in those undesirable roles. Just look to their parents' past.

As anthropologists, we have not given children their due. I make no claims to remedy that here but rather share my frustration and my own limitations. At one point early on in my research, it became clear that I needed to know much more about the anthropology of children. I headed to the Kroeber anthropology library at the University of California: in the stacks, I found there were no children there. With a few notable exceptions, somehow anthropology's interest in children stopped with Margaret Mead, a perverse disciplinary twist on "arrested development." I invite the skeptic to randomly select one hundred ethnographies. Read them and try to learn something about the lives of children in the societies studied. I do not mean what adults say about children but what the children themselves say and do.

Children are largely absent in our texts, missing from our studies of human life and cultural production. The absence of children in anthropological writing finds its parallel in studies of social memory. If transmission is what makes memory "social," then why are children peripheral to this literature as well? If we understand transmission not as mimesis but as the creative reelaboration of cultural forms, narrative conventions, and collective histories, one would suppose children would be key protagonists in the process. Unfortunately, as Nancy Scheper-Hughes notes, "As a whole, childhood is under-represented and under-theorized and anthropologists need to alter their conventional ways and methods of studying children."[13]

Among those conventions are the standard representations of children and war, a clunky literature I gloss as "war is bad for children and makes them draw helicopters." I acknowledge the recent surge of interest in child soldiers and the growth of child combatant literature and memoirs.[14] The child as victim cedes to the child as both victim and victimizer. This is an important corrective to earlier depictions, but between the two poles of child victim and child combatant lies a vast range of experience that remains largely unexplored. Between those two poles are many other ways in which children are political actors, producers of culture and history. Surely those activities contribute to the work of both commenting on and reconstructing social life. Yolanda certainly made me think so.

Yolanda Quispe Huamán was ten years old when we first met in 1997. Her skinny legs looked barely capable of holding up the layers of her heavily embroidered skirts. Her big felt hat sat low on her forehead, and long black braids the size of baguettes framed her face. Hers was not the face of a child; the features had no round-eyed, button-nosed anything about them. Just angles. She came to introduce herself, staying to talk about life in Carhuahurán. It was several hours later when she left, turning to tell me, "I'll be back tomorrow because I have so many more things to say."

The next day Yolanda had rounded up her gang: Edith and her potbellied brother Jonny; Máximo and his little brother (I called him Mínimo, but his name was Víctor), and Edgar. They were playing amid the broken clods of adobe that had been part of the watchtower outside my room. Máximo and Mínimo pretended to be soldiers, walking around with the swagger that distinguished them from nonconscripted *campesinos*. Edith and Jonny played villagers frantically wondering where their large rooster had gone. Distraught, they looked under every broken adobe, searching with their eyes and their hands. Their rooster was nowhere to be found.

Their efforts futile, Edith and Jonny took their case to Edgar, justice of the peace. They insisted it *must* be the soldiers who had taken their rooster and they demanded that Edgar bring them in for questioning. Máximo and Mínimo came swaggering by, the former concealing something bulky under his jacket. All eyes indicted him on the spot. About this time, Yolanda appeared, insisting that Edgar do something. He shrugged his shoulders in response: "Yeah, but what am I going to do?" Yolanda grabbed Máximo's arm and shook him. Out came the rooster, feathers ruffled. Yolanda insisted again that Edgar do something: "Yeah, but what I am going to do?" Turning her back in disgust, Yolanda grabbed her *manta*, filled it with boiled potatoes and toasted corn, and announced she was off to the judge in Huanta "because there is no justice here."

Children's games are their historicizing, but the chapters are open-ended and sometimes they outwit the adults around them, subverting relations of power and injustice that operate in their everyday lives. This is serious play—a political commentary on events that demonstrates their moral sensibilities and political subjectivity.

This political subjectivity was made clear in another circuitous manner. The president, and subsequently mayor, of Carhuahurán was Feliciano Rimachi, who reveled in his power, which was based in part upon his role as a hero of the war and an authoritative historian of the armed conflict. He began to notice that many of the children were permanent guests in my room. I had crayons, hot chocolate, and books, and had declared my room a "no corporal punishment" zone.

Don Rimachi took me aside to let me know that children are *sonsos* (senseless) and only speak *tonterías* (nonsense). He encouraged me to ignore what they said. However, as I later learned, on the winding road back from the market in Huaynacancha he told all of the adults standing in the back of the Toyota truck to make certain their children stopped talking to me. Remember the Peruvian saying *Los niños y los borrachos hablan la verdad* (Children and drunks speak the truth)? Perhaps not *the* truth, but certainly children offer perspectives on political and historical events that are not identical to those expressed by the adults who raise them.[15]

Sharon Stephens suggests "The challenge is to grasp the specificity of childhood and children's experiences in different world regions, national frameworks, and social contexts, while also seeking to illuminate the historical processes that not only link particular social worlds but are also crucially important in shaping and transforming them."[16] Part of what has transformed their particular social world is war, but many other forces—including their own—shape their social worlds. I have barely scratched the surface in this book: we have a long way to go toward doing justice to children and the complexity of their lives, at peace and at war.

Parables: A Tale of Two Funerals

In those years when the Senderistas killed, the dead were scattered like rocks all over the path. When we woke up, those of us who had escaped tried bringing them to the cemetery to bury them. We buried them piled up on top of each other. Out of fear we couldn't even hold wakes for them. We just buried them with all their clothes on. Ay, all day long we kept carrying back the dead. We just couldn't bring them all. We women would carry the bodies, between two of us we carried them. While we were carrying them back, the dogs and pigs were eating the rest of the bodies. We were so frightened—what if they [the Senderistas] were watching us? Worrying about that, we buried them quickly, just covered them with dirt. Ay, there was so much fear!
—Salomé Huanaco, Carhuahurán, 1998

Moral reconstruction cannot be accomplished through judicial means alone; it is at once political, legal, cultural, moral, psychological, and spiritual.
—Elizabeth Kiss, "Moral Ambition Within and Beyond Political Constraints"

It was midday when they came to tell us that María Quispe Curo had died. Although Efraín and I had not known her, we gathered up a package of candles and matches to accompany her family in the wake. We walked the steep incline to her house, where many villagers sat on sheepskins. Outside, women sat in clusters with children in their laps or tied to their backs in shawls, chewing coca leaves and passing the bottle of *trago* that made its way outside to them. We were invited in and settled into the corner of the house, at the foot of the corpse. Her body was wrapped in old blankets and surrounded by lighted candles. I was struck by the sight of her tiny body and murmured, "How sad, she was so young to die." The man on my left corrected me: "*Señorita*, she was very old. She was don Antonio's mother. She was paralyzed for years, her body doubled over by *aya*." As he explained, *aya* grabs a person when they come in contact with the bones of their ancestors who have not found peace. Because she had suffered from *aya* for seven years, the elderly María's swathed cadaver resembled that of a small girl.

The candles burned down as the bottle of *trago* made its rounds, offered by María's relatives to all who were accompanying the family that day. Finally, don Antonio announced that it was time to head for the cemetery. Five men carried María's body from the house to the cemetery, gently lowering her to the ground in front of the crumbling stone altar. We kept chewing coca, sipping *trago*, and preparing to send María's soul on its way. Don Lucas was called upon to perform the burial. With a pink rose in his hand, he kept dipping the flower into a glass of water, using the flower to sprinkle the water on María's body. As don Lucas traced the length of María's body with the rose, several men nudged me: "This is how we bury people."

Everyone awaited the next phase of the ceremony and don Lucas began to look uncomfortable. Some suggested we must dance, while others insisted don Lucas lead us in song. The singing contingent won and everyone waited for don Lucas to sing. Silence followed as don Lucas looked at the family and shrugged, "I just don't remember the songs."

Miguel insisted, telling him to get out his book if he couldn't remember the words. Don Lucas snorted: "My book? I don't have that book anymore. When my son Sato entered *el Evangelio*, he burned my book. I don't have that book anymore."

Several people offered up remembered words from songs from the past, but no one was able to piece together the fragments into a hymn. After a period of awkwardness, people began looking around and arrived at an agreement: "We can't sing anymore, we don't remember the words." Don Lucas improvised with his cup of water and rose, sprinkling water on the body as he murmured a few words in an inaudible voice. Later a group of men lifted the body and carried María to a corner of the cemetery. They lowered her body into the hole Miguel had dug, placing planks of wood over her and shoveling in the dirt. Once again the mourners at my side nudged me: "This is how we bury people."

I have struggled to understand how people could forget their burial rituals in such a relatively short period of time. However, both remembering and forgetting are dynamic processes, permeated with intentionality. Many villagers recall the people who were killed in the *puna* and how they were forced to hurriedly cover their bodies with dirt before the next attack. I was told of others whose body parts were collected in *costales* and brought back in an attempt to piece them into something resembling a human form so family members could light candles and hold a makeshift wake. Perhaps selective forgetting is one way to ease anxiety about those who died a "bad death" and were improperly mourned, hurriedly buried—those whose souls wandered and cried out, agitating the lives of the living and, at times, beckoning them to follow.[17]

Thus the repeated nudging: "This is how we bury people." John Comaroff and Jean Comaroff have suggested that "Ritual is a vital force in constructing and transforming the social and natural universe. It need not be merely conservative. It is not simply an adhesive that holds together authoritative social arrangements and institutions. Under certain conditions, its power may be called upon to illuminate, interpret, and counter dissonance in the lived environment."[18] The debt to those improperly buried has not been settled, but with this reinvention of tradition people affirmed that a human soul would be departing this world. Sometimes people make amends as best they can.

I recognized most of the family seated at the head of the pantheon but did not realize that the man who had been seated to the left of María's body was her husband. He had remained dry-eyed throughout the ceremony, in contrast to María's son and daughter-in-law, who sobbed and needed to be held up by friends. Ana María, her daughter-in-law, almost threw herself into the ground with María, her grief causing her legs to give way beneath her.

The following day, I asked about María's husband. Teodoro, from the health post, said Julio Huamán Curo was *mal visto*—unfavorably viewed by the rest of the community. He had deserted his wife during her long illness, leaving her to the care of their son Antonio and Ana María. Many insisted he had no right to sit with the family when she was buried because he had behaved so badly toward her. "Not only that," Teodoro explained, "but he started living with a widow in Qanqayllo. The authorities of Carhuahurán intervened. They told him to stop the relationship until his wife had died, but he kept seeing her secretly." Teodoro shook his head in disgust.

On Wednesday evening, August 4, 1999—almost exactly one year later—Julio died quite suddenly. He had been working in the *selva* and evidently fell ill with malaria. The widow he had taken up with had lost interest in him, and Antonio and Ana María remembered how poorly he had treated his dead wife. Julio's other son had followed his wife to her village, and she did not approve of her husband returning to Carhuahurán to care for his philandering father.

It was don Feliciano who found Julio dead in his house. His dog had been sitting outside the door for several days, alternately wailing and petulantly refusing to move. Feliciano finally went by and pushed open the door, finding Julio's cold body. Antonio and Ana María prepared themselves for another funeral, although there would be no tears shed for Julio.

Efraín and I were invited to Antonio's house for the wake, huddling with the other mourners seated upon *costales* full of potatoes. *Trago*, coca, and cigarettes were shared, the large bottle of *trago* served in a small tin cup that was offered as the hosts moved around the circle. Antonio greeted Efraín and me warmly, remembering that we had been there for the burial of his mother, María. He grabbed my hand: "I'm lucky that the two of you have arrived to accompany us once again."

I pulled a package of candles and a large bag of coca leaves out of my jacket. I lit a candle and placed it with the others that were flickering in front of the dead body. Antonio's sister thanked me for the coca, placing the bag behind her and handing out handfuls of coca to each mourner throughout the wake.

Doña Benita and doña Flora sat together in one corner, Benita's cheek plump with a wad of coca. Flora, staunchly evangelical, declined both the *trago* and the coca, offering to share the sodas she had brought with her.

Don Manuel and Teofilo were seated across from me, already showing the effects of having tilted back the tin cup on each round. They began teasing me gleefully, asking me to tell them about life in the Estados Jodidos.[19] They doubled over as they asked the question, coca-leaf-green teeth bared and heads thrown back in hilarity. Antonio and Ana María joined in, and soon we were all laughing so hard we had to shift our bodies to keep from sliding off the *costales*. I was seated next to the cadaver and determined not to fall on Julio and mortify myself.

We continued the wake, candles burning into a waxen puddle on the adobe block set before Julio's body. His body was clothed in burlap from head to toe, his face covered loosely with the cloth. His feet were covered in *ojotas*, sandals made from sheepskin.

After some discussion, it was decided that Julio could not be buried with only *ojotas* on his feet. Alcon stepped out, heading to his house up the hill. He returned quickly, handing the thin white socks he had brought to don Lucas. Don Lucas carefully removed the *ojotas* to put on the socks. He kept struggling to stretch the small opening over the stiff, unyielding feet. I crouched down to help him fit the socks over Julio's swollen feet. The nails were long, discolored, and bent, his feet those of a *campesino* who had walked through these hills barefoot from the time he was a toddler.

Don Lucas kept poking the swollen yellow flesh with his finger, showing me just how sick Julio had been. We worked together in the poorly lit corner to thread a large needle for sewing the *ojotas* over the socks and onto Julio's feet. Don Lucas tried to thread the needle several times, finally passing the needle and thread to me with a resigned laugh. Don Lucas was Julio's senior, his eyes far beyond threading such thick thread through so small a hole. I kept trying to lick the end of the thread, fraying like the piece of unraveled twine that it was. Finally my jabbing paid off, and I passed the threaded needle to Lucas and then held the thick sheepskin together as he sewed the pieces into sandals around Julio's feet.

Lucas then tied a thick cord around Julio's waist, forming the bow into the shape of a cross on his chest. He explained that the cord was important because it would allow Julio to defend himself against the large dog that guards the path to heaven.

As don Lucas finished preparing the body, Antonio came back in to invite us to eat, suggesting everyone move outside. I nestled next to Salomé. Bowls of soup were ladled out, and large piles of potatoes and *mashua* were served on brightly woven shawls unrolled at our feet. Before long, children gathered around for leftovers, kicking the dogs that tried to cut in front of them in line.

Once we had finished eating, five of the men tied Julio's body to a wooden frame in order to carry him down the slope, across the river, and up the mountain to the new cemetery. As they lifted him into the air, they cautioned everyone to walk behind them so that Julio's spirit would not call them into the next world.

The procession followed the body down the path that ran above the soccer field, then down around the school, through the thick green bushes and down to the river. We waited as various people offered their advice regarding where we should cross. Some women grew impatient; they lifted their skirts and simply waded through. I finally followed a group who crossed from rock to rock and then up the front of the mountain to the new cemetery.

Once we arrived, the women sat grouped together and so did the men. The children gathered around their mothers. Skirts opened as coca was shared and chewed. I sat between the men and women, listening to the conversations. Miguel Quispe began digging the hole to one side of the field; however, a foot or two down he hit hard rock and had to begin digging again. While he dug the hole, don Tomás and Manuel took turns praying and *rociando* the body.

At one point don Tomás, his eyes already blurry with *trago*, rose to pray and became annoyed with the animated conversations occurring all around him. He raised his voice and admonished the mourners: "*Carajo*, nobody pays attention here!" Those of us seated near him did hush as he prayed and attempted to lead us in song.

Miguel finally dug a hole that satisfied him and the crowd of men who kept peering into the earth to determine whether the hole was deep enough. Several men picked up Julio's body, freeing it from the wooden frame, and lowered him into the hole. As they moved him, the cloth fell from his face and I had to turn away. He was laid on top of a *pellejo* (sheepskin), and rock slabs were gently placed above him, fitted into the earthen sides of the hole so as not to touch the body. Tomás prayed once more, and the dirt was shoveled in.

The cold drove Efraín and me back down the hill, and we headed to the health post to cook dinner with Teodoro. He joined us there, having refused to attend Julio's funeral. He told us how many times he had taken food to María, *postergada en su cama* (left behind in her bed). Her legs had atrophied from *aya*, her body doubled in paralysis. One day he had passed by and saw Julio standing in his doorway; his anger prompted him to scold, "Just as you have abandoned your wife, you'll die the same way—alone and abandoned." Teodoro kept shaking his head in disgust.

A small shadow appeared in the door and we collectively jumped. It was Edgar. This was not a night for shadows to appear along adobe walls. Edgar laughed at our fright before eagerly eating his pasta with tuna.

We finished dinner in the near dark and I pulled my poncho tight around me for the walk back up to my room. Both Efraín and Teodoro asked if I thought I would be able to sleep alone that night. The possibility of a wandering soul scaring me in my solitude was broached, but I decided to place sticks against the inside of the door and not think any more about death for the night.

I walked across the soccer field, my flashlight bobbing across the stubbly grass and rocks. As I climbed the large rock stairs, I reminded myself of what El Piki had told me. When I asked him what I should do if suffering from *daño*, he told me *daño* could not harm me because I didn't believe in it. *Daño* can only make you sick or kill you if you believe. I hoped spirits worked the same way. I kept murmuring under my breath as I looked over my shoulder into the immense dark of night, "I don't believe, I don't believe," until the chant carried me back to my room.

There was a great deal of discussion the following day about Julio and how he had died. A group of men working in a *faena* building adobes told us they had not wanted to attend the funeral, although they did want to offer their commentaries on his death. One man shook his head, noting that Julio had left for the *selva* just a month ago, seemingly healthy.

Certainly he must have died of malaria. He had refused to go to the health post and seek treatment, even though several people had encouraged him to sell a goat and get himself some help. "Well, he died then just like his wife—abandoned." A round of nods.

Yet another voice joined in, pointing out that Julio had repeatedly ignored the communal authorities and their insistence that he care for his ailing wife and stop seeing the widow in Qanqayllo. "He ignored the authorities—he just wouldn't listen." Another round of thoughtful nods, and then a final commentary: "He died one year later, almost to the day."

There was a general consensus that Julio's death was just; that it was a form of reckoning. He died alone, abandoned just as he had abandoned María; only his dog had stood watch over his dead body; no tears were shed as he was buried; he had not been a good man. By the end of the day, the story in circulation emphasized that God had punished Julio for abandoning his ailing wife and ignoring repeated demands that he correct his ways. The story, told in the collective voice, became a parable illustrating the importance of family and the futility of assuming that because one ignored village authorities, he or she would be spared a higher justice.[20]

Julio was but one example of people's faith that each person would meet his or her rightful destiny at the Tribunal of Christ, and I have chosen this case precisely because Julio was not a former militant and his was not a war-related death. Invocations of divine justice did not just spring up as a result of the internal armed conflict and the tensions between victims and perpetrators; these are not merely communities of *ressentiment*.[21] I resist reducing people's long-standing, abiding faith that God judges and settles accounts to a morality forged from a position of structural weakness and simmering, suppressed rage. It is too dismissive.

Nigel Biggar, a Christian moral theologian, offers a sustained reflection on divine justice in his book *Burying the Past: Making Peace and Doing Justice After Civil Conflict*. Departing from a certain acceptance of the limits of human justice—an acknowledgment that echoes throughout these communities—he suggests we consider "eschatological hope."[22] Although such hope acknowledges the impossibility of proportionality in the face of grave harm, it is not inimical to secular forms of seeking justice, nor does it mean sinking into despairing inertia. Rather, eschatological hope "is necessary to render rational and possible an acceptance of the severe limits of secular justice that is not acquiescent but expectant, not resigned but resolute."[23] It is the steadfast faith that victims will be vindicated, and it best captures what I have seen and heard in Ayacucho. This faith is a resource in the aftermath of the *sasachakuy tiempo*, offering hope to those who feel they are victims. This same hope hangs over the heads of the perpetrators who enter the *evangelio* in an effort to make amends with their *prójimos* in the here and now and with Tayta Dios in the realm that lies beyond. Eschatological hope is not just the morality of the weak; this hope works in powerful ways.

Caridad and the Stranger

> Let brotherly love continue. Be not forgetful to entertain strangers: for thereby some have entertained angels unaware.
> —Hebrews 13:1–2

People loved Efraín. He was kind to everyone. He could make a *queña* (wind instrument) out of discarded plastic tubing; he knew when to joke and when to just listen. One afternoon in May 1998 he returned to our room with a bag of *olluca* (a tuber) a *warmisapa* had given him. He had helped Asunta that day and she was grateful. When I saw her later, she told me how hard it was to work as a day laborer on another's land. "What can I do?" she asked. "We widows work for others."

I commiserated with her, sharing some of my coca. Holding out her skirt to accept the leaves, she told me how good Efraín was, helping her carry wood up to her house. "You know, God always watches us to see if we help strangers. You never know—they might be the virgin, a saint, or even Jesús himself. You just never know."

Previously I suggested we consider a chronology of *caridad*—compassion or charity—when tracing shifts in moral sensibilities during the *sasachakuy tiempo*. This chronology influenced decisions regarding the pardoning (or not) of the *arrepentidos*; it also transformed a long-standing practice regarding hospitality and the stranger. Mama Asunta was one of many people who assured me that we must help a stranger in need because we could never be sure who that unknown person might be. At the time, I did not realize how much this gesture reflected the same religious exhortations that underlie our contemporary humanitarian discourse.[24]

The internal armed conflict ruptured this humanitarian gesture. During a time when family members and neighbors were resignified as enemies, even more distant strangers became a source of tremendous fear. Walking through the highlands during the *sasachakuy tiempo* and its immediate aftermath was dangerous; each community was armed, and the *ronderos* operated via a password system. Unknown people arriving to the village limits could be detained, roughed up, or even shot on sight if they did not shout out the correct password: perhaps they were *puriqkuna* coming to attack.

The drastic change was something I experienced firsthand. In 1996 I was visiting several communities in the *ceja de selva*—literally the "eyebrow of the jungle," referring to the zone in which the sierra begins ceding to the *selva* (jungle) region. I was with colleagues from World Vision, and we miscalculated the walking time between two communities. The sun had almost set by the time we finished stumbling down a steep, wet slope. As we approached the village, we heard Winchesters and Mausers cocked into readiness; soon the shouting began. We were with a *comunero* from another community, but he had not traveled this route in some time; the password had changed and his shouting did nothing to lower the guns. On the advice of my friends, we dropped on all fours to the ground and wrapped our hands around our heads.

Amid the shouting Elisabeth from World Vision called out, and thankfully several Evangelicals in the community recognized her voice and then her face. Soon the apologies began, followed by a friendly greeting, hot bowls of soup, and a warm bed for the night.

Fast forward to 2003. During the TRC, on our first visit to a community left unnamed here, we walked to the end of the bulldozed dirt highway and met up with the team of *comuneros* that was working on the road. We fell in step with them and walked to their pueblo, setting down our backpacks with a thud of relief. We began explaining who we were and mentioned the other communities we had visited. Soon we began swapping names of friends we had in common, and the initial coolness gave way to jokes and laughter. About an hour into our conversation, one of the men playfully slapped me on the knee. "You know, during the *sasachakuy tiempo*—if you'd arrived like you did just now, we would've already killed all of you and dumped your bodies down below in the ravine." He smiled widely, and soon we were all laughing. After all, no hard feelings: war was war.

And war left its mark. People lamented the loss of *caridad*—both the charity and compassion they could extend and that which they could expect from others. In his work with Cambodian refugees, Maurice Eisenbruch developed the concept of "cultural bereavement" to capture how people experienced their loss of social structures, cultural values, self and group identities.[25] Cultural bereavement includes mourning the loss of a way of life and conveys what I am getting at here. The loss of *caridad* referenced more than just the loss of reciprocity: it referenced the degree to which the violence snuffed out one pillar of human and humane conduct. This theme wove its way throughout my years of research, and with time I began to hear the ways in which people attempted to recuperate a cultural value that in part defined being *runakuna*.

This process was poignantly illustrated by *la loca* (the crazy woman) who found her way to Carhuahurán in late 1999. I had been away for about two weeks, spending time in Huamanga and Lima; however, I was told about her many times when I returned.

I arrived on the earliest truck at Friday's *feria*, and a group of children saw me through the window and began running after the truck into the field. After a round of hugs, Yolanda, Edith, Marina, Máximo, and Edgar began speaking in rapid-fire succession about the "crazy woman" who had stayed in my room. The children followed me to my room near the watchtower and stayed to describe *la loca* in detail. Her hair was long and disheveled, her clothes dirty and torn, her face scratched and scabbed. She said she had come from Huancayo and kept repeating sentences that no one could understand. The children pointed to Efraín's bed, which villagers had told her she could use. But no, she stayed curled up on the floor, rocking back and forth.

Over the next few days, many people—children and adults—told me about *la loca*. What was most striking was the nature of the stories they told about her. I had previously witnessed the detention of unknown wayfarers, who were brusquely questioned about their activities and asked to produce identity documents. Something was different now. There was no cruelty in their assessment of her, nor was there fear that a *desconocida* (stranger) had arrived. Rather, there was pity for her ragged condition, for her solitude, and for the fact she was *sonsa* (senseless).

Both Evangelicals and Catholics described her in detail and explained how the community had lodged her in my room, providing her with food and a safe place to sleep. The women had taken her food every morning and again at night, and the men had brought wood to the women who were cooking for her. She had spent three days, only able to state that she had walked from Huancayo and was tired and hungry. Everything else she said was incoherent. On the morning of the fourth day when mama Victoria brought food to her, *la loca* had already disappeared.

I wondered why she had not provoked fear and asked each person I spoke with what they thought. I was accustomed to heterogeneous responses on any and all issues. However, this question met with a uniform reply and with surprise that I did not know who she was: "*La loca* was a test from God. God sent her. Don't you know who she was?" (I did not.) "That was a saint or maybe even Jesúcristo in disguise. God sent *la loca* to see if after all the things we've done to each other here, are we still capable of having *caridad* for our fellow creatures [*caridaqa runa masinchinkpaq*]."

Villagers are trying—imperfectly, tensely, conflictively—to reestablish humane relationships in the aftermath of war. Part of communal reconstruction is the recuperation of trust and compassion; the capacity to recognize the humanity of others allows a rehumanizing of oneself. *La loca* was both a test and a lesson: for the adults, God had sent her to see if they could still show compassion after all the suffering endured *and* inflicted. They had passed the test. For the children, *la loca* was a lesson about social life, human decency, and extending *caridad* to someone in need, including the wayfaring stranger.

*   *   *

If we would start to talk about everything that happened here, all the old hatreds would come back again.
—Uchuraccay, 2003

Reconciliation is not a matter of confession offered once and for all, but rather the building of relationships by performing the work of the everyday.
—Veena Das and Arthur Kleinman, *Remaking a World*

I conclude this section by reflecting on communal justice and the micropolitics of reconciliation that *campesinos* in the highlands of Huanta have elaborated. In postconflict settings there is a great deal to learn by studying preexisting conciliatory practices that respond to the local needs of daily life and governance. Reconciliation is forged and lived locally, and state policies can either facilitate or hinder those processes, as we shall see when we look southward.

I stress the word "processes." Payam Akhavan has suggested that "Beyond a mere recital of objective facts, however, reconciliation requires a shared truth—a moral or interpretive account—that appeals to a common bond of humanity."[26] Reconciliation is an ongoing process of replacing antagonistic memories with memories of previous social bonds, and of replacing a recent history of fratricidal violence with a history that recalls long-standing practices that condemned the taking of human life.

I spent October 9, 2002, in Uchuraccay celebrating the Day of Return. The fiesta commemorates the refounding of Uchuraccay on that day in 1994. Edith and I were seated with a group of women when *comuneros* from a neighboring community began arriving for the festivities. The women's faces hardened as they watched them: "Here come the thieving assassins." Their bodies and voices tensed with rage. As the women explained, the *ronderos* from that neighboring community had arrived in Uchuraccay during the violence, robbing them and carrying off their livestock. Mama Saturnina spit the following words into the air: "Those thieves stole my animals, even the young ones. Now my animals keep on reproducing there in Carhuahurán while I only have two skinny goats." The stolen animals kept reproducing—offspring *and* resentment.

When a crowd had finally formed in the middle of the field, the mayor of Uchuraccay rose to welcome everyone and announce the beginning of the fiesta. In his speech, he thanked all those present and asked everyone "to remember to conduct themselves well."

> *Señores comuneros*, we are celebrating the anniversary of our return. Please, we need to proceed with our fiesta forgetting and forgiving our past errors. If we dance, we dance. If we drink, we drink. To the *señores comuneros* visiting from other communities, thank you for your visit. We should all enjoy ourselves and avoid starting fights. We have a *calabozo* [jail cell]. That's where anyone who picks a fight can wake up in the cold. Thank you.

Revelers were thus invited to bury one past and remember another.

During the PTRC, we discussed the concept of reconciliation with villagers. They nodded: "That's what *pampachanakuy* is." In Carhuahurán, Huaychao, and Uchuraccay, they performed various *pampachanakuy* during and after the political violence in an effort to repair social relations and implement a new moral order. These rituals occurred within and between communities. For example, when villagers in Uchuraccay returned to what was left of their community, they had a *pampachanakuy* among themselves to ask forgiveness for what they had done to each other during the internal armed conflict and to commit themselves to working together to rebuild their pueblo. Each villager then signed an *acta de conciliación*. As the mayor recalled, "So many people had been *engañado*. So there was a *pampachanakuy* in 1994. Everyone talked—the young and the old—about what we needed and what we had done. We pardoned each other. Families that had been killing each other before—now their children, who were just little back then, now they live here together. Some of them have even married each other."

However, although the emphasis is on burying the past, that which is buried is active in the lives of the living. I recall various funerals I attended in rural Ayacucho and the conversations regarding just how deep the hole should be or how tightly to pack down the earth because "This one just might try to get out" or "You know she'll be looking for some way to come back." The restless dead who wander, the earth packed tightly to keep the body there. That which is buried between us—*pampachanakuy*—is not settled once and for all. Rather, the earth may shift, the dead may rise, and that which was buried in the past lingers among us in the present.

PART IV

Looking South

Chapter 11

Living with "Those People"

Ay, we're never going to have peace with those people [*huk kuna*, referring to the former Shining Path militants]. They keep scaring everyone, especially when they drink. They walk around here as though nothing ever happened—walk around here with their heads held high! They take advantage of their past when they want to settle conflicts now. *Huk kuna* know everyone is afraid of them.
    —Claudia Bustios, Hualla, March 2003

IT WAS WITHIN the context of the PTRC that my research team and I began working with four communities that had been militant Shining Path support bases. While I had visited the provinces of Víctor Fajardo and Vilcashuamán before, these had been short visits driven by the syncopated rhythm of consulting projects. I remember being struck by the contrast between the *alturas* of Huanta and this region to the south. There was much less infrastructural damage. I was surprised to see so many buildings, including Catholic churches, standing intact. Yet those images were interlaced with others of elderly women passed out drunk in public, urine-soaked skirts turning the dust below them into patches of mud. I had never seen anything like that in Huanta. I also felt something I did not understand at the time: a sense of something turbulent beneath the surface of a physical landscape that was largely untouched, a certain unease, the feeling of being watched.

In contrast to the communities in the *alturas* of Huanta, where the revolutionary spark was lit by external agents who arrived to *concientizar* the villagers, throughout Víctor Fajardo and Vilcashuamán the Shining Path militants were overwhelmingly *lugareños*—people, especially young people, who were born and raised in the same communities in which they were waging the revolution. Of course there had been significant interest in Shining Path throughout the highlands of Huanta during the early years of the internal armed conflict. However, as we have seen, allegiances changed and this had narrative and political consequences. Villagers in the highlands of Huanta organized the *rondas campesinas* and collectively demonstrated their rejection of Shining Path. They "cleansed" their communities and their image and subsequently elaborated histories about their patriotic heroism, narratively erasing their sympathies with and participation in Shining Path.

The war and its legacies are different in the south. The communities of Accomarca, Cayara, Hualla, and Tiquihua are located in the region Shining Path considered its "Principal Committee."[1] Throughout the region, Shining Path cadres had begun their political work a decade before launching the armed phase of the revolution with their 1980 attack on Chuschi. Shining Path had much deeper roots in this region, and isolating militants and their sympathizers with the hope of expelling them was not feasible. Far too many people were implicated.

It was an afternoon in March 2003 when I had the opportunity to speak with Américo Paucar, the *teniente gobernador* of Tiquihua. I wanted to follow up on something many people in the community had told us: "It's much more painful to know that your own neighbor killed your papa." I asked Señor Paucar how they had begun to live together again.

"Well, it was difficult at first. We were so remorseful, so resentful!" He paused, choosing his words slowly. "But as time passed . . . *bueno* . . . we've learned to get along. But at times *huk kuna* [those people] have conflicts with other people. People pull out the truth and tell them what they were. 'You were a *terruco* and you killed people.' *Bueno*, I guess it's just normal."

"This remorse and resentment—do you think people will forget someday?"

He shook his head. "There will always be remorse and resentment inside. But remorse and resentment that you hear—that people talk about directly— not anymore. I don't think people will ever completely forget. They keep it in their hearts. Of course, they don't hit each other anymore, they don't mention it—but it's obvious the wounds are there, slowly healing. And the fear? That will only pass with time."

I commiserated with Señor Paucar and with the other people who assured us that coexistence was so difficult. I heard about the written death threats slipped under doors, at other times painted on the sides of dwellings. I grew accustomed to hearing stories about the former militants and the damage they had done, to people insisting that "everyone here" had participated in Shining Path, except for the speaker of course. When a glimpse of participation did slip out, it was overwhelmingly attributed to having been tricked or duped (*engañado*), illiterate or just plain ignorant. While I knew that degrees of militancy varied greatly, I was being served up a history of the vanquished, monochromatically stained with shame, remorse, ignorance, and regret. I was learning a great deal about the politics of memory but virtually nothing about the memory of politics. Surely there were other versions of the recent past in which people were protagonists of history rather than merely its victims or bystanders? Certainly *huk kuna*—or at least some of "those people"—must tell a different version of their own past and participation in Shining Path? Where were those other truths?

When the commissioners of the PTRC submitted their Final Report, Peru joined a growing list of countries that have engaged in a "truth-seeking" process to establish an official public record about a violent past.[2] However, while joining a growing trend, Peru also presents a series of exceptions. Peru was a triumphant state: there were no negotiations with the guerrillas of Shining Path (or the MRTA) because the leadership was largely incarcerated and the movement militarily defeated. Thus the commission was not a component of a peace process between opponents locked in a stalemate, seeking some sort of mutually acceptable compromise.

However, while most Shining Path leaders are in jail, many community-level militants are not, having been either released from prison or never incarcerated. They live on the margins, shunned by a society in which the subject of "subversion" remains taboo. Despite the country's massive truth-seeking effort, there is scant political or discursive space in Peru to explore *why* so many people joined Sendero and remained sympathetic to the movement even under military repression.

In the weeks leading up to the release of the PTRC's Final Report, the news headlines were striking.

> "There is no reconciliation possible with the assassins of Shining Path."
> —Alan García, *Correo*, August 14, 2003
>
> "With Shining Path there can be no pact, no political solution and no form of reconciliation."
> —Congresswoman and former presidential candidate Lourdes Flores Nano, *La República*, August 10, 2003

Even former president Valentín Paniagua, the man who led the country during the transitional government and signed the executive decree establishing the truth commission, insisted he had created the truth commission, with no "R."[3] Adding their voice to the cacophony were members of the armed forces, representatives of the conservative wing of the Catholic Church, and certain businessmen who were committed to the restricted circulation of the Final Report and its recommendations regarding accountability and reparations.

This flurry of declarations that rejected any form of dialogue with "terrorists" reflects the extent to which Shining Path remains monolithically demonized in Peru. This contrasts with other Latin American countries in which insurgent or guerrilla movements were perceived by many people to be fighting for social justice and at times eventually assumed legitimate political roles. Among the factors explaining this difference is the context in which Sendero began its armed struggle: Peru was not ruled by a military dictatorship but by a democratically elected civilian government. Additionally, although the original ideological discourse appealed to principles of social justice and equality, many Shining Path militants became increasingly authoritarian and lethally violent, unmatched by any other armed Leftist group in Latin America.

Obviously truth commissions operate within sensitive political contexts and amid polarized positions and group identities. In the Peruvian case, one particularly tense moment occurred when Commissioner Sofia Macher referred to Shining Path as a "political party." The media seized upon this statement, excoriating the PTRC for being "sympathetic to terrorists." The controversy was so vitriolic that the president of the commission, Salomón Lerner, was summoned before a congressional committee on July 15, 2002, to defend the use of the term "political party" in reference to Shining Path.

Dr. Lerner presented a list of dictionary definitions of "political" and "party" to explain why Shining Path could be defined this way without implying an "apology for terrorism."[4]

In such polarized contexts, truth commissions are structurally inclined to overlook the gray zone.[5] Truth commissions tend to construct a popular discourse that presents two distinct groups: victims and perpetrators. In Latin American truth commission reports, there is a regional version of this dualism: "between two fires," "between two demons," or "between two armies." These binary identities, however well-intentioned and conditioned by the nature of the political transition, prompt people to locate themselves somewhere within the victim typology, which in turn determines which sort of "truths" enter the public record and which do not. Truth commissions and their final reports establish the narrative terms of engagement and set the tone for public debate in the post–truth commission period. Final reports have a political and social afterlife.

In this chapter and the next I draw upon research in Accomarca, Cayara, Hualla, and Tiquihua to explore certain legacies of Peru's war on terror, as well as certain legacies of the TRC that was established to investigate that bloody period of violence and make recommendations to promote "sustainable peace and national reconciliation." I sought to understand what motivated people to join or sympathize with Shining Path, how they view their participation now, and how they interact within these communities as well as with the state. It is conversations with former militants that lead me to insist on disaggregating the category "Senderista" (which in Peru is used interchangeably with "terrorist") to reveal the vast variation in motivations, actions, and intent. The image of the terrorist is a key figure that organizes political discourse and action in our contemporary world. Yet beyond the abstract image of the terrorist—that free-floating signifier—what is the work of this figure in particular historical and political contexts? By disaggregating the category, I hope to contribute to a dialogue that has not yet occurred in Peru. This lack of civic debate in turn allows the category of the terrorist to be used to stifle social protests and to delegitimize opposition and civil society groups that voice their demands for change.

I begin with Accomarca to explore how Shining Path operated in one community. Most research on Shining Path has focused on the top cadres or political prisoners, leaving unexplored the trajectories of former militants and sympathizers who live in society. While each pueblo has its specificities, Accomarca illustrates regional patterns and served as an emblematic case in the PTRC's Final Report. In tracing the experiences of this community, I consider the consequences of Peru's war on terror and how they informed both the truth the TRC was able to tell and the communal memory projects people have forged in former Shining Path strongholds. We shall see how the logic of innocence affects individuals, collectives, and political life following the internal armed conflict, contributing to the contentious politics of victimhood and reparations in post–truth commission Peru.

"The Initiators"

The PTRC established that on August 14th, 1985, an army patrol, belonging to the "Lince" company from Huamanga, under the command of second lieutenant Telmo Ricardo Hurtado, assassinated sixty-two *comuneros*, including women, elderly people, and children, inhabitants of the district of Accomarca, the province of Vilcashuamán, Ayacucho. The massacre was carried out as part of the "Operative Plan Huancayoc," a counterinsurgency action planned by the military organization of the national security subzone 5, with contempt for the life of innocent civilians.
—PTRC, Final Report

Where were we going to bury our *paisanos*? They were dying everywhere. How would you bury them all? When we did want to bury them, the soldiers were watching and they'd kill you. We buried them later. We dug a big hole, and for those who died on the paths we just buried them there. How could we carry everyone to the cemetery? In Lloqllepampa, the soldiers killed everybody by locking them in the houses. They chose the women, young women, pregnant, little girls. They raped them all and then killed them afterward. Because they weren't dying, they threw grenades and then burned the house down. There weren't bodies anymore—just their bones, burned black. That's how we pulled them out of the house. We couldn't tell who was who. The smell was awful. The bodies stunk like *chicharrón* [deep-fried pieces of pork]. Human fat was running down like oil. We pulled out all of the bones and buried them to the side. All of those bones.
—Doña Aurelia, Accomarca, February 2003

Shining Path established an early presence in the provinces of Víctor Fajardo and Vilcashuamán.[6] At first it was one more party competing for political space and constituents, and promises to radically transform an unjust society were not limited to the Communist Party of Peru-Shining Path. In Vilcashuamán there were representatives from the Sindicato Único de Trabajadores de la Educación del Perú (SUTEP, the teacher's union), as a well as the Communist Party of Peru—Red Flag, the Revolutionary Student Front (FER), the Apristas, and Popular Action, among others. The initial growth of Shining Path coincided with increasing economic and social expectations, particularly among students and teachers, in part fomented by the reforms implemented by the left-leaning military government of Juan Velasco Alvarado (1968–75). Shining Path benefited from an atmosphere of social demands foiled by the economic crisis that struck the country in 1976.

Schoolteachers, one sector that was hard-hit by the economic crisis, comprised a group ready to listen and to mobilize. Thus within an environment in which many people were demanding a radical change in the economic and social order, Shining Path began spreading its message promising a "New Society" and social justice among a population of receptive schoolteachers and their students. The cadres capitalized on feelings of marginalization, state abandonment, and anger about the poverty and inequality that characterized the region.

A key site for *concientizando* was the Colegio General Córdoba established in 1966 in Vilcashuamán. General Córdoba (a secondary school) quickly became one of the most important schools in the entire province. Many future Shining Path militants studied at General Córdoba, and a number of them continued their studies at the San Cristóbal National University in Huamanga (UNSCH). One of the professors at the UNSCH was Abimael Guzmán, who began to fill the ranks of Shining Path with students who were, in many cases, sons and daughters of *campesinos*—and the first generation of their families to study at the university level. Those who returned to their communities were *letrados*: literate, educated, with the prestige such status conferred.

One such student was Primitivo Morales, who moved on from General Cordóba to the education department at the UNSCH. Upon completing his studies, he took up his first teaching job in a small pueblo in Chungui. "I taught there for three years," he recalled. "The people were all illiterate— we teachers were like authorities. Many times we had to act as judges, had to settle conflicts. That's how the teachers worked then." Primitivo subsequently requested a transfer to his own community, where he was placed in charge of the "indoctrination of young people" in Shining Path's *escuela popular*. With his four brothers, the Morales family were among the "initiators" of Shining Path in Accomarca.

Our conversations with Primitivo span several years. They began inauspiciously when Edith and I made our way to his house on the outskirts of Huamanga. Although a graying Primitivo opened the door, that first visit suspended chronological reason. When we asked about Accomarca during the 1980s, he replied that he had been "too young then" to remember anything. Even he let slip a fleeting smile at that mathematical sleight of hand. With time, he allowed us to tape our conversations; as we found with a number of former local-level Shining Path militants, their fear of exposure competes with a desire to have their version of history enter the public record in some way. I quote from one of our conversations.

"I had three younger brothers. My mama was fairly old and they paid no attention to what she told them. That was one of the reasons I asked for a transfer [to Accomarca]. When I arrived, there were already problems. In 1980 they'd already burned the ballot boxes [in Chuschi]. During those years, they were visiting the pueblo. They say they passed by at night, armed. Well, I met Gutierrez. He was a union member of SUTEP [the teacher's union]. And there was a group—the *senderólogos*.[7] One of them was Bernardo, a guy from Huamanmarca. When he came to Accomarca, he told us, 'This is the way it is.' Well, I was always challenging things so I replied, 'I see it another way.' But then he said, 'You must support me.' I told him I didn't think about it that way, but more and more often unknown armed people arrived. They weren't even our neighbors. I didn't want to join them, but you heard they were annihilating anyone who refused."

"But people did support them, didn't they?"

Primitivo nodded reluctantly. "We had to collaborate economically. Every pueblo had to collaborate. But at the time, we schoolteachers were the key support for Sendero—even more so if the teacher was from the community because then they were living directly with their pueblo. You had to support them, there was no other option. That's why we agreed in an assembly not to tell anyone who Sendero was. If you did, they killed you for being a spy. I also told the young people, 'Be very careful. It's better to be quiet.' There was danger from one side and from the other, so I told them to be very careful. I even told the young people to leave quietly—that's why many left for Lima, because of fear."

As Primitivo went on to explain, "those who were arriving" were Bernardo, Shining Path's military commander for the Zonal Committee, and Gutierrez, who was the political commander for the district of Accomarca. Bernardo was one of the commanders who had participated in the attack in

Chuschi. He was a sporadic presence in Accomarca, while Gutierrez—originally from the coast—married in to the community. His wife, Paulina Gamboa, spoke with us in 2005, seated on one of the tattered straw mats that also formed the walls of her makeshift shack on the barren outskirts of Lima.

Paulina had not set out to marry a revolutionary. Some women may plan such matrimonies, but I imagine many do not. It was her daughter's sudden illness that brought the new schoolteacher to her door, and the gossip came knocking shortly thereafter.

"Well, turns out my daughter studied with Gutierrez. One day she got really sick, and I went to look for medicine in the stores but there was none. I was crying, and another student heard my daughter was sick. He told the teacher, and Gutierrez asked the student to show him my house. He came in and said, '*Caramba*—she's really sick.' So he sent another student on horseback to the health post and told him to send medicine for an emergency. Ay, if my daughter hadn't gotten sick, he would never have come to my house and I would never have gotten married to him!"

Paulina had no idea that one of her neighbors had set her sights on Gutierrez and that his kindness would start a round of gossip aimed at besmirching her reputation. She shook her head as she recalled what happened. Both the gossip and her relationship with Gutierrez gave her much to regret.

"Gutierrez came to check on my daughter, and that woman said we were lovers! Well, I told him I didn't like it at all. And then her daughter started writing on the school walls: Paulina and Gutierrez are in love." Paulina's face made clear just how disgusted she had been by the escalating gossip.

"So I went to the *gobernador* and told him, 'This woman is dirtying my reputation.' I was a single mother! The *gobernador* said, 'Let's go make a demand so she stops.' But I told him that right in front of him I was going to break her snout and her daughter's snout, too!"

As it turned out, Gutierrez *had* been visiting for another reason and took the opportunity to make his intentions clear. Unwittingly, the neighbor's gossiping set their courtship on fast-forward. Gutierrez decided to put a stop to it all by letting Paulina know he was single and had the documents to prove it. While Paulina still insisted she wanted nothing to do with him, her mother had other plans.

"My mother heard it all. He told her he would take care of her. Oh, he spoiled my mama. He didn't want her to lack for anything. So that's how we ended up married, and things were all right at first. He worked as a teacher and had me collect his salary."

However, Paulina's happiness did not last for long. A few years and a young son later, she found out her husband was carrying on with another teacher who worked in Accomarca.[8] Her neighbors told Paulina that the teacher and Gutierrez were meeting secretly at night. At first she refused to believe it, but the gossip was too pervasive to ignore.

"People told me to follow him, and I finally decided they were right. You can't live well with gossip. I left our little son with my mama and told her I was going to town for a quick visit. I walked there and looked into one of the stores. There he was with the teacher! There they were, caressing each other! She asked him, 'How are you going to be with a *serrana*—an ignorant, illiterate woman like that! You were crazy. And having kids with her!'"

As if the teacher's insults were not enough, Paulina felt the sting of her husband's response. "Gutierrez answered her. 'My mama didn't want me to marry her either. My mama kept telling me to take my son and that she would raise him. She told me to transfer far away from here, and just leave her.'" Paulina shook her head in disgust as she described the scene.

Gutierrez headed home that night, with Paulina following silently behind him. She confronted him in a rage. "I grabbed him and started hitting him. I threw him to the ground. 'You aren't ever entering my house again! I'll break your snout—you'll leave beaten up.' He asked me, 'What's going on? My love, my shining star, beauty of my life . . . ' Ha! All those things he had been saying to the teacher, now he was repeating them to me! I yelled at him, '*Desgraciado*! I didn't believe it, but people told me the truth about you. And you think you can still come to my house? Get out of here!' He told me he'd leave but would take his son with him. I yelled at him, 'Oh, so you think you'll take my son? Get out of here with your lover!' I beat him some more and went to my house, but he followed me. I couldn't be standing there in the door arguing with him because if my mama heard, it would give her *mal de rabia*. So I let him in but told him in a low voice, 'Get out of my way, *desgraciado*.' He didn't know what to say. I told him again, 'People were right when they told me about you. You were tricking me.' He answered, 'But that's how it is. I'm a man. You've seen how she grabs me, how that woman adores me. What am I? Am I not a man? She looks for me.'"

Paulina snorted as she remembered what Gutierrez had said. "After that I lost all interest in him. We barely spoke to each other, as though he were a stranger. I kept telling him to leave but he stayed. I became jealous, mistrustful, but unfortunately that man did not want to leave my house. Later he asked me to forgive him."

We waited for Paulina to pause, not wanting to interrupt her. "Señora Paulina, Gutierrez did this bad thing. But other than this, what do you think of him? Was he a good man, a bad man?"

Paulina shrugged. "He was a good man. He was a good man and he'd never treated me with disrespect. Even now, even though I treat him with total disdain, he never talks back with ugly words. His biggest mistake was joining all that [Shining Path] because then things changed."

Paulina's ambivalent assessment of her husband was shared by Alfredo Bendezu, also known as the Huambalpino in reference to Huambalpa, his pueblo of origin. He recalled Gutierrez: "That guy was a real humanist. He was always giving things away to people. Now he is *mal visto* because he was one of the initiators. He and Cupe [Cupertino] were the first. They were *responsables políticos*. But for me Gutierrez was a good person, even though he wasn't afraid to kill people."

Neither was the Huambalpino, who served as Shining Path's local commissar in charge of organizing the obligatory "collaboration."[9] Alfredo had also been an in-marrying *yerno* (son-in-law), wedding Teodora Mendez, the youngest of the Mendez sisters. Each of the sisters married Shining Path commanders (*mandos*), so that the Morales-Mendez families formed a kinship network of local militants. The Huambalpino, who now lives in Lima, described those early days.

"*Bueno*, the terrorists—when they were in Accomarca, they weren't aggressive. They were human beings like me. They arrived armed. What could you do? For example, just now, if you come here armed, what could I do?"

We nodded. "Alfredo, for you—who *was* Sendero?"

He shrugged. "Well, when they first entered the people were surprised. It was something new, no? Nothing like that had happened around here. I thought they were foreigners who were coming here—that's what some people said."

"So you never knew who they were?"

"No . . . well, little by little. I just made the nighttime meetings. When I was in Huambalpa, they met in one of the houses. They told my dad, 'Let's go to the meeting, to the assembly. Who else is in the house?' He told them, 'My son who's come from Lima.' 'Tell him to come, too,' they said. There was a group of young people giving talks about their experiences participating. I wanted to meet them during the day because it was nighttime when they came. Later they came during the day. When they came during the day, there was more trust."

"How did you realize they weren't foreigners?"

"When I saw them at night, they had ponchos, their *pasamontañas*, their rifles thrown over their shoulders. They walked around with rifles, but they were just young guys. I didn't think they were foreigners. They asked my papa to take them food. You went to a certain house and they said, 'Here are the *compañeros*.' My papa told me, 'We're going to take them food—they gave me that assignment.' I helped him carry their food. There were a lot of them in that house. That's when I discovered they weren't foreigners. I verified it. There were about sixteen people who initiated Sendero Luminoso in Vilcashuamán. They began with the first action in Chuschi."

After a few of those nocturnal meetings, Alfredo was increasingly interested in what he was hearing. As he explained, once he understood the position of Shining Path and the objectives they were pursuing, he joined their ranks.

"There were quite a few initiators then. Anasto Morales, Hilario, Medina—I don't remember who else, but they were all young then. That's where the *escuela popular* began. But afterward, people don't acknowledge that. Now they place all the guilt on the people who were under their control [Shining Path]. They say, 'Those are the ones.' Necessarily, they use us, they point at us."

Alfredo shrugged. "For example, Andres was a professor. I knew him. He was from Huambalpa—was almost my contemporary. When he returned from Accomarca he looked for me. 'You know, we need a meeting. There's an action—come with me,' he said. 'Where?' I asked. 'Below.' I said I wouldn't go. I didn't want to, but they pulled me out of the house anyway. They took me to the meeting, and there were the initiators. There they were. They started to form *comités populares*. You couldn't escape. So I decided once and for all to stay. I was in for less than a month when they took me to Accomarca and I had to accept. I couldn't say no. They gave us cargos. I was twenty-four years old then."

"What position were you given?"

"They named me to the committee, as a political commissar. Each time the *fuerza principal* was planning, I had to prepare a report on the taking of pueblos [*toma de pueblos*]. We went to all the pueblos—there wasn't any problem. We walked around these pueblos and they didn't do anything to us, we didn't kill anyone—that's how we went."

"Who named the cargos?"

"Andres. He was the one who elected us and later came other commanders. Different commanders came. When they first arrived they would call a meeting with the commissars."

"But Alfredo, why did people join? Did they like the politics, or were they forced?"

"No, it was practically an obligation. Like I said, the pueblo was practically in their hands and we had to participate."

"But did you like it?"

"Of course! I liked it because of the work I did. I organized political work. For example, with Primitivo [Morales] we talked about what we needed to do—we needed to build a well. With sixty bags of cement, and in the school there were food supplies. We told the community, "We're going to make an irrigation system.' So we had a large well made, and the canals ran down the hill, making a mill to grind wheat. Everything that came out would be water for irrigation. I wish that some authority right now would see that and do the same. Collective work, it's what gave me the idea. It's where everyone can plan, or divide it in equal parts, or everyone plants the entire field together. The political work was in the form of *ayni*—that we did achieve because everyone participated."

The reference to *ayni* was striking. While the Senderista cadres in the *alturas* of Huanta viewed communal traditions as obstacles to their revolutionary project (which resulted in a "cultural revolution" that left most *campesinos* intensely alienated), in the central-south the cadres incorporated many communal practices into their political project. The "homegrown" demographics of the initial militants in communities such as Accomarca made a difference in terms of how the guerrillas implemented the revolution.

"Alfredo, were you part of the principal force [*fuerza principal*]?"

"No, the *fuerza local*. On site, that's all. I was involved in everything that was occurring with these pueblos. I had to prepare everything in a report. For example, during the month how much did we do? How many commissars were elected? Or, why weren't we able to organize? If the pueblo was difficult to organize, then maybe they hadn't accepted. I had to report on all of that."

"So you all gave monthly reports on the things that had happened?"

"Exactly. If we had erred in something, we offered a self-criticism of what we should not do, of how we should not act. For example, assassinating an innocent *campesino*—we were giving ground to the soldiers. Doing that, they gained ground easily and we were ruining things."

"And in Accomarca, were there *niños pioneros* [children recruited by Shining Path]? In some place peoples talk about the children, how they went around armed, watching things. If anything happened they informed immediately. Did that happen here?"

"Of course. The *fuerza principal*, at times they placed elderly people and children as guards. Whenever anything happened they sent up smoke to spread the word to people. They gave us tasks, and we had to fulfill them. They were well organized: the *fuerza principal*, the *fuerza local*, and the *fuerza base*. The *fuerza principal*—they were capable young people between the ages fifteen, nineteen—up to twenty, 'til thirty. They were the *destacados* [distinguished or prominent ones] and went on patrols for several months. The *fuerza local*, they were forty to sixty years old, the ones who only went out to nearby pueblos. And the *fuerza base* were the people who stayed in the pueblos—the elderly, women—they were the ones who assumed activities in the pueblo. Among themselves, they took care of each other. 'Whatever happens, we need to warn the others so there's no tragedy.'"

"How did the pueblos receive you?"

"*Tranquilo.* We arrived and would begin with an assembly. We would call the people together and talk, tell them why we were there. If we needed water, they gave us water. They brought us fruit. *Tranquilo.* Those of us who entered the pueblos, not one pueblo rebelled. Here people trusted us."

"Alfredo, what was it all of you wanted? Was it to form a communist community where everyone participated?"

He nodded forcefully. "That was the goal. That's what we were aiming for. We were achieving it, we were going to achieve it. If we'd finished the project we were building, with that the people would have decided. But when the massacre happened in Lloqllepampa, everything was lost. We lost all contact."

During those early years, Shining Path gained virtual control of the pueblo through a combination of persuasion and coercion. Anasto Morales—who insisted that he was *not* one of the five Morales brothers but rather "another type of Morales"—recalled how he joined the initiators because he believed Shining Path was comprised of intellectuals and professionals who "without a doubt" were looking for a better life for the poor and the marginalized, especially *campesinos*.

In one conversation, we asked Anasto why he thought so many people had voluntarily accepted Shining Path in his pueblo.

"It's obvious! They would talk *maravillas*, no? At first it was a good political project. They said, 'We're going to fight for the poor. We are going to be equal to the big *gamonales*—we can't be treated differently from them.' So people, because they have little knowledge, they easily accepted this."

"When people in the pueblo heard this, what did they say?"

"People believed them. They were educated, they were professionals. Think about it. Who was Abimael? Wasn't he a university professor? That's how it was."

"So the fact the leaders were professionals gave them more credibility?"

"Of course—more *confianza*."

Thus, during the early 1980s, almost everyone was living what one former militant called *la vida en común* (a life in common). Well, almost everyone.

Following a common pattern throughout Víctor Fajardo and Vilcashuamán, people continued to hold their fiestas and their markets and to celebrate religious masses. These aspects of communal life were not under attack. However, although they allowed certain features of communal life to continue even under their territorial dominion, the Shining Path commanders began systematically naming people to various posts within their organization, thus attempting to impose their "popular committees"—directed by their designated *responsables*—while demanding the resignation of traditional communal authorities. Although many communal authorities did resign under coercion and outright threats, two authorities in Accomarca found out what happened to those who refused. Alfredo the Huambalpino described what happened when Shining Path commanders encountered opposition in Accomarca.

"Alfredo, why did Sendero start to kill in Accomarca? We know they killed two authorities—in 1982, I think it was?"

He nodded. "They killed them in an assembly. The *fuerza principal* killed them. A guy from Cayara I think it was, a *zambito*.[10] They had given the authorities a deadline to turn over their rubber stamps [*sellos*] and renounce their positions.[11] They told us, 'Ask them for their *sellos*.' So we asked for them. I told Narciso, 'You know, you're my uncle. I advise you to resign, leave, or prepare a letter and turn over your position.'"

"You only said that to Narciso?"

He shook his head. "No, to all of the authorities. But they didn't want to. They said, 'No, we're elected by the pueblo.' We told them there couldn't be two authorities [the state and Shining Path] in the pueblo, only one, but they refused. The deadline arrived and we held an assembly. They [the *fuerza principal*] asked us, and we told them that the authorities refused to turn over their *sellos*. So they grabbed them and in front of everyone they slit their throats with a knife—both of them. It was the worst, slitting their throats with a knife. There was my cousin, Primitivo—we were all there. Primitivo had his knife and the *zambito* borrowed his knife to slit their throats.[12] I thought they were going to start killing all the authorities like that. They said they had a list of people—a black list—with names. Well, when they were going to kill Edmundo, I told them, 'He isn't an authority, and all his little kids—who will take care of them if you kill him?' My aunt was his wife. He was number two to have his throat slit. I said, 'No, don't kill him.' Well, they told me that because I was defending him, they would slit my throat instead. So they killed him."

"And how did you feel after they killed him?"

"I thought I was on the same path, and that any day someone would do the same thing to me. I couldn't do anything. It was really difficult to leave this pueblo, so I stayed. The *fuerza armada* [in this case, the armed members of Shining Path] was always watching to see where you went. The soldiers also came here, and that was frightening, too. But the soldiers? They were totally dejected. Their shoes were torn, they were hungry. Sometimes we offered them food and we asked them, 'Why are you killing people? Why are you scaring them?' And they told us, 'The lieutenant, the captain—they order us to kill. What can we do?'"

"And what about you? Did the *fuerza principal*, the *mandos*, ever force you to kill anyone?"

"No. That's why I say people are not to be killed. The policy was not to kill anyone. All of this was supposed to instruct people, to change their mentality. But out of ignorance some people committed errors, threatened others, and thus the other person acted violently."

"But why did they start to kill?"

He paused for a moment. "Well, the commanders didn't want anyone to summon them up for their bad actions. In Sendero they had to give reports, and a balance, no? Why did they kill? What was the reason? How many killed? You couldn't kill just to kill. So some commanders wanted to cover this up, and if someone said, 'No it wasn't that way'—well, they killed him. That's how it was. But in contrast, for me to be in the ranks of Sendero—it made me do things well. I was more disciplined, more of a soldier almost. See, Sendero's policy was twofold: the struggle of the two lines, critique and self-critique. They critique you until you almost cry, and you yourself, when you have an auto-critique, you unburden yourself [*descargarse*] of all the errors that you have, all the problems you have. That's how it was for me. Sometimes here [in Lima] I tell people about all we did to acknowledge our errors and correct ourselves."

"I wonder, who were the most bloodthirsty *mandos* in Accomarca?"

He exhaled loudly. "Edilberto [one of the Morales brothers]. He told me how he'd beaten poor people to death and laughed afterward. 'That's what we've done,' he told me. That's what I didn't like. For them, what was it to kill people? When a woman screams, when people look at you . . . ," his voice trailing off.

He paused, clearly recalling what it felt like to witness the last moments of someone's life. "For example, Edilberto killed his neighbor because they'd never gotten along. He killed her. Oh, how many people did he kill! Even though he's my kin, he killed a woman who was my aunt.[13] But now no one says anything. First he killed his neighbor, right in front of her son he killed her."

"People say he laughed while he killed?"

Alfredo nodded. "When he trapped people inside their homes, the family would cry, scream in desperation, shout—he enjoyed that. He was very violent."

"Did you ever ask him about it—ask him why he did this?"

"No. At the end, we didn't understand each other. He became a brute, really violent. Around that time, Primitivo and I also had some discrepancies, and Edilberto thought about liquidating me. That's just not how it's supposed to be."

"But didn't anyone inform his superiors about what he was doing?"

"No. You see, they *were* the commanders. They were the ones who gave the reports. Since he was in the *fuerza principal*, who was going to investigate him? You see, every *fuerza principal* had its military commander. They had to give the reports about the *fuerza principal, fuerza base, fuerza local,* same thing for each. That Edilberto was a *maldito*. He also killed a guy in Vilcashuamán, and you know why? Just to take his merchandise. The guy sold candies, gum, hair clips, things like that. What sort of money could he have had? At the most maybe he had five hundred *soles*. Well, every afternoon Edilberto would show up with ribbons, one after another. One day I asked him, 'Where did you get all these?' 'Oh, we killed Fernando.' Just like that. And they'd played with his cadaver. Some people really like money and that's why they participated in Sendero. As part of the *fuerza principal*, they lived better lives. They also went around raping. And us, we lived with the base, we were in charge of the population. We were doing everything we could do, while other people were ruining it. So not everyone *is* equal. That's what ruined Sendero."

"But didn't you clarify these things in meetings?"

"Well, in our zone they didn't commit so many things. They did that more in the places they went to. For example, from here they went out. One day maybe they get really drunk and commit some atrocity. What are people going to do? It depends upon each one and their auto-critique. They arrive in Chosica, for example, and they begin killing and raping. They have their contingent of, say, five, ten men and women. People know what they've done, but they send in their report: In Chosica, we killed so many spies, so many criminals, like that. There was no one controlling them because they were the ones making the reports."

"I get it. Was Edilberto someone Gutierrez really trusted?"

"No, he wasn't. Edilberto was the *fuerza principal*. Gutierrez was one of our trusted guys. Edilberto was part of the *fuerza principal* and he went around with two guys, Andres and Rodrigo. It's certain that some of the commanders in the *fuerza principal* were criminals—they became bloodthirsty, but mostly they wanted to rob. Another was a commander they called Arturo—from Huancavelica or Cangallo. I don't remember that well. He almost shot me in Accomarca because a few guys had disappeared with about twenty women. I was the only one who knew them. So he said to me, 'You know where they are.' 'No, I don't know. If you kill me you're ruining everything, you're losing credibility.' I told him that. That's how it happened—some people grew used to robbing, raping women, threatening—that's what didn't work and it was primarily the *fuerza principal* who did that."

"I'm curious—did you use hoods [*pasamontañas*] or masks?"[14]

"At first when taking a pueblo, it was *encapuchados* [heads and faces covered]. But when I was here, they didn't come hooded. Yes, *pasamontañas* for the cold but not masked. I never used a mask, just a *pasamontaña*."

"But why do people say they were masked?"

"They say they were disguised, covered their faces—but I never saw that. At first it might have been. Now another case would be when someone is a local. Participating the first time, you'd have to cover your face so no one recognizes you. But when it was people from another place, there was no need because no one knows you. The people who wear masks wear them because they're local. For example, let's say I'm going to kill my neighbor.

I have to cover myself so no one recognizes me. But if I'm from someplace else, there's no need to hide my face. I never saw people masked, not the ones I was with. Maybe they say that to throw off the investigation—just like I could say that to mark the limits of my responsibility. To be able to say, 'I did it with a mask because they obligated me.' Maybe that's why I'd dress like that. As I say, it would be because local people participated—or people from another pueblo would need to disguise themselves because their pueblo is nearby and of course they recognize each other."

"Did you walk around armed?"

"No. There was a machine gun without bullets—we carried that around so they would say we were armed and treat us with respect. Gutierrez, now he had a big pistol. He made me carry it once even though I didn't want to. It was an automatic pistol and it could just go off. But with the machine gun you have to put bullets in to shoot."

How Edilberto became so "bloodthirsty" is open to debate. However, he and his surviving brothers agree that a pivotal moment in their commitment to Shining Path occurred in August 1983: "The soldiers killed my family members in 1983. Sendero had disappeared someone in the *feria* in Pitecc—someone from Vilcas. So there was an investigation. Well, one of the teachers, Marcial Chavez, mistakenly said that the person responsible was in my family. He said it was my brother Cupertino. That's why they [soldiers] came to my house and killed my brother, mother, his wife, their little children, other family members. Eleven people in all. They swore they would wipe out the Morales family that day."

The murders were pivotal not only for the Morales family but also in terms of the history of Sendero in Accomarca. The Huambalpino described how the murders changed things in his pueblo.

"It was after the Fiesta Patronal, that's when it was. It was around three in the morning when the bullets started exploding. I woke up my wife, grabbed the radio, and we escaped. We returned at seven in the morning and people were gathered in the plaza. They'd killed my sister-in-law, her husband, their children, and others. I wondered how they could do this—envy, revenge? And the soldiers kept asking everyone, 'Who else? Who else?'"

"Why did they kill them?"

"It's Marcial's fault [*culpa*]. They say he was in Churia [a nearby pueblo] and got drunk. He climbed up a tower and started calling people to come to an *asamblea popular* [an assembly held by Shining Path]. Now, from what they tell me he wasn't even in Sendero, so I don't know why he did that. Then he came drunk to Vilcas, and Vilcas never lacked for people who disliked Sendero. The soldiers grabbed him and the horse and took him to the military base at Vilcas. They grabbed him and took him there saying, 'This is him.' I guess they tortured him. He must have given names. So they came and blew the lock off Cupertino's door with a gun. The same soldiers said, 'Come to the plaza.' They had people gathered there. They had rounded up all the Morales and said, 'We're going to totally eradicate them.' They killed them. Because of those things, the hatred began in people here."

"So that's when it began with force—when Sendero really grew?"

"Of course. How could it be, the body of a little child? Why did they have to kill them? A little baby just two years old, another four years old. They found them with the intestines falling out—they had cut them and shot them. I don't know what else. My sister-in-law, they'd shot her through the waist. They'd shattered her spinal column so she was doubled in two. They shot her husband in the throat. Their uncles and aunts, their mother. Some people began to marginalize Primitivo because he was alone there. His two other brothers were both in the *fuerza principal* and were traveling."

"Cupertino, Primitivo, Edilberto, Nerio—and was there another brother?"

"Yeah, a younger one. He died—for having deserted [Shining Path], they killed him."

"When they killed the Morales family, what did all of you feel? What did people say?"

"There was no longer a family—practically no family left. Primitivo was the only one left, and I began to commit myself more because people began to hate him, to look for him. 'We should turn him in and kill him.' So I said, 'No, I'm here.' Some people really started to hate him. They wanted to know where he was, but I didn't know. Someone told me he was hiding below. Primitivo had escaped that night—he ran barefoot two kilometers down the hill."

The murder of the Morales family was a polarizing event in Accomarca. For some people who had not been sympathetic to Sendero, the army's brutality made them more receptive to the guerrillas' revolutionary message. For others, it was the militants themselves who were to blame for the military's actions; had they not been *comprometidos*, nothing would have happened. Moreover, another segment of the community wanted to turn in Primitivo as a demonstration to the army that they were against Shining Path—a demonstration they hoped would stave off further attacks. Finally, for the local militants, the murders were further evidence their cause was both necessary and just.

Indeed, not long after the Morales family was killed, Shining Path commanders decided to establish several encampments throughout the region with the goal of providing temporary respite for their "Popular Guerrilla Army." One such encampment was constructed down the steep slope from Accomarca; this encampment operated from 1983 through August 14, 1985, in Lloqllepampa, the site of one of Peru's emblematic army massacres.

"The Tragedy of Lloqllepampa"

> Brother, paisano,
> our beloved pueblo of Accomarca,
> we remember again,
> the massacre of Lloqllepampa.
> We remember again
> The river of blood that flowed.
>
> August 14, 1985
> My father and my mother were innocent
> They disappeared them without warning.
> Former president Alan Garcia
> What sort of conscience could you have had?
> My father and my mother were innocent
> Why did you disappear them without warning?
>
> That all of us, united and remembering
> All of your children demand
> Sr. President Toledo
> We ask you for support
> For the progress of our pueblo
> That you designate funding
> For the progress of our pueblo.
> —"La Tragedia de Lloqllepampa," composed and sung by the group (*comparsa*)
> New Heart of Accomarca, Carnival 2005

The PTRC's Final Report, volume 7, pages 147–60, begins with "The Facts." In the time leading up to the massacre on August 14, 1985, the army had multiple confrontations with different Shining Path columns and detained some alleged Senderistas. According to the statements taken (under torture), these detainees belonged to the Accomarca Company, comprised of thirty-two men organized into five platoons. Using the information they collected, the army began organizing an operative against the Shining Path presence in Accomarca. Operative Plan Huancayoc had as its objective the "capture and/or destruction of the terrorist elements in the Huancayoc ravine, the district of Accomarca." During the planning meeting, someone asked Infantry Captain Hélber Gálvez Fernández whether they should consider any resident of the area designated for the counterinsurgency action to be a "communist terrorist"; Captain Gálvez Fernández responded in the affirmative.[15]

The patrol was placed under the command of artillery lieutenant Juan Manuel Rivera Rondón and second lieutenant Telmo Ricardo Hurtado; Comrade Genaro, a captured Shining Path guerrilla, would accompany the patrol as a guide.[16] The patrol Lince 7 was transported by helicopter to the anti-guerrilla base in Vilcashuamán; they were subsequently transported to the *alturas* of Huambalpa and then continued on foot to Accomarca, where they spent the night in the pueblo. Early the next morning, a house-by-house search began. While the military subsequently declared they had confiscated "subversive material," the PTRC determined the patrol found no weapons, ammunition, or explosives.

Heading down the hill to Lloqllepampa, the soldiers gathered people in the open field. They began hitting the men and taking the women and girls aside to rape them. At approximately 11:00 a.m., the soldiers forced everyone into two dwellings that bordered the field. Telmo Hurtado gave the order to fire and then launched a grenade. Both structures, filled with men, women, and children, were burned to the ground. Sixty-two people were killed.[17] Upon completion of the operation, the soldiers occupied a house where they celebrated by drinking, dancing, slaughtering livestock, and shouting that they had "killed terrorists."

The carbonized bodies were unrecognizable, and survivors buried the collective remains to one side of the field. Not long after, the first in a series of investigative commissions was formed, this one at the congressional level. In issuing its findings, the congressional commission stated, "The Accomarca-Lloqllepampa Case was in our opinion a common crime and not a military one. Neither was it demonstrated that there was rape, because the witnesses only presume it and witnessed the acts from a distance. An expert investigation is impossible, and the rapes—except for recent deflorations—are not demonstrable."[18] Subsequent commissions absolved the accused of the most serious crimes, and in 1987 the War Room of the Second Judicial Zone of the army ruled that Telmo Hurtado had only committed the crime of "abuse of authority." He was sentenced to four years in prison and fined the equivalent of $830 in civil reparations. The sentence was subsequently absolved, and Telmo Hurtado resorted to the Amnesty Laws of 1995, which conferred amnesty on all acts that occurred during the "fight against terrorism." He remained in active service and continued to advance through the ranks until human rights organizations denounced him in 1998 when he was a major serving in a military base in Cajamarca. Even then, it was not until the Inter-American Court of Human Rights annulled the amnesty laws in January 2002 that legal justice was again possible. Shortly thereafter, Telmo Hurtado fled to Miami Beach, Florida, where he lived free until March 2007 when he was arrested for immigration fraud. As I write, he remains incarcerated at an immigration detention center in Miami, fighting extradition back to Peru, where he would face criminal charges.

In their investigation, the PTRC determined the military actions in Lloqllepampa-Accomarca were not the work of one person but the outcome of a joint decision that resulted in Operative Plan Huancayoc; moreover, they found that the highest army authorities in the city of Ayacucho participated in the planning, elaboration, discussion, and execution of the operation. Thus, the acts committed in Accomarca were part of a system of combat adopted by, consented to, and practiced by the infantry division of the Second Military Region. In sum, this was not a case of "excesses and errors" but rather a planned and endorsed counterinsurgency strategy. In summarizing the serial failed efforts to bring Telmo Hurtado and other participants in Operative Plan Huancayoc to trial, the PTRC notes the legal processes regarding Accomarca have been ruled in favor of impunity, such that this judicial history has been "lengthy, painful, and, in the final instance, an example of the denial of justice to victims."[19] I agree with the findings of the PTRC and hope my research may contribute in some way to bringing Telmo Hurtado to trial for his role in the massacre.

When sketching out this chapter, I was concerned about how my research might be used. One of my responsibilities as an anthropologist is to make certain my findings are not misconstrued. Was Shining Path active in Accomarca? Yes. Does the fact that a percentage of the pueblo was involved in Shining Path justify the military operation? Absolutely not. In part the history of Accomarca—and that of many other pueblos throughout Ayacucho—is one of counterinsurgency unleashed to horrible ends and counterproductive results. Killing unarmed civilians, among them pregnant women and children, alienates most people and foments deep and abiding resentment. Whatever short-term gains the military thought they secured with Operative Plan Huancayoc were offset by how greatly such actions sullied the armed forces as an institution and by the way those actions radicalized key sectors of the population. Military defeat cannot be equated with ideological defeat, as we shall see.

Paulina Gamboa, Gutierrez's wife, witnessed the events. "The day of the massacre, I saw the armed soldiers coming. I hid myself and was praying. I've always believed in God and I prayed to him, 'Help me, Señor, help me for my children's sake.' I knew—the soldiers, if they found you, they raped you, or they killed you. Or both. That's why I was saying, 'God help me, help me for my children. Save me.' I kept running until I found some bushes and hid. Rain was falling on me. The soldiers had seen me running, but I don't know what happened. They didn't find me. I was just grabbing onto my children, telling them to be quiet. Rocks were falling all around us because the soldiers were walking by, right above us. I kept thinking they were going to see us, but they just passed by. They were looking down below asking each other, 'Where are they?' They rounded everyone up in the valley. They tied people up and took them to the field. They raped the women."

The Huambalpino also escaped death by hiding farther up the slope. As he explained, ever since the Morales family had been killed he had been constantly alert. "That day, I thought why don't I have a camera? Or a video recorder? I could have filmed everything."

"What did you see that day?"

"It happened like this. The day before the massacre, I was at the *feria* in Pitecc. My wife was there, selling things in the *feria*. A man arrived—he was headed on to Vischongo with his harp, to play at a fiesta. He was in the truck, playing for the owner. Well, two of the guys from the *fuerza principal* were there and they played the violin, so they all started playing together. I love music so I was dancing. There I was, halfway drunk, dancing in my old tennis shoes. Well, a guy told me, "Oye, Alfredo, the *cachacos* [soldiers] are coming!' When I went to see, they were heading around Cayara—right around there. I thought to myself, well that must be where they're heading down, and they'll be here before too long. But then I realized they were already coming, ten meters, twenty meters away. They had their dogs. Well, that other guy had a machine gun strapped around his waist, so I told him, 'Don't involve people here—get out of here however you can.' Then I got my wife and told her, 'Get going—start walking because the *cachacos* aren't far off.' I headed out walking. The other guy, I guess he decided to follow me. I suppose he ran when they realized he had a gun. So the *cachacos* began to shoot. Then I fell to the ground, halfway drunk, and my tennis shoe ripped apart. I could barely walk, but the bullets were falling like rain. I was almost to the drop down to Lloqllepampa—there was a side path, and I went that way. I was halfway drunk, so I passed out! Then a woman came by pasturing her goats and asked me what I was doing there. She woke me up and told me the *cachacos* were looking for me down below. 'Wake up,' she said. I finally made it back to my house, and my wife showed up a bit later."

"The next day, August fourteenth, at seven in the morning we were eating breakfast. My wife was preparing soup and my papa showed up. He told me he'd woken up in the mountains and had no idea how he was going to make it to his *chacra*. That's when I realized that across the way in Lloqllepampa, about twenty or thirty soldiers were headed down there. They were taking someone with them—they had tied a rope around his neck. When I saw that I started telling people, 'The soldiers are coming!' There were even more of them coming down another hill. 'What's this? Let's get out of here!' Everywhere I looked there were soldiers. It was August so the mountains were bare—you could see everything easily. I told my wife, my father-in-law, my papa, 'Get out of here, *carajo*! We need to hide!' I took off with only a radio in my hand. I hid behind bushes, watching everything. The soldiers were everywhere, coming from all sides. At that hour, people were eating breakfast, cooking. So they gathered everyone up. No one escaped—only the people who had been attentive, on alert. The soldiers shot anyone who tried to escape. The soldiers made everyone get together in the field. They were there from about seven in the morning until three in the afternoon, everyone together. I kept watching and wondering what they were going to do to people. Then they made everyone march to the two houses. After they made everyone get in the houses, they began shooting. I heard bullets. Then I heard a bomb explode. Then they set the houses on fire—that's what happened. Afterward, they [the soldiers] went to my mother-in-law's house. She had quite a few animals she was raising. They started slitting their throats—they kept eating those animals until they were full. Then they headed back to the pueblo [Accomarca itself]. The next day, around eleven in the morning, we looked for survivors. We looked. I was the one who made people dig a large hole to bury the remains. The people were all burned up. You couldn't identify anyone. 'Who is this? Who is this?' There was no way to know. Gutierrez and I, we started making a list of all the dead."

The following day, both the Huambalpino and Gutierrez sent a report to President Gonzalo [Abimael Guzmán] about what had happened in Llo-qllepampa. According to both men, not a single Shining Path commander (*mando*) died that day—not one.

Pax Militar: Imposing Peace

A few months later, in December 1985, a military base was installed in Acco-marca, and many people who had fled after the massacre were encouraged to return to their pueblo now that the army was there to provide "security." Details about the founding of the *pax militar* came about in bits and pieces.

It was June 2003 when we met up with Ricardo González, a young man working as a vet tech in Accomarca. He had previously heard us talking with a group of his friends in a makeshift meeting in the park, and he wanted to set us straight on a few things. We had been talking about the Actas the community had elaborated when the military base was first established in the school back in 1985.

"Those acts exist," he insisted. "There are lots of documents. But before—when the authorities were finishing their terms—they warned the incoming authorities that no one unknown should see those documents. That's why the authorities hide them or say they don't have them."

"So you think they really do exist?" asked Juanjo.

Ricardo nodded. "But there's another agreement they signed later. No one, not a single authority could mention those documents. No one else could see them or review them. But they say they could turn them over in an official ceremony where provincial authorities and even departmental authorities were present. But I've heard the authorities ask, 'How could we give these documents to someone young or unknown?' There's distrust. Hey, only my papa and some friends have told me about this because I was just a kid when the base arrived."

"What sorts of things did they tell you?" asked Edith.

"They told me that those *puriqkuna*, they say there're a lot of them who still live here. Some of them repented saying they'd been tricked. Back then, people didn't know what to think—they just watched them without saying anything. People couldn't believe what was happening. On one side were the soldiers, on the other the *puriqkuna*, making peace. The cool thing is the soldiers arrived with a list, but saying 'Now we aren't going to kill. Now the government doesn't want us to kill. Before, yes, we killed—but now it's prohibited. All these Senderistas, have them come back and work in peace.' That's what the soldiers said. 'Tell them there's going to be a base. Tell them to come, that we're not going to do anything to them. Tell all of the *cabecillas*, tell them the soldiers are going to stay and they should come back. There'll be an *asamblea comunal* and we're calling everyone.'"

"So just like that they called everybody?"

"Well, they also told people that if they didn't come they would take all of our sheep and burn down our houses. So everyone decided to meet. But lots of people had communicated that they didn't want to come to the pueblo, saying it would be like other pueblos where the soldiers rounded everyone together and killed them. But it didn't happen. The soldiers said they wanted us to live in peace. They wanted the Senderistas to come and said nothing would happen to them. They said there would be peace, but the Senderistas didn't want to come. The *cabecillas* didn't come, they didn't participate. But when four or five of the *hatuns* [big guys] did come, they came without their sheep and the soldiers made them go back. 'Everyone must come with their sheep, with their animals, they have to come with everything. Here, we'll take care of them and nothing's going to happen,' the soldiers said. They made everyone gather and told them, 'Everyone come back because we're going to stay, we're going to take care of you, come with your sheep.' That's why we came back and we've stayed here. The ministers from Lima came and named the authorities because we didn't have any. They named the mayor, judge, president, and prosecutor.

Although I have never seen the Actas Ricardo referred to, I have seen something similar in the Libro de Actas in Hualla. The entry is worth citing because it gives us a sense of how these "Extraordinary Assemblies" worked.

ACTAS COMUNALES DE HUALLA, OCTOBER 11, 1984
ASAMBLEA EXTRAORDINARIA

In Hualla the eleventh day of October of 1984 gathered in the military base of San Pedro de Hualla under the control of the armed forces, we open this assembly with the following agenda items:

1st: The rising up of the community against the subversive criminals or communist terrorists;
2nd: Support for the forces of order or the army;
3rd: Naming of the district authorities.

> First: The community in general in the presence of the armed
> forces has committed to rising up against the defeated subversives
> and to not support in any moment or attend any meetings held by the
> terrorists
>
> Second: The entire community in general has committed to
> collaborating with the forces of order in every moment and to
> support them in any way whatever they may need
>
> Third: Under control of the armed forces, all of the community in
> general has committed to naming the authorities of their district

The Act is signed by various communal authorities, and by "Captain
EP . . . , Jefe Politico Militar, Huaya [who] gives faith with his signature to
the naming of the authorities of the district of San Pedro de Huaya [*sic*].

"Peace" in pueblos that were repeatedly razed by the army came in the form
of a militarized state of pacification. These communities were placed under
military control: as the Actas Comunales from Hualla and numerous interviews indicate, the local authorities were "puppets," several of whom were
Shining Path *cabecillas* identified by the population and forced to assume
communal cargos as part of repairing the damage they had done. Although
in later years serving as an authority could include an element of rehabilitation, in the early years it was a counterinsurgency strategy and at times a
form of revenge. Being a communal authority under military control meant
being at the beck and call of the officials in the base. In many conversations
we had in the central-south, people said the soldiers acted like *reyes, Dioses,
mandamasas* (kings, Gods, omnipotents).

Yet there is a certain ambivalence in people's recollections of the *pax militar*. We know that where there were military bases, the level of sexual violence was high and sustained. In addition, the soldiers frequently engaged
in theft, and their drunkenness appears in the Actas as a chronic problem.
However, fear works in many ways, including the ironic. At the end of a
long conversation about the abuses they had endured at the hands of the
soldiers, a group of women in Accomarca described the day the government
withdrew the base. "Oh, how we cried. We cried! The security they offered
us—when the soldiers were here, we could sleep at night. When they left, we
thought, 'Who will protect us now?'" The question, of course, is protect them
from whom?

From the neighbors.

The soldiers reintroduced *"arrepentidos"* into these pueblos under their watch. I use *"arrepentidos"* in quotation marks because the *cabecillas* had the opportunity to present themselves and renounce their militancy or be killed. The military exercised a monopoly on the use of violence; thus my insistence on a *pax militar*, as the following conversation illustrates.

Amadeus Palomino is thirty years old and has half a dozen children ranging from infancy to early adolescence.[20] He was very sweet with his children, and on most occasions when we met up with him he had one of the littlest ones in his arms and two or three others hanging from various limbs. We were cautious about the topics we broached in their presence, knowing that a number of the parents had picked up on the message one of the NGOs had promoted: talking about the past in front of children would traumatize them. Thus Juan José was pleased one morning to find Amadeus walking alone to his *chacra* and fell in step beside him. Their conversation spanned several hours, and at one point Amadeus described a communal agreement villagers had negotiated.

"There's so much distrust because life has taught us the burro only kicks once. That's why many people don't want to talk. When the soldiers arrived [referring to the installation of the base in December 1985], they had us all meet in the field so we could live in peace. We were all there that day, all the people who participated [in Shining Path] and all the people who didn't. Even the most *cabecillas* were there. With a communal agreement we decided not to talk about anything with anyone. The soldiers said that the guilty ones—well, the state had pardoned them so we could live tranquilly and in peace."

"So they came here just like that?"

"Well, they received some sort of punishment, I guess. They paid some price, the price of serving the pueblo as authorities, as servants of the *milicos* [soldiers]. That must have been really screwed for them because the *milicos* didn't trust them. They had to present themselves at whatever hour the *milicos* felt like. If the soldiers called them at midnight, they had to go running because if they didn't, the soldiers would go to their houses and beat them. Beating them, they would take them to the base and stick them in the hole. They made them suffer, they made them pay. The base made everyone who had served Sendero serve the pueblo. They had a list and they made them work, one by one, as communal authorities."

"But did they ask forgiveness in front of everyone?"

Amadeus shook his head. "Only the soldiers made them, so they'd accept that they were guilty for the disaster in this pueblo. But no one said anything about anything. What people want now is for them to *really* ask for forgiveness because now when we say anything about it, they tell us the state already pardoned them and they walk around as if nothing ever happened."

As Amadeus demonstrates, "reintegration" of the alleged *arrepentidos* reflected a change in military strategy rather than an initiative on behalf of the *cabecillas* or the population itself. The community served as little more than a mute audience regarding the demands of the military and their staging of "reconciliation." The manipulation of repentance in the service of counterinsurgency made an evaluation of sincerity superfluous. As Xabier Etxeberría argues, "Utilitarian 'repentance'—collaborating with justice in order to lessen my sentence, or repenting 'so that' a victim pardons me—falsifies the very essence of the act."[21] Military strategy served the goals of pacification, not those of promoting reconciliation.

In addition, while the sustained military presence did cause some *comuneros* to return from Huamanga, Ica, and Lima, that sustained presence also motivated some of "those people" to leave town. For example, Paulina decided it was no longer safe for her to remain in Accomarca: "At the time I had a sister in Huamanmarca. I went to her house. My pueblo was so dangerous—both the soldiers and the Senderistas. My sister had a little house but she told me, 'Better you leave for Ayacucho [referring to Huamanga].' She prepared food for me and I left for Huamanga. But I was worried about my mama. I sent her things from Huamanga and she sent me things, too. I was selling fruit in Ayacucho, but Ayacucho was dangerous, too. At night the soldiers entered, Sendero entered—people screamed and you couldn't even go outside. So I finally decided I had to leave. I went to Lima."

Alfredo the Huambalpino decided to leave as well, heading for the relative safety of Huamanga: "It was difficult for us to return to the pueblo. What was left for us? Better to go to another pueblo. Besides, after the massacre, the group [Sendero] had really low morale. How to continue? For example, to continue I would have had to contact another *fuerza base*—with the *fuerza principal*, they could take me with them. That was my only option. What other role would they give me? Give me the same place [Accomarca] to reorganize? Very difficult. I risked my life."

And yet another *mando* left—Primitivo Morales. I cite from conversations with one of the "initiators," in which he reflected upon his participation in Shining Path and the consequences of the massacre in Lloqllepampa.

"Why do you think people there [in Accomarca] didn't rise up against Sendero?"

"Well, as I understand it, because I oriented people very well so they wouldn't rise up. As a professor from the pueblo, I told them, 'Don't rise up because we will fall like dogs.' In other pueblos they lacked someone who could orient them like that and that's why so many people died at the hands of Sendero. Some *mandos* acted badly, the way they interpreted things was bad. I think it's a disaster so many people died, but who is guilty? The guilty are the owners of Peru [*los dueños del Peru*]. I think that here in the country there is no solution, nor will we see one for ten or fifteen years. What will happen is that the people will rise up and protest. That's how I think."

"Some people say you were very involved with Sendero."

"Oh clearly, some people. Someone told me people accused me. Initially everyone, including myself, was obligated. But those who know the truth about me—in the first place, those old people are no longer around. And the people who say I was involved are the resentful people."

"But so many people affirm your participation. . . ."

He shrugged. "For example, when they killed my family [the Morales family], if I had belonged to that group I would have secretly taken my revenge. No matter what, I would've got my revenge. People don't investigate well. If I had annihilated, had recruited—like the case of Gutierrez, who did a great deal of recruiting. I've done nothing because I have been present in the pueblo, including the day of the massacre. At dawn I was there because I was returning from a fiesta. After the massacre, I withdrew from Accomarca."

"How do you feel when people accuse you of being a former Shining Path *cabecilla*?"

"The accusations, that bothers me. It's fine ideologically—yes, that is. I accept that I told people, 'We need to be careful, we don't want to fight among ourselves.' That's how I oriented them. But what guilt do I have if I only oriented them?"

"Have you thought of clarifying what happened? There in your pueblo?"

"Yeah, I've thought about clearing things up in an assembly—including the young people because they have rancor toward me. One of them is my nephew and he says to me, 'Uncle, you're one of the *responsables*.' But I don't know what happens if the *responsables* live there in Accomarca. I was there with no problem, even when they were installing the military base. I was there passing my cargo at Christmas. But the following day, my older brother told me, 'Something could happen to you—you aren't going to stay.' So he brought me here."

"At any time did anyone accuse you to your face?"

He nodded. "Yeah, a drunk woman. 'You're guilty, you organized it,' she said to me. And I told her, 'I brought it but I didn't know they were going to kill people.' Yes, that happened to me. But take Felícitas—she and her husband were responsible. He should *concientemente* tell people the truth. But people in Accomarca are two-faced—they don't speak to you face-to-face."

A few days later we attended a fund-raiser in Huamanga for the Victim's Association of Accomarca. To our surprise, Primitivo showed up. He was quite drunk and outspoken: "Why do you look for me? Why do you accuse me? What's over is over. They had no cause to kill my mother and my brothers. Besides, how could we escape from there? We teachers were the nerve center—we were the ones chosen by Sendero. We couldn't do anything. Now the situation's a mess. There's no work. Another revolution will happen. The government? Tell me, what does it do? For the good of the pueblo, nothing."

We assured him we had only sought him out for conversation, and he slowly calmed down. "I'm a revolutionary and a revolutionary never dies. I'm a materialist, a Marxist. I was like a soldier of Spartacus. You know who Spartacus was? I was a revolutionary soldier like Spartacus. I was and I continue to be! I accept that I did what you said I did, but that was no reason to kill my mother, my family. Back then? We *all* supported it. And the situation now is bad. Nothing has changed. It stays the same or even worse. I'm certain there will be another revolution."

Alfredo also offered his assessment of Shining Path. According to most accounts, he and Gutierrez were the highest-ranking militants in Accomarca. The Huambalpino also left Accomarca shortly after the massacre and now sells groceries at a large open-air market in Lima.

"I worked in construction and later as a traveling merchant. Then this market was invaded [referring to a land invasion in which migrants seize unoccupied land]. I began to occupy this stall. Later, when they started to clear people out, people began buying and selling lots. We bought the stall—my wife also grabbed a small stall and sells chickens. But we don't get along well. She has a bad character. For example, in front of my children she says to me, "Assassin, *maldito*.' They hear that! I feel bad. I can't tell her, in front of my children, that she was also involved. We both participated. I can't say anything, so the only way to deal with it is to be quiet."

"What do your children say?"

He shrugged. "They don't say anything, they just listen. I tell them, 'We wouldn't be here. We would be in the sierra.' My goal was to live in the sierra because there you have life. So here we are in this situation, because of what happened. I tell them about what happened with me, and I tell them, 'Don't you ever get involved in things [*comprometerse*]. Because if you participate in that or in crime, it's the same thing because when you abandon it they'll kill you.' I tell them that."

"Alfredo, what have you learned from your experience? From all you've been through?"

He sighed. "I'll give you an example. The majority of people died at the hands of the military and the *ronderos* they organized, not Sendero. I even gave advice to the soldiers when they entered. 'Tell your captain to send the Intelligence Service. It's easy when an organization is not feasible for the society—the government has the Intelligence Service.' They send them to grab the primary leaders. But once the organization advances, they don't know what to do and they start to kill people. The policy of the military was, if you're able to capture ten *campesinos*, there will be one *terruco* in the group. How many people did they kill in Accomarca! I thought about that. They wanted to clean up their [army] image, so they placed weapons in the hands of people and took photos of them. Then they said they found them that way."

"Which ones of you died in the massacre?"

"Innocent people—people who had nothing to do with it, because we'd escaped. For me, the dead were heroes. They died just for being *pobladores*, nothing else. If it had been Sendero responsible there, then certainly the whole world would have said, 'They're responsible.' But they were innocent, they knew nothing, and they were executed."

"So, no one who had responsibility in the *fuerza principal* died there?"

He was adamant. "The *fuerza principal* did not die there. The *fuerza principal*, where would they die? In confrontations with the army, in an ambush they would die."

"So for you, everyone who died was innocent—like everyone tells us?"

"Yes, innocent, because there were pregnant women, children."

We nodded. "Could you tell us, what was Sendero's greatest achievement in Accomarca?"

Alfredo shook his head. "They didn't achieve anything. With the massacre it just fell apart. If there hadn't been the massacre, the pueblo would have advanced quite a bit. And the pueblo wouldn't have ended up killing other people—that was also bad. Because if we want to live in a communitarian society, united—for me, that's what we were looking for. But to achieve communism, there was a long way to go. According to history, you have to arrive at socialism. Oh, how many years would need to pass! Uff. It would arrive with the grandchildren of my grandchildren."

"Did you ever think about this back then?"

"Of course. That's why at that time, participating in that, I was more energetic, lively. I was brave. I liked it because there were no more criminals, rapists, bums, thieves—they died, necessarily. Think how many *campesinos* raise their little animals and the cattle rustlers take them for free! And when the police capture them, they offer them a bull and then they're free. I'm telling you, justice favors the enemy."

"But I wonder—what are you proud of, what did you do for the pueblo?"

"*Bueno*, just serving the pueblo for the time I was there. And organizing the *fuerza base*."

"And a weakness—perhaps an auto-critique?"

"That I didn't work harder. I should have been stronger. But there was weakness in the pueblo—it was hard to manage people."

"Alfredo, why do you think Accomarca didn't rebel against Sendero like other pueblos did?"

"They knew Sendero. If that had happened, Sendero could attack at any moment because they knew them. So it was preferable that we—that among us we know each other and have good relations. Because the people are like us. *If we rebel, then necessarily we're rebelling against our own kin—we would be rebelling against ourselves.*"

"And now what do you think—was it a failure or not?"

"Well, the failure was because of mercenary commanders who wanted to take advantage, charge people, assault, kill people even though those people were collaborators. The philosophy and the principles were good, but the leaders are what went bad. They mixed revenge—this is what ruined Sendero. They lost credibility and now they want to start up again, but the pueblo won't lend support easily. If those commanders, those militants had acted with humility, I know we would've achieved something. To arrive at that stage of change in a society is difficult, but they did learn something in the pueblo. Some people corrected their errors, they know how to work. They know in their *conciencia* that they achieved something."

"How do you feel now? Do you repent for having participated in that?"

"Repentance, no. It's that things had to happen one way or another, some time, like it would have to happen in any part of the world. If it weren't for that, maybe I would have been a criminal, maybe a thief. With that [Sendero] in Accomarca, many of us men corrected ourselves—not with fists, not with bullets. No, we corrected ourselves as human beings. There were people who abused their wives, got drunk, hit them, and we had to convoke a meeting and tell them, 'Why do you do this to a human being?'"

Alfredo paused for a moment. "On the other hand, the repentance I have is to have permitted those bad commanders within Sendero—that's what ruined it. And the people who just stood by, even though we were heading toward being criminals. If those commanders had conscientiously worked at their roles, it would have been different."

"Have you returned to Accomarca?"

"No, I haven't been back. I don't have a house, don't have family—only my sister-in-law."

"Do you still have a fear of going back?"

"Yeah, one way or another. Here the association [the migrant's association]—I don't approach it. I only went to a fiesta. Besides, there are some people, my uncles—they threatened me when I was there. Sometimes, even here, those who dedicate themselves to alcohol make problems—they offend others. They've said to me, 'You were one of them.' But if a person doesn't know, then why do they talk? They're just kids. Maybe they heard something. I just stay quiet. If I say anything, it would be worse—they'd want to kill me. So I don't want to humiliate myself. They marginalize a single person, but I wasn't alone. But everyone stares at me and accuses me."

"You don't want to humiliate yourself, you say. Humiliate yourself in what way?"

"After the massacre I came here [Lima] and the whole population thought I kept operating there. The soldiers searched for me, asking everyone, 'Where is he?' Someone had just tried to dynamite the base and they accused me, saying, 'He's out going around with Gutierrez.' There are people who, because of their ignorance, they talk like that. They still live in Accomarca, and that's how they talk."

"How do you feel when they think like that?"

"That in some corner there they have resentment toward me. Because I didn't fall—here I am."

"Have you tried to clear things up?

"No. I was going to one time, but . . . " He shrugged.

"What do you think they could do to you?

"Any old thing. Now a person could return there with another way of thinking, go back there peacefully. But like any political figure, any leader—they could assassinate you. Obviously not everyone would but some people, because they have a great deal of resentment."

"Have you wanted to apologize? Did you ever think of doing that?"

"In front of the association [of migrants in Lima], I didn't do it. But I did individually with some people. I've spoken personally with various people, but that's not the same as doing this with the association."

"What did they say when you apologized?"

"*Bueno*, they didn't say anything. For example, Pedro Ochoa, they told him I was guilty—told him that because of me his mother died. When I clarified things to him, why things had happened . . . well, because we didn't know. They would have killed all of us, *pues*. Luck allowed us to live, but the pain and disgrace are for all of us."

Alfredo continued. "Now, other people, even though they participated, they say nothing. But I've spoken with various people already. That's why I say, you shouldn't blame a person without knowing what happened. I think there should be reconciliation somehow or another because all human beings, we're equal. We all commit errors, but we're here to overcome with the experience we've had."

"Did you suggest there should be a reconciliation?"

"Yes, because no matter what, something would've happened. If the pueblo had denied [Shining Path] from the beginning, maybe they would have been left worse off—maybe like Uchuraccay, no? People who live in Lima don't think about that. They think simplistically—that a person just rose up armed and started to assassinate the population! This was happening at a national level so there was no stopping it. It had to happen."

"Why do you think Accomarca accepted this?"

"Accomarca is a pueblo with practically no means of survival. With the politics that began, they accepted it because they're poor people that don't even have irrigation. But they're hardworking people. I *know* them to be hardworking people. Besides, a small pueblo had to accept—and also because Sendero had been working there since the 1970s."

"Something else we've noticed is that many people who participated in Sendero are Evangélicos now. What do you think about that?"

He rolled his eyes. "*Bueno*, when I was in prison, there were some bloodthirsty people there. They told me they'd killed people like pigs just to keep their money. But each day, when it dawned and again at sundown, I saw them grabbing the Bible. 'We're cleaning ourselves,' they said. So I told them, 'Satan, do you believe you're going to be freed of your sin? You won't be freed. No one is going to clean you.' They just stared at me. Many entered the *evangelio* because they'd committed errors, sinned, because they killed people. That's why when an Evangelical comes with their book, I say I'm Catholic! I can't just enter. But I read the Bible from time to time. For me it's a guide to have a better life, to follow a path, to have my family. Besides, I say that Christ—well, the same as Sendero. He was chased, he went around hiding. He had few disciples to defend him. Almost no one was willing to stand up for him—they marginalized him, too."

Although Alfredo was dismissive of Evangelismo, some of the former militants insist that joining the church has allowed them to build a new life. Anasto comes to mind. Although he claims he is "another kind of Morales," most people we spoke with in Accomarca assured us that his branch of the Morales family tree also had deep roots in Shining Path. In one of our conversations, Anasto described his rebirth in 2001.

"Because God came to the world for the great sinners, God chooses you while you're still in your mother's stomach. The first day you're born, you're chosen. That's why I became a *hermano*. I used to reject the Evangélicos, but when God chooses you, God himself calls you in your dreams. I analyzed my dreams, and they were a call from God. I was born again. First you have to be reborn to be a *hermano*, and when you're born again all of your sins are forgiven and God pardons you. God then writes you down in the Book of Life. As a consequence, you're destined to be with Jesus Christ. When you're born again, all of your sins are forgiven. That's why God chooses the sinners."

"You mention forgiveness from God—did you also ask for forgiveness from the other *hermanos*?"

He nodded. "That's confessing. You're obligated to talk about what you were before knowing God. You have to recount it."

"What if someone doesn't tell?"

"That's bad. You'll always remember with remorse. Once you start to confess, you lose that remorse."

"Anasto, did you confess?"

"Of course. You're born again because up to the day you are baptized, you're full of sin. You feel your sins as though you were carrying them on your back in a *kipi* [shawl]. You're carrying all your sins. This load, by confessing you can let it down. Then you're forgiven. When you are baptized in water, then you're free from your sin. You're like a *nueva criatura*—all that evil that you had inside is totally forgotten."

We nodded and paused before asking, "Anasto, let's say I killed someone. That person's family could react strongly. They could even kill me, no? Do you know of anything like that happening?"

"Those who killed need to ask forgiveness. For example, if I killed a family member of my *paisanos*, I have to go ask for forgiveness. Now, what reaction would the family have? I don't know. I still haven't seen. But numerous people there were walking with Sendero."

"If you *had* done anything like that, would you have asked for forgiveness?"

"Of course—I did a while back. That's why I gave my testimony over the loudspeaker in Accomarca. I go there every once in a while now and the first thing I do is enter the house of prayer."

"And what sort of testimony did you give?"

"*Bueno*, I told people, 'Now I'm a *hermano*. I had to be born again so that God could forgive me for all my sins—that is what I asked God for. Now over this loudspeaker I'm asking our pueblo to forgive me for what I have done. You know what I've done. You all know me, know that I am a son of this pueblo, family to some of you.' That's how I had to speak. And when I was talking, another *paisano* who had come from Lima interrupted me just when I was going to keep talking. As soon as he heard my voice over the loudspeaker, he came to greet me. He wanted to tell everyone he's also a *hermano*. He wasn't a sinner anymore."

"Did he also participate in Sendero?"

"Yeah, but he also asked for forgiveness. Everyone knows that—they know us, and that's why we had to talk. Because God will call us before our death, and He will ask us why we never confessed. Many don't want to do it. I didn't want to either, but I had to. I couldn't stand my remorse any longer."

"And after you asked for forgiveness, how did you feel?"

"Happy that I changed my life. There's no more remorse."

"What motivated you to ask for forgiveness?"

He leaned forward. "Your own heart accuses you, your conscience. Your conscience says, 'You know. Why don't you talk?' It happened regularly. Ay, it's terrible. I was there in Accomarca for three days. The first day, the second day, my conscience was accusing me. I paid almost no attention. The third day, I was going to leave but the accusations continued. I got up at five in the morning to head to my sister's house, and it's across from the radio. The first and second days my conscience was accusing. I was still thinking, 'What am I going to say? Will they let me?' I wondered. Something just told me to talk. I entered and asked them to please loan me the radio so I could greet my *paisanos*. 'Yeah, uncle, go ahead.' So I started to talk."

As soon as he finished apologizing for what he had done, Anasto took his place in the *combi* that was waiting for him; if he stayed around, "Who knows what could happen?"

That depends upon whom one asks. I asked Celestino, a resident of Accomarca, what he thought might happen between him and the *huk kuna* he holds responsible for his losses. He was adamant in his response.

Everything that happened, to forget all that? We'll have to die to forget. While alive, we can't forget what happened. For example, take my case. I lost my mother. Forgetting that is *not* an easy thing to do. Even though it already happened, it's over—forgetting is *not* easy. How could it be that they burned my mother? Someone who never harmed anyone! I'll have to die to forget. In the meantime, I'm not going to forget. Now, even though they burned them, why? Who is responsible? Weren't they looking for someone? Weren't they looking for people from this same pueblo? A neighbor in this pueblo? Do you think the massacre was because the soldiers wanted it? No! They were provoked, and who provoked them? People from this pueblo! How can we want to reconcile with them when it's their fault the soldiers came! We lost many lives— not just sixty-nine lives but so many more. We have more than one hundred victims here. It's not easy to forgive—children died, children who were only a few months old. And people up to ninety years old. That's why this is very hard to forgive. Those people did so much harm.

To be sure, debates in Accomarca—as well as Cayara, Hualla, and Tiqui-hua—regarding *who* is to blame for what happened to these pueblos during the internal armed conflict are vociferous and ongoing. Assigning guilt, determining responsibility, and meting out punishment? These are complicated and arduous discussions, to which we now turn.

Chapter 12

Facing Up to the Past

Perpetrators have a history as well as victims, but in what sense do they share a narrative? In fact, their narratives intertwine just as all adversarial histories must.
—Charles Maier, "Doing History, Doing Justice"

ON HIS FIRST day in Hualla, José Carlos was taken aside and warned: "Be careful while you're here." During the weeks prior to our visit, there had been a volley of anonymous notes sent to various members of the community. Some of the notes had included death threats, while others assured the recipient that "sooner or later, the pueblo will judge you." Still others insisted "the pueblo will never forgive so much spilled blood." People's daily encounters with local-level perpetrators are a constant reminder of lives losts, accounts unsettled, and the burden of unpunished crime.

In this chapter I draw upon research in Víctor Fajardo and Vilcashuamán to further illustrate the competing logics at work when we introduce a politics of scale into our analyses of transitional justice. What may serve national goals—amnesties, top-down "reintegration" of former combatants in staged reconciliation ceremonies, and militarily enforced pacification campaigns—may unintentionally complicate local processes of social repair. Indeed, these policies contributed to the construction of two categories of "untouchables" who were placed beyond the reach of communal mechanisms of assessing guilt and administering justice: the former Shining Path *cabecillas* and the soldiers.

In contrast with the *propias prácticas* implemented in the northern communities, the southern pueblos are characterized by the lack of reconciliatory processes and by omnipresent discussions about *who* the guilty are and what should be done with them. Daily conversations resonated with what I have called local moral idioms—detailed discussions of responsibility, degrees of guilt, and processes of redress.[1] This is "justice talk" in another register, likely to involve references to aching hearts, lacerating ulcers, masks, faces and foreheads held shamelessly high. This local moral idiom is one of condemnation and transformation and provides great insight into how people conceptualize their elusive search for justice.

The "Untouchables": Living with Impunity

In Accomarca, Cayara, Hualla, and Tiquihua, people recall various assemblies in which the military had people gather together, collectively "repent" for their involvement in or sympathy with Shining Path, and promise they would "live in peace, as one reconciled community." Ricardo spoke a bit about one such event in Accomarca; there were others. In some cases, these ceremonies preceded the National Repentance Law (Ley de Arrepentimiento, #25499), in effect from 1992 to 1994, by which the Peruvian state offered Shining Path militants reduced prison terms in exchange for surrendering and for naming other members of the organization. During that period, the Peruvian government also orchestrated a series of publicized "repentance ceremonies" as one dramaturgical component of the state's war on terror.

However, although people referred to these ceremonies—which at times convoked *comuneros* from several pueblos, marching to the assemblies with white flags of surrender flying above their heads—equally common was the insistence that there has been no meaningful sort of *arrepentimiento*, much less punishment, for the ex-Senderistas at the local level. Rather, various people lamented that the ex-*cabecillas* "arrived here already pardoned," refusing to engage in any sort of public act that would indicate their willingness to submit to communal norms. There were no local processes of rehabilitation, leaving many *comuneros* feeling impotent in the face of those they consider "the guiltiest," the "most bloodthirsty." For example, mama Aurelia in Accomarca recalled the day the soldiers made everyone gather in the plaza beneath the Peruvian flag.

"The soldiers brought them from the prison—brought those *terrucos* so they would talk. They brought them here and told us, 'Now you're going to live as a community. You're going to pardon each other and reconcile.

You're going to reconcile and live like one community.' Those people [*huk kuna*] are still here. If we say anything, they could come at night and slash our throats with a knife. They could make us disappear and no one would ever know. When I remember everything that's happened, my heart hurts. It rises from my stomach to my chest, and I can't breathe. It reaches my heart and it's as though it wants to come out of my mouth but it can't. My eyes roll back, my heart aches—I tremble when I remember. I have it here in my thoughts," placing her hand on her heart. "Not even pills help me. What am I going to do? Sometimes I see them and I greet them. But I lower my head because I want to spit in their faces. But what if they come at night? What am I going to do? I can't do a thing."[2]

The idea of "making the *terrucos* talk" and the insistence they arrived "already amnestied" refers to counterinsurgency efforts prior to the National Repentance Law.[3] The military "reintegrated" the Senderistas in part so they would serve as informants and kept them under surveillance during the *pax militar*. It is important to note what happens to tests of conscience when they are reduced to mere instruments for gathering information. What was happening in the 1980s in the south—and during the subsequent repentance law—did not provide for conciliatory processes at the local level. Rather, the ex-*cabecillas* arrived with impunity, refusing local initiatives that would encourage them to publicly ask for forgiveness and repay the community for the devastation they had inflicted.

The sense of impotence with regard to "the guiltiest" extends to the current communal authorities. Under military pressure during the 1980s and early 1990s, many of the most committed Senderistas left for the cities of Ica and Lima. It is during the last decade that they have returned to their communities, bringing new conflicts with them. For example, communal authorities in Vilcashuamán indicated that some 135 ex-*cabecillas* had returned by the early 2000s. What to do about these returnees remains a concern.[4]

I had the opportunity to talk with two authorities in a community in Vilcashuamán. They described how they had gone to Lima as a commission to talk with the ex-*cabecillas* who had expressed an interest in returning to their pueblo. As they lamented, "We tried to talk with them about reconciliation. We told them that if they were really going to come back, they needed to apologize in front of the community. They refused. They came here and we can't do a thing. It hurts a person. They killed our family members and we can't do anything."[5]

Current social conditions in these communities illustrate the limitations of imposed peace and top-down "reconciliation" as foundations for the reconstruction of social life. The level of methyl alcohol consumption throughout these provinces is alarming, and many insist they began to drink "so we were prepared every day for death." These fears continue, and they are not unfounded. When José Carlos and Leonor reviewed the Actas de Denuncias (Complaint Log) in Cayara, they found that 80 percent of the complaints brought before the local authorities concerned death threats among community members. As the governor told Leonor, "The people have become aggressive. For the last ten years, they threaten to kill each other." Although some complaints of this sort did exist prior to the 1980s, they were a small percentage of the total complaints registered. Death threats increased dramatically during the late 1980s, assuming the dubious title of first place in the complaint log in 2002. Both men and women were denounced for threatening to kill other villagers, who would then request *garantías personales* (personal guarantees) to protect their safety.

Of course, obtaining *garantías personales* is a long-standing practice. However, even if the practice has been around for a long time, the content of the complaints and corresponding guarantees has changed. It is precisely the climate of impunity in these pueblos that has provoked the desire for revenge, either through witchcraft or with one's own hands. In each community many people lament how the ex-*cabecillas* "walk around without ever saying they're sorry. They walk around as though they'd never killed people." This defiant position generates resentment on many levels, including the phenomenological.

Indeed, it was in a conversation with the *curandero* Mario Aquise that the impact of the "untouchables" on those around them became clear. His visit to Accomarca coincided with one of ours, and in between treating his long line of patients he found a few minutes to speak with us. Señor Aquise explained that he visited the communities in a rotating fashion, with particular attention to those heavily affected by the political violence. In Accomarca the most common affliction he treats is ulcers: "Everyone has them."

Why ulcers? Silence has been imposed and there are secrets that eat away at a person from the inside out. In Accomarca, our conversations were punctuated with elbow jabs. Frequently the speaker was interrupted and exhorted to "Shut up!" What does it mean to live shutting oneself up? What is it like, in the words of several women, to spend so many years swallowing one's rage? When the women complain of irritation of the heart, they convey the physical and mental costs of spending so many years with such rancor. So many years swallowing their rage, and so many ulcers. Living with the "untouchables" is to live on a daily basis with the corrosive effects of impunity.

The Beneficiaries

Compensatory justice is one facet of the concept of justice that operates in these communities. The idea of repairing the damage one has done is a fundamental aspect of people's legal consciousness, and it is the violation of this principle that gives impunity its lacerating edge. And, once again, we must consider not only victims and perpetrators but also beneficiaries when we contemplate postwar tensions and hatred. While at times the categories "perpetrator" and "beneficiary" may be conflated, that is not always the case. In some contexts the beneficiaries may have no blood on their hands or burden on their hearts. However, the rage they provoke was powerfully conveyed to us in Cayara.

It was an early morning in February and the streets were empty and silent. The houses were shut, their owners sleeping and recovering from the night before, or perhaps still celebrating Carnival behind closed doors. We passed one house and responded to a voice calling us over. The words were mumbled but we recognized a ruddy face poking out the door.

We made our way in, greeting the revelers and fighting off the nausea that the smell of strong alcohol can provoke in the early morning hours. We sat among the guests, occupying as little space as possible on the crowded benches lined up along the walls. A very drunk woman pulled on Edith's sweater and held out a large metal cup. "'Señorita, drink some *chicha*. This is how we drink for Carnival. We don't drink every day—don't think we're drunks. Here in this pueblo we've suffered so much," she slurred. "Those disgraceful soldiers and *compañeros* [Senderistas] razed our community. It's their fault our children are far away. Many of our children continue to suffer in foreign lands. They live with resentment because they lost their family members. Those spies continue to live here. They live tranquilly and better than we do! God still hasn't punished them for having turned in innocent people. Those *terrucos*, they have nice houses, animals—they're *apus* [gods]. And those of us who didn't participate [in Sendero] are poor. We lost our families." The woman began to cry and several other women pulled her back to where they were sitting, telling her, "Shut up. Don't talk." Another woman staggered to her feet and approached us: "Please—we're drunk. We can say anything when we're drunk. Please excuse us." We assured her she owed us no apology at all.

The *wasisapas, ovejasapas, los apus*—those with many homes, many sheep, living like gods. I have suggested we consider a political economy of forgiveness, recognizing that reparation is a central step in opening up the possibility of a coexistence that is not prisoner to a fratricidal past. The forms of social reparation practiced in the north—working on behalf of the community, serving in the *ronda campesina*, engaging in public rituals of confession and punishment—facilitate the rehabilitation of perpetrators. They are also a way of redistributing resources and diminishing the economic inequality that stoke hatred and rancor, two emotions that smolder within Hermelinda Baldeón Chuchón and María Gamboa in Accomarca.

In one conversation during the PTRC, Señora Hermelinda was adamant: "We won't have forgiveness. First the guilty would need to kneel and ask for forgiveness, and maybe then we could pardon them—before that, no. What sort of reconciliation could there be between the good and the bad, between those who lost everything and those who gained everything? They came out of this ahead. They benefited! There'll never be reconciliation while there's inequality between us. Those who ruined our pueblo have not even apologized! Nothing. They say the government pardoned them, that the Big Daddies pardoned them, and that's why the community can't do anything to them."

Later that same day, María expressed similar feelings: "These people who ruined the pueblo continue to live here. It doesn't matter to them if they apologize—they don't want to reconcile with us. And the people who ruined this pueblo receive aid! They have a better life. But those of us who've suffered? We don't receive any aid and we just keep suffering in our poverty. If the government is going to provide some aid, they should do it directly with the affected and then we might find some justice."

"And should the people who participated receive any aid?" I asked.

"Ha! Those shameless people [*sinvergüenzas*] shouldn't receive anything! Better yet, they should go somewhere else to live. We don't want them around because we don't know what their hearts are thinking. Maybe they continue with the same thoughts? It offends us that they're authorities and they're the ones who receive aid! They only split it up with their families, and poor people like us get nothing. Oh, they're doing fine, not like us who're screwed, with nothing. And with this, there's hatred, there's envy. With all of this—I ask you, could there be reconciliation or not?" María quickly answered her own question. "No, there can't and if the authorities try, what moral right do they have? With what face could they do that? Never, because they're the guilty ones. Never!"

The term *qochasapakuna*—the "guiltiest ones"—echoed throughout our conversations in Víctor Fajardo and Vilcashuamán. However, just as the term was a constant in daily life, so were the debates about exactly who "the guiltiest ones" might be.

The Guiltiest Ones

We turn now to the complicated issue of guilt, one of the dominant moral emotions in so many conversations. On the one hand people consider degrees of crime (*grados de delito*), and one category consists of "the guiltiest." But just who "the guiltiest ones" are is something I have learned to ask rather than to assume. My research with these communities provides numerous examples of just how complex the assignment of guilt can be in the face of prolonged, intimate violence.

At times it has been tempting to think in terms of a social psychology of the victors and the vanquished. For the majority of people in these former Shining Path strongholds, they lost the war. With the exception of those who continue to be "very ideologized," there is no glorious history to tell. Quite the opposite: many people lamented, "It's our fault the soldiers came here. What happened is our fault. *El pueblo tiene la culpa* [the pueblo is guilty]."

Without falling into a Manichean reading, one simply does not hear this discourse of guilt in the north. Rather, as we have seen, the communal histories in the heights of Huanta emphasize their heroism in defense of La Patria. Even if these histories have been manufactured ex post facto—there was, after all, a triumphant state—these histories both reflect and mold psychological profiles. Additionally, these histories have permitted villagers to achieve a rapprochement with the state and to benefit from a state presence that goes far beyond the installation of a military base. The public works and infrastructure have altered the landscape and, although poverty continues to be extreme, the distance between the state and these northern communities has been greatly reduced.

The war and its legacies are different in the south. These communities were considered "red zones" and, given the outcome of the armed conflict, this history still confers a certain stigma. Of course some sectors continue to justify the actions of Shining Path, arguing that the political violence was the result of the marginalization and poverty that the Peruvian state was, and is, incapable of resolving. But for many people, there is a sense of guilt for the destruction they associate with their ties to Sendero Luminoso. For this group, responsibility for the violence of both Shining Path *and* the soldiers lies on their own shoulders for having allowed Shining Path to *engañar* their pueblos with promises of revolutionary change.

But certainly not everyone feels that way. Clearly national political dynamics shape local conflicts, both while they are waged and in their subsequent narration. While at the national level the public face of Sendero is dominated by the jailed leadership and lower-ranking political prisoners—and a few high-profile *arrepentidos* who accept the movement's defeat—at the local level the trajectories of former militants are characterized by diversity. We saw some of that diversity in the last chapter: former militants who are now Evangélicos; others who repent for the violence of Shining Path while defending the group's founding principles; those who dare not return to their communities because they fear for their lives; and still others who have returned and continue to terrify their neighbors. Now let's consider another group: the proudly defiant who deny any guilt at all.

In Chapter 2 I described the day when a man from Hualla came knocking on the large front gate of the PTRC office in Ayacucho, requesting psychological treatment for his pueblo. That was not our only conversation with him. Edith happened to be in Hualla for Semana Santa one year, and Hernán had arrived from Ica to celebrate with this extended family. He saw her walking across the plaza and waved her over.

The plaza was full of children playing, while adolescents sat in gender-segregated groups on the benches that bordered the plaza. Edith was surprised that he chose such a public place to talk, but as we learned more about him over the years, his high profile made sense.

Edith asked if she could tape their conversation, and he nodded. "I'm going to tell you what happened here." As he would in other conversations, Hernán readily admitted he was an "indirect participant" in Shining Path but denied participating in the killing of anyone.

"Here, the mayor was Juan Inca, and there was another authority, Demetrio Ipurre. They were people who had a bit more business than everyone else. The terrorists killed them."

"Why?"

"*Bueno*, I think it was revenge. They were really abusive. They were authorities, and they didn't respect anyone or anything. They kept appropriating land from the community, from their neighbors. If they saw someone was weak, they immediately bought their land at the price they wanted. They paid people next to nothing for their land. Both of them kept committing abuses against the community, against the little people [*la gente humilde*]. That's why the Senderistas killed them."

What was striking was Hernán's utter indifference regarding eavesdropping. He spoke loudly, forcefully, and—indeed—defiantly.

"Was that the first time they killed someone?"

He thought for a moment. "Yeah, that was the beginning."

"Was it a *juicio popular*?"

"Exactly. The Senderistas asked people, 'Should this miserable person die or not?' Everyone yelled, 'Yes! Kill him!' Maybe because he'd been so abusive and they couldn't stand it anymore. Like I said, he was the mayor. After they killed Juan Inca, people started dividing up everything he had in his store. The Senderistas dragged out everything—his store was left empty."

Children walked by looking; Hernán neither stopped nor lowered his voice. When Edith expressed her surprise, Hernán insisted it was better the young people learn about the armed conflict.

"How did Sendero begin here?"

"They came one day when I was just little. It was 1980. They were students from Hualla who were studying in Huamanga. They came with their flags, with the hammer and sickle. But I didn't really know what was going on because in the plaza they were yelling, 'Viva! Viva!' and writing on the buildings. We didn't even realize, but it had started. That was the beginning."

"After they killed Juan Inca, did the Huallinos support Sendero?"

"Yeah, after that they started to give them their support. That's because they formed *escuelas populares*, called meetings."

"What were the meetings like?"

"They had the books of Sendero, Mao, Lenin, Marxism, all of that. Almost every day in the schools, the teachers, the students—I mean, there was no more normal education. They destroyed it. It was education in Sendero. Every day there were classes and they taught us what Sendero was, why we needed to start the revolution, what was right and what wasn't, why the authorities were abusive and exploiting the *gente humilde*. They explained why the rich people were against the struggle. Only with armed struggle, only if we were willing to give our lives, would we someday have communism. Equality for everyone. No more rich. We weren't going to have to ask for favors from the president, not from anyone anymore. Everyone would earn enough with their work, there would be total equality. They were preparing us. Every day we had to run during physical education. We would leave the stadium and run through the mountains. When we'd get back, the teacher was already waiting for us and we had to form the army."

"Why do you think Sendero began?"

"*Bueno*, that's something we need to analyze," visibly warming up to the question. "The oppressed pueblos, people living as slaves—even worse in remote pueblos, like in parts of Ayacucho and Huancavelica where the government has never worried about us. We were forgotten regions [*zonas olvidadas*]. Whatever sort of project the authorities developed and took to the [government] offices were ignored. They ignored that we even existed. What was there for us? For people in the sierra, there was nothing. So people opted for a communist Peru, hoping things would change. Equality would arrive for everyone—that's what you heard. But that was without knowing they [Sendero] were going to have confrontations with the same pueblo, with the very people who were supposedly their cause."

Hernán fell silent for a while before a large smile appeared. "I think that in the long run, and seeing what our reality is—well, maybe if those men hadn't started an armed struggle, I think the authorities would never have fixed their eyes on places like this. That's what I say."

"So you're saying the struggle was necessary?"

"Of course it was necessary. Only that way did the authorities recognize the existence of these indigenous groups, of forgotten sectors. I think that without the violence, they wouldn't have been recognized or remembered. In exchange for the massacres, for the deaths, we have all of this," gesturing around the plaza. "Hualla has changed. We have basic necessities like electricity, water, sewers, parabolic antennas, public telephone, communications radio. I think it's thanks to those men who died for a real cause, and now their children can thank them for all of this. That's how I think."

As Hernán makes clear—and as other former militants also argued—they may have lost the war but they won some lesser battles. The history they tell is not that of the vanquished, the tricked, or the ignorant. Rather, they saw (and continue to see) themselves as part of a heroic effort to change rampant social inequality: their versions of history remain part of the counter-memories at work in Peru. Guilt is not an emotion they shoulder themselves but one that they place on the government and the armed agents of the state. Anasto, whom we met in the last chapter, is adamant that it is "the owners of Peru" who are to blame for what happened: "These were abandoned pueblos, forgotten zones—the state marginalized these communities for centuries." From this perspective, it is the "owners of Peru" who are the *qochasapakuna* and thus the ones who should be held accountable for the devastation of the internal armed conflict.

One final example to underscore the complexity of determining whom people hold responsible for their greatest losses and most abiding pain. A conversation with mama Benedicta turned my assumptions upside down and taught me that the issue of guilt is always a question to pose rather than an answer to assume—even in what might seem to be the most obvious of cases. This conversation has been seared into my memory since the day Edith and I spent with Benedicta, sitting in her rustic hut that overlooks Lloqllepampa. She described what had happened on August 14, 1985, the day of the massacre.

When the soldiers made everyone gather in the field, they had the women and girls line up separately from the men. One by one the soldiers then dragged the women off to the side to rape them. Benedicta was in line "waiting her turn" when she decided to run for it. She took off toward the mountains, struggling for air, her heart pounding as the bullets flew by. As she reached the cover of some scraggly bushes, she realized her two little children were running as fast as they could behind her. She was terrified they might accidentally be shot and told them, "*Mami, papi,* you go back down to the field and hide in one of the houses. You hide there and wait until I come for you. You'll be safe there. Wait for me." Benedicta continued her escape into the hills.

Her young children hid in one of the two houses that bordered the field; they were among the sixty-two people locked in the dwellings, machine-gunned, bombed, and burned into an unrecognizable mass of charred teeth and bones. Benedicta's mother also died that day, out in the field when she came to see what in the world was happening in Lloqllepampa. Her mother's remains were recognizable, and Benedicta had insisted on burying her mother separately from the mass grave in which the traces of the others were interred.

After the massacre, Benedicta had her husband, César, build her a little wooden lean-to alongside the field. I was surprised by this, thinking of all the painful memories that had sedimented in the earth around her. However, Benedicta explained why she had him build the hut. "I come here each day and sit, and I look out at the field. I can *see* my children. I can *still* hear my children's laughter. *This is my penance.*"

It took some time to absorb what she had said. I gently asked what she thought should happen to the soldiers who did those horrible things.

"Oh," she replied softly, "those poor little soldiers."

This was definitely not the reply I expected from someone who had lost three loved ones that day.

"Some of them talked to me," she explained. "They said, '*Tía*, this is happening all over. So many people are suffering—it's not just you, *tía*.'" Thus some of those "poor little soldiers" had comforted her, assuring her she was not the only one.

"What did they say about what happened here—about what the soldiers did?"

"They told me they had orders. They told me they had to obey, even if they did it with their eyes closed. '*Tía*, we have to obey orders or they shoot us, too.'"

I nodded, and decided to ask about the officer who oversaw the massacre. "Mama Benedicta, what about Telmo Hurtado? What would you do with him?"

Suddenly, she sat up straight, clenched her jaw, veins bulging in her neck, her body tense with rage. "If I saw that Telmo, I would grab him and slap his face! Then I'd piss in his mouth." Benedicta's voice grew louder as the revenge she had dreamed of played out before us. She thrust her arms into the air. "Then I would grab a rock and smash his head," repeatedly inflicting the imaginary blows. Next her right arm went up, elbow crooked and hand tightly clenched. "Then I'd grab a knife and stab him over and over again." Quick pause for another change of weaponry. "Then I'd kill him with machete blows, with bullets, with bombs—and then I would burn him like he did our family members. And then, maybe then, my soul would be calm."

Her voice softened back into sadness. "My soul and the souls of my mama and my two little children would be in peace. Now they keep walking from one place to the other, and the investigation continues. That's why their souls are walking, and until we have justice their souls won't be in peace."

Mama Benedicta paused, looking out again at the field. "After killing that damned Telmo, I could go anywhere, even to prison, even if they killed me, because now I don't have my younger children alive. Since they robbed me of my happiness when they killed my children, I don't want anything else. There's not much time before my suffering ends. When I die, I'll be tranquil and beside my children."

Benedicta illustrates how impunity wounds and outrages the person who lives with constant injustice. If indeed state policies contributed to making the ex-*cabecillas* "untouchables," the military officials are even further beyond the reach of communal justice. We must differentiate between vertical and horizontal reconciliation. In these communities, there exists the possibility of working on reconciliation, even if it is a lengthy process. In contrast, the state should assume a leadership role in terms of vertical reconciliation between the population and members of the armed forces who, for reasons of power, have remained unpunished. Justice for the massacre in Lloqllepampa remains one of the Peruvian government's glaring failures, and the possibility that anything will be done during President Garcia's administration is highly unlikely: after all, he is both the present and past president (1985–90) of the country.

But there is another reason this conversation with Benedicta has stayed with me: women and revenge. In both the highlands of Huanta and the communities to the south, all of the communal authorities were men. Communal justice requires personal sacrifice, and that sacrifice is unevenly distributed among the members of these pueblos.

A Thirst for Revenge

One of our visits to Accomarca in 2005 coincided with the election of communal authorities. We learned that Edilberto—one of the Morales brothers, described by some as the "most bloodthirsty" of the five—was running for office. Elizabet, a young woman whose father was kidnaped and disappeared by the Senderistas, took us aside to express her disgust. When Edilberto announced his candidacy, she was vehement: "He does not have the morals to be an authority! He wasn't just a Senderista—he was one of the leaders!"

Elizabet had the courage to stand up during the assembly and confront him. "'And he wants to be *gobernador*? That man who killed my father?' So I asked him how he thought a terrorist could be an authority! I said it right to his face. He stared back, while other people started to support me. And *huk kuna* [those people] want to be authorities now—*tiene cara todavia*![6] People here know very well that he killed their family members. People here say he should pay for what he's done. Some people say he should work for the pueblo, but I don't agree. I want to see him suffer. They all need to suffer like we did. Let them suffer and see their families suffer, and see how they like it."

Twenty-two-year-old Elizabet is already the mother of four and runs a small store in town. She had dreamed of being a "professional," but the disappearance of her father also marked the disappearance of her educational possibilities. The theme of revenge hovered over all of our conversations with her.

"What I most want is revenge. I could never accept a reconciliation with those people. Nothing can replace those years of pain."

"So you could never forgive the people who did this?"

"No. I look at them with rage. I'm capable of getting revenge. I'm capable of doing to them what they did to my father. I keep telling myself that someday I'll get revenge. Some of them are still here. Some are authorities, others just *comuneros*. I want revenge—so do my [female] cousins. They did the same thing to my cousin's father. They disappeared him along with mine. Because we aren't men, we'd have to end up being some sort of authority to be able to get our revenge. But we talk about getting revenge. Even if it's just talking, we talk about it. I know I'm capable of it! Those men who killed him—they say they came back with the *cabecillas*, carrying my papa's clothing. They said, 'We already killed that dog.' That's why my mama drinks. She just gets crazy. She's capable of throwing herself in the river, taking poison. She remembers my father and cries. In their *conciencias*, they know they killed him, but they don't say anything. The people responsible—they're men. Three of them are here." She named the three, and told us the rest are in Lima.

"One of them is Edilberto. The authorities haven't done anything! They say they're afraid, that those people might try to involve *them* in all of this. They say it's better for us to keep quiet, but I don't want to forget! With my rage, I'm capable of just about anything. When they drink, when people meet up with them, they say, 'You're an assassin, *terruco*. Get out of here.' Those people don't say anything back. It was even worse before. They say people are forgetting—what are we going to say? The *responsables* in Lima? I wish I had poison in my eye! I'd look at them and the poison would jump right out at them! They come here [from Lima] all friendly, saying, 'Cousin, cousin.' They have lots of family here. Those people who killed my papa—they say the leader is in Lima. His name is Alfredo Bendezu—they called him the Huambalpino. If someone could find him and punish him, then maybe we could be a bit calmer knowing he suffered like we did."

Elizabet then remembered her aunt who was nine months pregnant when the Senderistas killed her. Her husband was an authority in Accomarca, and the *mandos* had been threatening him. When they went to look for him, they found only his wife at home.

"They tied her feet and hands and broke her head open with a hatchet. Now her two sons are *licenciados* [former soldiers]. Well, two years ago they were drinking in a store and Edilberto came by. They carried him up to the base, and said, 'You killed our mother. Just the same way you killed her, now we're going to kill you.' Edilberto started begging, crying. He kept asking them to forgive him. 'I'm sorry, forgive me. It wasn't just me, several of us killed her.' I don't know what else he said, but they didn't kill him. I told my cousins, 'You're cowards. If I were a man, I'd kill him.' But those two told me, 'Cousin, we just couldn't kill him.' So I told them what cowards they were," she repeated in disgust.

There were two groups that most consistently expressed a desire for revenge: women and adolescent boys. In thinking about their motives, it occurs to me that both groups are marginal to the working of power and decision making in their communities. For the women, they can attempt to marshal public opinion to their cause, but ultimately it is adult men who administer justice in these pueblos. For the adolescent boys, they are frequently raised listening to family histories that include details about which of the adults played a role in their parent's murder. The transmission of memories can serve a variety of ends. While memory as a deterrent is part of the human rights logic, memories can be equally vital to transmitting a thirst for revenge. The following conversation offers insight into the stories parents tell and the young people who grow up listening to family histories infused with historical grievances and unsettled accounts.

Nancy is a young single mother in Accomarca. She never volunteered any information about what happened to her husband and it seemed rude to ask. She had strong feelings about *huk kuna*.

"I wish those people who always participated in Sendero would go somewhere else. They shouldn't live here. What if it appears again? Maybe it could all start up again because so many of them are still here. It's so difficult to forgive them. They killed people right here in the plaza, hanging them as though they were dogs. If I were an authority I'd kick them out because they aren't going to forget the ways they had. When the truth commission came, those people went to their *chacras*. They were afraid someone would say their name because the family of the victims had told them, 'I'm going to say you killed.' I don't think they really said anything, but *huk kuna* went to their *chacras* because they were afraid someone would talk. But they aren't really that fearful. Oh no, some of them, they're still *machos!*"

"During assemblies, when the authorities are present, do you ask them to tell those people to leave?"

She shook her head. "We don't say anything, and the authorities don't say anything either. I'm sure it's because they're afraid. During those times, people were terrified, they thought *huk kuna* were going to kill them. They haven't asked the authorities to pardon them, but people here won't accept them even if they do ask for forgiveness. Some of them have been authorities here, but it's only because they still have people who were on their side. We complain, but they always win. We can't do anything. So we live *tranquilo*, but with fear. To the *responsables*, the authorities don't say anything. You know, they hanged my uncle right there in the plaza. Well, two years ago during a fiesta, my aunt was drinking when she saw the man who killed him. She grabbed the guy and started insulting him. That man told her to shut up and bought her some *trago*. So my aunt shut up and didn't say anything. When they drink, they remember. They also transmit all of this to their children. They tell their kids, 'That family are all *terrucos*.' I've heard my own aunt say that to her kids. And the children say that when they grow up 'I'm going to kill them. Someday I'm also gonna get revenge, killing them like they killed my father.' What we want is for *huk kuna* to go somewhere else because they aren't going to forget their old ways."

"If you could kick them out, would life be tranquil here?"

"Yes, but they won't want to leave. Besides, they could come back at night and kill us to get even."

When presenting this research at conferences, I am frequently asked about the issue of revenge. Once I have mentioned the death threats, the menacing notes, and the proximity of the perpetrators and the victims, people want to know how much lethal violence is currently occurring in these communities.

Aside from witchcraft, virtually none. In all the years I have been working with these communities, I did not hear of anyone carrying out a revenge killing. There have been isolated homicides in certain communities located along present-day "drug corridors." There are different stories in play about the motives behind those few homicides, but settling old accounts is not one of them. People have been remarkably effective in staying the hand of vengeance. How have they done it? How do people live with the perpetrators among them?

The Mask and the Mirror

> Human beings, it seems, cannot bear too much reality—at least not all at once. Domestic social life often requires the drawing of discreet veils over difficulties. This may be because there is no obvious solution; the burden of history is sometimes too big and heavy and complex to manage.
> —Nigel Biggar, *Burying the Past*

In the great majority of our conversations, and in the testimonies compiled by the PTRC in Ayacucho, people insist the perpetrators were masked. Certainly there were masked armed actors during the internal armed conflict; however, more than the physical presence of these masked actors, what is intriguing is the reiterative image of "the masked ones" (*mascarayuqkuna*). What lies behind the masks that haunt these testimonies, particularly in communities in which the *mascarayuqkuna* were frequently family members and neighbors?

One component of this research involved a genealogy of moralities. During ambiguous moral periods, many aspects of daily life are in flux, including one's own identity. People became "two-faced," trying to manage the competing demands of the military and of Sendero, as well as their own shifting loyalties. Still others turned to hiding their faces completely: the masked ones wore black woolen masks that left only their eyes and lips exposed.

In his work on masks, David Napier suggests that masks are almost invariably related to transition and that masking is a means of transgressing boundaries because it provides an avenue for manipulating certain paradoxes.[7] In various conversations with men I was told, "You change when you put on a mask"—that "I'm another person when I have a mask on." The insistence on masking and changing one's identity is one component of a social psychology of both the violence and its dismantling. This process of "doubling"—of putting on a mask and creating a *shadow self*—functions in two directions.[8] It permits the aggressor to distance himself from his own actions, delegating said actions to his or her double, and it permits the rest of the community to maintain a certain level of denial with respect to the perpetrators among them—to not *encararse* (face up) to the perpetrators, a theme powerfully conveyed by don Feliciano Huamán.

We had just returned from Tiquihua and were interested in locating a few Tiqueños who had left during the violence to settle in the city. Many migrants had decided to stay in the city and start new lives, some because their children were accustomed to city life and others because they feared returning to their pueblos. There were still others who visited each year during fiestas or to check up on family members who had stayed behind to watch the land or livestock.

Edith and I headed for the outskirts of Huamanga, following the map someone had sketched on a piece of paper so that we could find their relative's house. We walked about utterly lost. It was almost impossible to find people in the barrios, a space not so different from the *campo* with children pasturing goats and sheep alongside their houses.

On one futile search we met up with an acquaintance and explained what we were doing. She wanted to help. "I'm from Canaria [near Tiquihua]. I was born there. It's been a long time since I've been back. I hardly remember anything because I was so little when we left, but my uncle could tell you about it. He's sick because of the violence. It affected him so much that for years he was in bed. He lives on pills and tranquilizers. He never wanted to talk with anyone about his problem. I'm going to see if he might let you visit, but I can't promise you anything."

Fortunately her uncle agreed to our visit, and it was late December 2003 when we headed toward his house. A handwritten sign to the side of the doorway said "Injections given here." Evidently don Feliciano was still working as a health technician.

We knocked on the aluminum siding that served as a door. A slender elderly man peered out. "Good morning. Are you Señor Feliciano Huamán?"

"Yes. You've come to talk to me, no?"

We nodded, and he swung the door open to let us pass. He could barely walk. He dragged his feet behind him and his hands were trembling uncontrollably. We followed him into the kitchen, and he gestured toward chairs around the table. He sat across from us, offering us a glass of *chicha*.

Señor Feliciano Huamán was sixty-nine years old and lived in Huamanga, returning to Tiquihua infrequently to check up on his land. Both his wife and children had tried to convince him not to keep going back, and they refused to accompany him when he did so. The motives behind their refusal became clearer when don Feliciano and his wife told us about how the war years had changed their lives.

Edith and I took out our notebooks and began to set up the tape recorder when he slurred to us, "Wait, don't turn the recorder on yet. Let's wait a few minutes until this passes. I took my pills half an hour ago—they're starting to calm me. Look, my mouth doesn't work, my hands tremble, my feet, too. They say it's Parkinson's." He leaned over and began rubbing his hands together, trying to control their movements. "I have to take tranquilizers so I don't get like this." He sat back, and several minutes passed before his hands were still. "Now we can start."

"When did you start to have Parkinson's?" I asked.

"Ever since the Senderistas harmed me."

"What happened? Can you tell us about it, don Feliciano?"

"*Bueno*, the Senderistas arrived on August 4, 1982, at 12:30. Four masked people entered my house, pointing a machine gun at me. I had a dog, Rintintin. He lunged at them and they almost killed him. I held him back, thinking they were good people. But one of them pulled a machine gun out from under his poncho and yelled at me: 'Shut up, shit. Fuck your mother, damn it!' Don Feliciano shook his head. "He mentioned my mother that way. So I asked him, 'What's wrong, friend? I haven't offended you—I don't know you. Why are you talking like that about my mother?' 'Shut up, damn it!' he shouted at me. They tied my hands behind my back. Kicking me, they dragged me out the door to the church. My wife wasn't there. She'd gone to Huamanga to pay the rent on our house. I was alone with my three little children, and they were crying. They hit them and locked them in the kitchen. Well, they had me from one until six in the afternoon. I prayed fifty Our Fathers. I was there to die. I didn't even remember I was a person. At six o'clock they came for me, for a *juicio popular*. They asked me, 'All right—talk, damn it!' So I asked, 'What am I going to say? I don't know anything,' I said. 'Why are you doing this to me? I haven't harmed anyone. Oh, I must have some enemy—let him say it to my face. I haven't robbed, I haven't done anything. I've helped people in this community. Ask them.' But there people were, looting my store. My wife had everything, stacked in large quantities. Rice, sugar, noodles. Dammit—they took everything, even our clothes. There were no blankets left either. So at six in the afternoon they made me speak to the pueblo. 'Talk, dammit, talk!' they shouted."

And then, as he would at various points during our conversation, don Feliciano suddenly shifted into the present tense. "But I can't talk. I have no saliva. They're putting a red rag in my mouth. . . ." Don Feliciano did not move for several minutes. The table began to shake, his trembling hands rocking it and the water glasses. He was staring intently toward a corner of the room.

After several minutes he turned back toward us. "So they put a rag in your mouth?"

Don Feliciano looked at us intently and replied, "Everything. They made me open my mouth and put a pistol in it. I almost bit his hand, but I controlled myself. I had no saliva, dry already. . . . People knew me—there was a teacher there from Canaria. She spoke well. 'Why are you harming this man? He's a good person, he's cured me for free. Why are you doing this?' One of them said, 'Oh, damn it! You're his *comadre*!' It was just because I was an employee. They said, 'Pimp of the government, that's what these are. Have to kill all of them.'"

Don Feliciano took a deep breath "They gave me a *juicio popular*. Everyone was there. They didn't talk. Some of them were drinking beer—I had about forty cases. The store was full."

"Then they let me go and took me back to my house. 'I'm going to turn you over to your kids, you're saved. You have to fight with us, you have to take care of the flag.' They raised the hammer and sickle in the tower. 'You're going to take care of this. Make sure no one touches it. If someone does, you're going to tell me.' I said to him, 'But I won't be here, I'm leaving. You've taken everything I have. My medicines—how will I settle my accounts?' He said, 'Tell your boss the Senderistas took everything and nothing will happen to you. If they say anything, tell me.' They gave me fifteen days to take care of the flag. Well, my wife arrived: 'Enough. Let's get out of here.' So I came to Huancapi. That night they got an ambulance ready and brought me to Huamanga. They wanted my statement, but I didn't tell them anything. If I'd talked, they would've killed my wife and children for revenge. That's why I didn't talk. The *comandante* said, 'Surely you know where they're from.'"

Don Feliciano stopped talking. His whole body trembled, and he was biting his lips to hold back his tears. He began repeating, "I can't talk, I can't remember more. I've forgotten." A few minutes passed before Don Feliciano wiped his mouth. "I'm going to keep talking. It's already passed. For a few seconds I stopped existing. I lost my sight and died. Like at night when you close your eyes and you die in your dreams. At times it's like that, when I remember. But I'm a new man now. Those are the things they did to me. I'd prayed fifty Our Fathers and a creed to die. I prayed since one o'clock until six in the afternoon."

"Until late in the afternoon?"

He nodded. "They're giving me a *juicio popular*. What was I going to do?"

"And then what happened?"

"They wanted to kill me. They wanted to crucify me. But because I have El Señor here," showing us his crucifix, "that's why they couldn't. It's blessed and they couldn't kill me. Later I went to my house and my children were there. They were in the kitchen. The Senderistas said to my son, 'We're giving you back your father alive.' That's when they gave me the order to take care of the flag or they would kill me."

"Why did they do this to you, don Feliciano?"

"Because I was a state employee," he explained.

"Just because you worked for the state?"

He nodded. "I'm a sergeant with the air force. So they wanted me to teach people how to use weapons, but I refused."

"Oh, I see. I wonder, where were they from?"

"They were from Hualla, from other pueblos. They all came to kill me."

His wife suddenly spoke up. "They ran *escuelas populares* in Hualla, Tiquihua, Cayara. The people had been *concientizada* with all of that. But us, we didn't know anything. People came for us—we didn't know them."

"But lots of people participated, no? Like in Accomarca, Hualla?"

"Oh, lots of them! Everybody. Yes, it must have been everyone. Everyone was afraid. Only I was against them." Don Feliciano began to describe his store and the merchandise he had. "That's where the *envidia* started. They swept my store clean. They didn't even leave anything to eat."

Edith gently pursued a theme of great interest to us. "Don Feliciano, who did this? Was it people from Tiquihua, or did they come from somewhere else?"

"People came to incite them. People kept joining, *pues*," he explained.

"Of course," she nodded.

He returned again to the theme. "They were all from Tiquihua. Everyone is coming."

"But people from Tiquihua—well, I imagine they knew you?" I asked, hesitantly.

"Yes," he replied slowly.

"Do you know who they were? And those who came. . . . Who put the rag in your mouth, don Feliciano?"

"The Senderistas were masked. I don't know who they were."

"They were masked?"

Don Feliciano stared at the wall for several minutes before answering. "*I can't see their faces. Well, more or less. I imagined who they were. Their faces are covered with masks.* Some have guns, grenades—they have everything. That's how it is."

"And they're all masked?"

"*The ones who took my statement, all of those, they're masked. The ones I don't know—they don't wear masks.*"

There was a pause before don Feliciano began to speak again. "They did these things to me in Tiquihua. I haven't been back since."

"You've never been back?"

"As an employee I never went back. As a *vecino* [neighbor] of the pueblo, yes. I went just recently, after all those years."

"And how did people act?"

"All the people who knew me came to visit. 'Don Feliciano, how are you?' But the people who harmed me—*no me dan la cara*.[9] When I approached, they left immediately. They went pale, they're afraid of me. Back then, they thought I was going to denounce them. They thought I was going to put them in jail, but I didn't. Oh God, I know so many of them, about thirty authors [*autores*]."

"Did you note their names?"

"Every single one. They're alive now. Killing their own people, they killed."

"Don Feliciano, for you, what would justice be after everything that happened?"

"Among human beings, it seems there is no justice. There isn't. Only God makes justice."

"So you've left it to God?"

He shrugged. "I only ask. I'm already old. The authorities earn money with lies—they borrow, they bribe. There's no justice."

We nodded, familiar with hearing people's stories of frustration with the legal system. "And for you, what would be reconciliation with them?"

"Oh, well that's good. Forgiving their sins. Making friendship, giving them my hand. If I'm going to hate them, what good is that for me? Hating would be worse—I look for friendship. If I were to denounce them, sooner or later their family would seek revenge. That's why I say that Jesus Christ will work justice."

"And with this do you feel calm now, or do you remember sometimes?"

"Sometimes I remember. The *pensamientos* come to my head and I cry. . . . "

Feliciano's wife finished his sentence. "Yes, he gets angry, outraged, desperate," her voice rising with each adjective. "Bothered. Sometimes he curses people. He gets like that, and then after a few hours he calms down. I'm the same way. I see those people and just the sight of them alters my blood. I have to control myself and leave so I don't . . . " Her voice trailed off. "In confession the priest keeps telling me, 'You always have to forgive.' But I don't know. When I see them or remember, I feel sulfur flow through my veins. I have to control myself—it's better I just leave."

Facing Up

> If people here began to face up to everything they've done, we'd have even more problems. There would be no way to live.
> —Cayara, 2003

Our conversation with don Feliciano touches upon a variety of key themes, among them the "masked ones" who were not anonymous at all. Although he has a list of thirty "authors," don Feliciano has never said anything for fear of retaliation against him or his family. He lives trying to manage the images that torment him, erasing the faces, insisting on the masks: "I can't see their faces. Well, more or less. I imagined who they were. Their faces are covered with masks." Evidently it is a bit easier to live with what he knows if he does not have to see the faces of his tormenters in his mind's eye. Anonymity, even when artificial, permits some distance between a fratricidal past and a haunted present and provides one way of managing painful proximity.

We have discussed the processes of exteriorization that operate in these pueblos, at the individual level with the *males* (afflictions) that "grab" the person, as well as at the community level and the insistence that the "violence arrived here." Part of reconciliation is processing what people have done and *interiorizing who Sendero was*. Many people live seeing others they consider the *qochasapakuna* on a daily basis and these encounters are painful. The masks keep covered a constant source of rancor: the faces of the perpetrators. There is a process of revelation, of removing the masks little by little so that some people may interiorize the acts they committed, while others try to tolerate the people with whom they live. The insistence on "the masked ones" may provide a form of "plausible deniability" that has permitted people to process a bit more slowly the tensions between them. Slowly they are removing the masks, assimilating what they have done "between brothers." There is a liminal space between remembering and forgetting, and not putting a face to one's grief or loss may be a temporal strategy that curbs retributive emotions.

In their insightful trilogy, Veena Das and Arthur Kleinman have contemplated "how people engage in the tasks of daily living, reinhabiting worlds in full recognition that perpetrators, victims and witnesses come from the same social space."[10] Perhaps strategies that permit people to delay that full recognition—that permit people to mask the unbearable truth of intimate, lethal violence—are key to staying the hand of vengeance.

Recall how much guilt and shame contoured conversations in the south—guilt and shame ascribed, as well as assumed. The mask works in both directions. For example, in Cayara people spoke at length about the *soplón* (spy, traitor) who "sold his own brothers" and still lives in the community. As one man insisted, "No one says anything to him because they're afraid that he might bring the soldiers again and kill them all. That's why they don't say anything. We were afraid of our own brothers—we weren't afraid anymore of the witches, the condemned. We were terrified of our neighbors. *Everyone here muddied themselves with that situation, and now no one wants to recognize himself because of shame*." Recuperating shame implies *facing* another human being and being seen by him or her.[11] The following conversation, framed by local moral idioms, illustrates the centrality of faces and facelessness in people's efforts to remoralize their social worlds.

José Carlos and I were headed to the cemetery in Hualla when we met up with Feliciana Ipurre, doubled over beneath a heavy load of cornstalks. José Carlos offered to carry the load for her, but she was distrusting at first and rebuffed his offer. However, as we fell in beside her the heavy bundle on her back became more persuasive than words, and finally her deeply creased face folded into a smile. "Ah, *papacha*, which of the souls has sent you?"

We walked in silence for a few minutes, and her eyes kept darting back and forth. As we rounded the corner, an elderly woman reeking of *trago* came stumbling down the path. Feliciana shook her head disapprovingly and murmured a few words beneath her breath.

"Did people drink like this before the *wañuy tiempo*?" I wondered.

"*Manam*! Not a single woman drank. We learned to drink during that *mal tiempo*—we all started to drink as we waited for death. It was only with *trago* that we could sleep. We lived in fear. As soon as the sun began to set, we escaped to the caves. Everything was death here. There were dead people everywhere and we couldn't gather them up—they wouldn't let us. The dogs and the pigs ate our dead. *No one could see each other face-to-face. Was it out of shame or fear, but we all ran without seeing anyone. We lived without seeing anyone—we lived without seeing faces.* We couldn't talk with each other, as though we all had been grabbed by the *mal de rabia* [rage]."

We circled back around, arriving at mama Feliciana's house. She grabbed José Carlos's arm: "What I've told you—don't tell anyone because something could happen to us. We live with fear because those filthy Senderistas still live with us. I think this pueblo is blind. They've never punished them—they should cry in front of us like we cried. Now it's their turn! It's their turn to cry, to learn to suffer like we have. Then we'd be better. How are we going to live well with them if they don't apologize? We'll always be bad, fighting, insulting each other. That's not the way to live well."

The insistence on "facelessness" in doña Feliciana's description of the war years is striking. Her lament was coupled by those of others, who insisted, "We want authorities with faces now, not like it was before. *We want faces again*." What does the erasure of the human face mean? I believe that talk about masks, faces, and facelessness is talk about morality and immorality and that there is a phenomenology of justice and injustice in these pueblos.

The work of Emmanuel Levinas has been helpful in understanding the complexity of postwar social life. In his philosophy of ethics, Levinas insists upon the primacy of the face of the other as the basis for any sort of ethical system. He argues that justice responds to a call: "The absolute that upholds justice is the absolute of the interlocutor. Its mode of being and of making its presence known consists in turning its face toward me, in being a face."[12] The human face is thus the condition of possibility for ethics.[13] Levinasian ethics is grounded in an embodied exposure to the other, and an ethical relation is one in which we *face* the other person.

In the abundant literature on honor and shame, the concept of "face" is also central and is seen in part as a regulator of human interactions. In his work on war and apologies, Barry O'Neill writes, "Face involves the group's common belief about how much deference will be given to someone, especially in interactions that are face-to-face and publicly known. It sets behavior toward the individual by giving each group member expectations about how others will behave and what the individual will accept."[14] He also suggests that face is involved in making a credible commitment and that apologies grant the other person face, and thus the promise of better treatment in the future.[15] It is important to note that apologies work in two directions: they grant face (dignity) to the other and allow perpetrators to regain face (moral standing and accountability) vis-à-vis those they have wronged. An apology engages the interlocutors in a moral discourse, and calls for apology are conspicuous in "ongoing moral projects."[16]

These ideas resonate with what doña Feliciana questioned: How to live with people who refuse to recognize the harm they have done and the legitimate demands of those they have wronged? How to live with the "guiltiest ones" who have never apologized—in fact, who live "with the heads held high as though they had never killed people"? At this point, surely we can imagine how that must feel.

Apologies and Other Moral Projects

The truck we were riding in had just arrived in Huancapi, the capital of the province of Víctor Fajardo, and the driver announced there would be a brief rest so that passengers could have breakfast. The park was full of people we already knew from our previous visits, including several teachers from Tiquihua, Vladimiro among them. We invited him to join us for breakfast, and the winding conversation led us around to apologies. This surprised us because in Tiquihua he had not wanted to talk about much of anything.

"Do you remember how you asked me about apologies, reconciliation?" he said. "Well, this idea of apologizing, of pardoning—there was something like that in Tiquihua. In a communal meeting an ex-Senderista was participating in decisions and the majority rejected him. They insulted him, calling him '*terruco*,' 'evil'—telling him, 'You assassinated the pueblo.' But his reaction wasn't what we expected. He didn't try to shut up the people who were insulting him. He just bowed his head and very humbly apologized."

Vladimiro sat back, still surprised by what he had seen. "He asked people to forgive him because no one can live with a bad conscience. 'We've all made mistakes. Why did we act like that? Was it the water we drank or maybe the blood that flows in our body? Maybe that's what made us so bad, such demons. But now I'm apologizing in order to live tranquilly with myself and my family.' When he finished talking, he started to cry, but some women kept on insulting him and saying they could never pardon him. They said they would never forget everything that happened if he was living with them because his presence made them remember too much suffering. That was in 2000, when that guy had just come back from Lima. I tell you, that guy was macho to apologize because people were going to react. But the authorities calmed them down, saying that they shouldn't keep on resenting him in their hearts. They kept saying we should learn to forgive each other because all of our lives we're going to be here and we shouldn't keep on hating—living with envy, rancor. They told people, 'At least he's not like the others who live in the pueblo without saying a thing, as though nothing ever happened.'"

The desire for justice has led some people to demand the ex-*cabecillas* apologize for what they have done. Why are apologies so powerful? Philippe Defarges has argued, "Only the losers repent, those who see that history is not on their side."[17] If indeed repentance is a gesture of the vanquished, then the refusal to repent or to apologize has various implications. I have been told the ex-*cabecillas* continue to be very *idolizados*, referring to their continued embrace of Sendero's revolutionary ideology.

Campesinos are distinguishing between military and moral defeat. Sendero no longer represents a credible threat to the Peruvian state; however, this reality does not reflect local experience. Without local-level juridico-religious rituals designed to administer both retributive and restorative justice, these *campesinos* have not had the symbolic "departure from violence" that could frame the atrocities in the past tense. The lack of apologies means that these ex-Senderista leaders are not sorry for what they have done, nor have they had the "change of heart" that accompanies moral conversion. Consequently, the refusal to apologize implies that history is still in the making, echoing the Senderista refrain "the leadership never dies." Rather than the desired guarantee of nonrepetition, the past continues to be very present in these pueblos, personified in the faces that slip out from behind their masks.

In his work on public secrets and "defacement," Michael Taussig suggests that through a "drama of revelation . . . unmasking amounts to a transgressive uncovering of a 'secretly familiar.'"[18] The secretly familiar in these communities is a recent history of fratricidal violence. While coexistence is based upon a complicated alchemy of remembering, forgetting, and remembering to forget, I am convinced that coexistence is impeded by the sense of injustice that permeates these communities. If unmasking implies a confrontation with what is secretly familiar, it also implies some sort of reckoning. That reckoning—that settling of accounts—will at some point require that people can look themselves and one another in the face. Coexistence involves both the mask and the mirror.

Histories of Innocence

> We went to Lima to demand our rights, but nobody paid any attention. For *campesinos* there is no justice. If you demand your rights, they say you're a *terruco* from Cayara.
> —Anonymous

While conversations about guilt have been central to my research in these southern communities, equally present is the insistence on innocence.[19] As I mentioned earlier, in the polarized debates about Sendero Luminoso in Peru, it is controversial to even suggest that Sendero was a political party. This polarization in turn informs the debates about human rights. In sum, only the "innocent" have rights in Peru.[20] That is, any sympathy that one may have had for Sendero disqualifies the person from being the subject of rights. This game has been extremely useful to the armed forces, to the Apristas, and to members of the conservative Catholic Church: Implying that a person or group had something to do with Sendero has been used to justify violence against them, both in the past and in the present.[21]

This dichotomy between the guilty and the innocent has shaped how people in former Shining Path strongholds press their claims. In Chapter 5, I analyzed two focus groups that were held in one of the southern communities for what they revealed about the gendered dimensions of war and the economics of memory. Here we explore another facet: the reiterative emphasis on innocence. The men kept returning to this theme, moving from trembling children and women, to innocent people, and on to the insistence that "our pueblo was innocent." In turn, the women insisted that no women in their community had participated in Shining Path, although they had heard of female participation elsewhere. In subsequent conversations, former militants and *comuneros* insisted on the innocence of those who died at Lloqllepampa, assuring us that no Senderistas were killed that dreadful day. People felt compelled to construct the permissible victim, the Andean community passively caught between two fires.

My point is not to question the veracity of these claims but rather to note how they reflect the logic of innocence with all of its limitations. Whether or not people participated in or sympathized with Sendero, no one deserved to be raped, shot, burned, or blown up on that bloody field. No one should be tortured regardless of their affiliations, real or imagined. Innocence should not be the basis upon which we confer or respect human rights.

Additionally, although it is socially acceptable to demonize Sendero Luminoso, there is much less space to talk about why people supported Shining Path. There is a Faustian bargain here: the *campesinos* of the central-south can exercise protagonism today if they retrospectively adopt the role of passive victims during the internal armed conflict. The less they portray themselves as protagonists then, the more persuasive their demands on the state are today. Thus most people in these communities attempt to construct their life histories at a sizable distance from any sympathy whatsoever with Sendero.

On several occasions, someone pulled aside a member of my research team to assure them that everyone else was exaggerating their losses during the violence: "Oh, look at how he plays the victim—but that's not how it was! He was one of those *puriqkuna*. And now he wants to say he was a victim!

Me? Yes, I really was a victim—but he wasn't." People compete for a higher rank on the hierarchy of victimhood. This "innocence" is based on a logic that has guided the discourse of human rights in Peru: the subject of rights is the subject without moral taint, the innocent subject. However, in tying the right to redress to an individual's "innocence," the Peruvian state distorts the content and practice of citizenship. The right to voice dissent and to peacefully place demands upon the state are rights that should belong to all Peruvians, not just those who are forced to erase their past in the hope of securing their future.

Mahmood Mamdani writes on the Rwandan genocide, in which civilian participation in the killing was massive. He juxtaposes "victor's justice" with "survivor's justice," advocating for the latter as a means of combining the logic of reconciliation with the logic of justice:

> To transcend the previous oppositional terms is to forge a new community of survivors of civil war, the survivors being those who continue to be blessed with life following war. The concept of the "survivor" seeks to transcend the bipolar notions of victims and perpetrators.[22]

According to Mamdani, the price of victor's justice is very high. The victor must be permanently vigilant for fear that the winner's booty be snatched away. The winners live fearing the next cycle of violence, when those they squashed rise up in revenge. Consequently, the price of victor's justice is either a continuation of civil war or permanent divorce. When the enemies have been intimate, permanent divorce is not really an alternative. Thus the work of justice and the work of coexistence are intertwined, and both require a reorganization of power and resources. Within this reorganization, it is necessary to formulate multiple subject positions that do not freeze people into roles they assumed in the past.

The contentious politics of victimhood were magnified by Peru's July 2005 reparations law and how the law defines "victim." In circumvention of international human rights law and the principle of nondiscrimination, Article 4 of the reparations law states that "members of subversive organizations are not considered victims and thus not beneficiaries of the programs enumerated in this law."[23] To be a "good victim" now requires disavowing political protagonism in the past.

I am convinced the discourse of innocence paralyzes the process of reconciliation in Peru. In these former Shining Path strongholds, I asked people how they viewed the Peruvian state and the possibility of reconciliation. In Cayara, where the military committed a massacre on May 14, 1988, on the grounds that the villagers were Shining Path militants, one of the communal authorities explained why his is a *pueblo resentido* (a resentful town):

> If there are people [military] who have participated and are alive, the TRC should sanction them, according to the law. Maybe not punish the soldiers because they were under orders. It's more that they should punish the intellectual authors like General Valdivia and Dr. Alan García because he came here with such arrogance and called us *terrucos*. At least, as former president of our country, he should explain all of this. To achieve reconciliation between the state and us, there would need to be an agreement between the two and it would have to be after the sanction we were talking about. Reconciliation means, for me it means, that both sides reconcile, to live in peace and tranquility, and that there is justice. That is reconciliation.

Striking was his demand that the "intellectual authors" be punished, citing both the general who oversaw the massacre as well as former and current president Alan García. This conversation occurred in March 2003 and was echoed by many other members of the community who insisted that when García arrived following the massacre, "he called us all terrucos. He called our dead family members terrucos and said they deserved to die. He even said our pigs were *terrucos!*"

During the subsequent 2006 presidential campaign, many people in this community (and another that had suffered a military massacre in 1985) told my research team how worried they were: "If García is elected again—oh, he must be angry that we denounced the massacre to the human rights people. This time, he'll make certain they kill us all so that no one is left alive to tell." While these fears may seem extreme, the fear was palpable. That such worries were deemed credible provides an important and powerful insight into how these Peruvians view their government.

In addition to these concerns, the logic of innocence has other corrosive effects. It does not permit the construction of a more just society because if only the "innocent" have rights, then there will certainly be those who feel entitled to do whatever they want with the "guilty." The PTRC's Final Report leaves little doubt regarding the deadly consequences of that approach. As long as there is no space to talk about why so many people joined Sendero and, in some cases, remained sympathizers even under military repression—as long as there is no space immune to the Faustian bargain— there will be a repressed history of struggle that continues to generate bitterness in these *pueblos resentidos* of the central-south.

Afterword

MY PERSONAL AND professional commitments in Peru continue, and I imagine they will for the rest of my life. Books, however, must end. Thinking about how best to end this one was a struggle. I realize that readers might feel emotionally taxed by the time they reach this afterword; might feel a certain despair when contemplating the tremendous cruelty that human beings can inflict on one another. That is undoubtedly part of the story contained in these pages, but it is only one part. Any effort to understand postconflict reconstruction must be attuned both to devastation as well as to people's tenacity for life.

I share one conversation from among many with Marcos Rafaelo in Carhuahurán. Late one afternoon he described the worst years of the *sasachakuy tiempo*. The *ronderos* patrolled in the frigid cold of the mountaintops or sat up all night in drafty stone watchtowers. People took to sleeping fully clothed so they could run in case shots rang out warning of an enemy attack. Entire families sought refuge in the damp, dank caves at night, the rabid bats and the bones of the gentiles further disturbing their sleep. He recalled the pain of seeing loved ones murdered, slaughtered much like the livestock that were decimated during the war. Vast tracts of land lay fallow, while empty bellies rumbled and mothers gave their children water flavored with salt in an effort to "trick their stomachs" and still their tears. He recounted it all in a stoic monotone.

Eventually the conversation turned to his family, and I asked him where he had met his wife, Demetria.

"In the caves," he replied without skipping a beat.

"What? The caves?"

He sat back and looked at me slyly. "It was really cold in those caves. We had to do something to keep warm at night."

Time and again across these many years, villagers made it clear that although violence can horribly reduce human life, life cannot be reduced to that violence. What presses up against the reduction? I am still not certain I have an answer, but I do know I have an incalculable responsibility to the question.

I have explored what people say they suffer from and how they attempt to set things right. This required me to hold present both suffering *and* resilience. If the term "resilience" bothers you, then substitute one that allows you to imagine what it is that permits people to get up in the morning and believe—despite all evidence to the contrary—that there might be a better day ahead of them and a future for their children. This remains the most enduring memory of my fieldwork. When I close my eyes, I remember life in these villages as so much more than tragedy. I recall moments doubled over laughing, dancing until we could no longer stand up, children running into my room and piling on my bed, singing until the candles burned down and there were only stars streaming through the cracks in the corrugated aluminum roof. I remember more than endurance. There were also moments of joy that stretched into hours that in turn became days. Perhaps this is the small stuff of which everyday life is remade.

Notes

Preface

1. Abimael Guzmán, the founder of Shining Path, stated that "Ayacucho is the cradle" of the guerrilla organization during an interview with the PTRC (2003: vol. 1, p. 79).
2. A key theorist of the "new wars" is Mary Kaldor (1999).
3. Levi (1959) 1995.
4. See Shaw, Waldorf, and Hazan 2010; Stover and Weinstein 2004. Arthur Kleinman, Veena Das, and Margaret Lock, with other colleagues, have published an influential trilogy on violence and its consequences (1997, 2000, 2001).

Chapter 1

1. Degregori 1990; Gorriti 1990; Palmer 1992.
2. See interview with Francisco Morales Bermúdez, PTRC 2003: vol. 1, p. 77.
3. For an excellent overview in English of Shining Path, see Stern 1998.
4. *Campesino* communities are both historically situated, strategic identities and collective rights-bearing entities recognized as such in the Peruvian Constitution.
5. The other guerrilla organization was the Tupac Amaru Revolutionary Movement (MRTA in its Spanish abbreviation). The MRTA was more urban focused, and though they managed to stage some high-profile attacks—for instance, taking over the Japanese embassy—they were lesser actors in the broader history of the internal armed conflict. Additionally, given my focus on Ayacucho, Sendero Luminoso is far more significant.
6. When government troops stormed the Japanese embassy, members of MRTA (who had held dozens hostage for several months) were killed after they had

surrendered. One of the images repeatedly shown in the media was Fujimori strutting through the rubble in a flak jacket.

7. See Shaw 2005 for a discussion of the "Western culture of memory."

8. See Bickford 2000.

9. See Teitel 2002, 2003.

10. For a general discussion, see Hayner 2001.

11. For further discussion of how Peru's truth commission was exceptional in foregoing amnesty for criminal investigations, see Laplante 2007.

12. Laplante 2007.

13. America's Watch 1992.

14. PTRC, Final Report, 2003: conclusions.

15. See Peralta 2000.

16. For an excellent article in English analyzing the aftermath of the killings at Uchuraccay, see Mayer 1991.

17. For an analysis of the role of colonial records and social scientists in the construction of the Iquichanos, see Mendez Gastelumendi 2005.

18. Vargas Llosa et al. 1983: 38.

19. Vargas Llosa et al. 1983.

20. Murra 1975.

21. *Caretas* 1983: 28–34. Author's translation.

22. Burga 1986; Flores Galindo 1986.

23. Mayer 1991: 476.

24. Ortega 1986.

25. Carhuahurán was of interest in part because it was a "resistant community": villagers remained largely in situ during the *sasachakuy tiempo*.

26. White 2000.

27. I feel I can now name the four communities with which my research team and I have worked; the PTRC's Final Report is part of the public record regarding the alliances forged by certain members of these communities during the internal armed conflict.

28. I offer more detailed regional histories at the beginnings of Parts III and IV.

29. Cavell cited in Das 1997: 69.

30. Favret-Saada 1980: 9.

31. Ibid., 9–10.

32. Taussig 1984: 476.

33. White 2000: 65.

34. *Daño*, also known as *alcanzo*, is caused by offending the mountain gods when a person sits or steps where one should not. This lack of respect causes serious illness; healing involves speaking with a *curandero* who takes a sacrifice (*pagapu*) to the gods (*apus*).

35. This was a veiled way of suggesting that don Teodoro worked with a book of spells.

36. See, for example, Nash 1993; Scheper-Hughes 1995; Sluka 1996; and Warren 2000.

37. Scheper-Hughes 1995: 411.

38. Fisher 1997: 455.

39. Benjamin 1969: 264.

Chapter 2

1. For a fascinating history of the concept of traumatic memory, see Hacking 1995; for a genealogy of the diagnostic category PTSD, see Young 1995; for a genealogy of trauma, see Leys 2000.

2. See, for example, Hermann 1992; her work on trauma has been very influential.

3. See, among others, Eisenbruch 2007; Jenkins 1991; Kirmayer 1996; Kleinman and Desjarlais 1995; Summerfield 1999, 2000, 2002; Pupavac 2001; and Theidon 2004.

4. For a discussion of how "trauma brokers" and "trauma portfolios" work within the aid economy in Haiti, see James 2004.

5. See Good 1992.

6. Fassin, Rechtman, and Gomme 2009: 278.

7. Appadurai, Gupta, and Ferguson have all, in various ways, eloquently critiqued the conflation of place, culture, and people. To assume these are isomorphic obscures far more than it illuminates about globalization and the transterritoriality of culture and can lead to what Appadurai calls the "spatial incarceration of the native" (1998). However, I temper their critiques with Escobar's work on the reassertion of place as a key strategy in subaltern struggles and social movements, as well as an important arena for rethinking Eurocentric categories of analysis (2001: 141). Merging the insights of phenomenology with those of political economy, he argues that however globalized the world may be, we still experience that world from *some place*—a place one may care a great deal about. In making his arguments, he provides one of my favorite lines: "We are, in short, placelings" (ibid., 143).

8. See Breslau 2004.

9. Wilson 2003: 377.

10. Ibid.

11. See Das and Das 2007: 90.

12. I think here of Kleinman and Desjarlais, who argue that PTSD medicalizes problems as psychiatric conditions that elsewhere and for much of human history have been appreciated as religious or social problems (1995: 181).

13. PTRC 2003: vol. 3, chapter 2.6, p. 276.

14. See PTRC 2003: vol. 8, part 3, chapter 2, pp. 292–98 for an analysis of these 401 testimonies.

15. As Breslau suggests, it is important to explore how the discourse of trauma moves in local social and political fields (2004).

16. Manrique 2003.

17. Huaychao, February 2003.

18. See De la Cadena 2000.

19. Marcos Cueto has conducted outstanding research on the history of the health care system in Peru and the vertical organization of the public health campaigns (1997). The early years of my research were conducted against the backdrop of an aggressive "family planning" campaign. During the latter half of the 1990s, the Peruvian government (with funding from USAID) carried out the enforced sterilization of an estimated three hundred thousand women, the majority of whom were urban and rural poor. For a discussion of the sterilization campaign, see Getgen 2008.

20. Cited from the *Situational Needs Assessment of the Health Post*, Cayara, 2003.

21. PAR 2002.

22. Julian literally said, "Daño, llakis—son creencias y nada más. Son cosas de los ignorantes y los analfabetizados."

23. The literature in medical anthropology is vast; for an example based upon research conducted in the Andes, see Malamud-Crandon 1991.

24. During final revisions to this chapter, I read Pandolfo's eloquent chapter in *Postcolonial Disorders*, based upon her work on psychiatry, postcolonialism, and subjectivity in Morocco. She analyzes how colonial histories shape psychiatry, informing who is made a "cultural" subject and who is made a "universal" subject (2008: 330). She asks readers to ponder what it means for patients to live in a symbolic order made incommensurable by relations of power. I read her chapter thinking about Quechua speakers and their "inconceivable" afflictions that could not exist. I also share Pandolfo's concerns that studies of ethnopsychiatry can lead to a folklorization of culture. I hope to have avoided that pitfall and am certain people will let me know if I have not.

25. Das and Das 2007: 67.

26. My conversation with Hernán captured one of my enduring concerns with the "everyone is traumatized" or "traumatized pueblo" approach. If the category of trauma confers victim status, then what happens when social groups as a whole are described as "traumatized"? I cannot accept the moral elasticity of a category that includes both victims and perpetrators; "traumatized" also tells me nothing about the experience of collectives in which victims and perpetrators find themselves living together again.

27. PTRC 2003: vol. 8, part 3, chapter 2, p. 292.

28. Kleinman and Kleinman 1991: 277.

29. I am *not* issuing a veto on mental health services but rather on reducing mental health to trauma—and to reducing the world of suffering and resilience to what a biomedically trained physician can perceive of it.

30. *Promotores de salud* are a fascinating group of men and women who have been recruited from these communities, given training in biomedical models, and then serve as intermediaries between medical systems.

31. The most eloquent argument for the violence of hunger is Scheper-Hughes 1993.

32. Feldman 1995: 243.

33. Good 1992: 201.

34. Csordas 1994.

35. As Lock argues, "It cannot be assumed, therefore, that dialectics exist between an infinity of cultures and a universal biology, but rather between cultures and local biologies, both of which are subject to transformation in evolutionary, historical and life cycle time bytes, and to movement through space" (1993: 145–46). See also Kleinman 1998: 360.

36. See Connerton's suggestive work: "Performative memory is bodily. Thus, I want to argue, there is an aspect of social memory which has been greatly neglected but is absolutely essential: bodily social memory" (1989: 71).

37. Stoller 1997: 54.

38. Carhuahurán, March 1999.

39. Das 1997: 80. See also Boddy 1989 for a discussion of historical consciousness and women's bodies. For a fascinating book on bodily signification, social memory, and the mnemonic schemes inscribed upon the body, see Comaroff 1985.

40. The work of Tousignant has been helpful to me. In "*Pena* in the Ecuadorian Sierra: A Psychoanthropological Analysis of Sadness," he notes that *pena*—*llaki* in Quechua—is an illness that results from an intolerable accumulation of suffering and that the body occupies a predominant place in the phenomenon of *pena*. He suggests that claiming one is ill with *pena* could be a way to demand justice through legal procedures but does not develop this idea further in his exploratory article (1984). I found that people used the term in both its singular and plural form: *llaki* can be a noun we would translate as pain or suffering; it can also be used in the plural to refer to memories that cause the suffering and fill the body.

41. In his work on *susto*, Rubel (1964) notes the centrality of water imagery in healing throughout Latin America.

42. See Tousignant 1984; and Stevenson 1977. Stevenson studied *colerina* (epileptiform attacks) in the Peruvian Andes and argues that such attacks constitute a demand for moral solidarity and trigger a chain of mutual aid.

43. I was struck by this shift when reading a book of testimonies that were collected in 1985. Various conjugations of the verb *ñakariy* appear in those testimonies; in contrast, in my research conducted from 1995 to the present, the most prevalent term for suffering is some version of *llaki* or *llakis*.

44. Jelin 2002: 29.

45. For example, Breuer and Freud (1895) 2000; Foucault 1994; Canguilhem (1943) 1991; and Janet (1923) 2010.

46. In her work with Somali refugees, Zarowsky found that emotions and "emotion talk" embedded people in moral webs of duty and care, which were not always fulfilled (2004: 189). For an overview of anthropological work on the emotions, see Lutz and White 1986, as well as the more recent Boellstorff and Lindquist 2004.

47. This presents a compelling contradiction: women's insistence on forgetting while at times tenaciously holding onto the memory of dead loved ones. This paradox may index the contradictory obligations women feel to the past, present, and future in terms of love and loss.

48. For nursing and the transmission of negative emotions in Brazil, see Scheper-Hughes 1993: 226. Paul Farmer has also written about "bad blood" and "spoiled milk" as a response to social distress and interpersonal conflict in Haiti (1988). Clearly this is a widely occurring phenomenon and worth further study. It would be particularly interesting to follow the children born and breastfed under these conditions.

49. See Zapata et al. 1992.

50. *Campo* is used in contrast to *city*; it refers not only to geography but to life in rural areas.

51. The line between *curandero* (healer) and *brujo* (witch) can be porous, underscoring that power is always ambiguous and can be harnessed to various ends. However, in most communities, and the *barrios* of Huamanga, people discern between the two when seeking services, and certain *curanderos* are renowned for their healing abilities.

52. Tousignant 1979: 357.

53. See Seguín 1979.

54. This resonates with the work of Mehta and Chatterji, who write, "Agency is attributed to the force of violence, not to its individual carriers, who are merely its tools. Violence erupts, invades, and establishes a time out of time, a period of normlessness" (2001: 229).

55. See Peña Jumpa 1998.

56. In her research in the Andes, Oths found that *debilidad* is most common among older menopausal and post-menopausal women. She suggests that highlanders use *debilidad* "to express the degeneration of the integral body due to the accumulated hardships of productive and reproductive labor" (1999: 295).

57. See Coronel 1995.

58. Scheper-Hughes 1993.

59. For an analysis of pathology and the role of strong negative emotions in the Peruvian Andes, see Shephard 2002.

60. The "repentant ones" refers to the ex-Senderistas who repented for their participation in, or sympathy for, Shining Path. I will address this term at length later in the book.

61. Rebhun's work on emotions in Brazil resonates with women's comments about rage and its embodied impact. Rebhun analyzes the expression "swallowing frogs," which women use in reference to suppressing anger, hatred, or irritation due to gendered proscriptions on expressing certain emotions. She writes, "Women speak of these sentiments taking up space in their bodies, pressing against the inside of the face, the chest, or the belly, and having to be restrained with a physical effort" (1994: 370). It is important to note that the illnesses associated with these emotions describe both a set of symptoms and a psychosocial situation (ibid., 361).

62. The literature on *nervios* (nerves) is vast. Two good places to begin reading—and to understand the role of nerves in offering commentary on one's difficult social context—are Jenkins 1991 and Scheper-Hughes 1993.

63. For studies on "traditional" medicine in Ayacucho, see Delgado Sumar 1988a, 1988b.

64. This refers to the early years of my research, 1997–99.

65. See Abercrombie 1998 for an analysis of Aymaran healers (*yatiris*) and their uses of memory and history.

Chapter 3

1. Biehl's book, *Vita: Life in a Zone of Abandonment*, provides useful questions for postwar contexts. When discussing the idea of humanness, Biehl insists, "I do not refer to the universal category of the human but rather to the malleability of this concept as it is locally constituted and reconstituted, with semantic boundaries that are very fuzzy. Above all, the concept of the human is *used* in the local world and it cannot be artificially determined in advance in order to ground an abstract ethics" (2005: 40).

2. In my attention to making humans and to emotional experience, I am not studying "Andean culture" as a foundational reality to be discovered but rather as the protean product of complex practices and discourses. This reflects an interest in situated knowledge—in the theories and practices people marshal in their efforts to rebuild individual and collective lives.

3. For a discussion of anthropomorphizing infants, see Scheper-Hughes 1995.

4. De Miguel 2000: 1597.

5. See Morote Best 1988.

6. See Shweder and Bourne 1984, in which they contrast "sociocentric" and "egocentric" constructions of the self. I do not suggest an "atomized West" and "relational rest" dichotomy that essentializes cultures and portrays them as timeless and unchanging. No anthropologist would make such an argument. Perhaps if we think of cultural contouring rather than absolutes, we can acknowledge that different social groups do emphasize relatedness more than autonomy and will have various ways of cultivating those values in individuals.

7. I was also struck by the mothers who told me the political violence had damaged their children, who were consequently born without the capacity to love. This would imply they were born without a central human capacity: one cannot foment love in these "damaged" children.

8. In their introduction to *Language and the Politics of Emotion*, Lutz and Abu-Lughod (1990) argue that in certain cultures emotions are discursively and socially produced in moments of exchange rather than existing as incipient or concrete sentiments waiting to be expressed. This leads me to insist on the centrality of "emotional management" in communal reconstruction.

9. See Rebhun's work on emotions in Brazil (1994), in which she argues that people live in a world in which others are dangerous and thus one is concerned about the emotions she inspires in an Other.

10. Allen 1998.

11. I refer here to Laura Nader's influential work on "harmony ideology" (1990).

12. *Muspay* literally means "to be confused or disoriented; to lose one's way." In common usage, *muspaypi qina* refers to being in a sleeplike or dreamlike state. Both madness (*locura*) and *muspaypi qina* (like being in a dream) refer to the loss of *conciencia* and the *uso de razón*. *Conciencia* can be translated as both "conscience" and "consciousness," and this double meaning is important. A "crazy person" may unconsciously go about his or her life, not fully aware of his or her actions or their consequences. Combined with the lack of conscience and the use of reason, the person also lacks the capacity to discern right from wrong and thus is not fully responsible for his or her actions. The "crazy person" cannot be held to the moral codes that normally govern interaction; thus the reaction to *locos* is frequently a mixture of compassion and fear.

13. Hualla, April 2003.

14. Tiquihua, December 2002.

15. "Killing someone again" refers to inflicting more violence on the body of someone who is near death or already dead.

16. I have found the essays in Biehl, Good, and Kleinman 2007 and Good et al. 2008 helpful in analyzing the centrality of collective madness in Ayacucho.

17. Aretxaga 2008: 52.

18. The *uku pacha* is also associated with the Earth Mother (Pachamama), reflecting the ambiguity of Andean deities. In contrast to Christian teachings, good and evil are not absolute within an Andean cosmology.

19. See Shephard's work in the Peruvian Amazon (2002).

20. See Holston's article on Brazil (2000) for a fascinating discussion of the religious imagination in Brazil.

21. Philpott 2007: 35.

Chapter 4

1. Robbins 2004: 117. The literature on the growth of Evangelical Christianity in Latin America is vast, and it is beyond the scope of this chapter to offer a thorough review of the relevant authors and their works. However, the explanatory frameworks tend to cluster around several key factors. The early works of Lalive d'Epinay (1969) and Willems (1967) were both theoretically informed by the concept of anomie and its explanatory power with respect to conversions. More recently, Burdick (1993) has argued that evangelical churches are "cults of affliction" for the poor. A similar argument is made by Chestnut, who suggests that evangelical growth reflects the need for solutions to what he terms the "pathogens of poverty"—the multiple health problems that stem from poverty and are addressed via the emphasis on faith healing and personal transformation (1997). Other key works are those of Stoll in Guatemala (1990) and Brusco in Colombia (1995). The former points to

political oppression under military dictatorship as the primary impetus for evangelical growth in rural regions of the country, while Brusco's feminist analysis argues that conversion to *evangelismo* represents a gender strategy on the part of women who seek to control destructive male behavior associated with *machismo* by joining religious groups that sanction promiscuity, drinking, and interpersonal violence. Joining these key works are those of Garrard-Burnett (1998) and Garrard-Burnett and Stoll's coedited volume of case studies (1993). In addition to these insightful works, I am persuaded by James Holston's critique of "compensation theories of evangelical conversion" that frame religious change among the poor and oppressed within a scheme of deprivation and revitalization: "Compensatory accounts tend to be mechanical in posting an action-reaction model of religion. They also tend to suppose that people are interested in religion—and hence that their collective actions take religious form—because religion is inherently about transcendental unity and, therefore, a means to reintegrate a shattered self and society. Such assumptions may be accurate, but they also close off discussion of other kinds of engagements people get out of developing their religious imagination" (Holston 2000: 613). Thus I draw upon the key explanatory models and certainly see elements of each in Ayacucho; however, I am motivated by a desire to understand those "other kinds of engagements" and the role they play in war and its aftermath.

2. See Del Pino and Theidon 1999.

3. In the Apurímac and Ene region of Ayacucho, Del Pino (1996) found that 50 percent of the population was *evangélico*. In her research in another region of Ayacucho, Caroline Yezer's household survey revealed that 80 percent of the population was *evangélico* (2007).

4. In 1984 in Peru, 60 percent of the 2,265 Catholic priests were internationals. PTRC 2003: vol. 3, chapter 3.3, p. 380.

5. I say "alleged" because this egalitarianism works in contradictory ways. See, for example, Gill's work in Bolivia, and her concern with the ways in which Evangelismo "affirms traditional relations of domination between men and women" (1990: 708).

6. O'Neill 2009: 24.

7. *Trago* is a generic name for alcoholic beverages.

8. *Pacha* (earth) and *manca* (pot) refer to cooking a meal in a large hole in the earth in which food is placed on the top of hot rocks or adobe bricks. The hole is then covered in dirt, and the food slowly cooks as the heat emanates from the rocks. *Pachamanca* is delicious and is prepared for special events.

9. Vidal's conversion narrative shared classic features with those of most of the men I spoke with. They contrasted their life before—filled with drunkenness, idleness, and generalized sin—with the new person they became once they embraced Jesus Christ. This is a formulaic male narrative. With women, life "before" was generally plagued by illness of some sort and a variety of bodily aches and pains. This narrative of rupture is, of course, characteristic of Evangelical testimonies.

10. An important exception was the Iglesia del Sur Andino, which refers to the Catholic dioceses of Cuzco, Puno, Juli, Sicuani, Ayaviri, and Chuquibambilla. In this

region, the Catholic Church maintained a high-profile presence in the rural areas and had been a key supporter of various peasant organizations. It was one region in which Shining Path made meager inroads. See Klaiber 1992; and PTRC 2003: vol. 3.

11. See Klaiber's various texts of the history of the Catholic Church in Peru.

12. Canessa notes a similar phenomenon in Bolivia, where institutional Catholicism was tightly bound to the hacienda system such that when the Agrarian Reform effectively abolished the haciendas, the power of the Catholic Church concomitantly declined in rural areas (2000: 131).

13. Gutiérrez 1986: 222–23, cited in PTRC 2003: vol. 3, chapter 3.3, p. 403.

14. Cipriani was named auxiliary bishop in May 1988 and ordained in July; in May 1991 he was designated apostolic administrator of the archdiocese of Ayacucho and was made archbishop in 1995. He is currently archbishop of Lima.

15. This information appears in the PTRC's Final Report. Cipriani subsequently denied the sign ever existed; however, many people I have spoken with in Ayacucho recall the sign and their despair.

16. PTRC 2003: vol. 3, chapter 3.3, p. 393. The Coordinadora Nacional de Derecho Humanos was founded in 1985; it is a collective of civil society institutions that work in the defense, promotion, and education of human rights.

17. Abimael Guzmán was also known as Presidente Gonzalo by his followers. Pensamiento Gonzalo (Gonzalo Thought) refers to his revolutionary ideology. For an excellent analysis of the "quasi-religious scientism" of Shining Path and the "religious fervor of Shining Path ideology," see Degregori 1989.

18. World Vision was an important actor in postwar Ayacucho, and Isaías was referring to their aid work. As in other postconflict and post-disaster settings, Evangelical Christian charities established reconstruction programs that emphasized both social and spiritual reconstruction. For interesting case studies on Protestant organizations and their impact, see Garrard-Burnett 1998; and Bornstein 2005.

19. Pastor Vidal is referring to the Concilio Nacional Evangélico del Perú (CONEP) founded in 1940 to represent the Evangelical community vis-à-vis the state. Their historical struggle was to obtain religious freedom; during the internal armed conflict, CONEP advocated for human rights, establishing the Department of Social Service "Paz y Esperanza" to attend to evangelicals affected by the violence. For more details on CONEP and their human rights activism, see PTRC 2003: vol. 3, chapter 3.3, p. 469; and López 1998.

20. Del Pino (1996) also recorded "holy war" narratives in the Apurímac Valley during this research in the mid-1990s, and the apocalyptic reading was widespread (AYNI 1992; Yezer 2007). I think this is due, in part, to Radio Amauta, the Bible movies, and the mobile local pastors who move between communities, as well as the coast, *sierra*, and *selva*.

21. See De Certeau 1984.

22. Numerous people described the wartime experiences in terms of an exodus and subsequent return, a finding also noted in Del Pino's work on the Apurímac Valley

(1996: 134). Between 1983 and 1984, approximately 50 percent of the population of the highlands of Huanta—approximately a thousand families—migrated to the capital city of Huamanga and to the valleys of Huanta, Tambo, and the Apurímac.

23. Appadurai 1991: 199.

24. See Viswanathan 1998.

25. Gupta and Ferguson 1992.

26. For an excellent discussion of "popular Catholicism," see Marzal 1997.

27. *Huacas* are sacred burial places; *wamanis* are the gods of the mountains.

28. See Gill 1990: 713. Her analysis of the contradictory implications of *evangelismo* in Bolivia is helpful, yet I diverge on one aspect. In referring to the emotional experience of religious conversion, Gill writes, "The experience infuses the converts with a new and stronger sense of God, who, they believe, actually exists" (1990: 714). I do not share her cynicism and find troubling the posture of many academics who study religious belief and practice. Too often religion stands as a mark of "Otherness," equated with a premodern state of being. The very terms "magic," "science," and "religion" are steeped in the evolutionary context in which they emerged, and they limit our capacity to ask new, interesting, and fruitful questions precisely because they are moored to a teleological mode of reasoning.

29. For an excellent overview of the relationship between Shining Path, the Catholic Church, and the Evangelicals, see PTRC 2003: vol. 3.

30. See Del Pino 1996 for a discussion of this process in the Apurímac.

31. See AYNI 1992: 63 for an early discussion of this pentecostalization. I also emphasize the different chronologies of Evangelismo in Huanta versus the central-south, where I have worked with several communities that were Shining Path strongholds. Whereas the massive conversions in Huanta occurred during the 1980s, it was not until the defeat of Sendero Luminoso (SL) that the number of Evangélicos sharply increased in the central-south. These were two ideological projects in competition, and with the defeat of SL both hearts and minds were more disposed to conversion. Additionally, as we shall see, the Evangelical growth is pronounced among former militants—according to others, especially those who "killed their *prójimos*."

32. Robbins 2004: 119. I might add that autonomy cannot be conflated with isolation, and these local pastors were part of the migratory routes that carried people and ideas across time and space.

33. Natalie Davis has criticized those who depict peasants as recipients of knowledge transmission "from above"; they are somehow incapable of religious innovation. Instead, she argues that popular religions arise from the creative processes of ordinary people—perhaps ordinary people living through extraordinary times (1974). The theologies elaborated are not a distorted revision of official religion or a debased attempt at mimesis. Rather, popular religion—in this case, *evangelismo*—can form a consistent system of symbolic meanings in its own right. I thank Philip Williams for bringing this text to my attention and for demonstrating the accuracy of Davis's critique with his own insightful research in Yungay, Peru.

34. I recall a conversation I had with another Presbyterian pastor in Huanta. When I shared with him some of the conversations I had had with *evangélicos* in the *alturas* of Huanta, he was startled: "But that's not what we told them!"

35. Kevin O'Neill discusses the image of the Christian soldier in his work on Guatemala. One young neo-Pentecostal pastor exhorted his parishioners to be "Kaibiles for Christ," invoking the Guatemalan army's most elite and brutal commando unit. The Kaibiles carried out many atrocities during the genocide, which makes the exhortation especially chilling. The parishioners were encouraged to carry out the sort of spiritual warfare that is a metaphor for Christian life in a world plagued by sin (2009: 87–88).

36. Del Pino, in his research in the Apurímac Valley, found that "the Evangelicals elaborated an ideological response that translated into practical action: for the Final Judgment, the earth would be cleansed of demons. Thus it was necessary, under God's protection, to fight against the forces of evil" (1996: 118). Author's translation.

37. Robbins 2004: 128.

38. Philpott 2007: 12.

Chapter 5

1. See Scarry 1985.

2. Veena Das has suggested that women's silence about rape may be a form of agency—perhaps the only form available to women—and thus silence does not necessarily signify the absence of linguistic competency but rather the active refusal to allow it (1997). See also Ross 2003; and Butalia 2000.

3. The Rome Statute of the International Criminal Court of 1998 included sexual violence as a crime against humanity in Article 7 and a war crime in Article 8.

4. Even though the TRC has gathered almost seventeen thousand testimonies, it is still impossible to determine the magnitude of sexual violence during the internal armed conflict. My research resonates with a study conducted in Ayacucho by COMISEDH, which determined that rape was systematically used as a strategy of war and that the number of rapes was massive (Falconí and Agüero 2003). Ultimately this is what the Peruvian TRC argued based upon the testimonies they received (PTRC 2003).

5. Minow 1998.

6. See Hayner 2001.

7. Ibid., 78.

8. I benefited from conversations with Roberto Garretón regarding the Rettig Commission in Chile, and Elizabeth Jelin has taught me so much about Argentina, past and present.

9. In South Africa, of the 21,227 testimonies given to the TRC, women accounted for 56.5 percent of the witnesses (www.peacewomen.org), and in Peru women accounted for 54 percent of the 16,917 testimonies at the national level and 64 percent of the testimonies given in Ayacucho (PTRC 2003: vol. 8).

10. See Mantilla Falcón 2005a, 2005b.

11. Bell and O'Rourke argue that "Efforts to 'add gender' to transitional justice have been most prominent with respect to the legal treatment of sexual violence in conflict" (2007: 26).

12. Mantilla Falcón 2005b: 2.

13. PTRC 2003: vol. 8, chapter 2.1, p. 89.

14. Hayner 2001: 77.

15. Mantilla Falcón 2005b: 2.

16. PTRC 2003: vol. 8, chapter 2.1, p. 64.

17. Ibid., 89.

18. Ibid.

19. PTRC 2003: vol. 8, chapter 2.1, pp. 89–90. Author's translation.

20. Mantilla Falcón 2005b: 3.

21. I would add another explanation centered on the war-peace continuum of violence against women. In rural communities, wartime rape was a continuation of long-standing patterns, albeit exacerbated and "massified." It was common practice in cases of rape for the family of the young woman to look for *un buen arreglo* (a good arrangement) that would entail the rapist marrying his victim or, in the case of pregnancy, at least recognizing the child with the father's name on the birth certificate. Sexual violence was thus resignified within the idiom of kinship. Indeed, until 1997 the Peruvian Penal Code stated that in the case of rape, penal action against the perpetrator would be terminated if the accused married his victim. See Villanueva Flores 2007.

22. Ross 2003.

23. One thinks here of the impact of militarization and the new forms of security *and* insecurity that a sustained military presence implies. For example, see Enloe 1988; and Jacobs, Jacobson, and Marchbank 2000.

24. Theidon 2003a.

25. See PTRC 2003: vol. 8, on women in Sendero Luminoso.

26. For a discussion of the logic and materiality of secrecy in Sierra Leone, see Ferme 2001.

27. Malkki, in her research with Hutu refugees in Tanzania, also noted the importance of knowing when to stop asking questions. As she wrote, "the success of fieldwork hinged not so much on a determination to ferret out 'the facts' as on a willingness to leave some stones unturned, to listen to what my informants deemed important, and to demonstrate my trustworthiness by not prying where I was not wanted" (1995: 51).

28. Rehn and Sirleaf 2002: 2.

29. Ross 2003.

30. In part I am troubled by the pedagogical use of another's suffering or grief as a means of sensitizing those who do not recognize an Other as capable of pain. I think here of the African women in the film *Long Night's Journey into Day*, whose legs gave

way beneath them as they wailed in anguish at police photos of the mutilated bodies of their loved ones during the amnesty hearings. I imagine the goal was to teach white people that darker others also grieve (although in this film it is the death of one young white woman that is foregrounded).

31. Theidon 2003a.

32. Patricia Connell's research on domestic violence was helpful to me as I analyzed what women talked about with us. Connell criticizes the use of agency and victimhood because they are too frequently conceived as mutually exclusive in relation to one another. She found that women often refused to characterize themselves as victims, leading her to argue that focusing on a woman's status as victim "creates a framework for others to know her not as a person, but as a victim, someone to whom violence is done" (1997: 122).

33. February 2002.

34. I have been asked why some women believed that pregnancy might protect them from rape. People believed, at first, that women and children would be spared. They were wrong. Over the course of the internal armed conflict, the atrocities themselves recalibrated notions of the possible and the impossible as the violence took on forms that exceeded anything people had experienced before. I understand this as an incremental loss of disbelief. I thank Andrew Canessa for the question.

35. There are several verbs women used to speak about sexual violence in a veiled manner: *abusar* (to abuse); *fastidiar* or *molestar* (to bother); and *burlar* (to take advantage of). It was only within the TRC context that I began to hear women in these communities use the verb *violar* (to rape).

36. I borrow this term from Veena Das, who, in writing about the massive raping that occurred during the Partition, argued that raping the women was a means of creating a future memory for the men who would look at them and thus remember the brutality of what had happened. In that context, she argues women learned to move the violation inward, thereby concealing it in a protective silence (2007: 55).

37. April 2003.

38. April 2003.

39. Tamayo 2003: 7.

40. December 2002.

41. See Theidon 1999.

42. See Rehn and Sirleaf 2002.

43. On the need for an anthropology of men and masculinity, see Gutmann 1997.

44. Foster notes that the South African TRC's report acknowledged the commission had neglected to study masculinity and violence, which prompts him to pose a series of questions: "What is it about masculinity that under certain circumstances renders such an identity form so noxious? What are the circumstances? All of this awaits research" (2000: 227). The comparative work of political scientist Elisabeth

Wood (2006) points to the differing prevalence and deployment of rape in various conflict settings.

45. Falconí and Agüero 2003: 12.

46. For a discussion of war rape and male bonding, see Enloe 1988.

47. Diken and Lausten 2005.

48. Ibid., 114. I thank Jean Franco for bringing this text to my attention.

49. I use the term "race" intentionally. While it may be more accurate to think in terms of ethnicity given that race has no biological basis, it is more appropriate to think of racism when analyzing discrimination in Peru. I met mothers who were eager to marry me off to their sons to "whiten the family" or "improve the race." There is a biological imaginary fueling these comments, which most certainly prompts the sorts of insults that Quechua-speaking peasants are routinely subjected to. See Theidon 2004.

50. Henriquez Ayin 2006: 69. Racial categories in Peru can be ambiguous; however, as a general rule the term *chola* (or *cholo*) is a racial category between "Indian" and "white" and has many demeaning connotations. *Mestiza* also reflects hybridity but implies a higher status on the hierarchy. "Indian" is considered a very insulting term, as is *chuto*. The literature on race and ethnicity in the Andes is vast; however, two very insightful books are De la Cadena 2000 and Weismantel 2001.

51. Henriquez Ayin 2006: 71. As this testimony indicates, there is a racialized geography in Peru, with coastal and urban locations conferring a higher status relative to people from rural areas, particularly the highlands. Thus the young women from the coast were privileged relative to the more rural *cholas*.

52. Theidon 2004: 53.

53. PTRC 2003: vol. 8, part 2, chapter 2.2, p. 123. Author's translation.

54. Drawing upon her research in Guatemala, Diane Nelson has written that "Reports of brutal barracks training suggest that internalized racism is a tool used to break the boys down so they may be remade as soldiers, in part by promising them marks of ladino identity (modern bourgeois practices like wearing shoes and eating meat) and of masculinity. Mayan men are often feminized in relation to traditional practices and in their limited power vis-à-vis the ladino" (Nelson 1999: 91). Military service, for all of its abuses, is thus a way to become "less Indian" in a context in which "The Indian is often coded as female" (ibid., 182). This holds true in Peru as well where young rural men swell the lowest ranks of the army.

55. Weismantel 2001: 169.

56. Ibid., xl.

57. Butler 1990: 144.

58. De la Cadena (1991) analyzes the themes of gender and ethnicity in Cuzco, suggesting that because women speak less Spanish and have less urban experience, they are considered "more Indian." Thus gender, race, and ethnicity are axes of differentiation that function in a multiplicative manner, prejudicing the women who find

themselves at the crossroads of these forms of categorizing people and constructing hierarchies based upon those categories.

59. See, for example, Diken and Lausten 2005; Kwon 2006; Milillo 2006.

60. There is much more that needs to be understood about the pleasure of the rapists. I found myself returning to Scarry's influential book *The Body in Pain* (1985). In her sophisticated analysis of torture, missing is the perpetrator's pleasure. In the case of sexual violence—and I imagine this would be true of other acts of torture as well—I believe the person or persons inflicting the pain are quite aware of the Other's suffering. That pain is part of the titillation. As repugnant as the idea is, the torturer's delight requires further reflection.

61. Theidon 2003a.

62. In her analysis of the gendered dynamics of armed conflict, Cockburn argues that "male-dominant systems involve a hierarchy among men, producing different and unequal masculinities, always defined in relation not only to one another but to women" (2001: 16).

63. Huaychao, February 2003.

64. The fact I am a woman may certainly contribute to men's silence about rape; however, I have worked with several male research assistants and they did not find men forthcoming on this topic either. This may be a more pervasive silence. Liz Kelly offers one way of understanding this: "Any 'peace' involves a reworking of power relations, not just between nations or parts of nations but between men and women. Attempts are made to conscript women into a 'rebuilding the nation' agenda in which their needs are subordinated to those of repairing the damage to men and 'the society.' One central, but universally neglected, element of this is that the violations women experienced during the conflict are silenced, since the male combatants need to be constructed as heroes rather than rapists" (2006: 62). This comment is suggestive, but it also requires attentiveness to the nature of the armed conflict and the construction of winners and losers, heroes and victims.

65. The silence of the perpetrators warrants further research. I was struck by Antje Krog's comment that, to her knowledge, no rapist applied for amnesty from the South African TRC (2001). As I completed revisions on this chapter, I also came across a fascinating piece by Roland Littlewood. In laying out a research agenda on military rape, he insists on the importance of understanding the motivations and experiences of the men, while acknowledging how difficult it will be to answer these questions given the "near impossibility of research on humans . . . and because of the post-conflict disgust, on the part of the principal and his surviving victim which prevents any sort of detailed contextual study" (1997: 13).

66. February 2003.

67. For a similar process in South Africa, see Ross 2003.

68. Jacobs, Jacobson, and Marchbank 2000: 82. I focus on women in this conclusion but hope I have demonstrated the importance of "gender-sensitive" strategies that take all genders into consideration.

69. Utas 2005: 408.

70. Krog 2001.

71. In a compelling editorial marking the fourth anniversary of the PTRC's Final Report, political scientist Martín Tanaka observed how little impact the report and the commission's recommendations had had to date (*Perú 21*, August 28, 2007). In contemplating possible explanations for this silence, he noted that "those who were in one moment perpetrators (the armed forces) ended up being labeled 'saviors,' celebrated by both former president Fujimori and current president Alan García for having saved the country from the 'terrorist threat.'" There is scant discursive space for saviors to be rapists. Additionally, among the TRC's stated goals was "refounding the social contract" and promoting national reconciliation. I am persuaded by Veena Das's work on post-Partition policies in India and the ways in which a new social contract may dictate the terms of new sexual contracts. Thus the reformulation of gender ideologies in the service of nation-building following periods of violence may have deleterious consequences for women. See Das 2007, particularly chapter 2.

72. The Peruvian TRC designed the Program of Integral Reparations (PIR), one of the most comprehensive truth commission reparations programs to date. One component of the PIR includes symbolic reparations, which would include public gestures, memorials, and media campaigns. For more information on the Peruvian PIR, see Guillerot 2006; and Laplante and Theidon 2007.

Chapter 6

1. PROMUDEH 2001.

2. INEI 1996: 29.

3. For example, see Arnold 1997; Harris 1978; and Isbell 1979.

4. Varallanos 1989: 7.

5. Ibid., 149–50. Similarly, Cuzqueño writer José Uriel García and Ayacuchano anthropologist Ranulfo Cavero Carrasco both establish the historical presence—and historicity—of *qarawi*, citing discussions of this singing in the chronicles of early colonial priests. For example, Fray Martín de Morúa wrote that people were singing their "*historias y memorias pasadas . . .* and other things they did not want to forget which were communicated to the young and the old" (ibid., 152).

6. See Theidon 2003a.

7. Interview with commander in Pampay, 1996.

8. Ortner 1990: 46.

9. See Cooke 1997.

10. For example, see Degregori et al. 1996. This volume, by an astute group of researchers, is crucial to understanding the course of the war in the northern highlands. However, it does present a masculinist version of the war as related by male

peasant patrollers. I appreciate the context in which the book was written and the authors' desire to demonstrate that peasants were actors with a political agenda.

11. Caldeira and Holston 1996: 717.

12. Mallon 1994: 1511.

13. See Mallon 1995 for a discussion of communal hegemony.

14. For a compelling analysis of the ways silence enters into historical accounts, see Michel Rolfe Trouillot's book on the first slave rebellion in Haiti (1995). Trouillot suggests there are four crucial moments at which silence enters into history: in the making of sources; in the creation of archives; when narrators themselves silence certain topics; and by the fact that not every narrative enters into the accepted corpus. Part of his persuasive argument is that the very idea of a slave rebellion in 1791 was "unthinkable" and thus formed part of a silenced history of the impossible.

15. Robert Desjarlais (1992) recounts a similar sense from his work in the Himalayas.

16. There are two forms of the first person plural in Quechua: *ñoqayku* and *ñoqanchik*. The first is the exclusive "we" that includes only the group of speakers and not the people they are addressing. In contrast, *ñoqanchik* is the inclusive "we" and includes all people present. Thus the women were also delimiting who was included in the collective experience they were narrating.

17. See Scott 1985.

18. I thank José Coronel for confirming this information. Personal communication with the author, October 4, 2006.

19. See Ramphele's work on political widowhood in South Africa (1999). As she argues based upon her own experience as the widow of an African National Congress hero, "The term 'political widowhood' reflects the appropriation of certain women's bodies as part of the symbolic armor mobilized by political movements in the contest for moral space following the fall of heroes in the struggle for power" (101). Thus, "[T]he widow embodies a desired social memory of the fallen hero and the nobility of the commitment he made to the struggle" (102). There is a slightly different process at work in Ayacucho, where many widows embody a tainted social memory of the guilty dead; that is, they lost their husbands on the losing side of the war.

20. Veena Das's sustained theorizing of the self that must endure and the complex transactions of body, pain, and language has been enormously helpful to me in my analysis (2007).

21. Green 1999: 13.

22. See Foucault 1977.

23. Felícitas in conversation with the author, October 2002.

24. Indeed, in the interviews we conducted during the TRC and in the testimonies given to the TRC, villagers concurred that Segundo Morales was the appointed representative (*responsable*) for Shining Path in Uchuraccay.

25. Kleinman 2006: 3.

26. For a summary of these findings, see PTRC 2004: 384–409.

27. Ibid., 385.

28. Warren 1998: 179–80.

29. In testimonies to the PTRC, peasants commented that communal forms of labor were disrupted because people lacked the trust necessary to work together. Zur (1998) and Green (1999) also found that traditional forms of solidarity in Mayan communities frequently collapsed during the war in Guatemala for similar reasons.

30. The Peruvian currency at that time was *nuevos soles*; the exchange rate fluctuated but generally hovered around 3 *soles* to the dollar.

31. See Foucault 1977.

32. In her work with rural widows in Guatemala, Zur (1998) noted a similar collapse in traditional systems of support following the genocide.

33. In her efforts to theorize a feminist approach to peace building, Donna Pankhurst argues, "It is also commonly assumed that women automatically benefit from 'community activities,' where there is considerable evidence to refute this" (2003: 167). This resonates with my observations.

34. For a discussion of these practices, see Leinaweaver 2008.

35. Linda Green heard similar comments from Mayan widows in Guatemala (1999).

36. Linda Green (1999) noted that postwar interventions tended to operate with an almost total ignorance of the local divisions that frequently served as obstacles to the successful implementation of those interventions. Indeed, they tended to accentuate the cleavages, albeit unintentionally. For an exploration of the economics of conflict, reconstruction, and vulnerability with regard to "genocide widows" in Rwanda, see Brück and Schindler 2009.

37. Das 2000: 209.

38. See Ferguson 2006.

39. Carhuahurán, June 18, 1998.

40. Carhuahurán, October 1999.

41. For excellent studies on women's organizing during the conflict, see Coral Cordero 1998; and Blondet 1991, 1995. The Mother's Clubs are a fascinating example of how women organized in the midst of war. As Coral Cordero explains, by 1995 the Departmental Federation of Mother's Clubs of Ayacucho (FEDECMA) had come to include eleven provincial federations, 1,400 Mother's Clubs, and approximately eighty thousand members (Coral Cordero 1998: 358–59).

42. February 2003.

43. See Merry 2006.

Chapter 7

1. One can look to classic studies of World War II (among them Arendt 1963; Browning 1992; Gross 2001; and Lifton 2000) for examples of the "banality of evil"

and bureaucratic indifference; for case studies of neighbors killing neighbors; for the impact of ideology and totalitarianism on human action; and for the compartmentalization and creation of a "double" that could engage in acts normally repugnant to the individual. There are also the Milgram experiments on authority and obedience (1974) and the Stanford Prison Experiments (Zimbardo et al. 1973), which indicated how quickly study participants could be socialized into inflicting pain on others. More recent work looks at military socialization (Goldstein 2001), violence workers (Huggins, Haritos-Gatouros, and Zimbardo 2002), the mobilization of semiotic and cultural repertoires (Hinton 2004), native-settler dynamics and colonial logics in the Rwandan genocide (Mamdani 2001), and the bodily construction of radical alterity (Malkki 1995; Theidon 2001a, 2004). For a helpful overview of various explanatory models, see Fletcher and Weinstein 2002.

2. Minow 1998: 5.

3. Kleinman 2006: 2.

4. For example, see Huntington 1991; and O'Donnell and Schmitter 1986.

5. Wilson 2001: 175.

6. For example, see Biggar 2003; Borneman 1997, 2002, 2003; Shaw 2005; Theidon 2004, 2006a; and Wilson 2001.

7. See Remy's (1991) analysis of these ritualized battles and critique of the "ideal informant" (frequently a *mestizo*) eager to provide commentary on the "violent nature" of Andean peasants.

8. Another term for these battles is *tinku*, and the literature on *tinku* is abundant. *Tinku* are annual ceremonial battles that affirm both group identity and complementary opposition. For example, see Allen 1988; Bolin 1998; Orlove 1994; Remy 1991; and Villalobos 1992.

9. I thank Roberto Rojas for conversations regarding the productive aspects of community life.

10. See Degregori 1990.

11. Peña Jumpa 1998: 192.

12. The literature is vast, but here I refer to Evans-Pritchard 1937; Favret-Saada 1980; Luhrmann 1989; Stewart and Strathern 2004; and Ashforth 2005.

13. December 2002.

14. Following the armed conflict, there was evidently a resurgence of witchcraft. This resonates with Ashforth's research on the upsurge in witchcraft accusations and killings following South Africa's democratic transition in 1994. The South African TRC was led by Archbishop Desmond Tutu, an inspiring figure. During the commission's work, he emphasized the concept *ubuntu*, arguing that it was a part of a distinctly African philosophy of ethics and personhood. As he wrote, "*Ubuntu* says I am human only because you are human. If I undermine your humanity, I dehumanize myself. You must do what you can do to maintain this great harmony, which is perpetually undermined by resentment, anger, desire for vengeance. That's why African jurisprudence is restorative rather

than retributive" (1999: 31). Tutu thus juxtaposed an alleged African jurisprudence with a "Western" approach, implying that retributive justice was a Western import. Ashforth, who lived and conducted research in Soweto, suggests we consider "negative *ubuntu*." In the midst of lives characterized by grave insecurity, social life was laced with the presumption of malice, and witches were its key agent. As with the Andean context, the sociocentric self was predominant, and people lived fully aware, and fearful, of the harm human beings could do to one another via an intermediary.

15. With regard to the banality of evil I refer, of course, to Hannah Arendt's analysis of Adolf Eichmann during his trial in Jerusalem. See Arendt 1963.

16. Manrique 1989: 148. Author's translation.

17. See Isbell 1994 and Berg 1994 for two interesting studies of Shining Path at the local level.

18. Isbell 1994: 83.

19. Ibid., 84.

20. Señor Alejandro Huamán was the president of Uchuraccay. The Senderistas killed him in late November or early December 1982.

21. *Caminar* (to walk) is a fascinating term. It implies the search for resources—and the *gestiones* (negotiations) necessary to secure those resources—for the good of one's community. Authorities "walk" as a way of bringing needed goods, services, and infrastructure to their constituencies.

22. Degregori 1997: 67.

23. Carhuahurán 1998.

24. See Scott 1992.

25. Mallon 1995: 10.

26. See Mayer 1991: 476.

27. For a fascinating study of narratives and history making among refugees in Burundi, see Malkki 1995.

28. Stern 1998, 2006: 1.

29. Apter 1997: 4.

30. Berg (1994) recounts one Senderista attack on the village of Pacucha in Andahuaylas. Villagers told him that the leaders of the attack were unknown Sendero militants but that the mass of the assailants were residents of a nearby village.

31. This is similar to Kay Warren's findings in Guatemala (1993). The period of terror was used as a temporal marker, and people spoke in terms of before, during, and after the terror.

32. See Mehta and Chatterji 2001: 230–31.

33. See Das and Kleinman 2000.

34. See Theidon 2004: 237. This conversation occurred in Accomarca in 2003.

35. Suárez-Orozco 1995: 243.

36. February 2003.

37. Doña Victoria's reference to ideology was part of the central-southern

dynamic, and she is one of several older people who lamented how they had "lost our children to that ideology."

38. Conversation with the author, January 2003.

39. See Peña Jumpa 1998; and Theidon 2001a, 2004.

40. White 1987.

41. I emphasize that villagers say "fallen out of humanity" rather than "lost their humanity." The image of the fallen is significant given the massive conversions to Evangelical Christianity in the highlands of Huanta during the internal armed conflict. God expelled Lucifer and his minions from heaven and they fell to earth. Again we see the condensation of images of evil; to have fallen out of humanity implies divine judgment as well.

42. Manrique 1989: 144.

43. *Caretas* 1983, no. 737.

44. For example, see Isbell 1978; and Silverblatt 1987.

45. Douglas 1966.

46. Del Pino 1998: 159.

47. See Ansión 1989; and Wiesmantel 1997.

48. Weismantel 1997: 12.

49. White 2000: 44.

50. See Weismantel 1997.

51. See Manrique 1989 for a discussion of how Shining Path ideologues ignored ethnic discrimination in their critiques of Peruvian society.

52. What was interesting was that I did not hear these sorts of descriptions in Uchuraccay. It may have to do with *where* people spent the war years, as well as what sort of violence they did or did not engage in. By 1984 Uchuraccay was deserted; the multiple attacks the community suffered at the hands of the army, the Senderistas, and the *ronderos* from Carhuahurán forced villagers to flee. The village was virtually empty until 1993–94. Thus people in Uchuraccay did not stay in the war zone, caught up in the protracted fighting and insecurity that characterized the region. They did not really wage war, although there was some killing within the community prior to 1984. There was simply less need to develop the elaborate psychology of war and of the enemy that was related to me in Carhuahurán and Huaychao.

53. Mayer 1994: 152–53.

54. I thank José Coronel Aguirre for an illuminating conversation regarding this topic.

55. Mellinkoff 1981: 1.

56. Goffman 1963: 43.

57. Ibid., 104–5.

58. Rabinow 1984: 60.

59. See Bourdieu 1990: 85–86.

60. See Bourdieu 1990.

61. Ibid., 73.

62. In Quechua, the suffixes *-sqa* and *-sqayki* indicate the speaker is not responsible for the event, that what the speaker is saying is "hearsay."

63. White 2000: 30.

Chapter 8

1. Jacoby 1988: 78.

2. See Duce and Perdomo 2003; and Moore 1986.

3. Moore 1986: 6.

4. Ibid., 322.

5. Mauss 1990: 79.

6. Minow 1998.

7. See Arendt 1958.

8. I am referring to James Scott's concepts of public versus hidden transcripts and what the discrepancies between the two tell us about the impact of domination on public discourse (1992).

9. Harvey 1991: 5.

10. See Das and Poole 2004.

11. Aretxaga 2000: 52.

12. See Steve Stern's work (1982) on the legal reforms implemented by Toledo in the early colonial era and the ways in which *indígenas* learned to use the legal system to try to lower *mita* requirements and taxes, while simultaneously maintaining autonomy from the state in other legal arenas. The mixed results point to the benefits and limitations of autonomy.

13. The Ley de Arrepentimiento (Repentance Law) was passed in May 1992 and remained in effect through November 1994. The law was part of broader counterinsurgency efforts, and in addition to the legal component the government staged "repentance ceremonies" in various parts of the country as a propaganda tool. See Tapia 1997 for an analysis of this law.

14. See Husson 1992.

15. Ibid., 45. Author's translation.

16. See Escriche 1918: 249–50.

17. As we saw in a previous chapter, intercommunal conflicts were quite common, and ritual battles were waged. However, although blood might have been drawn, these were not lethal engagements. I believe Marcelina was making that distinction in her comments.

18. I draw here from Del Pino and Theidon 1999.

19. This meeting took place in late 1982.

20. Asad 1993: 27.

21. Ibid., 47.

22. Brooks 2000: 2.

23. Ibid., 2.

24. Seider 1997: 42.

25. Tavuchis 1991: 7.

26. Starn 1999: 97.

27. February 2003.

28. Villagers in Huaychao made a communal decision not to give their testimonies to the TRC. This pact of silence reflected concerns that their testimonies would be broadcast on the radio, provoking Senderista reprisals. These sorts of fears were in part the result of the misinformation campaign waged by opponents of the TRC.

29. Jacoby 1988: 6.

30. Terdiman 1989.

31. Arendt 1958.

32. In her ethnography of a Quechua-speaking community, Allen (1988) describes a ceremony called Chacra Mañay. It takes place in February, when communal authorities distribute land that has returned to the community as a result of death or permanent outmigration of community members. The assembly I discuss here occurred in February 1986, following the worst years of the war in terms of death and displacement. I did not encounter another assembly of this nature in the Libro de Actas of this community, but it would be interesting to explore this practice in other communities that were affected by the internal armed conflict.

33. Again I think of Desmond Tutu's insistence that retributive justice was a "Western" imposition, at odds with an African emphasis on restorative justice. I do not believe that restorative and retributive justice are distinct or opposing forms of justice. Rather, I find that retributive emotions are very common and not intrinsically "Western" and that some form of punishment may be conducive to the reincorporation of the perpetrators as well as to restoring social relations between transgressors and those they have wronged. For a discussion of the centrality of vengeful emotions in the townships of post-apartheid South Africa, see Wilson 2001. For a fascinating analysis of how revenge comes to be considered a "base" emotion, see Jacoby 1988.

34. Tavuchis 1991: vii.

35. See Mauss 1990.

36. During my work with the TRC, I began research in the Apurímac and Ene River Valley (VRAE). In the VRAE there are many *recuperados* (recuperated people), referring to the former guerrillas, and the Comités Antisubversivos de Autodefensa Civil (DECAS, as the peasant patrols in the VRAE are called) played a key role in "recuperating" them.

37. See Nozick 1981.

38. For more on missionary justice, see Nader 1990: 444.

Chapter 9

1. See Hayner 2001.

2. These interviews were taped with people's permission. Although the men knew there was a possibility I would subsequently hear the tapes—we were very clear about why we were taping these conversations—my absence and the *trago* created a "men only" atmosphere.

3. I use his real name because he is a public figure and did not request anonymity.

4. In my conversations with several local authorities in the VRAE, they assured me that 50–60 percent of the population of the VRAE are *recuperados*. This refers to ex-Senderistas whose lives were spared if they repented and promised not to return to the ranks of the guerrilla. While the figure seems very high, it was consistent across conversations during my research in 2005.

5. I use his real name because he is a public figure and his name appears in the PTRC's Final Report.

6. This is reminiscent of the debates regarding collaboration, degrees of complicity, and guilt that Rigby discusses in the context of post–World War II European purges (2001).

7. Literally *runa masinchik* means "people like us" or "our fellow creatures." However, in daily use it also means "people we work with."

8. See Isbell 1978; and Peña Jumpa 1998.

9. Tamayo Flores 1992.

10. I thank Chema García for helpful conversations on the ethical dimensions of *ayni*.

11. See Stern 1982.

12. When Catholic priests were brought up to the villages to perform religious ceremonies, they did charge for their services. I think the fee charged for performing marriage ceremonies was conflated with the process of marching the women in a circle while the men selected partners; thus the notion that priests were actually selling the women.

13. Goffman 1963: 9.

14. See Gilligan 1993; and Ruddick 1995; for a critique, see Scheper-Hughes 1993.

15. Ortner 1995: 177.

16. Williams 1985: 75–76.

17. Peña Jumpa 1998; Williams 1985: 75–76.

18. See Nader 1990.

19. Huaychao, January 2003.

20. Minow 1998.

21. Jelin 2002: 6. Author's translation.

Chapter 10

1. See Fletcher and Weinstein 2002.

2. See Borneman 2002.

3. A "bad death" is abrupt or violent, making confession or last rites impossible. The status of these souls is ambiguous, wandering between this world (*kay pacha*) and an upper realm Christians would gloss as heaven (*hanan pacha*).

4. See Del Pino and Theidon 2000.

5. *Wachay* can be contrasted with *wachakuy*, which is used exclusively for childbirth.

6. Judith Zur found something similar in Guatemala: "The longer one was in *el monte* [the bush], the more of a guerrilla they were assumed to be" (1998: 86).

7. Portelli 1991: ix.

8. The Peruvian government did not implement a disarmament, demobilization, and reintegration (DDR) program for former combatants, as many other countries have during transitional periods.

9. During her research in post-genocide Guatemala, Judith Zur found that second husbands were not inclined to support children from a woman's previous relationship (1998: 58). This was also the case in Peru.

10. Harvey 1994: 86.

11. For an eloquent discussion of motherly love in conditions of chronic scarcity, see Scheper-Hughes 1993.

12. I acknowledge the studies done with second- and third-generation family members of Holocaust survivors; however, as Veena Das has suggested with regard to models of trauma and witnessing, the lessons bequeathed from "Holocaust studies cannot simply be transported to other contexts in which violence is embedded into different patterns of sociality" (2007: 103). I think this is also true of children, social memory, and the legacies of war.

13. Scheper-Hughes and Sargent 1998: 15.

14. For two eloquent examples, see Beah 2008 and Iweala 2007.

15. I was concerned that children might face some reprisal for the hours they spent with me and my research assistants. Thus I made a point of letting the adults see what we did with the children: painting, drawing, reading to them aloud in Spanish, singing, and practicing plays the children produced. Given the pitiful quality of rural education, combined with parents' fervent desire that their children learn Spanish and perhaps face less discrimination than they did, I found parents were generally pleased to have children spend time with us.

16. Stephens 1995: 4.

17. Zur found a similar anxiety in Guatemala, where Mayan people were not able to perform proper funerals and carry out their obligations to the dead (1998: 192). Shephard, working in the Peruvian Amazon, emphasizes that "death is contagious" and notes the power the dead hold over the living (2002).

18. Comaroff and Comaroff 1992: xxix.

19. Estados Unidos is Spanish for the United States. *Joder* means to fuck; thus Estados Jodidos is the Fucked States.

20. In her work in Burundi, Malkki heard many "mythicohistories" that were concerned with the moral order of the world. They were stories told in the collective voice, unmoored from any one author (1995: 56). I was struck by how quickly certain stories—Julio's death, the stranger (whom we will encounter shortly)—became communal stories, told and retold with remarkable uniformity. These occurrences become emblematic communal events not in the moment in which they happened but in the subsequent narrative work done in the name of the community.

21. I refer here to a Nietzschean understanding of *ressentiment* (1887) 1998. As I have written elsewhere, in the southern communities some people did describe their villages as *pueblos resentidos* (resentful pueblos) harboring resentment toward the state for the massacres carried out by the armed forces and toward certain Shining Path militants who continue to live defiantly among them. However, I do not conflate resentment with *ressentiment*. See Theidon 2004.

22. See Biggar 2003: 19.

23. Ibid.

24. The Christian roots of humanitarianism are well established, but the figure of the traveler or the stranger—and one's duty to show him compassion—is not limited to the Judeo-Christian tradition. For example, in the Muslim faith almsgiving (*zakat*) to the poor is a way of purifying oneself. However, the list of potential recipients is not limited to the poor; "sons of the road," the traveler, or the stranger are also people to whom charity is due. Benthall and Bellion-Jourdan 2003: 9–10.

25. See Eisenbruch 1991: 674.

26. Akhavan 1998: 738.

Chapter 11

1. I feel I can now name these four communities. The PTRC's Final Report is part of the public record regarding the alliances forged by certain members of these communities during the internal armed conflict.

2. See Hayner 2001.

3. Valentín Paniagua, *La República*, August 10, 2003. Mr. Paniagua was noting that he had created a truth commission, not a truth and reconciliation commission. It was his successor, Alejandro Toledo, who added "reconciliation" to the commission's name and mandate.

4. Lerner 2002.

5. Here I invoke Primo Levi ([1959] 1995, 1989) and his exploration of the "gray zone."

6. I struggled mightily with this material, concerned that something I wrote could endanger the people who spoke with us. I decided to provide scant personal details,

and that anonymity works both ways. I will use block quotations more frequently and avoid offering any physical descriptions of the former militants with whom my research team and I have spoken. Nor will I identify, in most instances, which of us conducted the interview. I want to avoid compromising any of us and our ability to continue to conduct research with former Shining Path members.

7. His use of the term *senderólogos* is worth a few words. Within the Peruvian academic community, Los Senderólogos refers to a group of researchers who extensively studied Shining Path. Primitivo uses the term here to refer to the Senderista cadres, who were well versed in the group's ideology.

8. His lover was a teacher from Cuzco. From what we were told in 2005, she was either in prison or had been recently released from Santa Mónica Prison on terrorism charges.

9. The majority of interviews we have conducted in Accomarca indicate that Gutierrez and Alfredo the Huambalpino were the two highest-ranking and most active Shining Path militants in the pueblo.

10. *Zambo* is a Peruvian term used to refer to people with African ancestry.

11. *Sellos* are rubber stamps bearing the various communal authorities' elected positions. These stamps are used in preparing documents, signing Actas Comunales, and in the exercise of other official duties.

12. In other versions I heard, Primitivo did not lend his knife to a member of the *fuerza principal* but rather killed the authority himself.

13. Alfredo is married to one of the Mendez sisters, each of whom was married to one of the local Shining Path commanders. Cupertino Morales was his uncle, thus Edilberto is Alfredo's uncle's brother. Edilberto still lives in Accomarca, as we shall see.

14. *Pasamontañas* are akin to balaclavas, and they leave the eyes and lips exposed.

15. PTRC 2003: vol. 7, pp. 148–49.

16. Both Telmo Hurtado and Rivera Rondón attended arms orientation courses at the U.S. Army School of the Americas from 1981 to 1982 during the height of military repression.

17. People in Accomarca insist that sixty-nine were killed because seven other people were killed in various incidents during the operation.

18. PTRC 2003: vol. 7, p. 153.

19. Ibid., p. 152.

20. Accomarca, June 2003.

21. Etxeberria 2002: 98.

Chapter 12

1. I am, of course, influenced by Arthur Kleinman's body of work on local moral worlds, as well the medical anthropology of local idioms of distress.

2. Señora Aurelia Choccña, Accomarca, November 15, 2002.

3. See Tapia 1997 for an analysis of the Ley de Arrepentimiento.

4. I thank José Coronel for sharing this information with me.

5. Authorities in another central-southern community attempted this same strategy with the ex-*cabecillas* who returned to their pueblo. Their efforts were refused.

6. With *tiene cara todavía*—literally "they still have face"—she is referring to their audacity to show their faces and run for office.

7. Napier 1986.

8. I think of Lifton's work on the Nazi doctors who delegated the horrible medical interventions they conducted to their "Auschwitz self," thereby maintaining some sense of themselves as decent people (2000).

9. *Dar la cara* is literally "to give the face." It can mean showing one's face; it also implies having the courage to face up to someone.

10. Das and Kleinman 2000: 2.

11. Braithwaite (1989) has written powerfully about "reintegrative shaming" and the role it plays in many rituals such as those we saw in the *alturas* of Huanta.

12. Levinas, Smith, and Harshav 1998: 22.

13. Critchley and Bernasconi 2002: 21.

14. O'Neill 1999: 139.

15. Ibid., 191.

16. Tavuchis 1991.

17. Defarges 1999: 35.

18. Taussig 1999: 51.

19. I thank Nelson Manrique and Isaías Rojas Pérez for helpful conversations on this theme.

20. For an excellent discussion of the contradictory tensions in Peruvian human rights law and practice, see Laplante 2007.

21. "Aprista" is someone who belongs to the political party Alianza Popular Revolucionaria Americana (APRA).

22. Mamdani 2001: 272.

23. For an excellent discussion of the debates regarding the applicability of the "Clean Hands Doctrine" in Peru, see Guillerot and Magarell 2006 and Laplante 2007. The "Clean Hands Doctrine" dictates that the wrongdoing of an injured party may limit his or her claim to reparations. However, as Laplante skillfully argues, this doctrine violates human rights principles and laws, having been developed for common law disputes seeking to balance blame in determining causation of injury of harm between equal parties, such as states. The tensions that arise when applying this doctrine to human rights violations are multiple: if only those with "clean hands" are legitimate subjects of human rights protection, then the stigma of past militancy—or even accusations to that effect—are sufficient to sully far more than an individual's hands.

Glossary

acta. A binding agreement made between individuals or in communal assemblies.

apu. Mountain deity.

arrepentido(a). A repentant person, in this case referring to former Shining Path members who repented for their participation in the guerrillas.

ayni. Reciprocal labor exchange, which can establish solidarity, hierarchy, and indebtedness.

calamina. Corrugated aluminum sheets used for roofs and doors.

cargo. A communal charge or responsibility.

caridad. Charity or compassion.

campesinos. Peasants.

chacra. A plot of agricultural land or small farm.

chapla. Round wheat bread.

comunero(a). Member of a peasant community (*comunidad campesina*).

comunidad campesina. A legally recognized, rights-bearing entity.

costal. Burlap sack.

curandero. Healer.

daño. Literally harm; also an illness caused by stepping or sitting where one should not, thus angering the mountain gods (*apus*).

engañado. Tricked or duped.

envidia: Envy.

faena. Obligatory communal labor.

formaciones. Meetings held, in addition to communal assemblies, with a tendency to focus on security issues.

gamonal. Local political boss.

hacendado. Owner of a hacienda (large ranch).

huk kuna. "those people"; used to refer to former Shining Path militants.

ichu. Straw.

iskay uyukuna. Two-faced; said of a person who cannot be trusted.

juicio popular. A term used by Sendero Luminoso. Literally a "people's trial"; refers to justice meted out, frequently lethally, by the militants.

llakis. Suffering or pain, associated with heartache and memories.

prójimo. Fellow creature, neighbor, brother.

puna. Grasslands in the high Andes.

puriqkuna. Literally "those who walk" in reference to the Shining Path guerrillas.

quejas. Literally complaints; also refers to legal cases brought before communal authorities.

ronda campesina. Armed peasant patrols. In Ayacucho, the *rondas* began during the internal armed conflict.

rondero(a). Male or female member of the armed peasant patrol.

runakuna. Quechua for "people," "human beings."

sasachakuy tiempo. The difficult time; one of the terms Quechua speakers use to refer to the internal armed conflict.

sinvergüenza. Shameless.

susto. Soul loss due to fright.

terrucos or *tucos.* Slang for "terrorist"; used to refer to members of Shining Path.

trago. Alcohol.

umasapa. Literally "big head"; community leaders.

varayoq. Literally one who holds a staff, referring to one form of community leadership and hierarchy. (Although the plural of *varayoq* is *varayoqkuna*, people frequently just say *varayoqs*.)

Selected Bibliography

Abercrombie, Thomas. 1998. *Pathways of Memory and Power: Ethnography and History Among Andean People.* Madison: University of Wisconsin Press.

Akhavan, Payam. 1998. "Justice in the Hague, Peace in the Former Yugoslavia? A Commentary on the United National War Crimes Tribunal." *Human Rights Quarterly* 20, no. 4: 737–816.

Allen, Catherine J. 1988. *The Hold Life Has: Coca and Cultural Identity in an Andean Community.* Washington, D.C.: Smithsonian Institution Press.

Americas Watch. 1992. *Peru Under Fire: Human Rights Since the Return to Democracy.* New Haven, Conn.: Yale University Press.

Ansión, Juan María, ed. 1989. *Pishtacos: De verdugos a sacaojos.* Lima, Peru: Tarea.

Appadurai, Arjun. 1991. "Global Ethnoscapes: Notes and Queries for a Transnational Anthropology." In *Recapturing Anthropology: Working in the Present,* ed. Richard G. Fox, 191–210. Santa Fe, N.M.: School of American Research Press.

———. 1998. "Putting Hierarchy in Its Place." *Cultural Anthropology* 3, no. 1 (1998): 36–49.

Apter, David. 1997. *The Legitimization of Violence.* New York: New York University Press.

Arendt, Hannah. 1958. *The Human Condition.* Chicago: University of Chicago Press.

———. 1963. *Eichmann in Jerusalem: A Report on the Banality of Evil.* New York: Viking Press.

Aretxaga, Begoña. 2000. "A Fictional Reality: Paramilitary Death Squads and the Construction of State Terror in Spain." In *Death Squad: The Anthropology of State Terror,* ed. Jeffrey A. Sluka, 49–69. Philadelphia: University of Pennsylvania Press.

———. 2008. "Madness and the Politically Real: Reflections on Violence in Postdictatorial Spain." In *Postcolonial Disorders,* ed. Mary-Jo DelVecchio Good, Sandra Teresa Hyde, Sarah Pinto, and Byron J. Good, 43–61. Berkeley: University of California Press.

Arnold, Denise Y. 1997. Introduction to *Más allá del silencio: Las fronteras de género en los Andes*, ed. Denise Arnold, 37–65. La Paz, Bolivia: CIASE/ILCA.

Asad, Talal. 1993. *Genealogies of Religion: Discipline and Reasons of Power in Christianity and Islam*. Baltimore: Johns Hopkins University Press.

Ashforth, Adam. 2005. *Witchcraft, Violence and Democracy in South Africa*. Chicago: University of Chicago Press.

AYNI. 1992. *Diagnóstico de la Iglesia Presbiteriana Nacional del Perú*. Huanta: AYNI.

Beah, Ishmael. 2008. *Long Way Gone: Memoirs of a Boy Soldier*. New York: Farrar, Straus, and Giroux.

Bell, Christine, and Catherine O'Rourke. 2007. "Does Feminism Need a Theory of Transitional Justice? An Introductory Essay." *International Journal of Transitional Justice* 1, no. 1: 23–44.

Benjamin, Walter. 1969. "Theses on the Philosophy of History." In *Illuminations: Essays and Reflections*, ed. Hannah Arendt, 253–64. New York: Schocken Books.

Benthall, Jonathan, and Jerome Bellion-Jourdan. 2003. *The Charitable Crescent: The Politics of Aid in the Muslim World*. New York: I. B. Tauris.

Berg, Ronald H. 1994. "Peasant Responses to Shining Path in Andahuaylas." In *Shining Path of Peru*, 2d ed., ed. David Scott Palmer, 77–100. New York: St. Martin's Press.

Bickford, Louis. 2000. "Human Rights Archives and Research on Historical Memory: Argentina, Chile and Uruguay." *Latin American Research Review* 35, no. 2: 160–82.

Biehl, Joao. 2005. *Vita: Life in a Zone of Abandonment*. Berkeley: University of California Press.

Biehl, Joao, Byron Good, and Arthur Kleinman, eds. 2007. *Subjectivity: Ethnographic Investigations*. Berkeley: University of California Press.

Biggar, Nigel, ed. 2003. *Burying the Past: Making Peace and Doing Justice After Civil Conflict*. Washington, D.C.: Georgetown University Press.

Blondet, Cecilia. 1991. *Las mujeres y el poder: Una historia de Villa El Salvador*. Lima, Peru: Instituto de Estudios Peruanos.

———. 1995. *Hoy, Menú Popular: Comedores en Lima*. Lima, Peru: Instituto de Estudios Peruanos.

Boddy, Janice. 1989. *Wombs and Alien Spirits: Women, Men and the Zar Cult in Northern Sudan*. Madison: University of Wisconsin Press.

Boellstorff, Tom, and Johan Lindquist. 2004. "Bodies of Emotion: Rethinking Culture and Emotion Through Southeast Asia." *Ethnos* 69, no. 4 (December): 437–44.

Bolin, Inge. 1998. *Rituals of Respect: The Secret of Survival in the High Peruvian Andes*. Austin: University of Texas Press.

Borneman, John. 1997. *Settling Accounts: Violence, Justice, and Accountability in Postsocialist Europe*. Princeton, N.J.: Princeton University Press.

———. 2002. "Reconciliation After Ethnic Cleansing: Listening, Retribution, Affiliation." *Public Culture* 14, no. 2: 281–304.

———. 2003. "Why Reconciliation? A Response to Critics." *Public Culture* 15, no. 1: 199–208.

Bornstein, Erica. 2005. *The Spirit of Development: Protestant NGOs, Morality and Economics in Zimbabwe.* Stanford, Calif.: Stanford University Press.

Bourdieu, Pierre. 1990. *The Logic of Practice.* Stanford, Calif.: Stanford University Press.

Bracken, Patrick J., and Celia Petty. 1998. *Rethinking the Trauma of War.* London: Free Association Books/Save the Children.

Bracken, Patrick J., Joan E. Giller, and Derek Summerfield. 1995. "Psychological Responses to War and Atrocity: The Limitations of Current Concepts." *Social Science and Medicine* 40, no. 8: 1073–82.

Braithwaite, John. 1989. *Crime, Shame and Reintegration.* Cambridge: Cambridge University Press.

Breslau, Josh. 2004. "Cultures of Trauma: Anthropological Views of Post-Traumatic Stress Disorder in International Health." *Culture, Medicine and Psychiatry* 28: 113–26.

Breuer, Joseph, and Sigmund Freud. (1895) 2000. *Studies on Hysteria.* New York: Basic Books.

Brooks, Peter. 2000. *Troubling Confessions: Speaking Guilt in Law and Literature.* Chicago: University of Chicago Press.

Browning, Christopher. 1992. *Ordinary Men: Reserve Police Battalion 101 and the Final Solution in Poland.* London: Penguin Books.

Brück, Tilman, and Kati Schindler. 2009. "The Impact of Violent Conflicts on Households: What Do We Know and What Should We Know About War Widows?" *Oxford Development Studies* 37, no. 3 (September): 289–309.

Brusco, Elizabeth E. 1995. *The Reformation of Machismo: Evangelical Conversion and Gender in Colombia.* Austin: University of Texas Press.

Burdick, John. 1993. *Looking for God in Brazil: The Progressive Catholic Church in Urban Brazil's Religious Arena.* Berkeley: University of California Press.

Burga, Manuel. 1988. *Nacimiento de una utopia: Muerte y resurreción de la Inca.* Lima, Peru: Instituto de Apoyo Agrario.

Butalia, Urvavshi. 2000. *The Other Side of Silence: Voices from the Partition of India.* Durham, N.C.: Duke University Press.

Butler, Judith. 1990. *Gender Trouble: Feminism and the Subversion of Identity.* New York: Routledge.

Caldeira, Teresa P. R., and James Holston. 1996. "Democracy and Violence in Brazil." *Society for Comparative Study of Society and History* 40, no. 4: 691–729.

Canessa, Andrew. 2000. "Contesting Hybridity: Evangelistas and Kataristas in Highland Bolivia." *Journal of Latin American Studies* 32: 115–44.

Canguilhem, George. (1943) 1991. *The Normal and the Pathological.* London: Zone Books.

Carbonnier, Jean. 1994. *Sociología jurídica.* Paris: Presses Universitaires de France.

Chestnut, R. Andrew. 1997. *Born Again in Brazil: The Pentecostal Boom and the Pathogens of Poverty.* New Brunswick, N.J.: Rutgers University Press.

Cockburn, Cynthia. 2001. "The Gendered Dynamics of Armed Conflict and Political

Violence." In *Victims, Perpetrators or Actors? Gender, Armed Conflict and Political Violence*, ed. Caroline O. N. Moser and Fiona C. Clark, 13–29. London: Zed Books.

Comaroff, Jean. 1985. *Body of Power, Spirit of Resistance: The Culture and History of a South African People*. Chicago: University of Chicago Press.

Comaroff, Jean, and John Comaroff, eds. 1992. *Modernity and Its Malcontents: Ritual and Power in Postcolonial Africa*. Chicago: University of Chicago Press.

———. 1999. "Occult Economies and the Violence of Abstraction: Notes from the South African Postcolony." *American Ethnologist* 26, no. 2: 279–303.

Conklin, Beth. 1996. "Reflections on Amazonian Anthropologies of the Body." *Medical Anthropology Quarterly* 10, no. 3: 373–75.

Connell, Patricia. 1997. "Understanding Victimization and Agency: Considerations of Race, Class and Gender." *Political and Legal Anthropology Review* 20, no. 2: 116–43.

Connerton, Paul. 1989. *How Societies Remember*. Cambridge: Cambridge University Press.

Cooke, Miriam. 1997. *Women and the War Story*. Berkeley: University of California Press.

Coral Cordero, Isabel. 1998. "Women in War: Impact and Responses." In *Shining and Other Paths: War and Society in Peru, 1980–1995*, ed. Steve J. Stern, 345–73. Durham, N.C.: Duke University Press.

Coronel Aguirre, José. 1995. "Recomposición del Tejido social y el estado." Lecture, Foro Nacional sobre Desplazamiento Interno Forzado. Lima, Peru, July 13–14.

Critchley, Simon, and Robert Bernasconi, eds. 2002. *The Cambridge Companion to Lévinas*. Cambridge: Cambridge University Press.

Csordas, Thomas J., ed. 1994. *Embodiment and Experience: The Existential Ground of Culture and Self*. Cambridge: Cambridge University Press.

Cueto, Marcos. 1997. *El regreso de las epidemias: Salud y sociedad en el Perú del siglo XX*. Lima, Peru: Instituto de Estudios Peruanos.

Das, Veena. 1997. "Language and Body: Transactions in the Construction of Pain." In *Social Suffering*, ed. Arthur Kleinman, Veena Das, and Margaret Lock, 67–91. Berkeley: University of California Press.

———. 2000. "The Act of Witnessing: Violence, Poisonous Knowledge, and Subjectivity." In *Violence and Subjectivity*, ed. Veena Das, Arthur Kleinman, Mamphela Ramphele, and Pamela Reynolds, 205–25. Berkeley: University of California Press.

———. 2007. *Life and Words: Violence and the Descent into the Ordinary*. Berkeley: University of California Press.

Das, Veena, and Ranendra K. Das. 2007. "How the Body Speaks: Illness and the Lifeworld Among the Urban Poor." In *Subjectivity: Ethnographic Investigations*, ed. Joao Biehl, Byron Good, and Arthur Kleinman, 66–97. Berkeley: University of California Press.

Das, Veena, and Arthur Kleinman. 2000. Introduction to *Violence and Subjectivity*, ed. Veena Das, Arthur Kleinman, Mamphela Ramphele, and Pamela Reynolds, 1–18. Berkeley: University of California Press.

———. 2001. Introduction to *Remaking a World: Violence, Social Suffering and Recovery*, ed. Veena Das, Arthur Kleinman, Margaret Lock, Mamphela Ramphele, and Pamela Reynolds, 1–30. Berkeley: University of California Press.

Das, Veena, and Deborah Poole, eds. 2004. *Anthropology in the Margins of the State.* Santa Fe: School of American Research.

Das, Veena, Arthur Kleinman, Mamphela Ramphele, and Pamela Reynolds, eds. 2000. *Violence and Subjectivity.* Berkeley: University of California Press.

———. 2001. *Remaking a World: Violence, Social Suffering and Recovery.* Berkeley: University of California Press.

Davis, Natalie. 1974. "Some Tasks and Some Themes in the Study of Popular Religion." In *The Pursuit of Holiness in Late Medieval and Renaissance Religion*, ed. Charles Trinkhaus and Heiko Obermann, 307–36. Leiden: E. J. Brill.

De Certeau, Michel. 1984. *The Practice of Everyday Life.* Berkeley: University of California Press.

Defarges, Philippe Moreau. 1999. *Repentance et reconciliation.* Paris: Presses de Sciences Po.

Degregori, Carlos Iván. 1989. *Que difícil es ser Dios: Ideología y violencia política en Sendero Luminoso.* Lima, Peru: El Zorro de Abajo.

———. 1990. *Ayacucho, 1969–1979: El surgimiento de Sendero Luminoso.* Lima, Peru: Instituto de Estudios Peruanos.

———. 1997. "The Maturation of a Cosmocrat and the Building of a Discourse Community: The Case of Shining Path." In *The Legitimation of Violence*, ed. David Apter, 33–82. London: UNRISD/MacMillan Press.

Degregori, Carlos Iván, José Coronel, Ponciano Del Pino, and Orin Starn. 1996. *Las rondas campesinas y la derrota de Sendero Luminoso.* Lima, Peru: Instituto de Estudios Peruanos.

De la Cadena, Marisol. 1991. "Las mujeres son más indias: Etnicidad y género en una comunidad del Cusco." *Revista Andina*, no. 17: 7–29.

———. 2000. *Indigenous Mestizos: The Politics of Race and Culture in Cuzco, Peru, 1919–1991.* Durham, N.C.: Duke University Press.

Delgado Sumar, Hugo E. 1988a. *Ideología Andina: El pagapu en Ayacucho.* Ayacucho, Peru: Universidad Nacional de San Cristóbal de Huamanga.

———. 1988b. *Medicina tradicional en Ayacucho.* Ayacucho, Peru: Universidad Nacional de San Cristóbal de Huamanga.

Del Pino, Ponciano. 1996. "Tiempos de guerra y de dioses: Ronderos, evangélicos y senderistas en el Valle de Río Apurímac." In *Las rondas campesinas y la derrota de Sendero Luminoso*, ed. Carlos Iván Degregori, José Coronel, Ponciano Del Pino, and Orin Starn, 117–89. Lima, Peru: Instituto de Estudios Peruanos.

———. 1998. "Family, Cultural and 'Revolution': Everyday Life with Sendero Luminoso." In *Shining and Other Paths: War and Society in Perú, 1980–1995*, ed. Steve J. Stern, 158–92. Durham, N.C.: Duke University Press.

Del Pino, Ponciano, and Kimberly Theidon. 1999. "'Así es Como Vive Gente': Procesos deslocalizados y culturas emergentes." In *Cultura y globalización*, ed. Carlos Ivan Degregori and Gonzalo Portocarrero, 183–202. Lima, Peru: Red para el Desarrollo de las Ciencias Sociales en el Perú.

———. 2000. "'El Chino ya murió, Ayacucho lo mató': Crónica de una muerte no anunciada." *Ideele: Revista del Instituto de Defensa Legal*, no. 127 (May): 49–53.

De Miguel, Juan Palomar. 2000. *Diccionario para Juristas*. Mexico City: Porrúa.

Desjarlais, Robert. 1992. *Body and Emotion: The Aesthetics of Illness and Healing in the Nepal Himalayas*. Philadelphia: University of Pennsylvania Press.

Desjarlais, Robert, Leon Eisenberg, Byron Good, and Arthur Kleinman, eds. 1995. *World Mental Health: Problems and Priorities in Low-Income Countries*. Oxford: Oxford University Press.

Diken, Bülent, and Carsten Bagge Lausten. 2005. "Becoming Abject: Rape as a Weapon of War." *Body and Society* 11, no. 1: 111–28.

Douglas, Mary. 1966. *Purity and Danger: An Analysis of the Concepts of Pollution and Taboo*. London: Routledge.

Duce, Mauricio, and Rogelio Pérez Perdomo. 2003. "Citizen Security and Reform in the Criminal Justice System in Latin America." In *Crime and Violence in Latin America: Citizen Security, Democracy and the State*, ed. Hugo Fruhling, Joseph S. Tulchin, and Heather Golding, 69–93. Washington, D.C.: Woodrow Wilson Center.

Eisenbruch, Maurice. 1991. "From Post-Traumatic Stress Disorder to Cultural Bereavement: Diagnosis of Southeast Asian Refugees." *Social Science and Medicine* 33, no. 6: 673–80.

———. 2007. "The Uses and Abuses of Culture: Cultural Competence in Post-Mass Crime Peace-Building in Cambodia. In *After Mass Crime: Rebuilding States and Communities*, ed. Béatrice Pouligny, Simon Chesterman, and Albrecht Schnabel, 71–96. New York: United Nations University.

Enloe, Cynthia. 1988. *Does Khaki Become You? The Militarisation of Women's Lives*. London: Pandora Press.

Escobar, Arturo. 2001. "Culture Sits in Places: Reflections on Globalism and Subaltern Strategies of Localization." *Political Geography* 20: 139–74.

Escriche, Joaquin. (1847) 1918. *Diccionario razonado de legislación y jurisprudencia*.

Etxeberría, Xabier. 2002. "Qué entender por perdón." In *Verdad y reconciliación: Reflexiones éticas*, 107–20. Lima, Peru: Centro de Estudios y Publicaciones, Instituto Bartolomé de las Casas.

Evans-Pritchard, E. E. 1937. *Witchcraft, Oracles and Magic Among the Azande*. Oxford: Clarendon Press.

Falconí, Carola, and José Carlos Agüero. 2003. "Violaciones sexuales en las comunidades campesinas de Ayacucho." In *Violaciones sexuales a mujeres durante la violencia política en el Perú*, 8–13. Lima, Peru: Comisión de Derechos Humanos (COMISEDH).

Farmer, Paul. 1988. "Bad Blood, Spoiled Milk: Bodily Fluids as Moral Barometers in Rural Haiti." *American Ethnologist* 15, no. 1: 62–83.

Fassin, Didier, Richard Rechtman, and Rachel Gomme. 2009. *The Empire of Trauma: An Inquiry into the Condition of Victimhood*. Princeton, N.J.: Princeton University Press.

Favret-Saada, Jeanne. 1980. *Deadly Words: Witchcraft in the Bocage*. New York: Cambridge University Press.

Feldman, Allen. 1991. *Formations of Violence: The Narrative of the Body and Political Terror in Northern Ireland*. Chicago: University of Chicago Press.

———. 1995. "Ethnographic States of Emergency." In *Fieldwork Under Fire: Contemporary Studies of Violence and Survival*, ed. Carolyn Nordstrom and Antonius C.G.M. Robben, 224–53. Berkeley: University of California Press.

Ferguson, James. 2006. *Global Shadows: Africa in the Neoliberal World Order*. Durham, N.C.: Duke University Press.

Ferme, Marianne. 2001. *The Underneath of Things: Violence, History and the Everyday in Sierra Leone*. Berkeley: University of California Press.

Fisher, William. F. 1997. "Doing Good? The Politics and Antipolitics of NGO Practices." *Annual Review of Anthropology* 26: 439–64.

Fletcher, Laurel E., and Harvey M. Weinstein. 2002. "Violence and Social Repair: Rethinking the Contribution of Justice to Reconciliation." *Human Rights Quarterly* 24: 573–639.

Flores Galindo, Tito. 1986. *Buscando un Inca: Identidad y utopia en los Andes*. Lima, Peru: SUR.

Foster, Dan. 2000. "What Makes a Perpetrator? An Attempt to Understand." In *Looking Back, Reaching Forward: Reflections on the Truth and Reconciliation Commission in South Africa*, ed. Charles Villa-Vicencio and Wilhelm Verwoerd, 219–29. Cape Town: University of Cape Town Press.

Foucault, Michel. 1977. *Language, Counter-Memory, Practice: Selected Essays and Interviews by Michel Foucault*, ed. Donald F. Bouchard. Ithaca, N.Y.: Cornell University Press.

———. 1994. *The Birth of the Clinic: An Archaeology of Medical Perception*. New York: Vintage.

Garrard-Burnett, Virginia. 1998. *Protestantism in Guatemala: Living in the New Jerusalem*. Austin: University of Texas Press.

Garrard-Burnett, Virginia, and David Stoll, eds. 1993. *Rethinking Protestantism in Latin America*. Philadelphia: Temple University Press.

Geertz, Clifford. 1983. *Local Knowledge: Further Essays in Interpretive Anthropology*. New York: Basic Books.

Getgen, Jocelyn E. 2008. "Untold Truths: The Exclusion of Enforced Sterilizations from the Peruvian Truth Commission's Final Report." Cornell Law School Berger International Speaker Papers, Paper 8, Cornell Law School, Cornell University, Ithaca, N.Y. http://scholarship.law.cornell.edu/biss_papers/8.

Gill, Leslie. 1990. "'Like a Veil to Cover Them': Women and the Pentecostal Movement in La Paz." *American Ethnologist* 17, no. 4 : 708–21.

Gilligan, Carol. 1993. *In a Different Voice: Psychological Theory and Women's Development*. Cambridge, Mass.: Harvard University Press.

Ginzburg, Carlo. 1992. *Clues, Myths, and the Historical Method*. Baltimore: Johns Hopkins University Press.

Goffman, Erving. 1963. *Stigma: Notes on the Management of Spoiled Identity*. New York: Simon and Schuster.

Goldstein, Joshua S. 2001. *War and Gender: How Gender Shapes the War System and Vice Versa*. New York: Cambridge University Press.

Good, Byron J. 1992. "Culture and Psychopathology: Directions for Psychiatric Anthropology." In *New Directions in Psychological Anthropology*, ed. Theodore Schwartz, Geoffrey White, and Catherine Lutz, 181–205. Cambridge: Cambridge University Press.

Good, Mary-Jo DelVecchio, Sandra Teresa Hyde, Sarah Pinto, and Byron J. Good, eds. 2008. *Postcolonial Disorders*. Berkeley: University of California Press.

Green, Linda. 1999. *Fear as a Way of Life: Mayan Widows in Rural Guatemala*. New York: Columbia University Press.

Gross, Jan T. 2001. *Neighbors: The Destruction of the Jewish Community in Jedwabne, Poland*. New York: Penguin.

Guillerot, Julie. 2006. "Linking Gender and Reparations in Peru: A Failed Opportunity." In *What Happened to the Women: Gender and Reparations for Human Rights Violations*, ed. Ruth Rubio-Marín, 136–93. New York: Social Science Research Council.

Guillerot, Julie, and Lisa Magarell. 2006. *Reparación en la Transición Peruana: Memorias de un proceso inacabado*. Lima: APRODEH.

Gupta, Akhil, and James Ferguson. 1992. "Beyond 'Culture': Space, Identity, and the Politics of Difference." *Cultural Anthropology* 7, no. 1: 6–23.

Gutiérrez, Gustavo. 1986. *Hablar de Dios desde el sufrimiento del inocente: Una reflexión sobre el libro de Job*. Lima, Peru: Centro de Estudios y Publicaciones, Instituto Bartolomé de las Casas.

Gutmann, Matthew C. 1997. "Trafficking in Men: The Anthropology of Masculinity." *Annual Review of Anthropology* 26 (October): 385–409.

Hacking, Ian. 1995. *Rewriting the Soul: Multiple Personality and the Sciences of Memory*. Princeton, N.J.: Princeton University Press.

Harris, Olivia. 1978. "Complementarity and Conflict: An Andean View of Women and Men." In *Sex and Age as Principles of Social Differentiation*, ed. J. S. Fontaine, 21–40. New York: Academic Press.

Harvey, Penelope. 1991. "Drunken Speech and the Construction of Meaning: Bilingual Competence in the Southern Peruvian Andes." *Language in Society* 20, no. 1: 1–36.

———. 1994. "Domestic Violence in the Peruvian Andes." In *Sex and Violence: Issues in Representation and Experience*, ed. Penelope Harvey and Peter Gow, 66–89. New York: Routledge.

Hatzfeld, Jean. 2005. *Machete Season: The Killers in Rwanda Speak.* New York: Farrar, Straus, and Giroux.

Hayner, Priscilla B. 2001. *Unspeakable Truths: Confronting State Terror and Atrocity.* London: Routledge.

Henríquez Ayin, Narda. 2006. *Cuestiones de género y poder en el conflicto armado en el Perú.* Lima, Peru: CONCYTEC.

Hermann, Judith. 1992. *Trauma and Recovery.* New York: Basic Books.

Hinton, Alexander Laban. 2004. *Why Did They Kill? Cambodia in the Shadow of Genocide.* Berkeley: University of California Press.

Holston, James. 2000. "Alternative Modernities: Statecraft and Religious Imagination in the Valley of the Dawn." *American Ethnologist* 26, no. 3: 605–31.

Huggins, Martha K., Mika Haritos-Gatouros, and Philip G. Zimbardo. 2002. *Violence Workers: Police Torturers and Murderers Reconstruct Brazilian Atrocities.* Berkeley: University of California Press.

Huntington, Samuel. 1991. *The Third Wave of Democratization in the Late Twentieth Century.* Norman: University of Oklahoma Press.

Husson, Jean Patrick. 1992. *De la guerra a la rebelión: Huanta, siglo XIX.* Cuzco, Peru: Centro de Estudios Regionales Anclinos "Bartolomé de Las Casas."

Instituto Nacional de Estadística e Informática (INEI) (Peru). 1996. Tercer Censo Nacional Agropecuario (1994). Departamento de Ayacucho. Lima, Peru: INEI.

Isbell, Billie Jean. 1978. *To Defend Ourselves: Ecology and Ritual in an Andean Village.* Austin: University of Texas Press.

———. 1979. "La otra mitad esencial: Un estudio de complementaridad sexual andina." *Estudios Andinos* 12, no. 5: 37–56.

———. 1994. "Shining Path and Peasant Responses in Rural Ayacucho." In *Shining Path of Peru*, 2nd ed., ed. David Scott Palmer, 77–100. New York: St. Martin's Press.

Iweala, Uzodinma. 2007. *Beasts of No Nation.* New York: Harper Collins.

Jackson, Michael. 2002. *The Politics of Storytelling: Violence, Transgression, and Intersubjectivity.* Copenhagen: University of Copenhagen, Museum Tusculanum Press.

Jacobs, Susie, Ruth Jacobson, and Jennifer Marchbank, eds. 2000. *States of Conflict: Gender, Violence and Resistance.* London: Zed Books.

Jacoby, Susan. 1988. *Wild Justice: The Evolution of Revenge.* New York: Harper and Row.

James, Erica Caple. 2004. "The Political Economy of 'Trauma' in Haiti in the Democratic Era of Insecurity." *Culture, Medicine and Psychiatry* 28: 127–49.

Janet, Pierre. (1923) 2010. *The Major Symptoms of Hysteria.* Charleston, S.C.: Nabu Press.

Jelin, Elizabeth. 2002. *Los trabajos de la memoria.* Madrid: Siglo XXI.

Jenkins, Janice. 1991. "The State Construction of Affect: Political Ethos and Mental Health Among Salvadoran Refugees." *Culture, Medicine and Psychiatry* 15, no. 140: 139–65.

Kaldor, Mary. 1999. *New and Old Wars: Organized Violence in a Global Era.* Oxford: Polity Press.

Kelly, Liz. 2000. "Wars Against Women: Sexual Violence, Sexual Politics and the Militarised State." In *States of Conflict: Gender, Violence and Resistance*, ed. Susie Jacobs, Ruth Jacobson, and Jennifer Marchbank, 45–65. London: Zed Books.

Kirk, Robin. 1993. *Grabada en piedra: Las Mujeres de Sendero Luminoso*. Lima, Peru: Instituto de Estudios Peruanos.

Kirmayer, Lawrence. 1996. "Landscapes of Memory: Trauma, Narrative and Dissociation." In *Tense Past: Cultural Essays on Memory and Trauma*, ed. P. Antze and M. Lambek, 173–98. London: Routledge.

Kiss, Elizabeth. 2000. "Moral Ambition Within and Beyond Political Constraints: Reflections on Restorative Justice." In *Truth v. Justice: The Morality of Truth Commissions*, ed. Robert I. Rotberg and Dennis Thompson, 68–98. Princeton, N.J.: Princeton University Press.

Klaiber, Jeffrey. 1992. "The Church in Peru: Between Terrorism and Conservative Restraints." In *Conflict and Competition: The Latin American Church in a Changing Environment*, ed. Edward L. Cleary and Hannay Stewart Gambino, 87–103. Boulder, Colo.: Lynne Rienner Publishers.

Kleinman, Arthur. 1995. *Writing at the Margin: Discourse Between Anthropology and Medicine*. Berkeley: University of California Press.

———. 1998. "Experience and Its Moral Modes: Culture, Human Conditions and Disorder." The Tanner Lecture on Human Values, Stanford University, Stanford, Calif., April 13–16.

———. 2006. *What Really Matters: Living a Moral Life Amidst Uncertainty and Danger*. New York: Oxford University Press.

Kleinman, Arthur, and R. R. Desjarlais. 1995. "Violence, Culture, and the Politics of Trauma." In *Writing at the Margin: Discourse Between Anthropology and Medicine*, 173–92. Berkeley: University of California Press.

Kleinman, Arthur, and Joan Kleinman. 1991. "Suffering and Its Professional Transformation: Toward an Ethnography of Interpersonal Experience." *Culture, Medicine and Psychiatry* 15, no. 3: 275–301.

Kleinman, Arthur, Veena Das, and Margaret Lock, eds. 1997. *Social Suffering*. Berkeley: University of California Press.

Krieger, Nancy. 1999. "Embodying Inequality: A Review of Concepts, Measures and Methods for Studying Health Consequences of Discrimination." *International Journal of Health Services* 29: 329–52.

———. 2003. "Does Racism Harm Health? Did Child Abuse Exist Before 1962? On Explicit Questions, Critical Sciences and Current Controversies." *American Journal of Public Health* 93: 194–99.

Krog, Antje. 2001. "Locked into Loss and Silence: Testimonies of Gender and Violence at the South African Truth Commission." In *Victims, Perpetrators or Actors? Gender, Armed Conflict and Political Violence*, ed. Caroline O. N. Moser and Fiona C. Clark, 203–16. London: Zed Books.

Kwon, Heonik. 2006. *After the Massacre: Commemoration and Consolation in Ha My and My Lai*. Berkeley: University of California Press.

Lalive d'Epinay, Christian. 1969. *Haven of the Masses: A Study of the Pentecostal Movement in Chile*. London: Lutterworth Press.

Laplante, Lisa J. 2007. "The Law of Remedies and the Clean Hands Doctrine: Exclusionary Reparation Policies in Peru's Political Transition." *American University International Law Review* 23, no. 1: 51–90.

Laplante, Lisa J., and Kimberly Theidon. 2007. "Truth with Consequences: The Politics of Reparations in Post–Truth Commission Peru." *Human Rights Quarterly* 29, no. 1: 228–50.

———. 2009. "Commissioning Truth, Constructing Silences: The Peruvian TRC and the Other Truths of 'Terrorists.'" In *Mirrors of Justice: Law and Power in the Post–Cold War Era*, ed. Kamari Maxine Clarke and Mark Goodale, 291–315. Cambridge: Cambridge University Press.

Leinaweaver, Jessaca. 2008. *Circulation of Children: Kinship, Adoption and Morality in Andean Peru*. Durham, N.C.: Duke University Press.

Lerner, Salomón. 2002. "Inaugural Speech. Tareas de la Comisión de la Verdad y Reconciliación. Fundamentos teológicos y éticos." In *Verdad y reconciliación: Reflexiones éticas*, ed. Salomón Lerner et al., 15–32. Lima, Peru: Centro de Estudios y Publicaciones, Instituto Bartolomé de las Casas.

Levi, Primo. (1959) 1995. *Survival in Auschwitz*. New York: Touchstone.

———. 1989. *The Drowned and the Saved*. New York: Vintage.

Levinas, Emmanuel, Michael Bradley Smith, and Barbara Harshav. 1998. *Entre Nous: Thinking of the Other*. New York: Columbia University Press.

Leys, Ruth. 2000. *Trauma: A Genealogy*. Chicago: University of Chicago Press.

Lifton, Robert J. 2000. *The Nazi Doctors: Medical Killing and the Psychology of Genocide*. London: Macmillan.

Littlewood, Roland. 1997. "Military Rape." *Anthropology Today* 13, no. 2: 7–16.

Lock, Margaret. 1993. "Cultivating the Body: Anthropology and Epistemologies of Bodily Practice and Knowledge." *Annual Review of Anthropology* 22: 133–55.

López, Darío. 1998. *Los evangélicos y los Derechos Humanos: La experiencia del Concilio Nacional Evangélico del Perú, 1980–1992*. Lima, Peru: Ediciones Puma.

Luhrmann, Tanya. 1989. *Persuasions of the Witch's Craft: Ritual Magic in Contemporary England*. Cambridge, Mass.: Harvard University Press.

Lutz, Catherine, and Lila Abu-Lughod, eds. 1990. *Language and the Politics of Emotion*. Cambridge: Cambridge University Press.

Lutz, Catherine, and Geoffrey M. White. 1986. "The Anthropology of Emotions." *Annual Review of Anthropology* 15: 405–36.

Maier, Charles S. 2000. "Doing History, Doing Justice: The Narrative of the Historian and of the Truth Commission." In *Truth v. Justice: The Morality of Truth Commissions*, ed. Robert I. Rotberg and Dennis Thompson, 261–78. Princeton, N.J.: Princeton University Press.

Malamud-Crandon, Libbet. 1991. *From the Fat of Our Souls: Social Change, Political Process and Medical Pluralism in Bolivia.* Berkeley: University of California Press.

Malkki, Liisa H. 1995. *Purity and Exile: Violence, Memory, and National Cosmology Among Hutu Refugees in Tanzania.* Chicago: University of Chicago Press.

Mallon, Florencia. 1994. "The Promise and Dilemma of Subaltern Studies: Perspectives from Latin American History." *American Historical Review* 99, no. 5 (December): 1491–1515.

———. 1995. *Peasant and Nation: The Making of Postcolonial Mexico and Peru.* Berkeley: University of California Press.

Mamdani, Mahmood. 2001. *When Victims Become Killers: Colonialism, Nativism, and the Genocide in Rwanda.* Princeton, N.J.: Princeton University Press.

Manrique, Nelson. 1989. "La década de la violencia." *Márgenes* 56: 137–82.

———. 2003. "Memoria y violencia: La nación y el silencio." In *Batallas por la memoria: Antagonismos de la promesa peruana,* ed. Marta Hamann, Santiago López, Gonzalo Portocarrero, and Víctor Vich, 421–33. Lima, Peru: Red para el Desarrollo de las Ciencias Sociales en el Perú.

Mantilla Falcón, Julissa. 2005a. "La experiencia de la Comisión de la Verdad y Reconciliación en el Perú: Logros y dificultades de un enfoque de género." In *Memorias de Ocupación: Violencia sexual contra mujeres detenidas durante la dictadura,* 67–89. Chile: Centro Regional de Derechos Humanos y Justicia de Género.

———. 2005b. "The Peruvian Truth and Reconciliation Commission's Treatment of Sexual Violence Against Women." *Human Rights Brief* 12, no. 2: 1–5.

Marzal, Manuel. 1977. *Estudios sobre religión campesina.* Lima, Peru: Pontificia Universidad Católica del Perú.

Mauss, Marcel. 1990. *The Gift: The Form and Reason for Exchange in Archaic Societies.* London: Routledge.

Mayer, Enrique. 1991. "Peru in Deep Trouble: Mario Vargas Llosa's 'Inquest in the Andes' Reexamined." *Cultural Anthropology* 6, no. 4 (November): 466–504.

———. 1994. "Patterns of Violence in the Andes." *Latin American Research Review* 29, no. 2: 141–77.

Mehta, Deepak. 2000. "Circumcision, Body, Masculinity: The Ritual Wound and Collective Violence." In *Violence and Subjectivity,* ed. Veena Das, Arthur Kleinman, Mamphela Ramphele, and Pamela Reynolds, 79–101. Berkeley: University of California Press.

Mehta, Deepak, and Roma Chatterji. 2001. "Boundaries, Names, Alterities: A Case Study of a 'Communal Riot' in Dharavi, Bombay." In *Remaking a World: Violence, Social Suffering and Recovery,* ed. Veena Das, Arthur Kleinman, Margaret Lock, and Mamphela Ramphele, 201–49. Berkeley: University of California Press.

Mellinkoff, Ruth. 1981. *The Mark of Cain.* Berkeley: University of California Press.

Mendez Gastelumendi, Cecilia. 2005. *The Plebeian Republic: The Huanta Rebellion and the Making of the Peruvian State, 1820–1850.* Durham, N.C.: Duke University Press.

Merry, Sally Engle. 2006. *Human Rights and Gender Violence: Translating International Law into Local Justice*. Chicago: University of Chicago Press.

Milgram, Stanley. 1974. *Obedience to Authority: An Experimental View*. New York: Harper and Row.

Milillo, Diana. 2006. "Rape as a Tactic of War: Social and Psychological Perspectives." *Affilia: Journal of Women and Social Work* 21, no. 2 (Summer): 196–205.

Minow, Martha. 1998. *Between Vengeance and Forgiveness: Facing History After Genocide and Mass Violence*. Boston: Beacon Press.

Moore, Sally Falk. 1986. *Social Facts and Fabrications: "Customary" Law on Kilimanjaro, 1880–1980*. Cambridge: Cambridge University Press.

Morote Best, Efraín. 1988. *Aldeas sumergidas: Cultural popular y sociedad en los Andes*. Cuzco, Peru: Centro de Estudios Rurales Andinos "Bartolomé de las Casas."

Murra, John. 1975. *Formaciones económicas y políticas del Mundo Andina*. Lima, Peru: Instituto de Estudios Peruanos.

Nader, Laura. 1990. *Harmony Ideology: Justice and Control in a Zapotec Mountain Village*. Stanford, Calif.: Stanford University Press.

Napier, A. David. 1986. *Masks, Transformation and Paradox*. Berkeley: University of California Press.

Nash, June. 1979. *We Eat the Mines and the Mines Eat Us*. New York: Columbia University Press.

Nelson, Diane. 1999. *A Finger in the Wound: Body Politics in Quincentennial Guatemala*. Berkeley: University of California Press.

Nietzsche, Friedrich. (1887) 1998. *On the Genealogy of Morality*. Cambridge: Cambridge University Press.

Nozick, Robert. 1981. *Philosophical Explanations*. Cambridge, Mass.: Harvard University Press.

O'Donnell, Guillermo, and Philippe C. Schmitter. 1986. *Transitions from Authoritarian Rule: Tentative Conclusions About Uncertain Democracies*. Baltimore: Johns Hopkins University Press.

O'Neill, Barry. 1999. *Honors, Symbols and War*. Ann Arbor: University of Michigan Press.

O'Neill, Kevin Lewis. 2009. *City of God: Christian Citizenship in Postwar Guatemala*. Berkeley: University of California Press.

Orlove, Benjamin. 1994. "Sticks and Stones: Ritual Battle and Play in the Southern Andes." In *Unruly Order: Violence, Power and Cultural Identity in the High Provinces of Southern Peru*, ed. Deborah Poole, 133–64. Boulder, Colo.: Westview Press.

Ortega, Julio. 1986. *Adiós Ayacucho*. Lima, Peru: Mosca Azul Editores.

Ortner, Sherry. 1990. "Gender Hegemonies." *Cultural Critique* 15 (Winter): 35–80.

———. 1995. "Resistance and the Problem of Ethnographic Refusal." *Comparative Studies in Society and History* 37, no. 1: 173–93.

Oths, Kathryn S. 1999. "Debilidad: A Biocultural Assessment of an Embodied Andean Illness." *Medical Anthropology Quarterly* 13, no. 3: 286–315.

Palmer, David Scott, ed. 1992. *The Shining Path of Peru*. London: Hurst.

Pandolfo, Stefania. 2008. "The Knot of the Soul: Postcolonial Conundrums, Madness and the Imagination." In *Postcolonial Disorders*, ed. Mary-Jo DelVecchio Good, Sandra Teresa Hyde, Sarah Pinto, and Byron J. Good, 329–58. Berkeley: University of California Press.

Pankhurst, Donna. 2003. "The 'Sex War' and Other Wars: Towards a Feminist Approach to Peace Building." *Development in Practice* 13, nos. 2 and 3 (May): 154–77.

PAR (Programa Para el Apoyo al Repoblamiento, Perú). 2002. *Informe resultado talleres de recuperación: Asesoría Técnica*. Lima, Peru: Ministerio de la Presidencia.

Peña Jumpa, Antonio. 1998. *Justicia comunal en los Andes: El caso de Calahuyo*. Lima, Peru: Pontificia Universidad Católica del Perú.

Peralta, Víctor. 2000. *Sendero Luminoso y la Prensa, 1980–1994*. Lima, Peru: SUR.

Philpott, Daniel. 2007. "Religion, Reconciliation and Transitional Justice: The State of the Field." Social Science Research Council Working Papers, October.

Portelli, Alessandro. 1991. *The Death of Luigi Trastulli and Other Stories: Form and Meaning in Oral History*. Albany: State University of New York Press.

Povinelli, Elizabeth A. 2002. *The Cunning of Recognition: Indigenous Alterity and the Making of Australian Multiculturalism*. Durham, N.C.: Duke University Press.

PROMUDEH (Ministerio de Promoción de la Mujer y de Desarrollo Humano). 2001. *Censo por la Paz: Situación de la población afectada por la violencia política en el Perú*. Lima, Peru: PROMUDEH.

PTRC (Peruvian Truth and Reconciliation Commission, Comisión de la Verdad y Reconciliación). 2003. *Informe Final de la Comisión de Verdad y Reconciliación*. 9 vols. Lima, Peru: Comisión de la Verdad y Reconciliación.

———. 2004. *Hatun willakuy: Versión abreviada del informe final de la Comisión de la Verdad y Reconciliación*. Lima, Peru: Comisión de la Verdad y Reconciliación.

Pupavac, Vanessa. 2001. "Therapeutic Governance: Psychosocial Intervention and Trauma Risk Management." *Disasters* 25, no. 4: 358–72.

Rabinow, Paul, ed. 1984. *The Foucault Reader*. New York: Pantheon Press.

Ramphele, Mamphela. 1999. "Political Widowhood in South Africa: The Embodiment of Ambiguity." *Daedalus: Journal of the American Academy of Arts and Sciences* 125, no. 1: 99–118.

Rebhun, Linda Ann. 1994. "Swallowing Frogs: Anger and Illness in Northeast Brazil." *Medical Anthropology Quarterly* 8, no. 4: 360–82.

Rehn, Elisabeth, and Ellen Johnson Sirleaf. 2002. *Women, War and Peace: The Independent Expert's Assessment on the Impact of Armed Conflict on Women and Women's Roles in Peace-Building*. New York: UNIFEM.

Remy, María Isabel. 1991. "Los discursos sobre la violencia en los Andes: Algunas reflexiones a propósito del Chiaraje." In *Poder y violencia en los Andes*, ed. Henrique Urbano, 189–210. Cuzco, Peru: Centro de Estudios Regionales Andinos "Bartolomé de Las Casas."

Rigby, Andrew. 2001. *Justice and Reconciliation After the Violence*. Boulder, Colo.: Lynne Rienner Publications.

Robbins, Joel. 2004. "The Globalization of Pentecostal and Charismatic Christianity." *Annual Review of Anthropology* 33: 117–43.

Ross, Fiona. 2003. *Bearing Witness: Women and the Truth and Reconciliation Commission in South Africa*. London: Pluto Press.

Rubel, Arthur J. 1964. "The Epidemiology of a Folk Illness: Susto in Hispanic America." *Ethnology* 3, no. 3: 268–83.

Ruddick, Sara. 1995. *Maternal Thinking: Toward a Politics of Peace*. New York: Beacon Press.

Scarry, Elaine. 1985. *The Body in Pain: The Making and Unmaking of the World*. New York: Oxford University Press.

Scheper-Hughes, Nancy. 1993. *Death Without Weeping: The Violence of Everyday Life in Brazil*. Berkeley: University of California Press.

———. 1995. "The Primacy of the Ethical: Propositions for a Militant Anthropology." *Current Anthropology* 36, no. 3 (June): 409–20.

Scheper-Hughes, Nancy, and Carolyn Fishel Sargent, eds. 1998. *Small Wars: The Cultural Politics of Childhood*. Berkeley: University of California Press.

Scott, James C. 1992. *Domination and the Arts of Resistance: Hidden Transcripts*. New Haven, Conn.: Yale University Press.

Seguín, Carlos Alberto. 1979. *Psiquiatría folklórica*. Lima, Peru: Pontificia Universidad Católica del Perú.

Seider, Rachel. 1997. *Customary Law and Democratic Transition in Guatemala*. London: University of London, Institute of Latin American Studies.

Shaw, Rosalind. 2005. "Rethinking Truth and Reconciliation Commissions: Lessons from Sierra Leone." Washington, D.C.: United States Institute of Peace.

Shaw, Rosalind, Lars Waldorf, and Pierre Hazan. 2010. *Localizing Transitional Justice: Interventions and Priorities After Mass Violence*. Palo Alto, Calif.: Stanford University Press.

Shephard, Glenn H. 2002. "Three Days of Weeping: Dreams, Emotions, and Death in the Peruvian Andes." *Medical Anthropology Quarterly* 16, no. 2: 200–229.

Shweder, Richard A., and Edmond J. Bourne. 1984. "Does the Concept of the Person Vary Cross-Culturally?" In *Culture Theory: Essays on Mind, Self and Emotion*, ed. Robert Alan LeVine and Richard A. Shweder, 158–99. Cambridge: Cambridge University Press.

Silverblatt, Irene. 1987. *Moon, Sun and Witches: Gender Ideologies and Class in Inca and Colonial Peru*. Princeton, N.J.: Princeton University Press.

Sluka, Jeffrey A. 1996. "Reflections on Managing Danger in Fieldwork: Dangerous Anthropology in Belfast." In *Fieldwork Under Fire: Contemporary Studies of Violence and Survival*, ed. Antonius Robben and Carolyn Nordstrom. Berkeley: University of California Press.

Starn, Orin. 1995. "To Revolt Against the Revolution: War and Resistance in Peru's Andes." *Cultural Anthropology* 10, no. 4: 547–80.

———. 1999. *Nightwatch: The Politics of Protest in the Andes*. Durham, N.C.: Duke University Press.

Starr, June, and Mark Goodale, eds. 2002. *Practicing Ethnography in Law: New Dialogues, Enduring Methods*. New York: Palgrave Macmillan.

Stephens, Sharon, ed. 1995. *Children and the Politics of Culture*. Princeton, N.J.: Princeton University Press.

Stern, Steve J. 1982. *Peru's Indian Peoples and the Challenge of Spanish Conquest: Huamanga to 1640*. Madison: University of Wisconsin Press.

———. 1998. *Shining and Other Paths: War and Society in Peru, 1980–1995*. Durham, N.C.: Duke University Press.

———. 2006. *Remembering Pinochet's Chile: On the Eve of London 1998*. Durham, D.C.: Duke University Press.

Stevenson, I. N. 1977. "Colerina: Reactions to Emotional Stress in the Peruvian Andes." *Social Science and Medicine* 11: 303–7.

Stewart, Pamela J., and Andrew Strathern, eds. 2004. *Witchcraft, Sorcery, Rumors and Gossip*. Cambridge: Cambridge University Press.

Stoll, David. 1990. *Is Latin America Turning Protestant? The Politics of Evangelical Growth*. Berkeley: University of California Press.

Stover, Eric, and Harvey Weinstein. 2004. *My Neighbor, My Enemy: Justice and Community in the Aftermath of Mass Atrocity*. Cambridge: Cambridge University Press.

Stoller, Paul. 1997. *Sensuous Scholarship*. Philadelphia: University of Pennsylvania Press.

Suárez-Orozco, Marcelo. 1995. "A Grammar of Tenor: Psychocultural Responses to State Terrorism in Dirty War and Post–Dirty War Argentina." In *The Paths to Domination, Resistance and Terror*, ed. Carolyn Nordstrom and JoAnn Martin, 219–59. Berkeley: University of California Press.

Summerfield, Derek. 1999. "A Critique of Seven Assumptions Behind Psychological Trauma Programs in War-Affected Areas." *Social Science and Medicine* 48: 1449–62.

———. 2000. "Rethinking PTSD." *British Medical Journal*. http:/bmj.com/cgi/content/full/325/7372/1105.

———. 2002. "Effects of War: Moral Knowledge, Revenge, Reconciliation and Medicalized Concepts of 'Recovery.'" *British Medical Journal* 325: 1105–7.

Tamayo, Giulia. 2003. "Documentando la violencia sexual: Definiciones, metodología y exigencias de justicia." In *Violaciones sexuales a mujeres durante la violencia política en el Perú*, 2–7. Lima, Peru: COMISEDH.

Tamayo Flores, Ana María. 1992. *Derecho en los Andes: Un estudio de antropología jurídica*. Lima, Peru: Centro de Estudios País y Región.

Tapia, Carlos. 1997. *Las fuerzas armadas y Sendero Luminoso: Dos estrategias y un final*. Lima, Peru: Instituto de Estudios Peruanos.

Tapias, Maria. 2006. "Emotions and the Intergenerational Embodiment of Social Suffering in Rural Bolivia." *Medical Anthropology Quarterly* 20, no. 3: 399–415.

Taussig, Michael. 1984. "Culture of Terror—Space of Death: Roger Casement's

Putumayo Report and the Explanation of Torture." *Comparative Study of Society and History* 26: 467–88.

———. 1999. *Defacement: Public Secrecy and the Labor of the Negative.* Stanford, Calif.: Stanford University Press.

Tavuchis, Nicholas. 1991. *Mea Culpa: A Sociology of Apology and Reconciliation.* Stanford, Calif.: Stanford University Press.

Teitel, Ruti. 2002. *Transitional Justice.* Oxford: Oxford University Press.

———. 2003. "Human Rights in Transition: Transitional Justice Genealogy." *Harvard Human Rights Journal* 16: 69–94.

Terdiman, Richard. 1989. "The Mnemonics of Musset's Confession," special issue, "Memory and Counter-Memory," ed. Natalie Zemon Davis and Randolph Starn. *Representations*, no. 26 (Spring): 26–30.

Theidon, Kimberly. 1999. "Domesticando la violencia: Alcohol y las secuelas de la guerra." *Ideele: Revista del Instituto de Defensa Legal*, no. 120: 56–63.

———. 2001a. "'How We Learned to Kill Our Brother': Memory, Morality and Reconciliation in Peru." Ed. Gonzálo Sanchez and Eric Lair, *Bulletin de L'Institut Français des Études Andines* (Bogota, Colombia) 29, no. 3: 539–54.

———. 2001b. "Terror's Talk: Fieldwork and War." *Dialectical Anthropology* 26, no. 1: 19–35.

———. 2002. "Género y justicia." *Ideele: Revista del Instituto de Defensa Legal*, no. 145 (March): 16–23.

———. 2003a. "Disarming the Subject: Remembering War and Imagining Citizenship in Peru." *Cultural Critique*, no. 54: 67–87.

———. 2003b. "La micropolítica de la reconciliación: Practicando la justicia en comunidades rurales Ayacuchanas," special issue, "Justicia Comunitaria en los Andes," *Revista Allpanchis* 60: 113–42.

———. 2003c. "Memoria, historia y reconciliación." *Ideele: Revista del Instituto de Defensa Legal*, no. 133 (November): 58–63.

———. 2003d. "Entre prójimos: Violencia y reconciliación en el Perú." *Ideele: Revista del Instituto de Defensa Legal*, no. 157 (September): 91–96.

———. 2004. *Entre prójimos: El conflicto armado interno y la política de la reconciliación en el Perú.* Lima, Peru: Instituto de Estudios Peruanos.

———. 2006a. "Justice in Transition: The Micropolitics of Reconciliation in Post-War Peru." *Journal of Conflict Resolution* 50, no. 3: 433–57.

———. 2006b. "The Mask and the Mirror: Facing Up to the Past in Peru," special issue, "War and Peace: Anthropological Perspectives," *Anthropologica: Journal of the Canadian Anthropology Society* 48, no. 1: 87–100.

———. 2006c. "Toward a Social Psychology of Reconciliation." In *The Psychology of Resolving Global Conflicts: From War to Peace*, vol. 2, ed. Mari Fitzduff and Chris E. Stout, 211–28. Westport, Conn.: Praeger Press.

———. 2007. "Gender in Transition: Common Sense, Women and War." *Journal of Human Rights*, no. 4: 453–78.

———. 2010. "Histories of Innocence: Post-War Stories in Peru." In *Localizing Transitional Justice: Interventions and Priorities After Mass Violence*, ed. Rosalind Shaw, Lars Waldorf, and Pierre Hazan, 92–110. Studies in Human Rights. Stanford, Calif.: Stanford University Press.

Tousignant, Michel. 1979. "Espanto: A Dialogue with the Gods." *Culture, Medicine and Psychiatry* 3, no. 4: 347–61.

———. 1984. "*Pena* in the Ecuadorian Sierra: A Psychoanthropological Analysis of Sadness." *Culture, Medicine and Psychiatry* 8, no. 4: 381–98.

Trouillot, Michel Rolfe. 1995. *Silencing the Past: Power and the Production of History*. Boston: Beacon Press.

Tsing, Anna Lowenhaupt. 1993. *In the Realm of the Diamond Queen*. Princeton, N.J.: Princeton University Press.

Tutu, Desmond. 1999. *No Future Without Forgiveness*. New York: Doubleday.

Tylor, Edward Burnett. (1871) 2010. *Primitive Culture and Anthropology*. Cambridge: Cambridge University Press.

Utas, Mats. 2005. "Victimcy, Girlfriending, Soldiering: Tactic Agency in a Young Woman's Social Navigation of the Liberian War Zone." *Anthropological Quarterly* 78, no. 2: 403–30.

Varallanos, José. 1989. *El harawi y el yaraví: Dos canciones populares*. Lima, Peru: Concejo Nacional de Ciencia y Tecnología (CONCYTEC).

Vargas Llosa, Mario, et al. 1983. *Informe investigador sobre los Sucesos de Uchuraccay*. Lima: Editora Peru.

Villalobos, Bernadino. 1992. "De fiestas, ritos y batallas: Algunos comportamientos folk de la sociedad andina de los K'anas y Ch'umpiwillcas." *Allpanchis* 40: 147–72.

Villanueva Flores, Rocío. 2007. "Respuesta del sistema de administración de justicia peruano frente a los casos de violencia sexual contra mujeres ocurridos durante el conflicto armado interno." In *Justicia y reparación para mujeres víctimas de violencia sexual en contexto de conflicto armado interno*, 211–58. Lima, Peru: Consejería de Proyectos (PCS).

Viswanathan, Gauri. 1998. *Outside the Fold: Conversion, Modernity and Belief*. Princeton, N.J.: Princeton University Press.

Warren, Kay B. 1993. *The Violence Within: Cultural and Political Opposition in Divided Nations*. Boulder, Colo.: Westview Press.

———. 1998. "Indigenous Movements as a Challenge to the Unified Social Movement Paradigm for Guatemala." In *Cultures of Politics, Politics of Culture: Re-visioning Latin American Social Movements*, ed. Sonia E. Alvarez, Evelina Dagnino, and Arturo Escobar, 165–95. Boulder, Colo.: Westview Press.

———. 2000. "Death Squads and Wider Complicities: Dilemmas for the Anthropology of Violence." In *Death Squad: The Anthropology of State Terror*, ed. Jeffrey A. Sluka. Philadelphia: University of Pennsylvania Press.

Weismantel, Mary. 1997. "White Cannibals: Fantasies of Racial Violence in the Andes." *Identities* 4: 9–43.

———. 2001. *Cholas and Pishtacos: Stories of Race and Sex in the Andes*. Chicago: University of Chicago Press.

White, Hayden. 1987. *The Content of the Form: Narrative Discourse and Historical Representation*. Baltimore: Johns Hopkins University Press.

White, Luise. 2000. *Speaking with Vampires: Rumor and History in Colonial Africa*. Berkeley: University of California Press.

Willems, Emilio. 1967. *Followers of the New Faith: Culture Change and the Rise of Protestantism in Brazil and Chile*. Nashville, Tenn.: Vanderbilt University Press.

Williams, Philip. 2001. "Popular Religion and the (Re)construction of Community in Yungay." In *Christianity, Social Change and Globalization in the Americas*, ed. Anna Lisa Peterson, Manuela Vásquez, and Philip J. Williams, 63–84. New Brunswick, N.J.: Rutgers University Press.

Williams, Raymond. 1985. *Keywords: A Vocabulary of Culture and Society*. New York: Oxford University Press.

Wilson, Richard. 2000. "Reconciliation and Revenge in Post-Apartheid South Africa." *Current Anthropology* 41, no. 1: 75–87.

———. 2001. *The Politics of Truth and Reconciliation in South Africa: Legitimizing the Post-Apartheid State*. Cambridge: Cambridge University Press.

———. 2003. "Anthropological Studies of National Reconciliation Processes." *Anthropological Theory* 3, no. 3: 367–87.

Wood, Elisabeth. 2006. "Variation in Sexual Violence During War." *Politics and Society* 34, no. 3 (September): 307–41.

Yezer, Caroline. 2007. "Anxious Citizenship: Insecurity, Apocalypse and War Memories in Peru's Andes." Ph.D. diss., Duke University.

Young, Allen. 1995. *The Harmony of Illusions: Inventing Post-Traumatic Disorder*. Princeton, N.J.: Princeton University Press.

Zapata, Cecilia, Atalah Robolledo, B. Newman, and M. C. King. 1992. "The Influence of Social and Political Violence on the Risk of Pregnancy Complications." *American Journal of Public Health* 82, no. 5: 685–90.

Zarowsky, Christina. 2004. "Writing Trauma: Emotion, Ethnography and the Politics of Suffering Among Somali Returnees in Ethiopia." *Culture Medicine and Psychiatry* 28, no. 2: 189–209.

Zimbardo, P. G., C. Haney, W. C. Banks, and D. Jaffe. 1973. "The Mind Is a Formidable Jailer: A Pirandellian Prison." *New York Times Magazine*, sec. 6, pp. 36ff.

Zur, Judith N. 1998. *Violent Memories: Mayan War Widows in Guatemala*. Boulder, Colo.: Westview Press.

De Certeau, Michel, 90
Chacra Mañay (ceremony), 418n32
Chestnut, R. Andrew, 402n1
children: acquisition of human
characteristics, 54–55, 259, 401n2;
anthropological research on political
violence and, 303–5; born as result of rape
("soldiers' gifts"), 120, 123–24, 127, 137–
40; fathered by soldiers (as orphans), 293–
94, 295–300; games and historicizing of,
304–5; knowledge of security issues, 284;
kuyachicuyta yachana (learning how to
make others love you), 58–59, 302, 401n7;
and postwar families, 302–5, 420n15;
recruitment by Sendero in central-south
communities, 334; story of *wawa* Gloria,
55–57; in studies of social memory, 303–4;
and studies of transgenerational legacies of
war, 303, 420n12
Children of Jesus Soup Kitchen
(Carhuahurán), 36
Cipriani, Juan Luis, 80, 403n14
"Clean Hands Doctrine" in Peru, 423n23
coca, chewing of, 16–17, 167
Cochran, Nicholas, 75, 76
Cockburn, Cynthia, 410n62
Colegio General Córdoba (Vilcashuamán),
327
Comaroff, Jean, 307–8
Comaroff, John, 307–8
comités populares (popular committees),
332–33, 335
communal labor arrangements: and
arrepentidos, 247, 261–62, 292; *ayni*
(reciprocal labor exchange), 261–62, 333
Communist Party of Peru—Red Flag, 327
Communist Party of Peru-Shining Path
(Sendero Luminoso), 3, 327. *See also*
Sendero Luminoso
compassion and *caridad*: chronology
of compassion (hospitality and the
stranger), 249–51, 278, 313–16; and
communal justice, 249–51; contrasts
between the *antiguo tiempo* and return of,
233; and "cultural bereavement," 314–15;
and human rights discourse, 313, 421n24;
the internal armed conflict and loss of,
313–16; Judeo-Christian model of, 229,
230, 233, 313, 421n24; local moral idioms
and rebuilding a moral order, 188–89;
postwar economic changes and restricted

forms of, 166–68
conciencia, 55, 186, 211–12, 255, 259–60,
402n12
concientización, 194–95, 260, 322, 327
Concilio Nacional Evangélico del Perú
(CONEP), 86, 404n19
Connell, Patricia, 408n32
Connerton, Paul, 399n36
Consejo Nacional de Derechos Humanos
(CONADEH), 21, 80, 404n16
Coral, Isabel, 177, 413n41
Cordova, Milton, 146
Coronel, José, 257–58
Csordas, Thomas, 37
Cueto, Marcos, 398n19
curanderos, 45, 51–53; distinguishing
between the *brujo* and, 19, 400n51; don
Teofilo (El Piki) in Carhuahurán, 14, 50,
51–53; as memory specialists, 52–53

daño, 16–20, 33, 52, 311, 396n34
Das, Ranendra, 33
Das, Veena, 411n71, 412n20, 420n12; on
female bodily representations of suffering
and memory, 40; on medical pluralism, 33;
on rape and creation of "future memories,"
408n36; on reconciliation, 316, 384; on
widowhood, 172; on women's silence about
rape, 406n2
Davis, Natalie, 405n33
death penalty in Peru, 190–91
debilidad, 400n56
DECAS (Comités Antisubversivos de
Autodefensa Civil), 256, 257
Defarges, Philippe, 387
Defensor del Pueblo en Huamanga, 21
Degregori, Carlos Iván, 190–91, 199
De la Cadena, Marisol, 409n58
Del Pino, Ponciano, 216, 403n3, 404n20,
406n36
Desjarlais, R. R., 397n12
*Diccionario de la Lengua de la Real Academia
Española*, 30–31
Diccionario para Juristas, 55
*Diccionario razonado de legislación y
jurisprudencia*, 234
Diken, Bülent, 132
disarmament, demobilization, and
reintegration (DDR) programs, 420n8
"disjunctive democracy," 149–50
Duce, Mauricio, 229

economies: economic exploitation by Sendero, 199–201; economic impact of losing a husband, 119, 120; economies of war and reconstruction, 165–72; postwar reconstruction and aid distribution, 168–72, 413n33, 413n36; redistributive economic justice, 265; women's reduced access to wage-paying labor, 167–68

"Eight Martyrs of Uchuraccay," 8–11, 160–64; and Vargas Llosa commission investigation, 9–11

Eisenbruch, Maurice, 314–15

enemy, constructions of the. *See* Senderistas, non-human/evil terms for

Escobar, Arturo, 397n7

Escriche, Joaquin, 234

escuelas populares and indoctrination of young people, 327, 332, 369–70, 381

Etxeberría, Xabier, 350

Evangelismo (Evangelical Christianity), 66, 67–100; apocalypticism, 87, 404n20; and babies' acquisition of souls, 54; Bible Institute in Huanta, 68, 74–75; and the Catholic Church, 68, 71–73, 75, 77–80, 91–92, 403n4, 403n10; in the central-south/in the north, 96, 405n31; and collective memory production, 90; communal justice and repentance/forgiveness, 84, 237; and conversion, 74–76, 84, 91, 93–94, 403n9, 405n28; egalitarianism (alleged) and spiritual intimacy, 73–74, 403n5; the evangelical body, 92–94; the evangelical films, 77, 87–91; and experience of displacement, 91–94; and ex-Senderistas, 357; the Fiesta Espiritual in Carhuahurán, 83, 87; founding churches in rural communities, 76–77; growth in Latin America, 68, 75, 402–3n1; judgment and divine justice, 97–100, 406n36; local theologies (pentecostalization), 94–97, 405n31, 405n33; and madness, 61; medical services, 70; militant theology, 95–96, 406nn35–36; murder of six *hermanos* in Callqui (1984), 68–69, 85–86; and mutability of identity, 57; and North American missionaries, 75, 76, 77, 86; and postconflict reconstruction, 83–87, 404nn18–19; the PTRC Final Report on, 67; Radio Amauta, 68, 75, 76, 77, 84–85, 90; and *ronderos*, 82, 95; and Senderista

threat, 78–79, 80–82, 87, 94–97, 405n31

Falconí, Carola, 131

Farmer, Paul, 400n48

Favret-Saada, Jeanne, 14–15, 20; *Deadly Words: Witchcraft in the Bocage*, 14–15

Feldman, Allen, 36, 189

Ferguson, James, 91, 397n7

Ferrua, Fredy, 167

Fletcher, Laurel, 277

Flores Nano, Lourdes, 324

forgetting, 33–35, 39–43, 111, 112–13, 154, 158, 269–76, 399n47. *See also* memory

Foster, Dan, 131, 408n44

Foucault, Michel, 222, 242

Fujimori, Alberto: administration and corruption, 5–6, 227; amnesty law (1995), 7, 227–28; efforts to defeat guerrilla movements, 5, 233–34, 395n6; the 2000 presidential campaign, 278, 279–85

funeral rituals, 278, 306–13, 318, 420n17

Galeano, Eduardo, 48

Gálvez Fernández, Hélber, 342

García, Alan, 324, 373, 391, 411n71

Garrard-Burnett, Virginia, 402–3n1

Geertz, Clifford, 103

gender: and the administration of justice, 265–66; and one's "historical project," 292; and performative identity, 135, 409n58; postwar families and different treatment of daughters and sons, 302–3; PTRC Public Audiences and problem of gendered dualism, 117–18; truth commissions and testimony from women, 105–8, 140–42, 406n9, 407n11; war widows and gender roles, 146–47, 173–75

Gill, Leslie, 403n5, 405n28

Ginzburg, Carlo, 221; *Clues, Myths and the Historical Method*, 221

Goffman, Erving, 220, 264

Good, Byron, 37

gossip, 15–16, 176–77, 329–30; Las Chimosas (The Gossiping Women), 176; duplicity and doubling, 15–16; Ley Contra Chismes (Law Against Gossip), 16, 291; and rape, 130; and war widows, 176–77

Green, Linda, 158, 413n29, 413n36

Guatemala's civil war: economic effects on rural widows, 165, 413n32; traditional forms of communal solidarity and support

Acknowledgments

THE BEST REASON for finishing a book is not necessarily the most obvious one. Yes, it is pleasant to rejoin the world of the living, resume regular hygiene, and foreswear Trader Joe's frozen food section. However, the best reason for finishing is the opportunity to acknowledge the people who contributed to one's life and work. As I began to write my acknowledgments, I hesitated: "But I don't even know where to begin." I was mistaken: I did indeed know where to begin but had no idea where to end. I have encountered enormous intellectual and interpersonal generosity during my academic training, research, and writing. I have been fortunate beyond imagination.

So to begin. The first time I heard the anthropologist Nancy Scheper-Hughes speak was an intellectual conversion experience. Nancy's example of committed scholarship and her abiding belief that anthropology matters have greatly influenced me. I also hope that somewhere in this text are a few lines that begin to approach the literary beauty she brings to ethnographic writing.

I heartily thank Billie Jean Isbell, who has been both mentor and colleague; her insights have invariably enriched my work and provided clarity where there had been murk.

Kay Warren generously offered guidance and feedback at certain crucial moments, and I thank her for the model she provides of rigorous scholarship and collegiality. Barry O'Neill provided so much support and enduring friendship when I needed to sit and write, or move to another country and change my name. Andrew Canessa also brought his deep understanding of the Andean region to bear in reading drafts of this book and making helpful suggestions.

In the United States, I give my heartfelt thanks to Steve Bloomfield, Roberta Culbertson, Kathleen Dill, Jorge Dominguez, Merilee Grindle, Eric Hershberg, Katherine Hite, Stephen Kosslyn, Lisa J. Laplante, Sally Merry, Victoria Sanford, Rosalind Shaw, Steve Stern, Charles Versaggi, Richard Wilson, Elisabeth Jean Wood, and Caroline Yezer.

I have been generously supported by the Social Science Research Council; the Wenner Gren Foundation for Anthropological Research; the United States Institute of Peace; the Instituto de Estudios Peruanos; and the Weatherhead Center for International Affairs and the David Rockefeller Center for Latin American Studies at Harvard.

The intellectual community in Peru was always welcoming and supportive, and my intellectual and affective debts are innumerable. The late Carlos Iván Degregori influenced my project in many ways over the years. Carlos Iván was a public intellectual in the best sense of the term, combining his theoretical acuity with his political commitments. I am also deeply grateful to Nelson Manrique, Isaías Rojas Pérez, Ernesto de la Jara, Patricia Oliart, Narda Henriquez, Julissa Mantilla, Félix Reátegui, Viviana Valz Gen, Miriam Rivera, Marcos Cueto, Cecilia Blondet, Susana Villarán, Isabel Coral, Ludwig Huber, Enrique Mayer, Eduardo Gonzalez, the late Manuel Marzal, Rodrigo Montoya, Ponciano Del Pino, and Jaime Bayona for many illuminating conversations.

In Ayacucho and Huanta, I would like to thank Victor Belleza, Iván Caro, Gumercinda Reynaga, Fredy Ferrua, Mariano Aronés, Raquel Reynoso, Efraín Loayza, Madeline Pariona Oncebay, Noemí Cabana, Marilú Calderón, Germán Vargas, Elisabeth Cabezas, Vidal Trujillano, Demetria Montes, and Julian Aguilar. In particular, my deepest gratitude goes to José Coronel Aguirre, who is a model of commitment and decency.

Elizabeth Jelin has been generous in her insights. Her work on collective memory and political violence launched me on this research path, and conversations with "Shevy" have illuminated many themes for me. Additionally, I had the opportunity to discuss my research with the outstanding participants in the Collective Memory and Political Violence program, directed by Professor Jelin and funded by the SSRC. I learned so much during these exchanges.

The anthropology department at Harvard has been a lively and supportive environment for which I am grateful. I thank each of my colleagues.

In particular, I thank Arthur Kleinman for his extraordinary intellectual generosity; his comments on draft chapters improved my thinking. For their keen insights and helpful suggestions, I thank Kedron Thomas and Alex Fattal.

My editors at the University of Pennsylvania Press—Peter Agree, Bert Lockwood, and Pamela Haag—were a pleasure to work with. Having editors who read and engage with one's work and ideas is exceptional. Who knows? With editors like these, I just might write another book.

My partner, William Kurth, has been a delight, and his insistence that I lock myself in my room and write was just what I needed to finish this book. Thank you for locking me in, and for not throwing away the key.

In my family, I have been blessed with some great women. My sister Karen Card is at the top of the list. As a child I was the envy of all my friends for having the coolest big sister around; I am so thankful I still do.

La Familia Ríos in Pueblo Libre have been friends and family since my first research trip to Peru in 1987. They are dear people and held their breaths each time I headed to a protest. It mattered enormously knowing someone would be waiting up when I came home. Bless you, Anacha.

And so my acknowledgments wind back around to where they belong: Peru. I thank people in the villages in Ayacucho who gave me the opportunity to demonstrate I came to do no harm. I appreciate how greatly fear shaped life well into the 1990s and remain profoundly grateful that villagers allowed me to live with them. I share with the adults the desire for a future in which their children will be treated with a respect too rarely extended to their parents.

I dedicate this book to the children with whom I have lived and worked in Peru. They both challenge and inspire me to work for social justice.

A preliminary version of Chapter 5 appeared in "Gender in Transition: Common Sense, Women and War," *Journal of Human Rights* 6, no. 4 (2007): 453–78. One section of Chapter 12 appeared in "The Mask and the Mirror: Facing Up to the Past in Peru," special issue, "War and Peace: Anthropological Perspectives," *Anthropologica: Journal of the Canadian Anthropology Society* 48, no. 1 (2006): 87–100. An analysis of microreconciliation processes in one community appeared in "Justice in Transition: The Micropolitics of Reconciliation in Post-War Peru," *Journal of Conflict Resolution* 50, no. 3 (2006): 433–57. I thank the journals for permission to use these materials.